A study of the origin and development of the

India
IN THE NEW ERA

Indian Union and Pakistan, new nations in a changing Asia

By T. WALTER WALLBANK, *University of Southern California*

SCOTT, FORESMAN & COMPANY · CHICAGO · ATLANTA · DALLAS · NEW YORK

India in the new era

CREDITS

Design, cover, maps, and charts by Arnold Ryan.
Illustrations by Franz Altschuler.
Sources for the photographs in the two picture sections are
indicated beneath the pictures. The photographs which appear on
the cover were supplied by the Government of India
Information Services and Three Lions.
The author wishes to acknowledge the courtesy of The Bodley
Head, London, who have granted permission to reprint passages
from Jawaharlal Nehru's Autobiography, *the English*
title of Toward Freedom.

To My Wife, Mary Onclé Wallbank,
Good Companion on Historical Journeys

TABLE OF CONTENTS

Chapter

LIST OF MAPS AND CHARTS

The Asian revolution against colonialism

GOLIA   MANCHURIA   *parallel   SEA of JAPAN   *Tokyo

Peiping ☆   38th   Seoul   HONSHU   JAPAN

KOREA

YELLOW   KYUSHU

SEA

REPUBLIC

Nanking o
Shanghai

FORMOSA

1- U. S. Department of
State, Publication
No. 3747, Jan. 23, 1950.

oï

HAINAN   LUZON

Manila ☆

INDO-
HINA   REPUBLIC of the PHILIPPINES

on o

SOUTH   MINDANAO

CHINA

SEA

NO.
BORNEO

LAYAN FEDERATION

SARAWAK   CELEBES

BORNEO

Singapore

D O N E S I A

Jakarta ☆

JAVA

PACIFIC

OCEAN

prologue:

A BASIC upheaval is transforming Asia. A political and social revolution of cosmic proportions, compounded of nationalism, anti-imperialism, and the rising protest of the masses against bleak and grinding poverty, is agitating and convulsing the lives of one billion people. Since 1945, the close of World War II, eight new nations have come into existence in Asia and a vast structure of colonial rule has virtually disappeared, leaving behind it only a few shaky remnants of European imperialism in Malaya and Indochina.

In the process of this Asian revolution new constitutions are being written, landlords are being dispossessed or liquidated in favor of the peasantry, grandiose schemes for obliterating illiteracy and reducing the hazards of disease are being devised, and ambitious blueprints for industrialization are being drawn up. Never before have the lives and patterns of culture of so many people in such a large area of our globe been so rapidly changed. In China alone the population is estimated at 475,000,000 inhabiting an area of one and a half million square miles. India and Pakistan add another 400,000,000 souls and about the same land area. And Southeast Asia, a region of great geographical and racial diversity, including Indonesia, Siam, Burma, Indochina, Malaya, and the Philippines, supports more than 150,000,000 Asians on an area of about one and a quarter million square miles. Nearly everywhere among these teeming millions a new spirit is openly manifesting itself. Dean Acheson, the American Secretary of State, observed, "Resignation is no longer the typical emotion of Asia. It has given way to hope, to a sense of effort, and in many cases to a real sense of anger."[1]

While the present volume is a study of the various historical constituents which developed, converged, and interacted on each other to bring about, finally, the independent states of the Union of India and Pakistan, this introductory section will briefly survey basic conditions and trends in Asia as a whole. No one segment of Asia can be clearly understood without reference to the larger pattern of which it forms a part. Each nation is distinctive from its neighbors yet similar to them in that it reflects common basic needs, a new political nationalism, and new social urges. It follows, therefore, that Pakistan and India are each separate entities but also integral parts of the larger Asian whole, both influenced by and yet having influence upon events in Peking, Batavia, Rangoon, Singapore, and Bangkok.

As late as the closing decades of the nineteenth century people in this country could still speak of the "unchanging East." At this time China could be described as a sleeping giant under the torpid rule of the Manchu dynasty, and a popular school history published in 1863 in New York advised its readers that "China, a vast country of eastern Asia, may be almost said to have no history of any interest to the general reader, it has so few revolutions or political changes to record."[2] India and Southeast Asia were still under the firm control of British, French, and Dutch rulers, and were apparently satisfied with, or at least resigned to, their status as the White Man's Burden.

During the past half-century, however, revolutionary changes have taken place with amazing rapidity in Asia. There has been developing an accelerating movement whose objectives may be said to be "political independence, social equality, a rising standard of living, access to knowledge and the fruits of knowledge, and international security."[3] It was these aims that emerged early in the program of the Indian National Congress founded in 1885; they were back of the nationalistic crusade and subsequent martyrdom of José Rizal in the Philippines in 1896, and they inspired the publication in 1924 of Dr. Sun Yat-sen's *Three Principles of the People.*

What were the basic factors behind this modern awakening of Asia? In general, it was the impact of western culture that brought new economic forces and disturbing and challenging political ideas. The introduction of western education created a small intellectual elite that was stirred by the story of the growth of representative and democratic government in western Europe. The exploits of Giuseppe Garibaldi, Camillo Cavour, and Louis Kossuth and the gospel of nationalism of Joseph Mazzini created the spark and fanned the flame of nationalism. In short, as a former Lieutenant Governor-General of the Dutch East Indies has put it, ". . . This access to the storehouse of Western history and science revealed to him [the educated Asian] that nationalism was the concentrated force behind the exploits of Europe and the United States."[4] Christian missions throughout Asia also played an important role as centers for the diffusion of western ways of life.

Before the penetration of western imperialism, the mass of Asian people lived in their villages, isolated and self-contained. The impact of western economy brought with it a more widespread use of money, the introduction of cash crops, new legal concepts of property and with them frequently the increase of rural peasant debt, the decline of native handicrafts, and the drawing of the heretofore subsistence economy of the peasant into the vortex of world economic forces with their intermittent menace of depression. All of this economic impact was disturbing and unsettling, as the major direction and control of Asian economy passed into the hands of western businessmen.

This exploitation of the natural resources of Asia by western capitalism also stimulated the nationalistic movement in the area and gave it strong ammunition to attack western economic imperialism for its plundering and predatory techniques. In the case of India, we shall see that this accusation was a powerful motive force behind its nationalism. It may be said, however, that while one may easily find examples of ruthless exploitation by western capitalism in Asia, they have not been the rule.

A well known authority on the Dutch East Indies supports this view in this rich colonial area, claiming that the Europeans by reason of their managerial skill and technical knowledge "probably contributed more to the national income [of the Islands] than they received."[5] In taking into consideration the many business failures in tropical areas, it appears that most foreign capital has earned only moderate returns. "Thus while foreign participation in the financial development of Southeast Asia," writes an American economist, "has been called 'ruthless imperialism' by some, it has been largely responsible for such modern industrial development as has occurred. Without such participation the rate of industrial change throughout the area might well carry out the adage that the East is not to be hurried."[6]

While the Asian nationalist's indictment against the West's economic exploitation has been exaggerated, on every hand there has apparently been ample evidence to support his case, for compared with the standards of living in such nations as Canada, the United States, and Great Britain, the majority of people in Asia live amid conditions of unbelievable squalor, provided with barely enough food to keep alive, let alone to enjoy health. One

2- Marcius Willson, Outlines of History, *New York, 1863, pp. 286-7, quoted in Paul H. Clyde,* The Far East *(New York: Prentice-Hall Inc., 1948), p. 1.*

3- Harold H. Fisher, "American Policy and the New Asia," *Far Eastern Survey, XIX (August 16, 1950), pp. 137-138.*

4- H. J. van Mook, The Stakes of Democracy in Southeast Asia *(New York: W. W. Norton & Co., 1950), p. 79.*

5- Amry Vandebosh, "Indonesia," *The New World of Southeast Asia, ed. Lennox A. Mills (Minneapolis: University of Minnesota Press, 1949), p. 104.*

6- Roland S. Vaile, "Southeast Asia in World Economics," *The New World of Southeast Asia, p. 352.*

7- *Foster Bowman Hailey,* Half of One World *(New York: The Macmillan Co., 1950), p. 8.*

United States correspondent, after visiting the East, penned a depressing picture of Asian poverty:

Here is a problem to challenge the world's intelligence: over one-half the world's peoples living on one-tenth of the world's surface (and not by any means the most productive one-tenth), living there in want, in misery, breeding like guinea pigs and dying by the millions each year from preventable diseases or in periodic famines. From one end of Asia to the other one walks always with misery by his side.[7]

While in some instances—as will be shown in India—imperialistic rule can be charged with impeding industrialization or failing to carry through certain essential agrarian reforms, in the main the poverty of Asia can be attributed to customs, traditions, and institutions lying deep and tenaciously within the pattern of culture of the various societies. The mere act of achieving independence does not automatically solve deep-seated economic problems, a truth that such nations as India and Pakistan have been finding it difficult to understand.

In Asia there are too many people on too little land; this land is not tilled efficiently, and the wealth that is produced goes in large part into the pockets of rich merchants, moneylenders, and landlords. The population density has reached a high level in most Asian countries and, despite a high mortality rate, the annual pace of natural increase in some areas has reached 1.5 per cent. The significance of this can be understood when it is pointed out that a natural increase of 1 per cent a year doubles the population in seventy years. Indonesia is a good case in point. Its population in 1800 was about eight million; in 1940 its teeming islands supported seventy million people. Java alone had a population of nearly fifty million crowded into an area no larger than our own state of New York.

In general, the same demographic picture holds true in other parts of Southeast Asia. The Philippines in its first census gave the population in 1903 as over seven million; by 1939 it was sixteen million, and in Burma during the same time span the increase was from ten to sixteen million. In the Indian sub-continent the advance of public health has brought about a distinct reduction in death rates but little change in the high birth rate, with the result that from 1872 to 1941 the population increased from 256 to 389 million, a gain of 52 per cent.

Population pressure does not necessarily bring about low standards of living, as witness the British Isles, which is a densely populated area with a relatively high standard of living. But Britain is a highly industrialized country and can command the latest developments in science and technology. In contrast, Asian countries are predominantly agricultural, industrial resources are underdeveloped, and all economic activity is characterized by low productivity. The highest wheat yield, for example, is less than one-third of that in Europe. Since the close of the Second World War in 1945 there has actually been a food deficit in China, Malaya, Ceylon, Japan, and the Indian Union. While this alarming situation stems basically from population pressure, civil wars and political instability have seriously interfered with agriculture, especially rice production, and to these factors have been added foreign exchange difficulties.

The net effect of all these negative economic factors is a low standard of living for the masses, and in many instances stark poverty. The per capita annual income in China has been estimated to be $23, in India $43, and in Indochina $35. Contrast these figures with an income per person of $1269 in the United States and $660 in the British Isles. Another way of appreciating the economic backwardness of Asia is to point out that four western nations (the United States, Britain, France, and Germany), while containing only 13 per cent of the world's population, yet own nearly 50 per cent of its goods.

The forces of social revolution and political nationalism now convulsing and transforming Asia are less than a century old. In the Philippines the "new thought," the impact of western political liberalism, came to the islands in the latter part of the nineteenth century. There was much criticism of Spanish rule, and the vice-like grip of the landlords on the land gave rise to mounting discontent. The Philippine national movement had its real birth when a group of young patriots, including José Rizal, formed the Young Filipino Party in the early 1890's. Rizal, a brilliant thinker and propagandist, exposed the evils of Spanish rule in novels like *The Social Cancer*. In 1896 he was arrested and shot by the authorities; this established his status as a martyr, and his memory served to strengthen the resolve of the Filipino nationalists to secure their freedom.

Ho Chi Minh

8- *Quoted in Claude Buss, "The Philippines,"* The New World of Southeast Asia, *p. 32.*

9- *Quoted in Charles A. Micaud, "French Indochina,"* The New World of Southeast Asia, *p. 228.*

The Spanish-American War in 1898 complicated the situation, for, after soliciting the aid of Filipino patriots to help defeat the Spanish forces, the United States was compelled to put down the "guerillas," led by Emilio Aguinaldo, who had demanded immediate independence. After the fighting ended in the spring of 1901 the United States took over the task of colonial administration. Our rule in the main was mild and paternalistic. Disease and illiteracy were attacked energetically and our educational system became a model for colonial dependencies everywhere.

A Legislative Assembly was set up in 1907 and from the outset the Nationalist Party, agitating for independence, became the most influential. This organization made sweeping promises: "After independence you will have no taxes, you will have to do less work to feed yourselves, and you will have plenty of time for fiestas."[8] This is not to imply that all or even the larger part of the appeal of the nationalists in the Philippines and elsewhere in Asia was misrepresentation; but undoubtedly wild promises were made to the masses and it was these promises of Utopia, so frequently made, which explain why there has been so much strife and discontent in the Philippines and other former Asian dependencies after independence failed to secure the millennium. As we will see in a later chapter, this has been the case in the Indian Union.

While the Congress of the United States as early as 1916 promised the Philippines independence as soon as stability was achieved, it was not until 1934 that outright independence was guaranteed following a ten-year transitional period. During this decade the Philippine Commonwealth, while practically self-governing, was to be subject to general supervisory powers retained by the government of the United States. In 1945 the Commonwealth was established with Manuel Quezon as the first president.

The growth of nationalism in the Philippines was paralleled in all the other Asian dependencies controlled by western nations, but elsewhere it did not receive the sympathy and encouragement accorded it by the United States. While Britain, it is true, did recognize the aspirations of nationalism in India, Burma, and Ceylon, her gestures in this direction were usually belated and half-hearted. And as for the Dutch and the French regimes in the East Indies and Indochina, there was only the pious hope that paternalistic government might continue indefinitely.

In Indochina, an area larger than Texas, where the peasants have had to endure a pitiably low standard of living and where in some areas overpopulation results in 60 per cent of the farmers owning less than one acre of land, the nationalists complained of the low wages paid to workers, the high taxes, and the refusal of the French to train the people for self-government. An educated minority was being produced in the French schools, but this articulate and ambitious group found little place for itself in the administration. There were warnings uttered by Frenchmen against this policy. One wrote in *Le Monde*, a Paris newspaper, "France cannot educate elite groups . . . unless she really intends to use them. Does one heat a boiler if one does not intend to use its steam?"[9]

By the end of the nineteenth century Indochinese nationalists avidly seized upon the teachings of Rousseau, read the lessons of the French Revolution, and admired the progress made by the Asiatic nation Japan. During the First World War 100,000 workers and soldiers were sent to western Europe, and they returned with strange and exciting ideas.

In the 1920's nationalism steadily forged ahead, and in 1930 a revolt was staged but was easily and ruthlessly put down. The most dynamic and best organized of the nationalist groups was the Communist, which had a very competent leader, Nguyen-Ai-Quoc, later better known as Ho Chi Minh. Born in Annam, this radical eventually made his way to France, where he joined the Communist party. After 1918 he went to Russia, where he learned well the trade of making revolution. Back in Indochina his party carried out underground activities and was the main support of the Viet Minh, or the "League for the Independence of Viet Nam," set up in 1939.

Nationalism in the former Dutch East Indies was born on the Muslim island of Java, where the influence of the Muslim revival in the Near East and Egypt in the late nineteenth century led to the founding in 1908 of an organization for the reviving and strengthening of Islam. Religious aims soon gave way to politics, and in 1913 a political congress asked for evolutionary self-government within the Dutch Empire.

After 1918 the Indonesian nationalist movement became more radical, and in 1926-1927 there were armed revolts in Java and Sumatra. In 1927 the Partai Nasional Indonesia was set up under the leadership of Sukarno, who ultimately was to become the leader of the Republic of Indonesia. Two years later this party was dissolved and its leader, Sukarno, arrested and interned.

Unlike the Americans in the Philippines, and more timorous and cautious than the British in India and Ceylon, the Dutch gave little encouragement to the nationalistic aspirations of their island wards. A representative body was indeed created for the islands in 1918, but it was far from being a real parliament; and, while Indonesians were widely used in the administrative services, 92 per cent of the officials in the higher brackets were European. Dutch rule was paternal and nowhere was tropical agriculture as well guided as in the East Indies. The population for the first time enjoyed a slight margin over bare subsistence and increased at a rapid rate. However, in the field of politics the Dutch followed a conservative policy utilizing what colonial administrators call "Indirect Rule," a system that utilized and worked through already existing native institutions whenever possible. We will see that the British followed a similar policy in those parts of India known as the Native States.

The origin and development of nationalism and social revolution in China parallels these forces that we have already briefly examined in other Asian areas with, however, certain significant differences. China was not on the surface an outright colonial dependency. Imperialistic control was exercised by a number of indirect techniques, such as the control of tariff revenues, extraterritoriality, and spheres of influence. In addition, reform in China had to be directed not only toward ending imperialistic controls but also toward modernizing its own governmental structure, which was hopelessly backward and inept. These efforts were also complicated by the fact that while Chinese leaders progressively succeeded in unshackling their country from old imperialistic bonds, they were confronted by the danger of having to accept far stronger and more painful manacles fashioned by their neighbors, the Japanese.

Omens of change and social revolt in China can be traced as far back as the Taiping Rebellion in 1850. This confused and ill-organized peasant re-

form movement failed, and it was not until the 1890's that a new revolutionary movement emerged, dedicated to the overthrow of the hated Manchu emperor and the abolition of the many galling privileges enjoyed by foreign powers in China. The final outcome was the October Revolution of 1911, the abdication of the Manchu dynasty, and the proclamation of a Republic. Behind this achievement were the personality and program of Dr. Sun Yat-sen, a reformer and nationalist who had dedicated his life to the creation of a new China. Dr. Sun's program is contained in his *Three Principles of the People*, in which he advocated (1) nationalism, or freedom of China from alien domination; (2) democracy, or government by the people; and (3) livelihood, or economic security for the people.

The new Republic did not find the going smooth. It came under the control of war lords and ceased to symbolize the spirit of reform in China. At Canton, however, Sun Yat-sen established a rival party, the Kuomintang, and a Nationalist government. This new regime received valuable aid from Soviet Russia at a time when the western powers were either lukewarm or openly hostile to the Nationalists. In 1925 Dr. Sun died, but his work was carried on by a capable disciple, Chiang Kai-shek, whose armies the following year carried out the famous Northern Expedition, destroying the predatory war lords and gaining control of the Yangtze Valley. By 1928 the Nationalist offensive had been completely successful and General Chiang was ensconced in his new capital at Peking.

In 1927, however, a split had occurred within the Kuomintang. One wing of the Nationalists, the left, followed Communist ideology and sought a far-reaching social revolution. The right wing, more conservative, represented the middle class and above all the wealthy financial groups. The result was a purge, the ousting and exile of the pro-Communists. "The purpose of the right-wing Kuomintang, now in the saddle, was to eradicate from party and government not only the Communists but also all liberal elements interested in fundamental political and social reform."[10]

During the decade 1927-1937 much was done by the Nationalist government to expand industry, to promote education and public health, and to bring in qualified engineers and technicians. Above all, the "New Tide," or the Chinese Renaissance, stimulated nationalism, changed old ways and

10- Clyde, op. cit., p. 548.

Sukarno

faiths, and expressed itself in a dynamic student movement that frequently demonstrated against Japan and against western imperialism. By 1931 China had 17,000 students in 34 colleges, and another 234,000 were in secondary schools. Scholarly journals appeared and university publications, like *The New Tide* of Peking University, became the vehicle for the diffusion of new ideas. A literary revolution was also carried out, in which the famous scholar Dr. Hu Shih sponsored the use of the popular language of the people rather than the classical form of the past.

A start had also been made by the Nationalist government in the direction of securing control over its tariff and removing the numerous privileges enjoyed by nationals of western powers. This program was abruptly halted when imperialism had to be combated from another quarter, Japan. In 1931 Japan seized Manchuria and subsequently began to expand into north China. Chiang ignored this threat from the north and instead concentrated upon crushing what he regarded as an even greater menace at home. The purge of the left wing from the Kuomintang had not eliminated Communist influence in China. In 1931 Communists had set up their own government in Kiangsi province, proceeding to carry out agrarian reforms and to wage guerilla warfare. Their two top leaders were Mao Tse-tung and Chu Teh. It was against the Communists rather than the foreign invader that Chiang concentrated his military power and in a full scale offensive in 1934 the Communists were scattered and forced to retreat in their Long March of some six thousand miles to a new base at Yenan.

As Japan pushed relentlessly into China from the north, there was increasing dissatisfaction, especially from the student organizations, with Chiang's civil war against the Communists. Finally, in December 1936, a measure of unity was restored, with Nanking and the Communists pledged to fight the common foe. But it was an unstable alliance. The Nationalist regime had moved far to the right since the early days of Sun Yat-sen's idealistic program. It was a highly conservative, one-party government. On the other hand, the Communists championed a program of nationalization and reform whose every plank was anathema to Chiang and his bourgeois supporters. In essence, the Japanese invasion merely furnished a temporary distraction; once it

was removed, both forces would inevitably return to the original struggle.

As the Indian sub-continent is the main theme of the chapters that follow, there is no need at this point to discuss the rise of nationalism and the many-sided effects of the impact of western culture upon Indian life and institutions. It may be said, however, that in India, as in the greater part of Asia, the following conditions held true: (1) Western powers controlled the great majority of the capital invested in modern real estate, plantations, trade, and industry. (2) The masses of the people were mainly tillers of the soil; a small proportion went to the cities for factory employment but usually failed to better their economic status. (3) A great socio-cultural transformation was taking place compounded of new educational methods; the decay of old faiths and loyalties; the rise of feminism; the establishment of a modern press comprising periodicals and newspapers; and the strong overriding belief of the western educated intellectuals that much of the indigenous pattern of culture must be swept away, or at least modified, in favor of democracy, technology, and modern science. (4) As in all of the Asian regions we have discussed, it was the middle class that was the spearhead for reform. Gladstonian Liberalism, with its belief in suffrage reform, representative government, justice in the courts, and an efficient civil service, was the program of most early twentieth-century Asian nationalists. It was not until the late 1930's that one could discern the rise of a definite socio-economic movement having socialistic and even communistic goals. (5) The prevailing idea of most nationalists was that independence would solve all; that once the imperialist was expelled, his Asian victims would at once enter a promised land.

It was the onset of global war in 1939 that accelerated the tempo of Asian nationalism. Throughout the United Nations there was much sincere discussion of "What do we stand for?" and "What are our peace aims?" and at the same time there was a recognition of the fundamental contradiction inherent in fighting Nazi imperialism while, at the same time, the democratic nations maintained their species of imperialism over much of Africa and Asia. The promulgation of the Atlantic Charter in 1941 by the president of the United States and the prime minister of Great Britain, with its announcement that "They respect the right of all

Chiang Kai-shek

peoples to choose the form of government under which they will live . . . ," seemed to Asian nationalists a pledge by the great imperial powers of the voluntary liquidation of their colonial empires. The Cripps mission to India in the spring of 1942 and the British emissary's pledge that at the conclusion of the conflict India would be free to frame its own form of government also encouraged the aspirations of Asian nationalism. Wendell Willkie in his widely read book *One World* called upon the imperial powers to liquidate their empires and draw up a definite time table of freedom. The former United States Under-Secretary of State, Sumner Welles, declared in a widely quoted statement that victory must bring with it the liberation of all peoples, that the age of imperialism was ended. The right of a people to their freedom would have to be recognized and the principles of the Atlantic Charter be guaranteed to the world as a whole.

On the field of battle Japanese victories destroyed the widely held belief that western nations, especially Britain and the United States, were invincible. As they occupied the Dutch East Indies, the Philippines, French Indochina, British Malaya, and Burma, the Japanese disseminated a continuous stream of anti-western propaganda. In the Dutch Indies they launched the so-called "Three *A* Movement," which advertised Japan as the Light of Asia, the Protector of Asia, and the Leader of Asia. In the occupied areas the Japanese paid careful attention to the impressionable youths and students, giving them military drill and indoctrinating them with Japanese ideology.

It is little wonder, then, that after the wave of Japanese conquest had subsided the colonial dependencies, in most instances, had no intention of returning to the *status quo ante bellum*. Ultimately, in the disturbed five years that followed VJ Day, six new nations emerged: Burma, Ceylon, the Indian Union, the Republic of the Philippines, Pakistan, and Indonesia. In a slightly different category were two additional new governments: Communist China, which had triumphed over the Nationalist regime of Chiang Kai-shek, and the Republic of Korea, which had been sponsored by the United Nations.

The young nations liberated from the yoke of western imperialism have not found much tranquillity in their new status of independence. Burma is a good case in point. During the war Aung San

had emerged as the outstanding champion of Burmese nationalism, first against the British and then against the Japanese. With the achievement of peace, Aung San succeeded in obtaining the promise of independence from the British Labour government, but, even before this could be realized, factional disputes had broken out in Burma which culminated in the brutal assassination of Aung San and six of his ministers. A new leader, Thakin Nu, became the head of the Burmese government, and independence was celebrated on January 4, 1948, amid the chants of yellow-robed Buddhist priests and volleys of gunfire. While these ceremonies were being carried out, however, the country was in a state of chronic unrest; and, as the Burmese Chief Justice of the High Court observed, "It should be a happy time for us, this day of our independence. But I look upon it with foreboding. What do you see when you look out of my window? Armed guards. Is this what 'freedom' means?"[11]

Events soon justified this official's disquietude, for in the spring of 1948 the country was rent by civil war that quickly assumed a highly confused character. At least four main dissident groups, including "Red Flag Trotzkyite" Communists and the "White Flag Stalinist" Communists, were engaged. In the ensuing struggle some thirty thousand lives were lost, millions of dollars of damage was done to property, and the country was brought to the brink of bankruptcy. No wonder that a Burmese high official later declared that independence was a "gamble that went wrong."[12] In 1950 the situation improved somewhat. Many of the rebels were rounded up and the British Commonwealth countries eased the desperate financial situation by granting a loan of six million pounds to Thakin Nu's government. Much remains to be done, however, before law and order is achieved. Government forces are in possession of the main towns, but the Burmese countryside is still virtually a "no man's land."

The new Dominion of Ceylon is a notable exception to the conditions of financial stress and political instability found in Burma and in most of the liberated Asian countries. This beautiful little island just off the southernmost part of India is prosperous, well governed, and happily busy with promising schemes for social and educational reform. Ceylon's great neighbors, the Indian Union and Pakistan, have not been so fortunate. As we

11- *United Press, Jan. 4, 1948.*

12- The New York Times, *Nov. 28, 1948.*

Quirino

will see in a later chapter, independence for these new states was accompanied by wholesale massacre and the migration of millions of refugees. India in particular has been plagued by a serious food shortage.

As for the Philippines, the prospect is none too reassuring. The expulsion of the Japanese from the Islands brought freedom but also left behind gutted cities, smashed docks and harbors, and disarranged communications. While the United States committed itself to make free grants of more than two billion dollars to help in rehabilitation, the burden of removing the scars of war has proved to be a heavy one for the young Republic. The Philippines are rich in natural resources but the masses of the people are poor. The *taos* (peasants) are mainly illiterate, easy-going, and lax. Much of their money goes to the landlord and the moneylender. Because of the wide gap between the wealthy middle class and the agrarian aristocracy, on the one hand, and the peasants on the other, social unrest was rising rapidly on the eve of World War II. Since 1945 unrest has reached serious dimensions. In 1942 the guerilla organization called the Huks had been formed to harry the Japanese invader. In addition to fighting against the foreign overlord the Huks began to carry out agrarian reforms, and in the process many landlords were killed. Following peace the farmer-guerillas refused to disarm, kept the land they had taken, defied the government of President Manuel Roxas, and continued their terroristic activities against the landlords, and then against the police and soldiery of the government which sought to destroy them.

Five years after the close of the war, unrest, outrages, and sporadic fighting still existed in the Philippines. And, to make matters worse, there were disturbing evidences of corruption in the government. While Luis Taruc, the Huk leader, claims to be a Filipino first and seems to have no intention of accepting dictation from Moscow, there is little doubt that he follows Communist ideology. It was evident, also, that the government was not living within its means. The huge credits supplied by the United States were exhausted and the government was borrowing heavily. By 1950 it was apparent that, unless the government were purged of scandal and graft and unless basic agrarian reforms were initiated, President Elpidio Quirino's administration might well suffer the

same fate as befell the Kuomintang Nationalists in China. The Huks and their allies would come to power and no one could hazard whether they would be free agents or would become the satellites of Russian communistic imperialism.

It is hard to present an adequate discussion of postwar trends in Indonesia. The general picture has been one of confusion and bewildering complexity. Following Japanese surrender it was six weeks before British troops arrived to round up enemy prisoners and establish an interim allied authority. Two days after the surrender, however, the Indonesian Nationalists, Sukarno and Hatta, proclaimed the independence of the Republic of Indonesia. There followed five years of negotiation punctuated by intermittent fighting. The British occupation forces soon turned over their responsibilities to the Dutch, who attempted to work out some satisfactory agreement with the Indonesian Nationalists. In 1946 the Netherlands government offered self-government qualified by a few special powers retained by the Dutch.

Little progress was made toward a solution, however, and in July 1947 the Dutch forces took "police action" against the Republic. In the following summer the quarrel was brought before the United Nations, and this body appointed a special Committee of Good Offices to mediate between the contestants. Agreements were signed, but mutual suspicions and intermittent outbreaks of terrorism blocked a satisfactory solution, and again in December 1948 Dutch forces initiated their second "police action" against the Indonesians. The final outcome was a Round Table Conference held at the Hague from August to December, 1949, in which nearly complete agreement was reached between the Dutch and Indonesian negotiators.

Sovereignty was turned over to the Republic of the United States of Indonesia, a federal government consisting of fifteen states of which the dominant one was the Indonesian Republic. At the same time a Netherlands-Indonesian Union was created which provided for a loose, consultative partnership between the Dutch and the Indonesian federal governments. It is doubtful whether in practice this partnership will really mean very much. The Indonesians mean to be masters in their own house, and the consultative partnership was mainly a face-saving formula for the Dutch. Independence, however, did not write the last chapter in the turbulent post-war history of Indonesia. Differences broke out between the Indonesian Republic and some of the smaller federal states, who were inclined to resent and fear the dominance of the former in the federal structure. It was apparent that federalism as well as the union with the Netherlands was to be merely a theoretical figment as the Indonesian Republic strove to extend its authority over all parts of the Indonesian Union. The result was civil strife and military actions.

In all of Asia, the most acute disappointment and even tragic development to the democracies of the western world, especially the United States, has been the course of events in China. At war's end in 1945 Nationalist China seemed to have reached all of its objectives. Not only had the Japanese been expelled from the homeland but China's old territory, including Formosa and Manchuria, was to be restored. China also had been given a seat in the Security Council of the United Nations, sitting alongside the greatest powers in the world. Yet, in spite of these happy auguries and the fact that the United States gave in aid, after 1945, more than two billion dollars, the regime of Chiang Kai-shek steadily deteriorated and finally collapsed before the Communist armies of Mao Tse-tung.

During the war liberals such as Sun Fo had criticized the Kuomintang regime for its ultra-conservatism. This worthy son of the great Sun Yat-sen commented in 1944: "We must frankly admit the fact that . . . the machinery and practice of the Kuomintang have turned in a wrong direction, inconsistent with the Party Constitution drafted by Dr. Sun Yat-sen in 1923 and contrary to the spirit of democracy."[13] Following the surrender of Japan, the forces of the United States, both army and navy, cooperated with General Chiang, assisting his divisions to take over strategic areas, especially in North China and in Manchuria. But civil war broke out almost immediately between the Communists and the Kuomintang. The former had been helped by Soviet Russia's conveniently abandoning in Manchuria large supplies of arms which Mao Tse-tung used to equip new divisions.

It was the policy of the United States to try to encourage agreement and compromise between the warring factions. Our government was ready to assist Chiang financially, but urged that his regime be broadened by the inclusion of moderates and liberals from all groups. General George C. Marshall was sent to China to help work out some such solution, but he failed because of the obstruction by fanatics in the Communist camp and by the reactionaries in the Kuomintang. In effect Marshall castigated the extremists in both groups and declared in his Report that China's salvation lay with the liberal middle-roaders who were patriotic, moderate, but powerless.

The Marshall Report meant that the United States was to wash its hands of the Chinese civil war, cease the thankless task of mediation, stop sending money to Chiang, and let nature take its course. It did not take long for the last named result. The Nationalist government squandered its initial post-war superiority in men and material. Its ranks were weakened by internal schisms; its leadership was static and ineffectual, its rule corrupt and often brutal, and its military strategy suicidal.

On the other hand, the strength of Mao Tse-tung steadily increased. Most of the supplies provided Chiang by the United States ended up in some fashion or other in Communist arsenals. Mao's land reforms earned the support of the peasants, while the intellectuals in the cities became disgusted with the Kuomintang and deserted it, providing Mao with the essential cadre of leaders to organize the Chinese masses. Steadily the Communist armies drove southward until all effective resistance by the Nationalists had been destroyed and a rather forlorn exile regime of Chiang Kai-shek on the island of Formosa was all that was left. There have been numerous explanations for the triumph of the Chinese Communists. Perhaps as good an explanation as any was that the Communists merely filled a vacuum which had been created by the collapse and actual self-destruction of the Kuomintang. In a sense, there was really no government to overthrow, for it fell of its own weight. In the final analysis, neither the United States nor Russia dictated the course of history in China.

Following the end of World War II the Soviet Union saw its opportunity to increase its own national power and discredit the prestige of its rivals in the West by directing the Asian flux to serve its own ends. Russian statesmen sensed the shift of the Asian revolution from a purely political program to one that stressed economic changes and social reform as well as nationalism. The

13- *Quoted in Agnes Smedley, "The Social Revolution," China: The United Nations Series, ed. Harley F. MacNair (Berkeley: University of California Press, 1946), p. 187.*

Mao Tse-tung

Soviet Union claimed to be the opponent of all economic privilege and exploitation anywhere and at any time. It offered its ideology, its training methods for would-be revolutionary leaders, and on occasion both arms and money to those Asians who wished both to be free and to be rid of the rapacious moneylender and landlord. In reality, of course, this championship of Asian social reform and anti-colonialism was a technique for the expansion of Soviet imperialism. The Tsars had their own particular methods, which were largely ineffectual, for advancing the geopolitical aims of Imperial Russia. The present rulers in the Kremlin have utilized Communism. As one observer has sagely commented: "Even Lenin failed to see what Stalin saw — that Russia could not be trimmed and snipped to fit the Communist coat, but the Communist coat had to be cut to the Russian measure. Stalin was no more taken in by Marx than Henry VIII of England, say, was taken in by St. Augustine."[14]

The opportunity provided in Asia after 1945 by suffering brought on by the war, by the rise of social unrest, and by the inexperience and weakness of the newly created governments was too good to be missed. Wherever possible, Communist Russia intervened, covertly and indirectly at first but by 1950 openly. In Burma Communist organizations were directed to carry out strikes and oppose the government by force. In the Union of India the Communists, estimated to number perhaps one hundred thousand, resorted to terrorism and sabotage, especially against the railroads and all transportation agencies. Malaya is the best example of sheer obstruction and terrorism which can hardly claim any legitimate reformist or idealistic objective as their justification. In British Malaya there is no question of a demand for self-government on the part of the Malays, who are now outnumbered by the Chinese and Indians, immigrant communities whose loyalties reside in their original homelands. In 1948 a band of Communists, estimated to be only 5000 in number and mainly Chinese, began a systematic campaign of terrorism, shooting down influential Malays and their own countrymen who refused to aid them, murdering plantation managers on the rubber estates, and damaging equipment in the tin mines. This entire effort was aimed first at paralyzing all business in Malaya, thus striking a body blow against capitalist Britain, which was earning many

14- Lewis Galantiere, "Through the Russian Looking Glass," Foreign Affairs, XXVIII (October 1949), p. 124.

dollars by its sales of rubber and tin to the United States, and, second, at so terrorizing the populace that they would support a Communist republic in Malaya.

Over two hundred acts of terrorism were carried out in one week, and the British government was forced to send a division of regular troops and to organize a Malayan constabulary of some 50,000 men. By the end of 1950 some progress had been made in extirpating the terrorist bands, but the almost impenetrable jungle made a thorough mop-up impossible, and the Communists still continued to carry on their hit-and-run campaign.

The situation in Indochina is not as clear cut as in Malaya, for in the former there is an undeniably strong nationalist movement which has joined forces with the anti-French Communist leader, Ho Chi Minh. Just what the relative proportions of nationalism and Communism are in the revolutionary movement it is difficult to say. The basic question may well be whether the Communists think of themselves as the most powerful tool Indochinese nationalism can utilize to gain its aims or whether they look upon nationalism as only a cloak for the victory of Communism. The French in 1946 recognized an Indochinese Federation in which the Republic of Viet Nam— the most nationalistic part of Indochina—would enjoy a large measure of independence within the larger framework of the French Union. In 1949 the French signed an accord with the former emperor of Annam, Bao Dai, setting up Tonkin, Annam, and Cochin China as the autonomous state of Viet Nam, which with the kingdoms of Laos and Cambodia formed the Indochinese Federation.

Ho Chi Minh and his Viet Minh Party, however, have refused to accept the French offers, and guerilla warfare has been carried out by his followers since 1946. France has had to keep 150,000 of her best troops in Indochina and the campaign is costing her millions of francs. Most Indochinese apparently regard Bao Dai as a French puppet and refuse to give their full support to French authorities. Whether France could win over their approval by more generous offers of colonial self-government, similar to British Dominion status, is a moot question. It is probable that the extremists in the Communist group would refuse even this gesture, as their apparent goal is not a free Indochina, friendly and allied to France, but a communistic Indochina, bound to Russia and unfriendly to her former imperial ruler and to the West in general.

In the spring of 1950 the situation in Asia became critical. The Soviet satellite state of North Korea, aided and abetted by Russia, invaded its neighbor, South Korea, the creation and the ward of the United Nations. Acting for this international body, large forces of the United States, together with small contingents from Britain, Australia, and other U.N. member countries, carried on full-scale war against the aggressors during the last half of 1950. On the eve of seeming U.N. victory, however, the Chinese Communist regime of Mao Tse-tung intervened and sent several armed divisions to the Korean battlefront from Manchuria. Intervention in this war seemed to indicate that Mao's military alliance with Russia meant something after all and that the Chinese Communists were ready and willing to fight against nations dubbed as enemies of Communism by the U.S.S.R. and as Western imperialists by many Asians. Another disturbing development was the Chinese Communist invasion of Tibet, which will be discussed in a later chapter in connection with the post-war foreign policy of India.

As the democratic world, and the United States in particular, witnessed these developments, the dread possibility of an entire Asia bound to and controlled by the U.S.S.R. emerged. Even worse, there appeared the prospect of a third world war. As Stewart Alsop sized up the situation:

> The best way to understand the process that is now at work is in terms of the homely pastime of bowling. What may now happen in Asia is precisely what happens when a good bowler hits the head pin hard. The head pin was China. It is down already. The two pins in the second row are Indochina and Burma. They are visibly wobbling. If they go, the three pins of the third row, Siam, Malaya and Indonesia, are pretty sure to topple in their turn. And if the rest of Asia falls, the resulting psychological, political and economic magnetism will almost certainly drag down the four great pins of the fourth row: India, and Pakistan, Japan, and the Philippines.[15]

As the strongest power and the leader of the democratic West, the United States was seriously aroused by the advance of Communism in Asia. In western Europe American efforts to contain Russian expansion had been, on the whole, successful. The Truman Doctrine had resulted in our intervention in Greece and the eventual destruction of the Communist forces that had threatened to take over the country. The Marshall Plan, initiated in 1948, enabled the western European nations to rebuild with American money their shattered economies and thus achieve for their people a better standard of living. And the North Atlantic Alliance definitely banded the free states of Europe together to resist Russian aggression. These measures, initiated largely by the United States, halted the westward march of Communism in Europe.

The situation in Asia, however, was infinitely more complex. A great socio-economic revolution was in progress and Russia was taking full advantage of it. The United States was not against social revolution and the establishment of economic justice and political freedom in any land. In fact our national traditions placed us squarely against colonialism and economic exploitation. We were, however, seriously alarmed at social revolution being tied to and made the dupe of Russian imperialism. The dilemma of the United States was how to encourage and cooperate with the forces of social change in Asia without delivering them into the hands of the Kremlin.

At the end of 1950, the State Department of the United States was feverishly considering every available means at its disposal to help the Asian nations solve their problems, especially mass poverty, and at the same time halt the expansion of revolutionary Communism. It was in these circumstances that the Indian Union and Pakistan took on unusual importance. While both these states were confronted by serious problems, they exhibited a stability and a unity not found in the other Asian nations. Above all they were relatively untouched by Communism and were strongly influenced by democratic traditions.

It would seem that India and Pakistan are the logical national units around which may be built a new and stable, and, it is hoped, a prosperous Asia, which may stand as a buttress against the expansion of Russian Communism. In these states there is yet the opportunity for America and the British Commonwealth to study and assist the economic and social transformation that is now in progress throughout Asia. Since all the basic problems and conditions of Asia are reproduced, more or less, in miniature form in the Indian subcontinent, it is logical to choose India and Pakistan as case studies for analysis.

5- Stewart Alsop, *"We Are Losing Asia Fast,"* Saturday Evening Post *(March 11, 1950),* 127.

In the years immediately following
the end of World War II, Asia with its
half of the population of the globe
was convulsed with social and
political revolution. This was the
situation in the Indian sub-
continent, where nationalism had
reached its highest peak of intensity.
The demands for independence came to
a head just at a time when Great
Britain was emerging from a world
conflict weak and impoverished and
in no condition, even had she so wished,
to maintain her imperial control over
four hundred million unwilling
subjects. In 1947 she gave
up all authority in India.

THE QUESTION naturally arises, what
was India like in the year of her independence after nearly two centuries
of British rule? What were the
problems faced by her two new states
of Pakistan and the Union of India
when British governors, district officers,
and their regiments sailed from
Bombay and Karachi in the fall of
1947? The Indian sub-continent is
racially, religiously, and linguistically one of the most complex areas
in the world. Even to the English, to
whom it should be best known, India
has in many respects remained a myste-
rious and incomprehensible land, while
to most Americans it has been a
distant and strange country compounded
of such elements as the Black Hole
of Calcutta, the Taj Mahal, the Burning
Ghats, and the enigmatic figure of
Mohandas Gandhi.

TO PEOPLE of the western world, and
especially to those in the United
States, it is becoming more and more
evident that myths and ignorance about
Asia and especially India must be
superseded by adequate unbiased knowledge
and sympathetic interest. One must,
therefore, go figuratively into the
700,000 villages in the Indian
sub-continent and its great cities
to discover how farmers, businessmen,
and industrial laborers live.

The facts of

Indian life

chapter 1

IF A map of the Indian sub-continent were superimposed on one of Europe, it would stretch north to south from Norway across the Mediterranean and almost to the African coast; and east to west it would cover an area from within England to well inside Russia. India is a sub-continent of 1,600,000 square miles, as large as western Europe without Russia, nearly twenty times the size of Great Britain, and about half the size of the United States. The large land mass stretches over twenty-nine parallels of latitude, with its northern area in the same zone as California or Virginia and its southern in the same as that of Nigeria or Venezuela.

India is a huge peninsula jutting down from its massive mountain base into the Indian Ocean and shaped like a great triangle. No country has ever been more influenced by its geographical features. India's hot climate has undoubtedly conditioned the attitude toward life and the social organization of its people. Its dependence upon the monsoons —the life-giving rains—has always given nature a cruel whip hand over man. Above all, the Himalayan mountain chain has walled India off from neighboring lands and made it a distinct geographical entity. While not offering complete protection from invasion—for many invaders have come through the passes—the Himalayas have isolated India and go far to explain both her distinctive culture and the remarkable continuity of her civilization.

The Land and the People

India can be divided into four main regions. The Hill Country and the Mountain Zone in the extreme north contain such great peaks as Everest (29,141 feet) and Kanchenjunga. This wild and beautiful section, while sparsely populated, has valuable forests and great water-power resources. At the foot of the Hill Country lie the great northern plains, stretching two thousand miles and watered by three river systems—the Indus, the Ganges, and the Brahmaputra. These plains can be thought of as stretching, crescent fashion, west to east, from the Arabian Sea to the Bay of Bengal. The plains of the Indus are largely barren. Rivers are used for irrigation in what is known as "Dry India," and the Indus River serves the same function as does the Nile in Egypt. The eastern half of the plains country is the fertile Ganges valley.

Enjoying plentiful rainfall and endowed with rich alluvial soil, it is one of the most productive areas in the world, with a population estimated at almost 175 million. All this plains region has been known throughout history as Hindustan and has been the traditional center of Indian culture. Directly to the south of Hindustan is the great tableland of the Deccan. Shaped like the larger triangle of the Indian sub-continent, its base is formed by the rugged Vindhya Mountains, which separate it from the plains country. Not far from the coast the walls or scarps, called Ghats, of the Deccan fall abruptly down to the sea. The soil of the tableland is not rich but it possesses great mineral resources. Between the Ghats and the sea is yet another region, the long and narrow coastal plains, and in the far south, where the eastern plain broadens out somewhat, is an area called Tamil Land.

The population of India in 1941 was 389 million, constituting one of the three great population masses of the world. Perhaps the most striking feature of its people is their diversity in culture, race, and religion. India has well been called one of the greatest ethnographical museums in the world. The reason lies in the many streams of invaders who have come through the mountain passes. An English anthropologist well expressed this fact when he declared, "The sub-continent of India has been likened to a deep net into which various races and peoples of Asia have drifted and been caught."[1] Three of the main racial groups of the world, the so-called yellow, black, and white, are represented in India, and these in turn have been further divided into seven distinct racial types.

Perhaps the most simple classification would be as follows: First, there are Indians, many of whom are tall, fair-skinned, and long-nosed, whose language is derived from Sanskrit. Known as Aryans or Indo-Aryans, these people live mainly in the north, and most of the high castes belong to this group. The people in the south, the second group, are darker and shorter and speak languages altogether different from the Sanskrit-derived tongues of the north. These southern Indians are referred to by the generic term Dravidians. In addition to the Indo-Aryans and the Dravidians, a third group is made up of some twenty-five million members of primitive tribes living in more or less isolated areas in the hills and

1- *J. H. Hutton*, Caste in India *(Cambridge: Cambridge University Press, 1946), p. 1.*

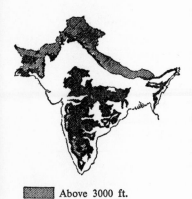

Above 3000 ft.

1000 to 3000 ft.

Below 1000 ft.

2- H. N. Brailsford, Subject India (New York: John Day Co., 1943), p. 119.

3- A. M. Lorenzo, "Atlas of India," Oxford Pamphlets on Indian Affairs, No. 16 (Bombay: Oxford University Press, 1943), p. 8.

4- Cambridge History of India, I (Cambridge: Cambridge University Press, 1922), p. 38.

jungles. The lot of these backward, childlike people has been an unhappy one. The impact of modern civilization has brought demoralization, the loss of their land, the decay of their old traditions with their ancient dances and myths, and the spread of disease. The fourth racial group is the Mongoloid. This type is found in Burma, Assam, Nepal, and the northern fringe of the United Provinces, the Punjab, and Kashmir. These people have a yellowish complexion, beardless faces, and high cheekbones. The mountain Gurkhas of Nepal, renowned for their military prowess in the British Indian army, are a good example of this Mongoloid type.

With so many ethnic groups it is natural that the linguistic situation is most complex. One language survey has found 179 languages and 544 dialects in India. This analysis, however, tends to overemphasize language complications, as many of the dialects are spoken by only a few tribes, and at least two dozen of the languages are relatively insignificant. There are only fifteen major languages, the most important of which is Hindustani. This language in its spoken form is understood by 150 million people. Unfortunately its written form is divided into High-Hindi, using the Sanskrit script, and Urdu, based on Persian script. Hindustani and related Indo-European languages are spoken by 70 per cent of the Indians, and these languages "are so closely akin that a quick-witted man who speaks one of them can with very little practice understand most if not all the others."[2] In the south of India, people speak Dravidian tongues, their users numbering some seventy million people.

During the past century English has occupied a unique place in India. It has been the lingua franca in what otherwise would have approached very close to a Tower of Babel, enabling educated men from all parts of India to understand each other. In 1931 out of twenty-eight million who could read and write, three and a half million could speak English.

While there has been a tendency on the part of English writers to exaggerate the linguistic complexity and for Indians to gloss it over, there is no doubt that the language problem is a serious one in India. There is no getting round the fact that in 1941 the All-India Radio was broadcasting in sixteen languages. We will return to this language problem in a later chapter, when we will see that it caused much controversy in the Indian Union after independence.

Most of India is either subtropical or intertropical. Generally speaking, it is an extremely hot land. The plains of the north are much warmer than the same latitudes in North America, the temperature often reaching 125 degrees Fahrenheit. Briefly summing up, it can be said that in the north the short winters are moderate but during the rest of the year temperatures are very high, and elsewhere—although extremes do not exist to the same degree as in the plains—it is always hot.

India is dependent upon the monsoons for its rain, especially the moisture-laden winds from the south-west that start in May. The months from June to September are always anxious ones in India, for if the monsoon fails famine results. An Indian geographer discussing the monsoon observes: "In a variable climate, such as we find in India, one year may be warm and wet, and full of crops, and another hot and dry, and famine stricken, one region may be inhabited by a healthy and prosperous peasantry, such as we find in the Punjab, and another by a half-starved mass of humanity, such as we notice in Central India."[3]

All in all, India is one of the most complex and diverse countries in the world. In its geography there are all kinds of contrasts: aridity and the heaviest rainfall in the world; lands of eternal snow and the humid, baking plains of the south; the highest of mountains and the flat plains at their feet. Racially and linguistically the human material is also infinitely complicated. There are also wide differences in the culture levels of the people. Professor E. J. Rapson has pointed out:

We now find, at one extreme of the social scale, communities whose members are contributing to the advancement of the literature, science, and art of the twentieth century, and, at the other extreme, tribes still governed by their primitive constitutions, still using the implements and weapons, and still retaining the religious ideas and customs of their remote ancestors in the Stone Age.[4]

As subsequent chapters will show, there are additional complications in human organization in India. There is caste, for example, and in religion there is more diversity than in all of Europe. India, with its immense size and population and its many contrasts in geography, race, and culture, is a fascinating land and one that has a strong

lure for its thinking sons and daughters, who are deeply moved by its rich variety. Jawaharlal Nehru had all this in mind when he wrote:

When I think of India, I think of many things: broad fields dotted with innumerable small villages; of towns and cities I have visited; of the magic of the rainy season which pours life into the dry, parched-up land and converts it suddenly into a glistening expanse of beauty and greenery, of great rivers and flowing water; of the Khyber Pass in all its bleak surroundings; of the southern tip of India; of people, individually and in the mass; and above all, of the Himalayas, snow-capped, or some mountain valley in Kashmir in the spring, covered with new flowers, and with a brook bubbling and gurgling through it.[5]

The Political and Economic Map of India

A political map of pre-independent India presented a bewildering mosaic of British provinces and Indian Native States all jumbled together in a confusing patchwork. Slightly more than half of the total land area of India had by conquest and annexation come under the direct rule of the British government. Known as British India, and usually colored red on the map, its territory often surrounded or mingled with that of the Native States, which were ruled by Indian maharajas and nawabs under the benevolent protection of Great Britain.

At the outbreak of World War II, British India was administered by the Government of India Act of 1935 and consisted of eleven provinces, among them Bombay, Madras, Bengal, and the Punjab. Some of these provinces were as large as a single European nation of fair size and supported a comparable population. Madras, for example, was as large as Italy, with a population of forty-seven million. Within these provinces, which had their own legislatures and provincial officials, there was a considerable degree of autonomy. However, their executives, the British Governors, were endowed with special powers enabling them to intervene in the event of a deadlock in the legislature or in the case of a threatened breakdown of law and order.

Apart from the provinces, where the people were British subjects and the land British territory, were the Native States, 562 in number, comprising an area of 715,000 square miles inhabited by 90 million people. More than half of the area of the

States belonged to the twenty-four largest; some of them, like Hyderabad, Mysore, Travancore, and Kashmir, were veritable countries. Hyderabad, for example, had an area of 82,000 square miles, with a Nizam—the ruler—who had sixteen million subjects. On the other hand, many of the States were quite diminutive, incongruous vestigial remnants from a remote past. More than three hundred of them had altogether a land area of barely six thousand square miles with a population of less than one million. In some instances the State might consist of only a few acres with a population of less than fifty.

Generally speaking, the people of the Native States were less influenced than those of British India by the impact of western civilization brought in by the European rulers. In the States much of the color, the picturesqueness, and sometimes the barbarity of medieval India lingered on. Here the courts of the maharajas, supported by prodigious funds supplied by poor peasantry, sponsored costly festivals, tiger-shoots, elephant processions, and entertainment for visitors on a lavish scale. Outside the courts of the rulers the rich traditions and culture of the past survived among the people in their handicrafts, their colorful costumes, and their ancient ceremonials.

Much has been said and written in denunciation of the Native Princes, whose domains have been defined as "anachronistic pools of absolutism in the modern world."[6] The best of the maharajas were benevolent despots presiding over progressive and well-governed States such as Baroda, Mysore, and Travancore; the worst of them were cruel tyrants or irresponsible spendthrifts. Many of the maharajas lived like English country gentry. They traveled widely and were quite at home on the boulevards of Paris or in Park Lane in London. Great sportsmen, they spent huge sums on their stables and frequently were mighty hunters, stalking the lion, tiger, hippopotamus, and buffalo. Above all, a Native Prince was proud of the gun salutes accorded to him by the British. Only those Princes with an eleven gun salute merited the title of "Highness." There were only five rulers enjoying what was the ultimate in status—a twenty-one gun salute; and of the entire number of Princes almost three-quarters, regarded as small fry, were granted no right to gun salutes whatsoever.

The Native States, as will be seen in succeeding chapters, originated in their modern form when

5- *Jawaharlal Nehru,* The Discovery of India *(New York: John Day Co., 1946), p. 51.*

6- *John Gunther,* Inside Asia *(New York: Harper and Brothers, 1939), p. 444.*

their rulers in the latter part of the eighteenth century and early in the next accepted the suzerainty and protection of the British crown. While in a sense independent, the Native States had to recognize what came to be known as the principle of Paramountcy, by which Great Britain controlled the foreign affairs of each of the States and also reserved the right to interfere in a State's domestic affairs in the event of maladministration and gross injustice on the part of its ruler. Such interference was rare, however, and most States ran their own affairs. The position of the Native States in relation to Great Britain has been expressed by an Indian publicist thus:

> Though they vary in size, population, revenue, and the extent of the rights they enjoy, there is one fact which is common to them, that is, their territory is not British and their people are not subjects of the Crown. British Indian Courts have no jurisdiction inside even the smallest States and the laws passed by the Indian legislature do not, except in certain cases in relation to British subjects, extend to the states. Legally, they are foreign territory.[7]

7- *K. M. Panikkar, "The Indian States,"* Oxford Pamphlets on Indian Affairs, *No. 4, 1942, p. 3.*

Of all the Native States, Hyderabad was regarded as the most important. Only Kashmir exceeded it in area, by a few thousand square miles, and in population and wealth it was without question the premier State. Its ruler, the Nizam, occupied an office that had first been established by the Mogul emperor in 1713. This potentate was often referred to as the richest man in the world; his treasure-trove in gold bars alone, excluding fabulous wealth in jewels, was estimated to be worth two hundred and fifty million dollars. Until 1911 Hyderabad was a pure autocracy, but in 1919 an Executive and a Legislative Council were set up. The powers of these bodies were limited, however, so that in practice the authority of the Nizam remained absolute. While there was little government by the people, the rule of the Nizam was benevolent. About 40 per cent of the public revenues were earmarked for public departments, like health and education, that served the people. There was much attention given to irrigation projects and industry was encouraged. As for the capital, Hyderabad city, it ranked as the fourth largest in India and was the home of the famous Osmania University, an institution sponsoring writing and research in the Mohammedan language of Urdu. The last striking feature

to comment upon in Hyderabad is the fact that the Nizam and his two million Mohammedan co-religionists constituted the administrative hierarchy over some thirteen million Hindus. This fact was to have signal importance in affecting the destiny of Hyderabad in the post-independence era.

Another Native State deserves attention. Kashmir covers an area of 85,000 square miles tucked away in the north-west corner of the Indian subcontinent. This State is sometimes called the "House of Many Storeys," composed as it is of lovely valleys, inviting lakes, and snow-capped mountains. It is famous for its scenery and for the artistry of its handicrafts. Unlike the situation in Hyderabad, the great majority of the people were Muslims and their ruler a Hindu maharaja. There was much dissatisfaction, with occasional revolts on a minor scale by the Muslims against the maharaja and the ruling Hindu class. A serious uprising in 1932 resulted in the British government's creating a Commission of Inquiry which exposed the corruption of the police, the lamentable neglect of education, and the resort of officials to forced labor. As in the case of Hyderabad, Kashmir was to play an exceedingly important role in the Indian drama immediately following independence.

It should be understood that in the 1930's there was no organic political integration between British India and the Native States. Under the Government of India Act of 1935, however, there was provision for the establishment of a federal structure in which the States and the British provinces were to be dovetailed into a common central government. This objective of federalism was not realized before World War II, but with the achievement of Indian independence in 1947 the question of the political future of the States was to become a major issue.

While India in the decade preceding its independence enjoyed a considerable measure of self-government, the ultimate authority lay with the Viceroy, who was the highest executive official and the representative of the British government. Assisting the Viceroy were less than three thousand British officers, for the great bulk of the administrative staff in the 1930's was Indian. In all of the country there were only 117,000 persons of British stock, men, women, and children, and this figure included 70,000 troops. The Indian Civil

Service, the inner steel frame of the entire administration, was staffed less than half by British officials, who in such services as the medical, the police, and the railways, formed a small minority. While the percentage of British officials in the Indian government steadily declined after World War I, as India became more self-governing, the fact is that even in the heyday of British rule in the nineteenth century the English controlled India with amazingly few men. Indeed, in the long history of imperialism there has been nothing approaching British control of India. For the fact was that a nation of some forty million living on a small island off the coast of western Europe was able to project its power six thousand miles to govern more than three hundred million subjects.

Great Britain, that nation of traders and shopkeepers, had good reason to maintain its position in India. Apart from its value as a market for British goods, huge sums had been invested in this country. In the 1930's the British stake was around three and a half billion dollars, of which some two billions were invested in public utilities and British-owned companies doing business in India, the remaining one and a half billion dollars constituting the public debt owed by the Indian government to Britain. Loans had been raised on the London market and the great bulk of the funds had been used for productive purposes, such as building railroads and irrigation projects. The interest on this debt ran to fifty million dollars yearly. While the British investment in India was considerable, its importance has often been exaggerated. Excluding the sterling debt owed to Britain, this country's investments in India were matched by approximate sums in Canada, Australia, South Africa, and Argentina.

Turning from things political to the socio-economic structure in India, we might first note the distribution of population between country and town. As we have already seen, the population of India in 1941 was 389,000,000, a figure one and a half times that of the western hemisphere and the second greatest population mass in the world, next to the Chinese. The great majority of these millions are peasants living in more than 700,000 villages. Out of every one hundred people in India ninety live in the villages, and of these, seventy-two are directly supported by agriculture.

Rural life may be dominant, but urbanization is an important trend. During the decade 1921-1931, city population increased more than six million, to a total of nearly forty million town dwellers. In the 1930's the rate of increase became more rapid, cities of 100,000 increasing in number from thirty-five to fifty-eight with a total population of sixteen and a half million. Calcutta almost burst at the seams as its population passed beyond the two million mark, with Bombay's figure increasing to one and a half million. Other cities, such as Cawnpore, Ahmadabad, and Jamshedpur, also made important population gains.

Although predominantly agricultural, India had by 1930 undergone a kind of industrial revolution that made her an important element in world trade. In fact, judged by her external commerce, India was surpassed as a world trader only by the United States, Great Britain, Germany, France, and Canada. As an Asian economic power India was not in the same industrial category as Japan but was well ahead of China. India's railway mileage was five times that of China, and in mileage of paved roads the superiority was again almost five to one.

Up to 1914 Indian industry was limited mainly to cotton textiles, coal, and iron, and in this year the number of workers in factories employing more than twenty hands was only 951,000. In the 1920's, however, industry forged ahead in steel, glass, soap, jute, sugar, leather, and cement. By the 1930's two million workers were employed in large scale industry, and India was rated as one of the eight industrial powers of the world. Compared to her huge population and to her resources, however, the degree of industrialization was quite meager and insufficient. The only great industries employing more than 100,000 by 1940 were the cotton mills engaged in spinning and weaving, the mills ginning and pressing cotton, factories processing jute, and the railway shops.

Life in Village and Town

To know India one must understand her villages, for here live the bulk of her many millions, and here exist in their strongest form the basic institutions of the Hindu way of life. The average village consists of a few hundred acres supporting perhaps fifty to one hundred families. As one approaches the typical village one sees no paved roads, no

running water, and no modern system of sewage disposal. Glancing about, one finds that, while certain signs of modernity may be noted, village life has changed little in fundamentals during the past five hundred years. Cattle live practically as part of the family. Sugar cane is crushed in a hand mill, wooden ploughs are used, bullocks at harvest time accomplish the thrashing by treading out the grain, and in harvesting people squat on the ground using sickles.

The huts—one cannot dignify most of them by the word house—are ramshackle edifices of mud and thatch with no chimneys or windows. Inside there are dirt floors, rarely tables and chairs, often no beds, and only a few chests and brass pots and pans. Filth and smells are everywhere. Sewage runs along the narrow alleyways. During the rainy season there are noxious pools full of mosquitoes. Garbage and filth litter the village. A recent American observer of Indian village life has given us a graphic and repulsive picture of its dirt, disease, and dung. He writes, "The smells rose too, smells of spice and of urine, of garlic and curry powder and dysentery stools, all the assorted smells of the Indian village, all the smells of life, decay, and death."[8]

The village is changing. Events in the outside world, especially the influences of modern business and city life, are causing it to alter its ancient ways. But the tempo of change is slow. The villagers are the most immobile of all the people; many live and die without traveling as much as fifty miles from the place of their birth. The village is the great fortress of conservatism. Without benefit of education, only vaguely understanding the slogans of his political leaders, and suspicious of new methods of agriculture, the Indian ryot, or peasant, dimly appreciates the fact that his standard of living is tragically low but, at the same time, he is often the despair of those who try to improve his lot.

India has her thousands of villages but, at the same time, she has great cities such as Calcutta, a metropolis second to London in the British Empire. In these cities one may see great government buildings, banks, hospitals, factories, and slums—especially the latter. For the impact of western civilization, particularly that of its economics, during the past half-century upon urban life in India has been singularly uneven, leading to all kinds of amazing contrasts, some good and

some evil. In the great cities, elements of the old and new exist side by side or mingle to form unhappy combinations heretofore unknown in either India or western Europe. Within the city are smartly dressed businessmen attired in western clothes; there are also Indians in their traditional *dhoti,* or dressed in a form of loose pajama-like trousers and jacket. Here and there are scantily clad coolies, practically naked fakirs, and at night hundreds of people sleeping on the pavements. Automobiles mingle with bullock carts. Hawkers shouting their wares pass by ultra-smart western-style shops, and from time to time a sacred cow meanders down the street.

Like any city in the United States, its Indian counterpart has the usual economic classes, from bankers, manufacturers, professional men, and shopkeepers to factory workers. As the last named class is by far the most numerous and its status the most unsatisfactory, attention at this point will be focused on the urban worker. He usually arrives in the city with little knowledge of its conditions, especially its snares and pitfalls. Only failure of his crops, loss of his land, or often threat of actual starvation has driven him to the city for employment. Work can be secured only by procuring the services of a middleman, the jobber (known variously as the *maistri, sirdar,* or *mukadam*). Payment of a kind of bribe puts the new worker into the debt of the jobber, a condition in which he often remains permanently. The jobber is actually employed by the factory management and in a sense is an essential intermediary between the employer and his men; in fact, he is usually a petty tyrant who gets rich on bribes and frequently graduates into the ranks of the moneylenders.

Wages, housing, food—these elements constitute a basic economic trinity which may or may not mean happiness and the good life for the urban worker. As far as housing is concerned, the situation in the 1930's was tragic. In most Indian cities housing for the workers was squalid, unhealthful, inadequate as to space, and unbelievably expensive. Bombay had its *chawls,* blocks of flats, in which there was little ventilation for the middle rooms, lavatory facilities were insufficient, and most household filth and refuse was dumped outside. Thirty-three per cent of the population lived in rooms occupied by more than five persons. A large number, estimated to be

8- *John Frederick Muehl,* Interview With India *(New York: John Day Co., 1950), p. 30.*

80,000, existed in rooms which were occupied by from ten to nineteen persons. And some people did not even have hovels and had somehow to live on the streets; and so one reads of the "night population" and of the "pavement sleepers." A graphic picture of these housing conditions is given by an Indian investigator:

> In one room on the second floor of a *chawl,* measuring fifteen by twelve feet, I found six families living . . . On enquiry, I ascertained that the actual number of adults and children living in this room was thirty . . . Three out of six women were shortly expecting to be delivered . . . When I questioned the nurse who accompanied me as to how she would arrange for privacy in this room, I was shown a small space 4 feet by 3 feet which was usually screened off for the purpose. The atmosphere of that room at night, filled with smoke from the six ovens and other impurities, would certainly handicap any woman with an infant both before and after delivery.[9]

Similar conditions are found in the industrial slums of other large cities such as Cawnpore, Calcutta, and Ahmadabad. In Madras the slums are called *cheries,* and consist of dilapidated hovels constructed of mud and kerosene cans. In one area it was estimated that there were only 460 faucets for 183,000 people, and everywhere there were open sewage, garbage, filth, and flies. In spite of the squalor the rents are high and the Indian landlords often secure a return of 35 per cent on their investment.

Trade unions for workers came relatively late to India, the first being organized in 1918. In 1935 only 270,000 workers were members of permanent unions. There are many serious obstacles hindering the growth of unions in India. Much of the industrial labor is migratory, there has been a lack of responsible leadership, workers are too poor to pay dues, and there is the general ignorance of the worker, who has little idea of what a union proposes to do. There has also been the opposition of jobbers, of employers, and, on occasion, of the government.

In 1934 a fairly adequate Factory Act was passed which reduced working hours, provided for better working conditions, and limited all adult labor (fifteen years and over) to a ten-hour day and fifty-four-hour week. This Act, unfortunately, did not apply to "unregulated factories," i.e., establishments employing less than twenty workers or where mechanical power is not utilized.

9- Quoted in B. Shiva Rao, The Industrial Worker in India *(London: George Allen and Unwin, 1939), pp. 108-9.*

In these small workshops, where millions of workers were employed, operations were carried on twenty-four hours a day. The rooms were dark and poorly ventilated, the floors often of mud, and it was not uncommon for children of five to work twelve hours a day under the strictest discipline.

As might be expected, the wages of the Indian urban worker are miserably low. Children get from ten to seventy-five cents a month, an average wage for a factory worker is one dollar and a quarter a week, and a casual farm laborer gets five to eight annas (about ten to fifteen cents) a day.

In most cities there is a disparity in numbers between males and females, the former sometimes exceeding the latter two to one. It is frequently the case that the villager will leave his wife behind, or that a young bachelor will come to the city with the idea of saving a small sum and then returning to the village. In any case, this sex disparity encourages immorality; and, in addition, squalor of surroundings and lack of adequate recreation encourage workers to drink to excess and to take drugs, such as opium. On the whole the state of the urban worker is a desperate one and his plight is perhaps more degraded than that of most of his fellows whom he left in the village.

The Arithmetic of Impoverishment

In the previous section the life of the peasant and city worker was surveyed in general terms; now we must proceed to analyze more concretely the socio-economic pattern of Indian life in terms of income, diet, health, life expectancy, and literacy. In 1930 the average per capita income was reckoned at twenty dollars, a figure exceeded seventeen times in England and twenty-two times in the United States. There have been numerous studies dealing with the income of the peasants. One such estimated that an average ryot had an annual income of about one hundred dollars (to estimate the money worth of his small crop). Above what he and his family needed for food he was able to sell thirty-nine dollars' worth of produce. With this cash sum in his pocket he was able to pay his land tax of six dollars, leaving a little more than thirty dollars for the clothing, amusements, and medicines needed by his family. But the ryot was in debt to the sum of eighty dollars to the moneylender, or bania, who demanded the exorbitant sum of twenty dollars each year for interest. Thus the peasant was not even able to pay the annual interest, but each additional year settled more and more securely into the clutches of the bania.[10]

With low income necessarily comes inadequate diet, and in this respect the Indian masses suffer both qualitatively and quantitatively, from not enough and from the wrong kinds of food. In certain sections of India the average daily intake of calories for an adult male has been estimated at only 1700, while the number required to maintain health would be 2500. In 1939 the director of the Indian Medical Service calculated that 39 per cent of the people were well fed, 41 per cent poorly nourished, and 20 per cent near a starvation diet. It has been estimated that 20 per cent of the population are always hungry.

The food that is consumed is not well balanced. The diet shows a deficiency of fats, vitamins, and proteins. Little milk is consumed and not enough green vegetables, eggs, fish, and fruit. Meat is an unknown item to the great majority of Hindus, because of both economic and religious factors. Actual experiments have been carried out to test the dietary habits of various sections of India. One such experiment used rats of the same size, weight, and age, and gave to some the best diets found in the country, to others the poorest. It was found that the weight differential after 80 days ran from 235 to 155 grams. There can be no question that India is a poorly nourished nation, with the inevitable evil results upon physical stamina, health, and life expectancy.

Every year nearly six million deaths result from preventable disease. Chief among these is malaria, which infects 100 million persons a year; only 10 per cent of these are able to secure adequate treatment, and one million of them die annually. Other diseases, such as tuberculosis, hookworm, leprosy, cholera, smallpox, and typhoid take a heavy toll. The factors which bring about heavy decimation from otherwise preventable disease are (1) contaminated water, (2) lack of sanitation, (3) bad housing, (4) mosquitoes and flies, and (5) malnutrition.

As long as malaria, fevers, and tuberculosis take life prematurely by the million, India will have one of the lowest rates of life expectancy in the world. The general death rate in 1941 was estimated to be 21.8 per thousand and for infants

under one year, 162. For New Zealand the corresponding figures were 9.1 and 31, for Australia 9.4 and 38, and for the United States, 12 and 55. The life-expectancy at birth in New Zealand and Australia was, respectively, 65 and 63 years; in contrast, India was 26. In India 65 per cent of the people die before 30, and no mother has a better than even chance of raising her child to manhood. It has also been pointed out that, of every 100,000 babies born alive, only a little more than 50 per cent live over five years.

India has desperately needed adequate public health facilities. But there have been only one doctor available to every 6000 people, one nurse to every 43,000, and one dentist to every 300,000. The country has needed adequate education, for much of the disease resulted from ignorance and superstition. In 1941 only 12.5 per cent of the population of British India was literate in its own language; only 2 per cent was literate in English; and for all of India only 14 per cent was estimated to be literate. While the number of literates increased from 23 to 47 million during the decade 1931-1941, the number of illiterates increased from 315 to 341 million. Merely to hold her own in the race between literacy and illiteracy India must educate three and a half million of her youth each year to read and write. Most serious is the lack of schooling for girls. In the 1920's only 35,000 girls were in classes above the elementary school, and in the latter the usual ratio is one girl to four boys. In 1941 barely 5 per cent of all women were literate.

A basic problem in Indian education is the large percentage of drop-outs in the upper grades of the elementary schools. Half-educated, these boys return to their villages with their lack of books, newspapers, and any form of adult education, and they naturally lose what little learning they possess. Commenting on this matter a school inspector observed: "The great majority of our ex-students, in less than ten years after leaving school, can neither read, nor write, nor cipher. From having nothing to read, having no occasion to write, and no accounts to keep, they gradually forget whatever they learn, and are as ignorant as if they had never been at school."[11]

All this is part of the arithmetic of impoverishment: low income, poor diet, ravages of disease, inadequate public health facilities, illiteracy, and low life expectancy. The over-all picture is a

10- C. F. Strickland, "The Indian Village and Indian Unrest," Foreign Affairs, X (October 1931), pp. 70-80.

11- Quoted in Cambridge History of the British Empire, V (Cambridge: Cambridge University Press, 1932), p. 342.

melancholy one. After studying these problems, not by benefit of statistics on the printed page but by the observation of daily life in India, an American writer, appalled by what he had seen, expressed his reaction thus:

> It was the fact of the atrocious poverty of village India; even starvation and famine could not measure its depths, for it was like something malignant with a life of its own. This memory I could no longer differentiate; it was a mass of hoarse cries and protruding bones, the smell of disease in a thousand villages, the smoke of a hundred burning ghats. . . . India was neither simple nor happy but complex and miserable, involved and squalid, the breath of its people coming labored and uneven through the weight and mass of superstition and ignorance.[12]

Religion: The Great Divider

India, like ancient Egypt, is a land saturated with religion; its people are obsessed with the destiny and status of man in the hereafter. Nearly every aspect of life, every thought and action, is conditioned by faith and dogma, whether in business, in politics, or in social behavior. The dominant religious community in India is the Hindu, whose followers in 1941 constituted 65 per cent of the entire population compared with a Mohammedan community of 25 per cent. Hinduism is impossible to define in a terse and neat statement, for it comprehends a way of life, rather than a narrow, church-going creed, and affects a man's social status, his marriage, the very food he eats, the friends among whom he can mingle, and the occupation he follows. In the following chapter something will be said of the origin and development of Hinduism and its theological and philosophical beliefs. At this point, however, a discussion of the caste system is appropriate, for it is the structure within which Hinduism has its being and at the same time the machinery which gives practical effect to the objectives of this faith.

The caste system is the classification of all individuals according to the occupation they traditionally follow, the circle within which they must marry, and the group with whom they can mingle socially. Birth lays down the caste to which a Hindu belongs, and there is not any possibility for him to switch to another. In ancient times, as will be explained in the next chapter, there were four basic castes—the Brahman, the most revered; the Kshatriyas, the nobles and warriors; the Vai-

syas, the traders; and the Sudras, the serfs. Today, however, this fourfold classification has been blurred and complicated by the development of more than three thousand separate caste groups. The easiest way of understanding the status of these many castes is to know that there are three main caste categories. The first group includes the Brahmans; the Rajput clans, representatives of the ancient Kshatriyas; and the traders who claim descent from the Vaisyas, all of whom constitute the Twice-Born. The second group embraces the traditional Sudra castes that are now all lumped together as being not Twice-Born. At the bottom are the Untouchables, also known as the Depressed Classes or Scheduled Castes. There is, consequently, a definite hierarchy from the debased and "unclean" ranks of the Untouchables up through the higher castes of those not Twice-Born, on into those who are, culminating in the Brahman castes. So ingrained is this concept of differential status that there are even various grades among the Untouchables, "each superior grade considering the inferior . . . as polluting as the highest class of the caste Hindus regard the worst grade of Untouchables. Further, among the same grade of Untouchables there are sections, each considering itself different and distinct from any other, prohibiting inter-dining and inter-marriage."[13]

Each caste is an exclusive group. It is endogamous, for a man must select his bride from within his own group. Furthermore, each caste has its *dharma*, its rules regulating the kind of food that may be eaten, the manner of its eating, and with what other castes there may be social intercourse. Rules of eating are especially complex, dictating the people from whom one can take water, the correct ritual at the table, the specific people who can cook one's food, and the companions one may have at the table.

Closely related to caste is the traditional Hindu institution known as the joint family, which consists of a father, his sons and grandsons, together with all their womenfolk until they are married and enter other joint families. The family is joint in food, worship, and estate, and the income of the ancestral property and the current earnings of all members are placed in a common fund.

Traditionally each caste followed a specific occupation, but new castes are constantly growing up and a caste may also take up a new occupation. Unless there is a rapid decline in the occupational

14- *Robert Neville, "Caste Is the Curse of India,"* Life, *XXII (May 19, 1947), p. 106.*

15- *Louise Ouwerkerk,* The Untouchables of India *(London: Oxford University Press, 1945), p. 3.*

16- *Gunther, op. cit., p. 397.*

17- *Quoted in Lord Meston,* Nationhood for India *(London: Oxford University Press, 1931), p. 51.*

18- *Nehru,* The Discovery of India, *p. 532.*

characteristics of the caste system, it is possible that the growth of industrialism in India may result in a further bewildering multiplication of castes to conform to the complex variety of modern industrial occupations. One American correspondent observes: "So far no subcaste of typists or airplane mechanics or locomotive engineers has been reported. But it could happen."[14]

At the bottom of the caste system are the Untouchables, some fifty million people, described as "the largest subordinate racial group in the world."[15] They are the menials of India, doing the dirty and degrading tasks, being the scavengers, the tanners, washers of dirty clothes, and handlers of dead carcasses. Untouchability has been defined as "Jimcrowism on a fantastic scale."[16] Untouchables must live apart, segregated from the rest of their fellow villagers. Their touch, contiguity, and sometimes even their shadows are considered to be polluting to the higher caste Hindus. In the past they were denied access to Hindu temples, they could not draw water directly from the village wells, and their children could not attend school along with the other Hindu students. They have even been forbidden to walk on the public roads. In many villages the higher-caste Hindus have done many things to stress the inferiority of the Untouchables. These unfortunates are not supposed to dress well, may not ride on a horse, cannot build a two-story house nor use brass vessels in their kitchens. It is natural that the Untouchables as a class usually have a bare subsistence living and are paid pitifully low wages. If, as sometimes happens, a member of the Depressed Class is able to obtain a good education and make a mark for himself as a businessman or lawyer, despite all the culture and the wealth that may be accumulated this "self-made man" remains an Untouchable, the social inferior of the higher castes who is barred from their society. This is somewhat less true today than in the past, especially since the legal abolition of Untouchability.

As we will see in the next chapter, certain deep and ingrained beliefs cause the vast majority of Hindus to accept their caste status without question. In most castes there is also the governing body, the Panchayat, which meets like a court of law—or perhaps one might say like the executive committee of an American trade union—to punish any rash members who have broken the traditional rules of their caste. Punishable offenses might be breaches of caste etiquette, killing a sacred animal, and breaches of the marriage law.

Like all human institutions, wherever found, caste did not just happen. Originally it served a positive function and even today it has certain commendable features. The Hindu emphasizes the fact that as a result of numerous racial invasions of his country, which will be discussed in later chapters, India became inhabited by many people with various levels of culture, and it was the caste system that enabled all the various groups to live together. In cases of western countries, however, backward peoples in like circumstances were either exterminated or enslaved. In its operation today Hindus point out that a caste is a kind of brotherhood, democratic within itself, within which all the members are equal regardless of their wealth.

Caste moderates personal ambition and checks the bitterness of competition. It gives a man, whatever his station in life, a society in which he can be at home even when he is among strangers. For the poor man, it serves as a club, as a trade union, and a mutual benevolent society, all rolled into one. It ensures continuity and a certain inherited skill in the arts and crafts. And in the moral sphere it means that every man lives content with that place which Destiny has allotted to him, and uncomplainingly does his best.[17]

There may be mitigating features in the caste system but on balance it is a way of life utterly inconsistent with the basic forces that are now influencing our contemporary world. Nehru, India's renowned statesman, has written that "in the social organization of today it has no place left," and that it "has to change completely, for it is wholly opposed to modern conditions and the democratic ideal."[18] One of the crusades of Mahatma Gandhi was against Untouchability.

Is caste declining? In the last census there were nearly seven million Hindus who refused to indicate any caste membership, and in the past half-century it is indisputable that the impact of British rule and western influences in general have weakened to some extent the hold of caste. Marriages outside caste have been legalized, and the law protects the property of a caste renegade who is threatened punishment by his caste Panchayat. Above all, modern conditions of life, especially in the city, where trains, busses, and factories throw people of all castes together, tend to break down the old system. Many Hindus are increasingly ignoring the old food taboos and restrictions and from time to time there are intercaste marriages. Despite these changes, however, caste is still the most powerful institution and its essential principle, that of caste endogamy, has been little weakened.

Religion has divided Hinduism within itself while at the same time there is the wide fissure between it and Islam. In 1941 there were ninety-five million Muslims, equivalent to 24 per cent of the population. The great majority are of the same stock as their Hindu neighbors, and in the province of the Punjab, where there is the largest percentage of foreign origin among the Muslims, such origin is computed at only 15 per cent. A later chapter will show how the bulk of present day Muslims are descendants of Hindus who accepted Islam voluntarily, often to escape low caste status, or who at times chose it as the preferable alternative to death at the hands of the invading Muslim hosts or discriminatory taxes by Muslim rulers.

If Mohammedanism were primarily and exclusively a matter of theology, the unfortunate rivalry and even hatred that developed between it and Hinduism in the present century might not have come about. Like Hinduism, however, Islam is more than a religion; it is a way of life, a veritable culture all its own. Unlike the former, it believes in the fundamental equality of all men and repudiates any notion of caste. Islam is iconoclastic, an idol-smashing faith, in contrast to the voluptuous polytheism of Hinduism with its variegated array of deities. The Muslims reject child marriage and eat meat, especially that of the cow.

Because of the exclusiveness of the caste system there can be little or no contact between these two religious communities, and intermarriage is out of the question. It has been pointed out that even in the case of the long traditional enemies, France and Germany, a young Frenchman going to the latter country to study might easily secure residence with a German family and eventually marry the daughter of the house. No Muslim could live on such terms in the large majority of Hindu homes. A Muslim leader commented:

Any of us Indian Muslims travelling for instance in Afghanistan, Persia, and Central Asia, among Chinese Muslims, Arabs, and Turks, would at once be made at home and would not find anything to which we are not accustomed. On the contrary in India we find ourselves in all social matters total aliens when we cross the street and enter that part of the town where our Hindu fellow townsmen live.[19]

In contrast to the contemplative and elaborate edifice of Hinduism with its many gods, Islam is simple, unadorned, and dynamic. The Mohammedan creed tersely affirms, "There is no God but Allah and Mohammed is his Prophet." In addition there is simply the belief in Allah's teachings as revealed in the Koran and in a final resurrection and judgment. The following chapter will explain how complex, passivistic, and subtle is Hinduism and will indicate its striking antithesis to the religious system we have just described.

During the past seventy-five years differences and rivalries have grown keener between the Muslim and Hindu communities. The former lagged behind the latter in taking up the new western education, thus giving the Hindus a monopoly in governmental service and in the professions. The Muslims were also disinclined to go into business, one important reason being the Koran's prohibition against lending money for interest. Naturally, Hindus came to dominate business, to be the moneylenders and landowners. More and more the Muslims came to resent being the "House of Have-Not" in India and much of the communal antipathy of the past two decades undoubtedly had some economic source.

Muslims eat the flesh of the cow; Hindus regard this animal as sacred and not to be killed under any circumstance. The matter of the cow has played an important part in stirring up trouble between the two religious groups. Once a year good Muslims celebrate the anniversary of Abraham's sacrifice on Mount Moriah. Several Muslims will come together and buy a cow for the rite. In the process Hindu neighbors are often baited and mocked and when the animal is decked out in garlands and led noisily to slaughter through the streets, a first-class riot ensues. On the other side, Hindus have taken an impish delight in conducting their noisy religious processions, including the loud playing of musical instruments, just outside the local mosque where the faithful are at prayer. The Muslims rush out to protest, stones are soon substituted for words, and another communal riot begins.

- Quoted in Sir John mming, ed., Political India *32-1932 (London: Oxford iversity Press, 1932), p. 104.*

In addition to the two dominant socio-religious communities, the Hindus and the Muslims, there are four minority groups deserving brief identification. The Parsis, a small community of about 100,000, are centered largely in Bombay. Originally they were followers of Zoroaster and their home was in Persia, which they left in the eighth century to escape coming under the rule of Islam. While almost a microscopic element amid India's millions, the Parsis have exerted an extraordinary influence on the cultural and economic life of their adopted country. They have proved themselves to be an unusually intelligent and enterprising group and were among the first communities to take to western science and culture. One of the greatest political figures in the early days of Indian nationalism, 1890-1910, was the Parsi Dadabhai Naoroji, who was a prominent member of the Indian National Congress. In the field of business the reputation of the Parsis is known throughout the Far East. The great Tata Iron and Steel Company, for example, was founded by a Parsi, the late J. N. Tata.

The members of the Sikh community, defined as "neither a race, nor a nationality, nor a caste, but primarily the followers of a religion,"[20] number almost six million concentrated primarily in the Punjab. This sect traces its history back to the founder, *Guru* (Great Teacher) Nanak, who lived in the fifteenth century and who opposed caste, idolatry, and the supremacy of the Brahmans. Known as Sikhs, and led by a line of famous *Gurus,* his followers fought back against the persecution of Muslim Mogul emperors who were ruling the country at this time. Gradually the Sikhs developed into a strong, militant brotherhood, famous throughout India for their military prowess. Early in the nineteenth century they gave evidence of becoming a strong imperial power in northern India, but they were conquered by the British. Their military tradition, however, was perpetuated by their service in the British Indian army, where the Sikhs gained fame for their heroism and soldierly qualities. They not only served in the Indian army but became a familiar sight as policemen in such British colonies as Singapore and Hongkong.

One result of British conquest and rule of India was the creation of a small community of mixed blood known first as Eurasian and after 1911 officially as Anglo-Indian. Never numbering more

20- *Ibid., p. 124.*

than 150,000, this group has illustrated, sometimes tragically, the effects of a biological blending of two proud peoples, both of whom often reject the new product of the union. The Anglo-Indians usually thought of Britain as their spiritual home and tried to associate themselves with the English community in India. The English, however, wanted little to do with them, while the Indians tended to despise this hapless group as renegades supporting the rule of the alien imperialist. So difficult was the economic status of the Anglo-Indians that the British sought to guarantee employment for them, mainly in the postal service and on the railways. As the day for Indian independence began to materialize in the mid-1940's, the leaders of the Anglo-Indian community began to urge its members to forget their British inclinations and to go with the new India as loyal sons and daughters.

Christian missionary enterprise has been very active in India, not only spreading the Gospel but making significant contributions in education, establishing pioneer printing presses, and developing the Indian vernaculars into literary languages. By 1941, while very small in following compared to Hinduism and Mohammedanism, Christianity had reached the position of the third religious community in India, with a little more than six million members. Most of these converts have come from the lower castes, especially the Untouchables. Compared with the population as a whole, the Indian Christians are remarkably advanced, especially in education. Their rate of literacy is far above the average.

Factors in Indian Poverty

Now that life in the village and town, the prevailing conditions of impoverishment, and the structure of the caste system have been described, it is logical to inquire somewhat more concretely why India is so poor. There have been in the past two basic approaches to this problem. One, the nationalistic school, has argued that all of India's problems, especially economic impoverishment, have sprung from the evils of British rule. It is argued that British imperialism has discouraged industries, prevented the creation of necessary tariffs to encourage Indian industry, established a parasitic landlord—zamindar—class, taxed the Indian masses too much, and neglected social services, such as education. The other school, in analyzing Indian poverty, finds its causes in fields other than the political or strictly economic, maintaining that it springs from socio-religious traditions and customs within the pattern of Indian culture. To this school it is naïve to believe that a fundamental improvement in standards of living can be secured merely by adopting a new constitution without a thorough reconstruction of Indian society. As later chapters take up in detail some of the charges made against British rule, it is appropriate at this juncture to comment upon socio-religious factors in Indian life that bear upon the problem of poverty.

Of utmost importance in its bearing upon the economic well-being of the masses is the prevailing attitude toward life inculcated by Hinduism in general and the caste system in particular. Later chapters will refer to the passivistic attitude, the principle of the unimportance of this life, and the spirit of resignation, all of which spring from Hinduism and its doctrine of transmigration. Nehru has bitterly complained of the undue influence of religiosity and the obsession with the supernatural that prevents Hindus from utilizing their energies in scientifically studying the socio-economic problems around them and keeps them from seeking to control the forces of nature to serve the legitimate needs of man.[21] Many Indians besides Nehru now criticize the Hindu outlook as not conducive to progress; one of them declared:

> The general outlook upon life in India is too gloomy to permit sound individual or social development. Far too common is the belief that life is merely a transitory stage in the passage of the soul to another world. That notion chills enthusiasm, kills joy and promotes fatalism. In some cases the joint family system tends to produce drones; some Indians actually take pride in the number of persons they maintain in idleness. While Indians feel that life is a burden, people in the West are full of hope and are intensely active.[22]

There are some authorities who maintain that it is not so much overpopulation, landlordism, or chronic indebtedness that explain the poverty of the peasant but rather his psychology and how he

looks at life. The Indian ryot is bound down by custom, caged within the confines of his caste, and usually a slave to tradition. Like so many backward people, up to quite recently at least, he tended to be satisfied with a bare minimum of subsistence, and he has in the past shown little interest in improving his lot. It has even been asserted that the Indian ryot seems to exhibit a kind of masochistic satisfaction in grumbling about the many evils that prey upon him.[23] Of all the cultural groups affected by the Asian revolution, the Hindu masses are most insulated by religion and custom against the suffering caused by their debased economic status. It follows that they will be the most difficult to arouse to the necessity of basic reforms.

There can be little argument that the village is the citadel of conservatism in India and that from the caste system with all its ramifications there stem many forces, usually malignant from the western point of view, that operate to bring about the tragically low standard of life in India. It is mainly by reference to Hindu beliefs that one can best understand the tremendous pressure of population in India today; appreciate the economic waste associated with the sacred cow and the principle of the sanctity of all life; and study the poverty of the average Indian village, which springs from debt created by uneconomic religious festivals and the wasteful fragmentation of agricultural holdings. Above all, there is the depressed status of Indian women, who are discouraged and even barred from making their potential contribution to the progress and wealth of their motherland. In discussing India's social problems it has well been said, "Of all the many changes likely to improve the welfare of Indian society, none is more important than these two—female education and marriage reform."[24] These problems of population pressure, the status of women, reform of the caste system, and the uneconomic use of the country's animal population will be discussed more in detail when we take up the stage in 1947 when independent India had both the challenge and the opportunity to embark on the great task of reconstructing the pattern of life of her masses.

21- Nehru, The Discovery of India, p. 520.

22- Sir M. Visvesvaraya, quoted in G. Findlay Shirras, Poverty and Kindred Economic Problems in India (Calcutta: Government of India, Central Publication Branch, 1932), p. 10.

23- Muehl, op. cit., p. 126.

24- Sir Edward Blunt (ed.), Social Service in India (London: His Majesty's Stationery Office, printed 1946), p. 74.

*Modern India as we know it today is a
product of the past century and a half.
The process of its creation began
in earnest shortly after 1800 and rapidly
advanced after reaching the mid-
point of the nineteenth century. It
is with this latter phase of modern
nation making in India that this volume
is mainly concerned. To understand
the India of Mohammed Ali Jinnah and
Mohandas K. Gandhi, however, one must
know something of what it started with
late in the eighteenth century on the
eve of the British conquest. For it was
out of the historical ingredients
existing at that time, found by the
officials of the English East India Company, together with what British
rule added, that modern India came to
be shaped.*

THIS CHAPTER, *therefore, concerns
the pre-British period of Indian history.
We will be concerned with its characteristics and will learn how they developed. More specifically, it will
be shown how India in its classical
age created a brilliant tradition
of civilization, especially during
the monumental rule of the Gupta emperors. Furthermore, it will be pointed
out that the most significant aspect
of this achievement of civilization
was the creation of an altogether
distinctive way of life, best simply
described as Hindu; and lastly, that it
was to these traditional historical
ingredients of India that another
element was added, the Islamic, which
conditioned and modified the Indian
pattern of culture and historical
development from early in the thirteenth
to the beginning of the eighteenth
century, just before the advent of
British conquest.*

Historical ingredients
of modern India

chapter 2

R. C. Majumdar, H. C. Ray-
[ch]audhuri, and K. Datta, An
[Ad]vanced History of India (Lon-
[do]n: The Macmillan Co., 1946),
[p.] 21.

UNFORTUNATELY, INDIA has few historical records compared with other countries. Lack of precise dates in its early history and the prevailing scarcity of comprehensive historical works down to modern times spring from three factors. There has been unusual difficulty in preserving records against the ravages of all kinds of insect pests and from the harmful effects of a harsh and humid climate. Throughout Indian history there have been numerous revolts, wars, invasions, and palace revolutions in the midst of which cities have often been put to the sword and priceless records and art objects destroyed. Then, most important, the Hindu savant never had his heart—or should one say soul—in the writing of history, the recording of man's failures and triumphs, for whatever man did in this world was completely unimportant in comparison with the hereafter. The best scholars turned away from politics and the study of the good society. Traditionally, great Hindu scholars, down to modern times, have not been political scientists, historians, or economists, but rather seers, prophets, and spiritual leaders.

The earliest precise date we have is that of Alexander the Great's invasion of India in 326 B.C. One looks in vain for the works of a Livy, Tacitus, or Herodotus in India, for the earliest work of history that has been handed down is a history of Kashmir, dated only in the twelfth century A.D. Without histories, India's ancient period has been laboriously reconstructed within the last century, mainly by European scholars. Through inscriptions on statues and tombs, coins, religious writings, and poetic literature, India's history has been rediscovered in what has been one of the most brilliant and fascinating stories of modern scholarship.

Archeology has given us the clue to the oldest chapter in Indian history yet found. As late as 1921 an important discovery was made of the remains of an ancient civilization in the Indus Valley. The specific sites were at Mohenjo-Daro (Mound of the Dead) in the province of Sind, and at Harappa in the North Punjab. Excavations under the direction of Sir John Marshall proved that India could well claim to be one of "the mothers of civilization." At a time when comparable achievements were being registered in the Nile Valley, in Mesopotamia, and along the Hwang-Ho in China, life in the Indus Valley had shifted from a nomadic existence to urban dwell-

ing, and writing, the use of metals, and the organization of government on a complex scale were achieved. The life span of this fluvial culture of the Indus has been estimated to run from 4000 to 2500 B.C.

Although the writing at Mohenjo-Daro has not been deciphered, much has been learned of life in India some five thousand years ago. We know that the people lived in large cities probably not duplicated at that time anywhere else in the world. Mohenjo-Daro had well planned streets, houses made of kiln-fired bricks and of several stories, and large, pillared halls that were probably municipal halls or palaces. There was a fine drainage system, and the most imposing edifice was a great municipal bath.

The state of the arts was well advanced in this ancient Indus Valley culture; there were skilled industries and an active commerce. Smiths worked skillfully with bronze and made beautiful beakers of copper, silver, and lead. Potters used the wheel in their craft and also were familiar with glazes. Cotton was grown and woven two thousand years before this textile was used in the West. The archeologist's spade has unearthed numerous beautiful carved soapstone seals and amulets or charms. The representation of animals on these seals is excellent. In addition, we have beautiful small figurines and samples of delicate jewelry.

What caused the downfall of the thriving cities in the Indus Valley? No one knows, but the end apparently came swiftly and completely about 2500 B.C. But, though some disaster seems to have overwhelmed Mohenjo-Daro, its culture in some unexplained fashion lived on. One of its deities apparently was a prototype of the Hindu Shiva, and various other elements in the Indus culture were passed down to the present pattern of Indian life. "We must therefore hold," writes an Indian historian, "that there is an organic relationship between the ancient culture of the Indus valley and the Hinduism of today."[1] This fact gives to Indian civilization an almost incredibly long continuity, a fact that naturally gratifies and stirs the modern Indian nationalist. Nehru in one of his books speaks of the thrill he felt standing on one of the mounds at Mohenjo-Daro and realizing that its ruins represented a civilization that was well developed five thousand years ago.

The next act in the drama of ancient India was the appearance of vigorous nomads who pushed through the mountain passes from Central Asia in successive waves from 2000 to 1000 B.C. Belonging to the Indo-European family, and thus related to the Greeks, Persians, and Romans, these Indo-Aryans as they are called were fair skinned, fine-featured, and tall. As they pressed down into the northern plains, the Aryans came into conflict with the Dravidians, who apparently were the most numerous indigenous group at this time. The invaders described these Dravidians as short, dark, and ugly and contemptuously referred to them as *Dasyu* or slaves. The Aryans set about the task of conquest with a will and "with the ferocity of the American pioneers in their struggles against the Redskins."[2]

The dark-skinned Dravidians were driven south down the Indian peninsula, where their descendants are mainly concentrated today. But in spite of this retreat there was considerable fusion of both blood and culture between the conquering Aryans and their foes. In order to try to preserve to some degree Aryan racial purity, a barrier which gradually developed into the complex caste system as we know it today was set up, apparently on a color basis, between the two races. It is believed that the Dravidians had a higher level of culture than their conquerors and that the Aryans borrowed numerous aspects of their pattern of civilization.

Our knowledge of the long period of conquest and Aryan settlement, 2000 to 1000 B.C., comes from the sacred Vedas, a mass of material handed down for centuries by word of mouth. The common usage is to classify this ancient literature into four Vedas (*Veda* means *wisdom*), the oldest being the *Rig-Veda*. This consists of 1028 hymns, addressed mainly to the gods, dealing with nature worship and prayers for long life, good cattle, and victory in war. In the *Rig-Veda* we find a brooding, probing spirit concerned with the mysteries of life and we note the element of mysticism that was to become so characteristic of Indian culture. Rabindranath Tagore, the famous Indian poet, has described the Vedas as "the poetic testament of a people's collective reaction to the wonder and awe of existence."[3]

The next important period in the development of Aryan civilization in India is called the Epic Age (1000-500 B.C.), mainly because our knowledge of events is gleaned from two famous epics. The *Mahabharata,* the longest poem in the world,

made up of 100,000 couplets, glorifies war as does the *Iliad* of the Greeks. The most famous part of this epic is the *Bhagavad-Gita* (*The Lord's Song*) of some seven hundred verses, the most beloved gem of Hindu literature and a piece of profound philosophy in poetic form. The *Gita,* as it is called, has been greatly admired in the western world and has been translated forty times into English, the most famous translation being *The Song Celestial* by Sir Edwin Arnold. The second epic is the *Ramayana,* which has been likened to the Homeric epic, the *Odyssey.* This poem deals mainly with peace and domestic devotion, with the wanderings of the hero and the dutiful steadfastness of his wife.

It has been said that perhaps no other pieces of literature have influenced so many people for so long a time as have these Indian epics. In a sense they are what the Bible, *Pilgrim's Progress,* Milton, and Shakespeare have been to the English-speaking people. Everywhere in India their characters are sculptured in the temples, carved in the woodwork of houses, or painted on the walls. Common people all over the land know and love the old plots and characters of these epics.

> Nightly to listening millions are the stories of the *Ramayana* and *Mahabharata* told all over India. They are sung at all large assemblies of the people, at marriage feasts and temple services, at village festivals and the receptions of chiefs and princes. Then, when all the gods have been duly worshipped . . . a reverend Brahman steps upon the scene . . . and sitting down, slow and lowly begins his antique chant, and late into the starry night holds his hearers, young and old, spellbound.[4]

These epics give us a vivid picture of life in India from 1000 to 500 B.C. By this time the Aryans had ceased to be nomads and the village had become the basic cell of society, as it has remained to this day.

Expansion by the Aryans was also taking place eastward along the Ganges, and numerous small kingdoms were established. Trade expanded and cities were built. By this time a fusion of cultures between invader and vanquished had been accomplished. This is referred to as the Aryo-Dravidian Synthesis, and was something like the fusion that took place between Roman and Germanic elements in Europe following the 5th century A.D. or the mixing in England between Saxon and Norman following William the Conqueror's victory in

2- H. G. Rawlinson, India: A Short Cultural History *(New York: D. Appleton-Century, 1938), p. 21.*

3- Quoted in Jawaharlal Nehru, The Discovery of India *(New York: John Day Co., 1946), p. 69.*

4- Herbert H. Gowen, A History of Indian Literature *(New York: D. Appleton-Century, 1931), p. 251.*

Shiva

Brahma

5- *Quoted in Nehru,* The Discovery of India, *p. 81.*

5- *W. H. Moreland and Atul C. Chatterjee,* A Short History of India *(New York: Longmans, Green and Company, 1945), pp. 20-21.*

7- The Bhagavad-Gita, *trans. Edward Arnold ("The Harvard Classics," XLV; New York: P. F. Collier and Son, 1910), pp. 806-807.*

1066. During the Epic Period caste began to harden. Four traditional castes crystallized: the Brahmans, or priests; the Kshatriyas, or soldier class; the Vaisyas, farmers and merchants; and the Sudras, or serfs. Beneath this caste hierarchy was the submerged group, the Untouchables or Outcastes. And, as we have seen, this caste system became closely tied in with religion.

Hinduism, or the Hindu way of life, is one of the most important historical ingredients of modern India. We say "Hindu way of life" because it is more than a religion as the term is usually understood. Hinduism has been termed a working hypothesis of human conduct; it took at least one thousand years to develop, but its seminal period was the Epic Age just discussed. It was during this period that the *Upanishads,* prose religious writings, were formulated. Philosophical in nature, these writings deal with the basic problems of existence and are replete with awe, wonder, and inquiry. This spirit is expressed in their words: "Lead me from the unreal to the real. Lead me from darkness to light. Lead me from death to immortality."[5] All of the main scaffolding of Hinduism is found in the *Upanishads.*

We may list these main elements in the structure of Hindu religious thought. (1) Life is evil. All things material are *Maya,* that is, illusion. In Christianity eternal life may be secured with the promise of individual existence. In Hinduism separate individuality is lost. The goal is not being but non-being, not separateness but absorption in the absolute. (2) The main object of true religion is *Moksha,* or deliverance, by which the soul becomes absorbed in the world soul or *Atma.* (3) This release is part of a cosmic and complicated process. The individual soul must go through a long series of wanderings, earthly reincarnations from body to body. The status of a man at any particular time is no fortuitous lot but depends on his soul's actions in previous existences. "At the moment of death, then, there is an accumulation of the consequences of past action, which determines the condition of the individual in the next birth, whether as a man or as a higher or lower animal."[6] Caste is the essential machinery for what is, in effect, the educative process of the soul as it goes through the infinitely long succession of rebirths from the lowest category in caste to that of the Brahman, who presumably is near the end of the cycle.

Hinduism has no canon, no precise doctrine, and it has room for the most primitive idol worshiper and at the same time for the believer in the most profound philosophy of monotheism. There are literally thousands of deities and godlings worshiped in India. One worships what or whom one pleases. Perhaps the essential characteristics of a Hindu are that he usually accepts the leadership of the Brahman caste and is usually content with his own position in the caste structure.

Pervading Hinduism is a passive attitude, a feeling of resignation, and a belief that death is only an essential incident in the foreordained cycle of rebirths. Quoting from the *Bhagavad-Gita:*

. . . . the wise in heart
Mourn not for those that live, nor those that die.
Nor I, nor thou, nor any one of these,
Ever was not, nor ever will not be,
For ever and for ever afterwards.
All, that doth live, lives always! to man's frame
As there come infancy and youth and age,
So come there raisings-up and layings-down
Of other and of other life-abodes,
Which the wise know, and fear not.
. . . .
Nay, but as when one layeth
   His worn-out robes away,
And, taking new ones, sayeth,
   "These will I wear to-day"
So putteth by the spirit
   Lightly its garb of flesh,
And passeth to inherit
   A residence afresh.[7]

Quite early in its development Hinduism appeared to some of its votaries as too priest ridden, too much concerned with ceremonies and sacrifices. In the sixth and fifth centuries B.C., therefore, a reform movement arose to challenge the dominance of the Brahmans. Led by the famous teacher Gautama Sakyamuni, later the Buddha, this movement denied the necessity of rituals and priests, fought against the dogmas of the Brahmans, and opposed caste. The gist of Buddha's teaching was that sorrow existed in the world; that it sprang mainly from individual self-seeking and love of material things; and that sorrow would continue as long as the individual was chained to the Wheel of Birth and Rebirth. Only successive life experiences could teach man's soul the illusion of self-seeking and show him that, finally, rest and peace would be achieved by reabsorption of the Soul into Universal Life or the state of Nirvana.

Buddha

8- *Quoted in Majumdar,
Raychaudhuri, and
Datta,* op. cit., *p. 226.*

It is too often not understood that the distinction between Buddhism and Hinduism was fundamentally, in India at least, only sectarian. Some of the basic ideas of Hinduism were accepted by this reform movement, such as *Maya* and Rebirth, and Buddha was regarded as a Hindu saint. Buddhism was a vital force in Indian religious life for almost one thousand years, but it was ultimately absorbed there by Hinduism, while it continued to live on in such areas as Ceylon, Tibet, and China. Although repudiated as a distinct sect in the land of its birth, it did exercise profound influence upon Hindu thought, especially in the realm of pacifism or *Ahimsa* (non-violence).

The first recorded contact of India with the West came in the sixth century B.C., when the Persian emperor sent an explorer who sailed down the Indus to its mouth, thence up the Red Sea to the present site of Suez. Shortly afterwards the Persians captured the Punjab, which became a satrapy (province) of their empire. The fourth century B.C. was destined to record momentous events. The Greek city-states collapsed, Macedonia rose to power, Rome began its amazing march to world empire, and Alexander the Great toppled over the mighty empire of the Persians. After this last feat, Alexander moved eastward and conquered first Afghanistan and then the Punjab. His aim was to conquer the rich Magadha Kingdom in the Ganges Valley. The conqueror, however, confronted with discontent and possible mutiny among his homesick troops, had to return to the West, and in 323 B.C. his grandiose plans of further conquest ended with his death. Alexander's Indian conquests were taken over by one of his generals, Seleucus.

It was at this time that a young man named Chandragupta Maurya appeared on the scene. Ousting the Greeks, he next conquered Magadha and established a great empire in north India. We have a vivid picture of his capital at Pataliputra from the pen of Megasthenes, ambassador from the court of Seleucus. The most illustrious member of the Maurya dynasty was Asoka, grandson of his house's founder, who became emperor in 273 B.C. We know more about Asoka than any other early Indian ruler. At the outset of his reign he was eager for military glory, but during one of his campaigns he experienced a revulsion against war and bloodshed, and was converted to Buddhism.

Asoka stands out par excellence as one of the best examples in world history of the benevolent ruler who had no thought but the welfare of his subjects. A staunch pacifist, Asoka abhorred the idea of taking any form of life. He went so far as to discontinue the royal hunts and forbade the kitchens of the palace to kill animals for the table. A devout Buddhist, Asoka sent numerous missions to various lands to propagate his faith. Missionaries were sent to Ceylon, to South India, Burma, Egypt, and Kashmir, and had great influence in disseminating Indian civilization.

Acting as the servant of the people, Asoka liberalized the laws, set up hospitals for the sick, and dug wells and planted shade trees along the roads. He was an eager builder, the first to use stone in India. His great palace, now no more, was in its day the wonder of the Chinese pilgrims. Asoka built many memorials, called stupas, to Buddhist saints. They were solid-domed structures of brick and stone built on a round base with beautifully carved balustrades and gateways. In addition to these the principal remains of the reign of Asoka are his magnificent pillars, huge sandstone monoliths, forty to fifty feet high, weighing some fifty tons. The pillars were surmounted by capitals ornamented usually by symbolic figures. The most striking of these capitals is the one at Sarnath, with its four magnificent lions, which is now used by the government of the Union of India as a symbol of the state. The late Dr. V. A. Smith has said, "It would be difficult to find in any country an example of ancient animal sculpture superior or even equal to this beautiful work of art, which successfully combines realistic modelling with ideal dignity and is finished in every detail with perfect accuracy."[8]

Under Asoka the Maurya Empire reached its height, including Hindustan in the north and much of the Deccan. In 232 B.C., however, the great ruler died, and the empire began to decline immediately with his passing. By 185 B.C. the Maurya Empire had collapsed. It fell before renewed invasions of Central Asian tribes, especially the Scythians, who in turn were overrun by Asian Nomads called the Kushans. After the extinction of the Maurya authority, with the exception of two relatively short periods, there was no political unity in north India for 1400 years.

The Kushans referred to above were invaders who took over the civilization of the people they conquered in north India. Under Kanishka (120-162 A.D.) they set up a large border state including north-west India and a large area of central Asia comprising Afghanistan. The Kushan capital was located near Peshawar. This state was the meeting place for many races and cultures; contacts with China were encouraged, and this was the beginning of a continuous interchange between the two countries, while Kushan relations with Rome were also very cordial. Kanishka became a Buddhist, a patron of the arts and of learning. Especially famous is the distinctive school of art, called the Gandharan, that flourished at this time. This art was Greek in technique but Indian in spirit, and its most important gift was the evolution of an image of the Buddha. Gandharan art spread through Turkestan to China and even to Japan.

After the death of Kanishka, events in northern India shaped themselves into a pattern that was to recur over and over in the political annals of the country. The Kushan Empire broke up and another dark period ensued. Little is known of the political history of northern India until the advent of the Gupta Empire in the fourth century.

While the invasions through the mountain passes spent their main force in the plains of Hindustan and interfered little with central and south India, political unity was just as evanescent in the Deccan and in Tamil Land as it was in the north. From time to time flourishing kingdoms arose giving promise of unifying south India, but this object was never achieved. The history of the Deccan and Tamil Land is the story of the rise and fall of kingdoms and of constant warfare.

Among the most important kingdoms of the south in Tamil Land were those of the Pandyas, Cholas, and Pallavas. In general, Tamil civilization was very advanced, based as it was on a flourishing sea trade. Tamil rulers, especially the Cholas, had great fleets which sailed to Ceylon, Burma, Java, and even the Far East. In 45 A.D. the use of the monsoon in navigation had been discovered and, taking advantage of these prevailing winds, ships could now cross the Arabian Sea instead of hugging the coast. The trade of Tamil Land with Rome was particularly active, as Europe greatly prized the spices, perfumes, precious stones, and textiles of south India. Several Roman colonies were set up in Tamil Land, and it has been estimated that the annual drain from Rome to India approximated four million dollars.

While, politically, kingdoms rose and fell and there was a fatal fragmentation, culturally the Tamil cities were on a par with the most advanced urban civilizations in the world. Flourishing cities were built, huge irrigation projects constructed, and remarkable progress made in architecture, as is attested by the temples at Tanjore and Madura. We are fortunate to have a picture of south India from the pen of Marco Polo, who visited the area on his return from China in 1293 A.D.

To return to north India, political disunity and confusion gave way in the fourth century A.D. to the orderly rule of one great paramount power. The dynasty known as the imperial Guptas began its rapid rise in 320 A.D., and by the time of its greatest ruler, Chandragupta II (not to be confused with Chandragupta Maurya), who was on the throne from 380 to 413 A.D., nearly all of north India was united in one empire. The Guptas gave India a glorious period of civilization, one which is to this land what the Periclean Age is in the annals of Greece.

A graphic picture of the glories of the Guptas has been handed down in the journal of a Chinese pilgrim, Fa Hian. He writes of an empire peaceful, prosperous, and well-governed. Art at this time enjoyed its classical period as definite types, conventions, and ideals of beauty crystallized. Gupta art, in keeping with fundamental esthetic Indian canons, was subjective and always sprang from a religious urge. This was the greatest period in Indian sculpture, and the artists of this time developed the standard type of divinity, both Buddhist and Hindu. Perhaps the Buddha images found at Sarnath, near Benares, constitute the finest sculpture yet found in India. Few examples of Gupta painting survive, the most famous being the Buddhist frescoes on the walls and ceilings of the Ajanta caves. The subjects of these paintings are the life of Buddha and scenes from court and domestic life in India. This most famous body of surviving painting gives evidence of being done over a period of five hundred years, and its scenes are valuable in giving us a picture of Indian social life fifteen hundred years ago. As for Gupta architecture, there is nothing to compare with the sculpture of Sarnath or the Ajanta frescoes, for little has survived. We know that spacious buildings were erected and imposing palaces built, but all these were destroyed by the ravages of the Muslim and Hun invaders.

The Gupta period witnessed a lush flowering of literature. This was the golden age of Sanskrit, the sacred language of the Brahmans. Knowledge was systematized, and the epic poem, the *Mahabharata,* was recast and put into its present form. A secular literature developed, consisting of lyric poetry, fables, and drama. The Gupta court was the patron of a group of famous writers, most outstanding being Kalidasa, the great master of Sanskrit. A great stir was created in Europe in 1789 when Europeans first learned of Kalidasa's masterpiece, the play *Shakuntala,* through the translation of Sir William Jones. One of the most important contributions of India to world literature has been its great storehouse of fables, fairy stories, and animal tales. Their themes have been borrowed by the writers of many nations, such as Chaucer, Boccaccio, Shakespeare, and Kipling in western Europe. The *Panchatantra,* a collection of animal tales, was carried to the courts of Baghdad, Byzantium, and Cairo and hence to Europe.

In science, scholarship, and industry, Gupta India had few competitors and many imitators. The greatest university, that at Nalanda, attracted students from all over Asia. Eight colleges and three libraries ministered to the needs of the students. A charming picture has been left us of how examinations were given and degrees conferred:

When a man's renown has reached a high distinction, he convokes an assembly for discussion. He judges of the talent or otherwise of those who take part in it, and if one of the assembly distinguishes himself by refined language, subtle investigation, deep penetration and severe logic, he is mounted on an elephant covered with precious ornaments, and conducted by a retinue of admirers to the gate of the monastery. If, on the contrary, one of the members breaks down in his argument, or uses inelegant phrases, or violates a rule in logic, they daub him with mud and cast him into a ditch.[9]

In mathematics the influence of Hindu mathematicians has been profound. The so-called "Arabic numerals," the zero, and the decimal place system all originated in India and gradually were transmitted westward to Europe. Advanced in chemistry and metallurgy, Indian industry was famous for its fine dyes and for the tempering of steel and iron. Above all, India was the home of fine fabrics; the methods of making many of these were taken over by the Arabs and from them by Europeans. The Arabs named one Indian fabric *quittan,* hence the word *cotton. Calico* comes from Calicut in India, and the terms *chintz, cashmere,* and *bandana* are also Indian.

A famous Indian philosopher has written, "Half the world moves on independent foundations which Hinduism supplied. China and Japan, Tibet and Siam, Burma and Ceylon look to India as their spiritual home."[10] This statement may appear extravagant to people of the West but what it refers to is India's past dynamic role in Asia, especially at its height during the Gupta period, when its culture spread, its maritime power was evident on many seas, and waves of colonists established numerous overseas kingdoms. Especially did China and India maintain intimate relations, with the former sending constant streams of devout Buddhist pilgrims to the latter's monasteries and to seats of learning like Nalanda. Although many cultural traits were borrowed from India, the Chinese were careful not to be too much influenced by the asceticism of their teacher. Perhaps this feeling was responsible for the following Chinese proverb: "If the government gets hold of you, they'll flog you to death; if the Buddhists get hold of you, they'll starve you to death."[11]

From the first century A.D. colonists from India sailed across the seas to Burma, Malaya, Borneo, Java, Indochina, and Ceylon. Many kingdoms were established in Greater India. One area of Indian colonization was in Kambuja (Cambodia), where several Hindu dynasties rose and fell. One of the most famous was that of the Khmer Kings who, about the year 1100 A.D., built the magnificent temple of Angkor Vat. Dedicated to Shiva, this edifice covered three and a half square miles. With its galleries covered with fine bas-reliefs of scenes from the Hindu epics, it must be acknowledged one of the greatest religious monuments ever constructed by man.

Another famous colonial Indian dynasty was the Sailendra, which built up a wide-flung empire in Malaya, Siam, Java, and Bali. Followers of Buddhism, the Sailendras built many splendid temples, including the greatest Buddhist shrine in the world at Borobudur in Java.

Referring to the diffusion of Indian culture to Indochina, Malaya, Sumatra, and Java, an Indian historian writes: "Indian religion, Indian culture, Indian laws and Indian government moulded the lives of the more primitive races all over this wide region, and they imbibed a more elevated moral

9- Quoted in H. G. Rawlinson, A Concise History of the Indian People *(London: Oxford University Press, 1946), p. 76.*

10- Sir S. Radhakrishnan, The Hindu View of Life *(London: George Allen & Unwin, Ltd., 1927), p. 12.*

11- Quoted in Nehru, The Discovery of India, *p. 193.*

Buddhist Emblem

spirit and a higher intellectual taste through the art and literature of India."[12] Toward the end of the Middle Ages, much of the area came into the hands of Muslim invaders and the Indian kingdoms were destroyed; but remnants of Indian culture survive in dances and legends originally brought from Hindustan and Tamil Land.

After giving northern India political unity and peace for less than two centuries, the Gupta Empire began to decline. Central Asian nomads, the White Huns, began to attack the Empire in 455 A.D., and the main Gupta army was defeated. The Huns were finally defeated, but before their setback, they had succeeded in dealing a death blow to the Guptas, whose empire collapsed in 480 A.D.

The curtain comes down on northern India for one hundred years, but out of the wreckage of the Gupta kingdom a powerful but short-lived state emerged. In 606 A.D. a ruler named Harsha came to rule a state located just north of modern Delhi. After much fighting nearly all the lands formerly held by the Guptas came under the control of Harsha. For forty-one years peace and strong government prevailed in north India. From the writings of a Chinese pilgrim we have an intimate picture of Harsha, who undoubtedly must have been a remarkable man. Tolerant of all religions, special patron of Buddhism, friend of poets, and himself no mean literary figure, Harsha stands out with Asoka and Chandragupta II as one of the greatest figures in Indian history.

On the death of this great ruler in 647 A.D., his empire collapsed. This was the last of the great native kingdoms of the north. Indian history again became the story of the rivalry and feuding of petty states, and north India had to wait for five hundred years for another paramount power.

About 1000 A.D., a definite deterioration in Indian strength, morality, and creativeness became apparent. The last great waves of colonization subsided and a spirit of complacency mounted as the invasions from the north ceased. Except for a toehold secured by Muslim Arab invaders in the Sind, there was no serious menace from the outside from the fall of the Guptas to the eleventh century. Contact with China diminished, and the result of this isolation was a spirit of smugness and superiority. A contemporary observer noted:

The Hindus believe that there is no country but theirs, no nation like theirs, no kings like theirs, no religion like theirs, no sciences like theirs. . . If they travelled and mixed with other nations they would soon change their mind, for their ancestors were not so narrow-minded as the present generations.[13]

Social organization and the caste system in particular became set in a rigid, inflexible mold that was inimical to innovation and progress. Nehru asserts that this led to a "decline all along the line —intellectual, philosophical, political, in techniques and methods of war, in knowledge of and contacts with the outside world."[14] Literature declined, in the arts there was representation of moral perversions, and in religion there came about the growth of such practices as the Devadasi system (generally referred to as temple prostitution). Although in southern India there were some kingdoms that could be called "national," enjoying the support of the people in general, in most of India the governmental structure was weak. The government of Indian kingdoms, in most instances, consisted of a corrupt bureaucracy in which the state was held together by the power of the ruling dynasty, not by the support of its subjects.[15]

All in all, India around the beginning of the eleventh century was hardly in a position to hold off a serious threat from without; but, before recounting its conquest at the hands of the Muslim invaders, it will be appropriate at this point to strike a balance sheet of the Hindu period from 3000 B.C. to 1000 A.D. In retrospect, Indian history during this period is largely one of numerous alien streams forcing their way into northern India. In spite of this constant ethnic interruption from without, the invading cultures were absorbed by the dominant racial stocks in India. The essential core was the Aryo-Dravidian Synthesis and to it such other elements were added and assimilated as Greek, Persian, Scythian, and Hun. Caste played an important role in the process, for it offered a place and a status for any type of culture. The absorptive capacity of Hinduism is also partly explained because of its tolerance. "Hinduism absorbs everything that enters into it, magic or animism, and raises it to a higher level."[16] Names mean little; Brahma, Vishnu, Kali, Buddha, are used indiscriminately for God the Absolute Reality. Linked to its absorptive capacity was its tenacity. Hinduism weathered many shocks. As we will see shortly, one of the most shattering blows came with the conquest of Islam, but Hindu-

12- Majumdar, Raychaudhuri, and Datta, op. cit., p. 222.

13- Quoted in K. M. Panikkar, A Survey of Indian History (London: Meridian Books, Ltd., 1948), p. 130.

14- Nehru, The Discovery of India, p. 221.

15- Panikkar, A Survey of Indian History, p. 137.

16- Radhakrishnan, op. cit., p. 47.

ism, unlike Christianity in the Near East, survived in the land of its birth.

In addition to tenacity and absorptive capacity, religiosity has been another important attribute of Hinduism. From Vedic times there has been preoccupation with the mystery of life. The qualities of mysticism, brooding, and asceticism have been much more pronounced than was the case even in the heyday of monasticism in medieval Europe. Religion dominated thought and art. This was true in the long era from the Vedas to 1000 A.D., and it continued to be true down to modern times. Unlike Europe, India, up to the twentieth century at least, never went through a potent secularizing process.

Another fundamental feature of the Indian traditional culture pattern has been its neglect of what we might call the science of society, and more specifically the art of government. Attention throughout the ages has been centered mainly on otherworldly matters. It is natural that mundane politics would hardly have much appeal in a society whose members considered existence an evil and an illusion, and who were primarily interested in escape from and not fulfillment in the world.

It is perhaps this emphasis upon metaphysical matters and the consequent neglect of humanistic values that explain what would seem to be a serious weakness in Indian development. The country has suffered constantly from political fragmentation. Even in those kingdoms that did achieve a modicum of greatness, "the political and administrative unity of the territory achieved spasmodically by able and victorious monarchs," writes A. R. Desai, "was surface unity."[17]

There is a tendency on the part of some Indian authors to make much of the "democratic tradition" of the Indian village, the basic cell of the country. Each of these villages had its little council, the Panchayat, and they have been referred to as "little republics." It should be understood, however, that what self-government existed functioned only within the village. The people never had an opportunity of extending their political activities outside the confines of their local Panchayat. "In spite of Indian claims," asserts an English authority, "hitherto the system of government has had no roots spreading right down among the masses of people."[18] The self-governing village Panchayat was a vigorous and hardy seed of democracy, but it was never nurtured into

anything on a provincial or national scale. It has been pointed out that popular parliaments or councils in the upper political brackets are not found in Indian history. These were to come only as a result of the impact of the West in the nineteenth century.

The Impact of the Muslims

Up to 1000 A.D. India had been able to assimilate the numerous invaders who had pushed through the narrow passes of her northern mountain wall. But not long after the death of King Harsha in the seventh century and the collapse of a strong government in the north, a new invasion movement began to take form that would seriously challenge the traditional capacity of Hinduism to absorb alien cultures.

As early as the year 711 Muslim Arabs came in conflict with Indians when an expedition of Arab marauders reached the mouth of the Indus and captured the area of Sind. Further expansion in this region, however, was blocked, and Muslim raids into India were started in earnest from the north-west late in the tenth century. Under the redoubtable Amir Mahmud of Ghazni, an Afghan Turk who began raiding in 998, seventeen looting expeditions were carried out. Few of the previous invaders into India matched the ferocity and ruthlessness of Mahmud's Turks. To his Muslim horsemen, India was a land handed over by Allah for pillage and plunder. Fiercely monotheistic, detesting idolatry, and believing in the equality of man, the Muslims abhorred the "Hindu infidels and unbelievers" with their idols and caste system.

The Hindus opposed the Muslim invader with desperation, and terrible battles were fought. No quarter was given on either side, thousands were massacred, and the cities and temples of the land were destroyed or despoiled. On occasion, when Hindu defenders of a stronghold realized that further resistance was futile, they carried out the terrible rite Jauhar, in which the men assembled their women and children, placed them on a huge pyre, and then, as the flames extinguished the lives of their families, sallied forth from the gates to die with sword in hand. Although resistance was desperate, the Hindu armies were no match for the invaders. Hindu military tactics were outmoded; their lumbering war elephants could not cope with the fast maneuvers of the horsemen from Central

Vishnu

17- *A. R. Desai,* Social Background of Indian Nationalism *(Bombay: Oxford University Press, 1949), p. 15.*

18- *Guy Wint and Sir George E. Schuster,* India and Democracy *(London: The Macmillan Co., 1941), p. 242.*

Asia. Furthermore, the defenders of India were not united and were additionally weakened by the fact that fighting was the traditional duty of only one caste.

A new chapter in Muslim invasion began in 1191 when Mohammed Ghori, an Afghan, not only raided India but began to occupy the country. By 1200 Mohammed Ghori controlled much of northern India, and on his death in 1206 one of his generals established a Muslim kingdom at Delhi. This Delhi Sultanate was in existence from 1206 until 1526. Its heyday was in the first century and a half of its rule, when the sultans reëstablished political unity in northern India. Military expeditions were also dispatched into the south, and the Hindu kingdoms in the Deccan and Tamil Land were conquered.

These Delhi sultans were a curious lot. While they were patrons of the arts, builders of magnificent mosques, tombs, and palaces, they were in general fierce fanatics and bloodthirsty tyrants. An American historian characterizes them thus: "In general they combined with their intolerance, insatiable avarice, lustful debauchery, and a positive genius for intrigue and murder."[19] After 1388 the Delhi Sultanate fell apart. Strong government collapsed amid the welter of warring small states, and in 1398 the dread Amir Timur, the Tamerlane of English literature and a Barlas Turk who had overrun Central Asia, invaded India and sacked Delhi. The city was pillaged, fifty thousand of its people massacred, and another hundred thousand carried off by the raiding army. It was said of Delhi, "The city was utterly ruined; the inhabitants who were left died, and for two whole months not a bird moved a wing in Delhi."[20] In 1450 the Delhi Sultanate was resurrected. Its rulers, however, were generally puppets who did not succeed in reuniting the old Delhi Empire. These sultans maintained a precarious existence until 1526, when they too, like their victims before them, fell prey to another invasion from the north. It was also in this last phase of the Delhi Sultanate that Portuguese Europeans secured a foothold in India and thus introduced yet another element into the chemistry of Indian life, an element which was to transform the destiny of the country.

Before European influence, however, came to play its momentous role in Indian affairs, another Muslim invader received the opportunity to work his will in India. In 1524 the chieftain Babur,

founder of the Mogul dynasty, invaded India. This hard fighting leader of men, a Turk descended both from Timur and Genghis Khan, had started out as a ruler of a small kingdom in what is now Russian Turkestan. In 1504 he captured the important Afghan stronghold of Kabul, and in 1519 began to move toward India. With a ridiculously small force, only twelve thousand men, Babur in 1524 pushed into India and two years later defeated the forces of the decrepit Delhi Sultanate at the decisive battle of Panipat. Thus the Mogul dynasty (*Mogul* comes from the Arabic word for *Mongol*) was established in India and was to be a dominant factor in the country's history from 1526 until 1707, the date of the death of the last great Mogul emperor.

The son of Babur had considerable difficulty in holding his own in northern India, and for a time was forced to flee the country. His son, Akbar, destined to be the greatest of the Moguls, succeeded to a weak throne in 1556. Though only thirteen years of age, the young ruler defeated a strong Hindu army and then proceeded to control and purge his conniving court. Akbar was resolute, strong, and efficient, and by 1576 he had eliminated all opposition in northern India and ruled over a submissive and dutiful empire stretching from the Himalaya to the Vindhya mountains.

Akbar had a noble vision: his central purpose was to unite Hindus and Muslims in a common loyalty to the crown. He accordingly abolished the *jizya,* the tax on non-Muslims. Hindus were employed in many branches of the government and religious toleration was offered to all. In particular, Akbar strove to conciliate the proud and martial Rajput Hindu princes. His policy of toleration was a significant departure from the bigotry of the sultans of Delhi.

Akbar was outstanding as a civil administrator. The empire was organized into a dozen provinces and placed in the hands of a well-paid and competent civil service. Well educated men from all parts of Central Asia flocked into India to become important administrative cogs in the Mogul bureaucracy; about 30 per cent of the officials, mainly in the middle and lower grades, were Hindus. An efficient system of land revenue was organized and a royal mint set up that produced coins not matched at this time, for design, in any other state in the world. The Mogul Empire at the beginning of the seventeenth century was probably the best

19- *G. Nye Steiger,* A History of the Far East *(Boston: Ginn and Co., 1936), p. 338.*

20- *Rawlinson,* A Concise History of the Indian People, *p. 133.*

Tamerlane

organized and most prosperous then existing in the world.[21]

Akbar as a man was an intriguing and appealing character. While not educated in a formal way and thus illiterate, he was one of the "best read" men of his day, for many books were read to him by his scholars. Akbar was a profound thinker and a patron of the arts and of learning. Nothing suited this Grand Mogul so much as to listen in on a brilliant conversation and so we learn that: "Crowds of learned men from all nations, and sages of various religions and sects, came to the court [where] they would talk about profound points of science, the subtleties of revelation, the curiosities of history, and the wonders of nature."[22]

Akbar at heart was a religious mystic who was searching for some eternal verity that somehow he could not find in Islam. The Emperor finally founded a new religion consisting, as he thought, of the best in all religions and one that could be accepted by both his Muslim and Hindu subjects. His famous minister, Abul Fazl, has left a verse from one of his poems that well expresses the religious outlook and purpose of Akbar:

O God, in every temple I see people that seek Thee; in every language I hear spoken, people praise Thee!
If it be a mosque, people murmur the holy prayer; if it be a Christian church, they ring the bell for love of Thee.
Sometimes I frequent the Christian cloister, and sometimes the mosque;
But it is thou whom I seek from temple to temple.[23]

Akbar must be considered one of the great figures of world history. In his own day he did not suffer one whit in comparison with such contemporaries as the French Henry of Navarre or Elizabeth of England. The successors of the great emperor, however, did not measure up to his greatness. His son Jehangir, who ruled from 1605 to 1627, was an indolent and ineffectual sovereign who ended his days a drunkard. There was little expansion during Jehangir's reign, the one important development being the coming of English merchants to India.

Shah Jahan came to the throne in a welter of blood, and before the fighting was over he had killed most of his male relatives. This reign is supposedly the summit of Mogul power. The wealth of the emperor was enormous, the treasury holding the equivalent of more than one billion dollars. Shah Jahan was a magnificent builder, his masterpiece being the world-famous Taj Mahal, a beautiful white marble tomb built in honor of his dead wife. This structure, called "the miracle of miracles, the final wonder of the world," employed twenty thousand workers for fifteen years. Underneath the glitter and magnificence of the Mogul court, however, all was not well. The great mass of the people no longer prospered as under Akbar. They were heavily taxed and, what was worse, Shah Jahan reversed the tolerant policy of his grandfather and set about destroying Hindu temples.

The climax of the empire of the Moguls came during the reign of Aurangzeb (1659-1707). His path to the throne, like that of his father, was drenched with the blood of his victims, mainly his brothers. For the first twenty years of his reign he was occupied almost exclusively with domestic matters. Unfortunately, his object was to free the land of heretics. Muslim apostates were put to death. The poll tax was reimposed on the Hindus, while their temples were destroyed and the ranks of the bureaucracy purged and cleansed of nonbelievers. The noble ideal of a secular state comprehending men of various religions had been forgotten.

Having sought to restore a pristine orthodoxy to Islam in India, Aurangzeb embarked on his second main objective, the complete political unification of India under Mogul rule. The conquest of central and south India, directed mainly against independent Muslim kingdoms and the proud Hindu hill people, the Mahrattas, began in 1681. By 1690 all effective opposition had been crushed. For the first time in all its history the Indian subcontinent was under one sovereignty. From the Himalayas to Cape Comorin the writ of Aurangzeb was supposedly supreme. But not for long. Revolts broke out in various parts of the empire as its different peoples—Sikhs, Mahrattas, and Rajputs—rose in rebellion. For more than fifteen years Aurangzeb moved his great unwieldy army across the country trying to crush his foes, above all the Mahrattas; in the end he completely failed. Aurangzeb passed away while in the field at the age of eighty-nine, with the forces of rebellion, whose ranks he had done so much to fill by his bigotry and intolerance, still defiant and undefeated.

The Muslim impact upon the pattern of Indian culture was profound and widespread in its influ-

21- *Rawlinson*, India: A Short Cultural History, *p. 308.*

22- *Quoted in Will Durant*, The Story of Civilization, *I (New York: Simon and Schuster, 1935), p. 469.*

23- *Quoted in Rawlinson, A Concise History of the Indian People, p. 183.*

ence. During the first phase of the conquest there was much brutality and even massacre. During this time the religious fanaticism of the victors all too frequently caused severe suffering among the subject Hindus. While the rich Hindus saw their goods and land confiscated, the lives of the masses of people in their villages were little touched by the new masters.

After this phase of conquest had been completed, there was a settling-down process. The Muslim rulers had to organize government, collect taxes, and stabilize their position. In the process there was bound to be a mixing of cultures. Hindus were employed in the civil service, especially in the subordinate posts. There was some intermarriage, especially between Turks and Moguls and Hindu women. In order to escape taxation, on occasion to be free from the incubus of caste, or to secure preferment in government, some Hindus were converted to Islam. The number, however, relatively speaking, was remarkably small.

Culture traits passed from one group to the other. The institution of purdah, i.e., the seclusion of women, was copied by the Hindus. Hindi, the Indian vernacular, was adapted by the Muslims as a kind of lingua franca; changed to Urdu by the use of Persian instead of Sanskrit script and by the addition of Persian and Arabic words, this modified Hindi became the common language of the day. Mogul manners were copied throughout the country. Just as the court of Louis XIV was imitated in Europe, the food, manner of dress, and system of etiquette prevailing at the Mogul capital were the models for both Muslim and Hindu princes in India. More fundamentally, Muslim thought, with its emphasis upon monotheism and democracy, made a deep impression upon Hinduism and led to the birth of important new movements that sought to reform and liberalize the native faith.

Culture reached a new height in India under the Moguls. Their courts were famous for their great luxury and for being the center of a galaxy of artists and scholars. Akbar employed many artists, lapidaries, artisans, and architects. While sculpture was neglected, Akbar founded an important school of Indo-Persian painting, which later was influenced by the Italian style. The exquisite work of this Mogul school of art can be seen in most of the great museums of the West. The official court language of the Moguls was

Persian, and many important Sanskrit works were translated into this language. While the classical Indian language, Sanskrit, was displaced, there was an important advance in the development of Indian vernaculars, especially in the north. The most famous poet of this new literature was Tulsi Das (1532-1623), often considered the greatest of all Indian poets.

It was in architecture that the Muslims made their greatest achievement, combining Persian and Indian elements into a distinctive new style. Indo-Islamic architecture began with the Delhi sultans, who introduced mosques and tombs and added to Indian forms the arch, dome, and minaret. With the Moguls the Indian influence declined. Their buildings were characterized by the use of the bulbous dome, the cupolas at corners on slender pillars, and lofty vaulted gateways. The city of Fathpur Sikri, built by Akbar, with its glorious mosque, tomb, baths, and palace; the Taj Mahal of Shah Jahan; and this latter emperor's palace at Delhi with its marble and richly inlaid pillars and its Peacock Throne—all attest to the rich architectural contributions of Islam in India.

The Muslim conquest introduced a new kind of invader into India with a culture both proud and militant and with no intention of being assimilated. The following statement, written by an Indian historian, would seem a correct evaluation of Islam as a historical ingredient in India:

The main social result of the introduction of Islam as a religion into India was the division of society on a vertical basis. Before the thirteenth century, Hindu society was divided horizontally. Islam split Indian society into two sections from top to bottom and what has now come to be known in the phraseology of today as two separate nations, came into being from the beginning. It was two parallel societies vertically established on the same soil. At all stages they were different and hardly any social communication or intercourse of life existed between them.[24]

By 1707, with the death of Aurangzeb, the Mogul empire rapidly fell apart. An Asiatic despotism, its cycle can well be described in the words of Edward Gibbon, "one unceasing round of valour, greatness, discord, degeneracy, and decay."[25] Although in theory the Mogul emperors sat on their thrones until 1858, they were increasingly impotent after 1707, *rois fainéants* with hardly anything left but memories of the glorious past. The Mogul cultural contribution remained.

24- Panikkar, A Survey of Indian History, *p. 162.*

25- Quoted in Stanley Lane-Poole, Medieval India Under Mohammedan Rule, 712-1764 *(New York: G. P. Putnam's Sons, 1903), p. 34.*

As the once all-powerful and strongly unified Mogul Empire declined, it left in the wake of its collapse a power vacuum in India. Several promising indigenous powers might well have risen to the challenge of creating again a structure of political unity for the country; but they failed to do so, leaving the European trading companies which were already on hand no other alternative than to intervene. It was out of this background of turmoil, as we shall see in this chapter, that the English East India Company emerged as the political sovereign of India.

THE NARRATIVE of the Company's conquest is an absorbing and even an amazing story of courage, audacity, and often downright chicanery; but much more important were the effects of Company rule upon Indian life and institutions. In the long chronicle of invasion, with the exception, of course, of the all-important Aryan incursions, no invaders—not even the Muslims—modified, influenced, and even reshaped the pattern of things in India as did the British rulers.

WESTERN RULE brought India into contact with the major historical trends—political, economic, scientific, and intellectual—that were agitating and influencing the European world. As we will see in this and the following chapter, these contacts had mixed results, good and bad. The important thing, however, is to see how a new India was created largely as a result of the British impact. This new India was effectively united, politically, for the first time. It began to become conscious of the importance of the humanistic and secular approach to life's problems. Eagerly its leaders imbibed and digested the food of European liberalism, with its emphasis on democracy, that was made available in the school system established by British rule. And in the area of economics, it was jarred out of the old avenues of barter and self-sufficiency into the highways of world markets, international finance, and at least the first stages of industrialization.

The rise of British supremacy in India

chapter 3

THE RETURN of the spice-laden ships of Vasco da Gama from Calicut to Lisbon in September 1499 marked the beginning of the European contact with India; from this time on steadily increasing European influence finally became control. Six years later, in 1505, a rapidly expanding trade justified the appointment of Francisco de Almeida as the first Portuguese Viceroy, or Governor of the East. Under his direction, control of the Indian Ocean was wrested from the Arabs, and his successor, Alfonse de Albuquerque, established Portuguese settlements at Goa, Malacca, Ormuz, and the island of Socotra off the entrance to the Red Sea.

For roughly a century the Portuguese commercial supremacy, built on the foundation of sea power, remained unchallenged. Tremendous revenues flowed to Goa, the capital of the Portuguese empire, and an immense trade monopoly was established. After 1600, however, the growing sea power of the Dutch and English, and the corruption, religious intolerance, and deterioration of Portuguese officialdom in the East combined to lessen the importance of Portugal as a power in Indian affairs.

By the mid-seventeenth century Portugal had ceased to be a factor in Indian development. Her rule had introduced Catholicism, popularized the use of tobacco, and given many words to Indian languages, but by the twentieth century all that remained of the once mighty Portuguese empire were a few decayed bits of territory on the west coast of India.

Between 1596 and 1602 fifteen Dutch expeditions were sent to the East, and in the latter year the great United Dutch East India Company was organized. These traders were determined to drive the Portuguese out of the Spice Islands and to challenge their trading monopoly in India. After capturing important Portuguese posts in the Spice Islands in the early 1600's, the Dutch expanded their empire, and by 1658 they were firmly established in Java, Goa, Malacca, and Ceylon. Dutch trading posts in India were opened at Surat, Masulipatam, and Pulicat before 1620, and other trading sites were acquired throughout the seventeenth century.

The first Englishman to come to India was Father Thomas Stevens, a refugee Jesuit who landed in Goa in 1579. As the reign of Queen Elizabeth ended, English interest in the trade of the East mounted rapidly. The leader of the first English traders to the East, Captain Lancaster, returned in 1594 from a three-year trip to Malaya. In 1599 Dutch merchants raised the price of pepper, and a group of English traders, having met in London to determine how they could escape the rising Dutch monopoly in the East, incorporated on December 31, 1600, as "The Governor and Company of Merchants of London trading into the East Indies." One hundred and twenty-five shareholders of the English East India Company subscribed £70,000 and were given exclusive trading rights and other prerogatives in the East for an initial period of fifteen years, after which these privileges were to be periodically renewed.

The English East India Company at the outset was mainly interested in the trading opportunities in Malaya and the East Indies, not those in India. Altogether, between the years 1601 and 1618, nine voyages were made, mainly to the Spice Islands. On the first of these expeditions (1601-1603) Captain Lancaster brought back to England one million pounds of pepper. The English, however, encountered the implacable hostility of the Dutch, and a species of undeclared war broke out. The final outcome was the so-called Massacre of Amboina in 1623, in which a small English factory, or trading post, in the Spice Islands was wiped out, its staff tortured and executed. By 1624 the Dutch had driven their competitors completely out of the islands.

Under these circumstances it was natural that the English should turn to the sub-continent of India, where pepper, albeit in smaller quantities, as well as silks, muslins, and calicoes, could be secured. The first landing in India was made by Captain William Hawkins, who disembarked at Surat early in 1609. Making his way to the Mogul emperor's court at Agra, he soon ingratiated himself with the chief officials and earned the favor of the emperor, Jehangir, by participating in his lusty drinking bouts. Hawkins succeeded in obtaining permission for the Company to erect a factory at Surat. In response the Portuguese began strenuously to bar English ships from Indian harbors, but in 1612 a small English naval squadron defeated a much larger flotilla of Portuguese vessels. Again, at the end of 1614, a much more decisive victory was gained by the English squadron over their European rivals.

East India House

1- C. M. Cross, The Development of Self-Government in India, 1858-1914 (Chicago: University of Chicago Press, 1922), p. 2.

2- Lord G. Elton, Imperial Commonwealth (New York: Reynal and Hitchcock, 1946), p. 83.

3- Quoted in W. H. Moreland, From Akbar to Aurangzeb (New York: The Macmillan Company, 1923), p. 53.

4- R. C. Dutt, The Economic History of India Under Early British Rule (2nd ed.; London: Kegan Paul, Trench, Trubner, and Co., Ltd., 1906), p. vii.

5- P. Padmanabha Pillai, Economic Conditions in India (London: George Routledge and Sons, Ltd., 1925), p. 29.

6- Sir John Cumming, ed., Modern India (London: Oxford University Press, 1932), p. 269.

The English East India Company was now free to proceed with the task of expanding its activities in India. Permission was obtained from the Mogul authorities to set up other factories at Agra, Ahmadabad, Broach, and Masulipatam. Much more important than these early factories was the actual acquisition of land by the Company in three widely separated but strategic spots. In 1639 a factor, Francis Day, secured a lease of land from a local Indian ruler on the Coromandel coast. On this strip of land, on the Cooum River, a fort named St. George was built; it was to grow into the modern city of Madras. In 1660 Bombay with its magnificent harbor came to Charles II as part of the dowry of Catherine of Braganza, when the English monarch married the Portuguese princess. In 1688 Charles handed Bombay over to the English East India Company. Calcutta, which has been described as "the third leg of the tripod on which England has built up its supremacy in India,"[1] was founded in 1690 by a Company official named Job Charnock on a desolate and marshy east bank of the Ganges, and nine years later a definite lease was secured from the Mogul government of the land on which was built Fort William.

In these early English settlements the officials lived under strict discipline. Their meals were taken in common as late as 1720. There were daily prayers, and the officer in charge, the president, had the power to impose fines on his subordinates for drunkenness, gambling, and brawling. An early factory of the Company has been described as "a large trade-household in which they [the Company's servants] lived under the authority of the President, very much like undergraduates in a strictly disciplined college."[2] There existed shortly after 1650 a regular hierarchy of ranks in the Company's service consisting of apprentices, writers, factors, merchants, and senior merchants. All ranks were paid scandalously low wages—a senior merchant received from £300 to £600 a year. The poor pay led the Company servants to borrow money to engage in private trade, a practice that soon led to peculation and many scandals.

Seventeenth-Century India

What kind of country did the English find when they arrived in India early in the seventeenth century? In comparison with other countries in this period before the Industrial Revolution it had important industries and an active and favorable balance of trade. Europe could supply few goods wanted by Indians, and in return for the pepper and textiles so avidly desired by the West her traders had to pay in precious metals, usually silver. Sir Thomas Roe, ambassador of the English East India Company at the Mogul court, referred to this situation when he remarked that "Europe bleedeth to enrich Asia."[3]

The manufacture of cotton cloth was the most important industry, while others of sizable dimensions were silk weaving; shawl and carpet weaving; the production of saltpeter (used in gunpowder); the making of paper, glass, and pottery. There has been a tendency on the part of some modern Indian economists to overemphasize the extent and importance of industry in Mogul India. For example, R. C. Dutt writes, "India in the eighteenth century was a great manufacturing as well as great agricultural country, and the products of the Indian looms supplied the markets of Asia and Europe."[4]

The truth of the matter would seem to indicate that the main industries were confined to a few large towns and that their products never enjoyed any wide market among the masses, who could not buy the luxury wares turned out by the urban workshops. Furthermore, the village—the heart of Indian life—was practically self-sufficient and economically isolated from the nearby town. In discussing these matters an Indian economist admits that "India was never a great manufacturing country in any adequate sense of the term."[5] Another index to the extent of Indian trade and manufacturing in the Mogul period has been expressed by the statement that in the time of Akbar a modern cargo ship of 5000 tons, sailing once a month, would have been sufficient to carry India's sea-borne trade.[6]

The social structure of India was bounded by two extremes. At the top there was a small but very wealthy aristocracy living on a palatial scale characterized by extravagance and pomp. The middle class was prosperous but numerically small and relatively unimportant. At the bottom of the social scale were the masses—perhaps more than 90 per cent of the population—whose condition in general was pitiful. The common man lacked adequate clothing, his work was usually not voluntary, and he suffered from the dread visitations of famine. In the seventeenth century, for example, there was an appalling famine in 1630-1631. European travelers have left us harrowing accounts of the misery of the population. There were eight other famines in the same century and a well known economic history dealing with this period says: "We must regard it [famine] rather as a spectre in the background, always visible to peasants, labourers and artisans, and coming forward from time to time to wreck the social and economic life of one region or another."[7]

Another aspect of Indian life in the Mogul period—and indeed even before the advent of Babur the Mogul—was the static life of the village in which the great majority of India's one hundred million people lived. The village was not only isolated; it was caste ridden and bound by custom. A modern Indian economist sums up the situation thus:

> The isolation of the village made the villager village-minded. The domination of caste over him in the minutest detail of his life, dictating to him not only what profession he should follow but how he should eat, marry and even die, made him caste conscious. The precarious nature of the economic life of the village population struggling against Nature with weak instruments of production and not in co-operation with people outside the village but as a solitary human group, made it defeatist and penetrated with a feeling of helplessness and frustration.[8]

All of this is not to imply that on balance India suffered in any marked degree by comparison with socio-economic conditions in contemporary Europe. After all, the *Travels* of the Englishman Arthur Young add up to a very dismal picture of the state of the countryside in eighteenth-century France. The economic conditions alluded to in Mogul India, however, do tend to correct the roseate picture that some writers have painted of a veritable Utopia existing in pre-British India.

The Fall of the Mogul Power

Whatever prosperity and tranquillity India enjoyed in the sixteenth and seventeenth centuries disappeared early in the eighteenth when the Mogul Empire broke apart. The most immediate cause of this breakdown was the religious intolerance of the Emperor Aurangzeb, which led to open rebellion in many parts of the realm.

It was to crush these revolts that the bigot ruler spent many years in the field, with immense armies consuming the revenues of the country and harrying the countryside. There were, however, more deep-seated causes. The corruption of officials, the extravagance of the nobility, and the oppression of the masses steadily drained away the empire's life blood. For some time there had been a noticeable deterioration in the character of the ruling Muslim caste. Wars of succession had wiped out the leading families, and new blood from Central Asia was no longer recruited for the higher governmental posts. Finally, the Mogul Empire was an alien regime. It continued to be so after Akbar's policy of conciliation was abandoned and it wore itself out trying to maintain its power against the ceaseless opposition, at times overt but always subsurface, of the discontented Hindus. In summing up the reasons for the decline Vincent Smith writes:

> The Mogul empire, like all Asiatic despotisms, had shallow roots. Its existence depended mainly on the personal character of the reigning autocrat and on the degree of his military power. It lacked popular support, the strength based on patriotic feeling, and on the stability founded upon ancient tradition . . .[9]

Following the death of Aurangzeb in 1707 the imperial authority became quite ineffectual. While emperors still sat on the throne at Delhi, governors of various provinces declared their own independence and established separate dynasties. In this fashion one of the imperial viceroys became the ruler, or Nizam, of the state of Hyderabad in 1724. The area of Mysore in 1761 fell into the hands of two Muslim soldiers of fortune, Hyder Ali and his son, Tipu Sultan. At the same time both Bengal and Oudh became in effect independent kingdoms.

While members of the Muslim aristocracy were founding their own dynasties, a notable revival had been taking place in Hindu power, especially in the case of the Mahrattas and the Sikhs. The former were a hardy hill people whose home was in the western ghats. The founder of their power was Sivaji, born in 1627, who became a kind of Robin Hood defying Mogul authority. Under their leader the Mahrattas built up a strong state with its center at the city of Poona. While Aurangzeb succeeded in crippling Mahratta power, he never quite extinguished it, and after his death

7- W. H. Moreland and Atul C. Chatterjee, A Short History of India (*New York: Longmans, Green and Company, 1945*), p. 248.

8- A. R. Desai, Social Background of Indian Nationalism (*Bombay: Oxford University Press, 1949*), p. 13.

9- *Vincent Smith*, The Oxford History of India (*2d ed.; London: Oxford University Press, 1923*), p. 465.

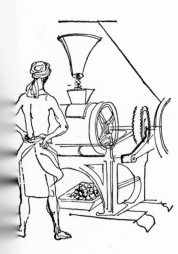

44

it quickly revived. New Mahratta leaders carved out their own states and quickly a great Mahratta confederacy was built up, covering all of the Deccan and extending its influence into north India.

About 1740 the Mahrattas decided to invade north India with the idea of seizing the imperial authority from the weak grasp of the Mogul emperor. Little opposition was met, and Mahratta forces reached the frontiers of Bengal in the east, and in the north-west occupied Delhi and annexed the Punjab. The Mahrattas, however, were not destined to become the heirs of the Moguls and thus unite India again. Their expansion was too rapid and their conquests were mainly predatory. They exacted *chauth*, or blackmail, from the conquered peoples and were continually raiding their neighbors for plunder. In 1761 whatever hope had been entertained by the Mahrattas of uniting Hindustan and the Deccan under their rule was shattered by the battle of Panipat, in which their main army was completely destroyed by Afghan forces that had been carrying out raids into the Punjab.

It was out of this confusion in north-west India that the Sikh power arose. As previously noted in Chapter I, the origin of Sikhism goes back to the teaching of the holy man Nanak in the fifteenth century. The new sect was persecuted by Jehangir and Aurangzeb, with the Sikhs fighting desperately for their faith. As a result they organized themselves into a kind of warring brotherhood proud of their military prowess. The founder and unifier of the Sikh nation was the famous Ranjit Singh, born in 1780, who united his people in the Punjab, created a splendid army, and established a strong kingdom in north-west India. The Sikhs did not play an important role in eighteenth-century India but waited until the 1840's to try to expand their kingdom into a great empire.

By 1740 the Mogul Empire was in its death agony. Only the year before the ruler of Persia had invaded India and captured the great imperial city of Delhi. The population was massacred and huge quantities of booty, including all the crown jewels and the famous Peacock Throne, were carted away by the invaders. From 1748 to 1762 there were repeated raids into north-west India. The incessant raids of the Mahrattas, the incursions of Afghans and Persians, and the rivalries of sol-dier adventurers as they fought among themselves for the tottering thrones brought about a collapse of law, order, and civilization unprecedented in the annals of world history.[10] Trade was disrupted, industry languished, and conditions of the masses in the villages were perhaps worse than they had been for the preceding five hundred years.

The Indian people were becoming a masterless multitude swaying to and fro in the political storm, and clinging to any power, natural or supernatural, that seemed likely to protect them. They were prepared to acquiesce in the assumption of authority by anyone who could show himself able to discharge the most elementary functions of government in the preservation of life and property. In short, the people were scattered without a leader or protector; while the political system under which they had long lived was disappearing in complete disorganization.[11]

In addition to the various new powers that were springing up out of the debris of the Mogul realm there were also present the European trading companies. The Portuguese no longer counted. The Dutch had had brilliant success until 1670, but after this date they began to lag behind the English East India Company. By the closing decades of the eighteenth century the Dutch had virtually been eliminated from India and today there are no Dutch possessions there; only a few quaint houses with Dutch tiles and carvings remain. There were also companies sent out by Denmark and Sweden, as well as the Austrian Ostend Company, but these had only an ephemeral existence.

The French came relatively late to India, for the French East India Company was not organized until 1664 by Colbert, the brilliant finance minister of Louis XIV. In the 1670's the Company became very active and established important and thriving factories at Chandernagore in Bengal and at Pondicherry on the Coromandel coast. Other trading posts were subsequently acquired, such as Mahé, Karikal, and Yanaon, and early in the eighteenth century the French obtained possession of the strategic islands of Bourbon and Mauritius in the Indian Ocean.

Five powers were possible heirs of the Moguls in India—the French, the English, the states of Mysore and Hyderabad, and the Mahratta Confederacy. There were several possibilities: some kind of balance of power or equilibrium between members of the above powers might be achieved,

10- *K. M. Panikkar*, A Survey of Indian History (*London: Meridian Books, Ltd., 1948*), p. 266.

11- *Sir Alfred Lyall*, The Rise and Expansion of the British Dominion in India (*London: John Murray, 1920*), pp. 64-65.

or there might be continuous shifting of combinations and alliances accompanied by endemic warfare. The last alternative might ultimately result in the unchallenged hegemony of one power that would destroy or assimilate all its rivals. As we will see, this last is what actually happened.

The first elimination took place among the European rivals. Neither the French nor the English companies had at first concerned themselves with political or military power in India. The officials of the English Company were specifically advised not to waste money on military adventures and, as the Company's first ambassador to the Mogul court put it: "Let this be received as a rule, that, if you will profit, seek it at sea and in quiet trade."[12] The growing turbulence and the absence of any effective central authority, however, brought about a fundamental change in policy. Joseph Dupleix, who became the Governor-General of the French Company at Pondicherry in 1742, carefully sized up the Indian situation. His policy was to participate in the rivalries of native powers, thus helping to put on the throne Indian rulers who would be at least his friends, and perhaps better his puppets. In order to increase the Company's military power Dupleix's officers trained and equipped native soldiers, called Sepoys.

Shortly after Dupleix became the head of the French Company, the growing Anglo-French rivalry that broke out in Europe in 1743 as part of the War of the Austrian Succession flared forth in India. Hostilities were carried on both at sea and on the land, and in 1746 French forces succeeded in capturing Madras. The final outcome of this first Anglo-French clash in India, however, was a return to the *status quo ante bellum*. Accordingly, Madras was returned to the English Company.

Dupleix was disappointed but not disheartened, and he proceeded to spin an ambitious web of diplomacy that would make the French paramount in south India and oust the English from this region. Taking advantage of a dispute between Indian claimants for the nizamship of Hyderabad, Dupleix in 1749 threw all his weight behind his candidate and insured his success over the opponent supported by the English. The pro-French Nizam was actually installed at Pondicherry with Dupleix dressed in Muslim garb taking part in the ceremonies. The year 1750 saw the French

Company at the height of its power. Dupleix next proceeded to try to dictate the outcome of another disputed office, this time the nawabship of the Carnatic. Realizing that a victory for the French protégé would spell disaster to their interests, English officials at Madras supported a rival candidate. In 1750 Dupleix had everything his own way, but in 1751 his plans were checkmated by a brilliant young official of the English Company, Robert Clive. It was the capture of Arcot by Clive in 1751 that was the turning point of the war and insured the success of the pro-English Nawab. Fighting continued until 1754, when an inconclusive peace was signed between the French and English Companies. As for Dupleix, he was recalled and died in poverty ten years later in France.

While the French and English were fighting in south India, their companies in Bengal were trading peacefully side by side. The reason was the existence of a strong and capable Nawab whose rule prevented any feuds between the European traders. In 1756, however, this ruler died and was succeeded by a young and impetuous nephew named Surajah Dowlah. The new Nawab distrusted the Europeans; perhaps he realized the significance of English success in south India. Whether justified or not, the ruler demanded that English measures to extend their fortifications at Calcutta be halted. Following the English refusal, the young Nawab gathered an army and captured Calcutta. Subsequently 146 English captives were imprisoned in a small dungeon and more than three-quarters of them died of suffocation during the night. This incident of the "Black Hole of Calcutta,"[13] as it is referred to by English historians, inflamed public opinion; and in October 1756 Robert Clive, now a lieutenant-colonel, embarked at Madras with an expeditionary force for Bengal. The small English army had little difficulty in recapturing Calcutta and forcing the Nawab to sue for peace.

The incident, however, was not closed with the vindication of English arms. Plots were hatched against the Nawab by his political rivals and by merchants he had fleeced, and they received the support of Clive, the final result being the defeat of Surajah Dowlah by forces of the English Company at the Battle of Plassey in June 1757. Robert Clive had won an astounding victory, and, while a new Nawab was placed on the throne, the real

12- Quoted in P. E. Roberts, Historical Geography of the British Dependencies, India, I (London: Oxford University Press, 1916), p. 37.

13- Indian historians now are inclined to discount the Black Hole incident and even to deny that it ever happened. In any event, amid the more fundamental plots and maneuvers of the time it was inconsequential, and its significance has been unduly magnified.

rulers of this great and rich province were not this Muslim official and his ministers but the English East India Company.

During the hostilities in Bengal the Seven Years' War (1756-1763) had broken out in Europe, and again England and France were antagonists, not only on the Continent but in America and India. The French sent out as their commander in India the Comte de Lally, an honest, fearless, and somewhat impetuous officer with a brilliant military record in Europe. Lally reached Pondicherry in April 1758 and opened a strong offensive against the English positions in the Carnatic in south India. In 1759, however, the tide began to turn in favor of the English, whose sea power prevented Lally from receiving reinforcements and badly needed supplies. The decisive victory scored by Colonel Eyre Coote at Wandewash in January 1760 destroyed French power in India and led directly to the surrender of Pondicherry in September of the same year. The Treaty of Paris in 1763 returned the French settlements to the Company, but they were to be unfortified and could exist only on the sufferance of the English.

Meanwhile, internecine war and predatory raids continued unchecked in India. The strength of the English East India Company, however, grew steadily. The main settlements of the Company were havens of security to which many important Indian traders and bankers made their way. It is estimated that as early as 1744 there were 250,000 Indians living in Madras.

One of the five main powers, the French, had apparently been eliminated, but hardly more than ten years after the peace of Paris had been concluded the English Company became involved in the most desperate and critical struggle of its rise to ascendancy in India. Warren Hastings was now Governor-General (1772-1785) and was determined to follow a policy of peace, yet he was constantly at war from 1775 to 1783. In 1775 he became involved, largely through the mistaken policies of subordinate officials at Bombay, in a war with the Mahrattas. Not long after these hostilities commenced, Hyder Ali of Mysore made an alliance with the Nizam of Hyderabad and also one with the Mahrattas, and declared war on the English. Hastings was now faced with an alliance of the three great native powers in India. In 1780 Company forces defending Madras were badly defeated.

In this crisis little help or succor could be secured from home by Hastings. While the Mahratta war was raging, Great Britain was confronted by the American Revolution, which soon merged into a world war as France, Spain, and Holland espoused the cause of the rebellious colonists. By herculean efforts, however, Hastings was able to hold the fort. He made peace with the Mahrattas and with Hyderabad, thus freeing himself to muster all his strength against Hyder Ali. In 1781 a French expedition arrived with help for Mysore, but this was offset by the arrival of English naval reinforcements. Early in 1784 the English and Hyder Ali signed a treaty ending hostilities without any conquests.

After all the fighting that had featured the administration of Hastings, it was hoped by the directors of the Company in London that the next Governor-General, Lord Cornwallis (1786-1795), would pursue a peaceful policy. He was ordered to avoid any attempts at conquest for the enlargement of British domains in India. Despite the best intentions, Cornwallis was soon involved in war with Tipu Sultan, ruler of Mysore. While Hyderabad and the Mahrattas were persuaded to remain neutral, Cornwallis had little difficulty in defeating Tipu Sultan (1790-1792), securing an indemnity, and forcing the cession of half of his territory, most of which was turned over to the Nizam. Given the existence of several independent political forces, each following a different policy, it was natural that the struggle of elimination should continue. A British historian observes: "The British Company for good or ill was now a political force in India, and came inevitably into collision with other powers, restless and bellicose, which considered themselves its equals and had no mind to allow the country to settle down to peaceful progress."[14]

For a few years following the conclusion of the Cornwallis governor-generalship in 1795 there was what has been termed a "period of timidity." Every attempt was made by the English authorities to avoid being implicated in the rivalries of the various powers, and the Company remained on the side lines while princes fought among themselves and the Mahrattas in particular robbed and pillaged. In 1798 a new Governor-General arrived for the East India Company. Lord Wellesley, older brother of the famous Duke of Wellington, was only thirty-seven but was a man of tremen-

14- James A. Williamson, A Short History of British Expansion (*New York: The Macmillan Company, 1931), Part V,* p. 131.

dous energy, military skill, and diplomatic astuteness. Three months after he arrived in India, Napoleon landed in Egypt and consorted with the Russian Tsar to plan an attack on India. At the same time contact was made with the ruler of Mysore, Tipu Sultan, who received French agents in his capital and organized a "Jacobin Club." Wellesley determined to extirpate what he regarded as a perennial menace to the Company's position in India. Cleverly he persuaded the Mahrattas to join him against Mysore and also secured the Nizam as his ally. Tipu Sultan was completely isolated, his army was defeated, and he himself was killed defending the walls of his capital.

English historians have a reluctant admiration for Tipu Sultan and most feel constrained to give him his due. One of them writes:

The death of Tipu Sultan removed from the Indian scene the most inveterate, the most implacable and the most fanatical, perhaps the most formidable enemy encountered by the Company in its contest with the "Native" Powers of India. But there was much in the career and character of Tipu, despite the vehemence of his anti-British sentiments, to extort respect and even admiration. If he had no more right than we had to claim territorial sovereignty in India, he had no less. . . . We were equally adventurers in the field of Indian policies. If we had the right to seek the aid of the Nizam and the Peshwa [the titular head of the Mahrattas] to subdue Tipu; Tipu had a right to call in the French to help in expelling us from the soil of India. We succeeded; he failed. But he displayed consistent courage, much persistence, and no little skill. While, then, we must rejoice in his defeat, we can respect his splendid effort to avert it.[15]

Wellesley not only eliminated an unfriendly Mysore under Tipu Sultan but he also initiated the policy of extending the East India Company's control over the existing Native States by making them in effect protectorates. This was accomplished by the system of Subsidiary Alliances, by which an Indian ruler agreed to disband his military forces, to dismiss any foreign officers in his employ, to place his foreign relations in the hands of the English, and to accept a force of English troops, the cost of which would be met by the revenues of a certain part of his territory. In return, the Company guaranteed to provide external security and maintain the Indian ruler's government. Wellesley made such a treaty with the Nizam of Hyderabad and with the Vizier (ruler) of another state named Oudh.

By 1800 there were really only two great powers left in India, the English East India Company and the Mahrattas. It seemed in the logic of history that one would have to give way to the other. The Mahrattas, it may be said, carried out their own destruction. Rivalries and feuds broke out between the various Mahratta chiefs and the leading one, the Peshwa, fled and sought refuge with the English at Bombay. Here a momentous treaty was signed in 1802, the Agreement of Bassein. By this subsidiary treaty the Peshwa—in return for English protection—agreed to receive at his court and maintain a subsidiary force of English troops and to pay twenty-six lakhs of rupees[16] in yearly tribute. This agreement constitutes one of the outstanding events in the story of the rise of British power in India. "The treaty," declares Professor A. B. Keith, "unquestionably must be accepted as giving the British the Empire of India, for it reduced the head of the Mahratta Confederation to a position of complete inferiority and, in matters external, of absolute subordination to the British."[17] Realizing the menace of the treaty of Bassein to their position, the Mahratta chiefs, except the Peshwa, declared war against the Company in 1803. The fighting was severe, as the Mahrattas had employed European officers, mainly French, to train their armies. By 1805, however, the issue was no longer in doubt, although some of the Mahratta forces had not been decisively defeated. Before Wellesley was able to complete his plan of entirely shattering Mahratta power, he was recalled by the London authorities, who were alarmed at his conquests. The peace subsequently made with the Mahrattas by the new Governor-General restored most of their territory to them but did nothing to solve the deep antagonism existing between the great Hindu Confederacy and the Company.

Although to his own mind his work had not been completed, Wellesley left to the Company a different India from the one he found in 1798. In six years he had changed the East India Company from one of several powers to *the* power in India. A glance at the map on page 48 shows the amazing expansion of English territory by Wellesley. Much of south India had now come under British rule; between Madras and Calcutta there was an uninterrupted corridor under Company rule; and in the Ganges Valley the British now not only administered Bengal but in addition

15- *Sir John Marriott,* The English in India *(London: Oxford University Press, 1932), p. 113.*

16- *16 annas = 1 rupee*
1 rupee = 30¢
a lakh of rupees = $30,000
a crore of rupees = $3,000,000
a lakh = 100,000
a crore = 10,000,000

17- *A. B. Keith,* A Constitutional History of India 1600-1935 *(2d ed.; London: Methuen and Co., 1936), p. 114.*

British India under Wellesley, 1799

So much of the story of the development of English dominance had unfolded by 1805 as to leave no doubt of the outcome, but there were several concluding chapters to fill in. The Mahrattas had not been completely subordinated. This task fell to Lord Moira, better known as the Marquis Hastings, who was Governor-General from 1814 to 1823. Hastings was sent out with the most specific orders not to engage in any wars. He was confronted, however, with growing lawlessness in central India. As the Company annexed territory and established the rule of law, large bands of mercenaries moved away to carry on freebooting in areas not under British control. These robber bands, known as Pindaris, found the Mahratta states a safe haven and from them continually harassed neighboring territory.

In 1816 a terrible raid was carried out by Pindari bands, and in one district of the province of Madras over three hundred villages were plundered. At this time it may also be pointed out that there was a military adventurer named Amir Khan who had an army of thirty thousand men and exacted tribute enough from the Rajput states alone to keep him in luxury and furnish his soldiers with an easy living. The Rajputs were a martial Hindu people living in such states as Bikaner, Jodhpur, and Udaipur, east of Sind and north of Bombay. They had a proud tradition of resistance to the Muslim invaders. In the face of these circumstances, Hastings decided he had no choice but to act, and in 1816 two great armies were set in motion. The Pindari bands were caught in a huge ring, much as a hunted beast of prey is encircled by game beaters. Many of the leaders were killed in the fighting, and their followers were given lands and encouraged to settle down to an orderly, if humdrum, existence.

The Mahrattas stood idly by while the Pindaris were being rounded up, but in 1817, perhaps realizing this was their last opportunity to resist the heretofore inexorable expansion of English authority, they suddenly attacked the Company's forces. Hastings' armies, however, were too strong and easily withstood the Mahratta attack, and by 1818 the chiefs had to sue for peace. One of the great Mahratta leaders, the Peshwa, was deposed, and his lands were taken to form the modern Presidency of Bombay. Other princes kept their titles but ceded some territory, and all definitely recognized the supremacy of the Company in

18- Despatch of July, 1804, quoted in Lyall, op. cit., p. 264.

had acquired far to the west the rich area between the Jumna and the Ganges rivers, in which were located the imperial cities of Agra and Delhi. It was in the latter city that victorious Company troops found a poor old man, the Mogul emperor, completely bereft of influence or wealth and blinded by a ruffian. The old emperor was made a pensioner of the East India Company, which, interestingly enough, continued the Mogul imperial titles on its currency until the Indian Mutiny in 1857.

The political significance of Lord Wellesley's Governor-Generalship is excellently expressed in a dispatch sent by him to the Company directors in London in which he declared:

A general bond of connexion is now established between the British Government and the principal states of India, on principles which render it the interest of every state to maintain its alliance with the British Government, which preclude the inordinate aggrandizement of any one of those states by an usurpation of the rights and possessions of others, and which secure to every state an unmolested exercise of its separate authority within the limits of its established dominion, under the general protection of the British power.[18]

subsidiary treaties. Furthermore, the Company proceeded to make treaties with the Rajput princes and thus brought them under the aegis of British authority.

To the north, on the mountain fringe of India, Hastings became involved in another conflict, albeit more limited than the Mahratta war, just before he launched his campaign against the Pindaris. For some time the Gurkhas, the "Highlanders of India," living in their mountain state of Nepal, had been raiding Oudh and Bengal. From 1814 to 1816 three campaigns were waged against the Gurkhas and finally peace was dictated by the forces of Hastings. The independence of Nepal was safeguarded although the western part was ceded to the Company. In this high hill country Simla, the winter capital of British India, was later located. After this conflict the Gurkhas proved to be loyal allies of the English and came to supply important contingents of troops for the Indian army.

Hastings, like Wellesley, was proud of his achievements in India, in particular his destruction of Pindari power and the subordination of the Mahrattas to Company authority. He had these accomplishments in mind when he declared:

> It is a proud phrase to use, but it is a true one, that we have bestowed blessings upon millions. Multitudes of people have come from the hills and fastnesses in which they had sought refuge for years, and have reoccupied their ancient deserted villages. The ploughshare is again in every quarter turning up a soil which had for many seasons never been stirred, except by the hoofs of predatory cavalry.[19]

By 1818 British raj, i.e., sovereignty, had reached the natural boundaries of the sea and of the Himalayan mountains to the north. There were two areas, however, where the frontier was weak and unstable—on the eastern edge of Bengal where the Burmese were penetrating, and in the north-west along the Sutlej River, which formed the frontier of an aggressive and restless Sikh kingdom.

While the English Company was building up its strength through the achievements of Cornwallis and Wellesley, Ranjit Singh had been consolidating the Sikh kingdom into a strong political unit. As long as this leader lived he was a friend of the English and agreed not to expand eastward across the Sutlej River, thus endangering

9- Quoted in Encyclopaedia *Britannica, Vol. XIII, 11th Edition, 1910-1911, p. 54.*

the British frontier. On his death, however, in 1839, the government became ineffectual and the state lapsed into anarchy. The real ruler of the Sikh kingdom was the army, some ninety thousand strong, trained by Europeans and regarded as the best native force in India.

The Sikh army thirsted for glory and was expansionist in spirit. In 1845 it crossed the Sutlej, which had been fixed as the British boundary. In this First Sikh War, 1845-1846, fought during the Governor-Generalship of Lord Hardinge, there were some desperate battles, in which the Company armies barely escaped defeat. But finally the British beat down Sikh resistance and dictated a peace at Lahore. A small indemnity was required, a new ruler placed on the throne, and a British resident stationed at the capital. In 1848 the Sikh army, not as yet convinced that the issue had been decided, revolted and sought to extirpate English influence. Sikh armies were again defeated and the Governor-General, now Lord Dalhousie, annexed their territory, the Punjab.

In the late eighteenth century the Kingdom of Burma was established by an aggressive native dynasty, the Alaungpaya kings, who, following the consolidation of this state, initiated a chauvinistic policy. Burmese armies began to advance westward across the mountains toward the plains of Bengal. In their advance they acquired the Kingdom of Assam in 1816 and in 1823 Burmese forces began to invade Bengal with orders to capture Calcutta. Up to this time the Burmese had not met European armies on the field of battle and their king was so ignorant that it is said he gave his general a pair of golden manacles with which to bring back the English Governor-General. This official, Lord Amherst, declared war in 1824 and several expeditions were sent to Burma by land and sea.

The campaign was fought under extreme difficulties, for the dense jungle and the rainy season impeded the advance of the Company's troops. The Burmese were also adept in jungle fighting, and their bamboo stockades proved difficult to find and harder to capture. Transport and medical facilities for the British troops had not been carefully planned and, in consequence, disease took a heavy toll. Rangoon was captured early in May but it was not until the cold weather of the next year, 1825, that a decisive victory was scored by the British.

The Treaty of Yandabo, signed in the spring of 1826, ceded the important Burmese districts of Arakan and Tenasserim, thus extending Company authority outside of India proper and making the Bay of Bengal a British lake. The frontier east of Bengal was stabilized by the Burmese cession of Assam, parts of which were organized as protected states with the remainder being added to Bengal. A little less than thirty years later, in 1852, hostilities again broke out between Burma and the English over what was charged to be the former's unjust treatment of English merchants. Having received no reply to an ultimatum sent to the Burmese government, Lord Dalhousie, the British Governor-General, dispatched an expedition that captured the important centers of Prome and Rangoon. The end of hostilities witnessed the British annexing the rich deltaic province of Pegu or Lower Burma; the upper part of the country with its capital of Mandalay remained independent. The East India Company now controlled all the eastern coast of the Bay of Bengal from Assam down to the Malay peninsula, and the Burmese kingdom was shut off from any contact with the sea. Rangoon, the port of the Irrawaddy River, became under British direction a great center for the teak and rice trade and one of the most thriving cities in the East.

In the case of Burma and the Sikh kingdom, the initial aggression had come from these states, not from the British; however, in the last case of Company expansion to be noted, in the Sind, there was absolutely no justification except the necessities of power politics and high strategy. The area of the Sind, located in the valley of the Indus, was important for strategic reasons. As long as its Amirs were independent, these rulers could deny the Company navigation rights on the Indus river and, furthermore, the Sind was an important territory for guarding and watching the north-west frontier of India.

In 1843 without any provocation the Amirs were badgered into war and defeated by Sir Charles Napier, who is supposed to have announced his success by the sardonic pun in a message to the Governor-General: "Peccavi" (I have sinned). He also admitted in his diary, "We have no right to seize Sind, yet we shall do so, and a very advantageous, useful, humane piece of rascality it will be."[20]

By the 1840's the entire Indian sub-continent had come under British control, either directly (as in Bengal, Madras, and Bombay) or indirectly by the subsidiary treaties in the case of the protected Native States. British power, exercised through the agency of the East India Company, had fanned out in all directions from the Indus on the west, the Brahmaputra River on the east, the mountain wall of the Himalayas on the north, and Cape Comorin in the far south of Tamil Land.

This expansion of British authority was a natural and indeed inevitable process, given the facts of the situation. There was an absence of national unity in the country, and the indigenous political forces were unwilling and unable to cooperate. Even more, at times they went so far as to assist the Company to strengthen its power by the defeat of some of its Indian rivals. This political ineptness is illustrated in the Mahratta Confederation's assisting the Company to crush Mysore. While originally committed to a policy of eschewing politics and sticking to trade, the menace of lawlessness and the collapse of effective central government forced the English to fend for themselves, and once this policy was initiated there was no turning back.

It is interesting that English historians argue that the British achievement of supremacy in India cannot be tagged simply as "foreign conquest." The Company in their view was merely one of several armed powers, several of which were hardly less alien than itself. And in view of the many invasions that have been written on the pages of the sub-continent's history, there is little evidence to show that Indians thought the rise to power of the Company to be an unnatural process. In fact, little hesitation or compunction was shown by them in fighting for the English Company. Sir John Seeley in summing up the march of British forces to supremacy declares, "Now this is not a foreign conquest but rather an internal revolution."[21]

Too little attention has been given to the role played by sea power in the achievement of British victory. It was neglect of the sea by the Mogul Empire that enabled the Portuguese to establish themselves, under the able direction of Albuquerque, in India and monopolize the trade routes of the eastern oceans. In the case of the English, it was command of the seas that enabled them to withhold supplies and reinforcements badly needed

20- *Quoted in Roberts,* op. cit., *p. 330.*

21- *Quoted in Guy Wint and Sir George Schuster,* India and Democracy *(London: The Macmillan Company, 1941), p. 61.*

by their French rivals or, if need be, following their own setbacks to rectify the balance by receiving additional supplies via the water. With command of the seas, English power was a well that never went dry. Before Hyder Ali of Mysore died in 1782, this astute ruler realized that English command of the seas in the long run must spell defeat to all those powers that stood in the way of the Company's achieving dominance in India. Great Britain, thus utilizing the strategic conception of Albuquerque, who had first realized the significance of sea power in this area, made herself ruler of an Indian empire through mastery of the Indian Ocean.[22]

The reading of the history of Great Britain's unification of India by the force of the sword is always interesting, at times complex, and often confusing. It is natural that there should be different interpretations of the process. In the case of the British the inclination is to regard the East India Company as an instrument of civilization, bringing the blessings of a restoration of law and order to an unhappy land. On the other hand, in the case of Indian nationalists, it is natural that the process should be interpreted somewhat differently, as expressed in these words of Nehru:

We are often reminded, lest we forget, that the British rescued India from chaos and anarchy. That is true in so far as they established orderly government after this period, which the Marathas have called "the time of terror." But that chaos and anarchy were partly, at least, due to the policy of the East India Company and their representatives in India. It is also conceivable that even without the good offices of the British, so eagerly given, peace and orderly government might have been established in India after the conclusion of the struggle for supremacy.[23]

The following, written by an American student of Indian affairs, constitutes one of the most objective and valuable analyses of the issue under discussion and hence is cited in full:

It must be kept in mind that this dominant position [i.e., of the English East India Company by 1850] was not wrested from a peaceful, honest and efficient government. Generally power was wrested from groups who at best were hopelessly inefficient and who generally ruled only because of their temporarily superior power. . . . The British went to India in the spirit of their time. Their primary interest was in trade, which at the time required considerable armed protection. Doubtless, in the spirit of the time, they were ready to use that limited force for advantage of any sort; but it was only because of Indian incapacity and disunion that they were in the first place compelled to protect their own interests with force and finally that their small contingents enabled them to become rulers. Indians, being what they were in the eighteenth century, had allowed their country to drift into the hands of rulers of their own race who were weak, inefficient and dishonest, and they have paid the logical penalty. In fact Indian society was so riddled with cultural and social barriers and Indian thought was so permeated with superstition and ignorant prejudice against other lands and peoples that it could not possibly produce a good government. From the viewpoint of modern democracy, the world is outraged when an outside power undertakes to rule any people, yet from the viewpoint of historical fact, no country of strategic importance either in resources or position, which has been undermined by inefficiency, superstition and contempt for other races and cultures, can hope to remain long its own master. The British came to India, not because they were thirsty for political power but because they were anxious to trade, the traders were forced to protect themselves and ultimately to govern. Britishers had occupied an important place in Indian economic affairs for a century and a half before they acquired political power. It is doubtful if any non-popular government of the time attained its power more legitimately.[24]

The narrative in this chapter has dealt largely with diplomatic maneuvering, alliances, wars, and treaties in which a half dozen powers competed against each other for supremacy. In these pages references have been made to the East India Company as the agent of Great Britain, and the terms Company and Britain—in India—have been used synonymously. What was the position of the Company? Was it a mere agent of the British government or did it preserve some degree of independence while acting in the name and with the authority of the British Crown?

In the following pages the status of the Company *vis-à-vis* the British government will be examined and the steps by which it became endowed with political rights and responsibilities recounted. Furthermore, after studying the rise of British supremacy in India, the logical question to raise is, "What was done with this power and how did it affect the destiny of the country and the lives and institutions of the Indians?" These matters, then, will be the agenda of the next two chapters.

22- K. M. Panikkar, India and the Indian Ocean *(London: George Allen and Unwin, 1945), p. 71.*

23- Jawaharlal Nehru, The Discovery of India *(New York: John Day Co., 1946), p. 280.*

24- D. H. Buchanan, The Development of Capitalistic Enterprise in India *(New York: The Macmillan Company, 1934), pp. 452-453.*

We have seen how a variety of factors,
such as geography, climate, contacts
with China and Southeast Asia as well as
numerous invasions, have conditioned
the course of India's historical development. Of all the extraneous influences,
none has been as momentous and significant
as that of the British, although this contact
was only really effective and widespread
for a period of one hundred and fifty
years, during which time India in whole
or in part was under British rule.
UNDOUBTEDLY THE foundations of modern
India are the traditions of the past,
going back to the days of the Mauryas
and the Guptas, to the thought of the
Upanishads and the ideals of the great
epics; and to these must be added the
cultural heritage brought to India
during the Mohammedan conquest. All
of these elements constitute the ground
floor of the Indian structure, but the
upper and most modern stories were
added during the period of British
occupation: the rule of law; parliamentary government and basic democratic
freedoms, interest in science and a
growing secular spirit; the advance of
industrialism and the addition of the
technological paraphernalia of posts,
telegraphs, railways, and harbors. This
chapter will recount the history and
the nature of the British impact on
India in the realm of politics. The
following pages will discuss such topics
as the initial period of crass British
exploitation in India, the rise of a
sense of trusteeship and responsibility,
causes and consequences of the Indian
Mutiny, and the governmental framework
of control that was built up during
the last half of the nineteenth century—
the golden age of the British raj
in India.
THE EFFECT of such other influences as
Victorian rational thought and western
ideas of political liberalism and
nationalism, together with the significant changes brought by British
economic enterprise and capital, will
form the theme of the following chapter.

The structure and spirit
of British ru

chapter *4*

ROBERT CLIVE, with his victory in 1757 over the ruler of Bengal, had made the East India Company the *de facto* power in this rich and populous province. The Nawab, still the titular ruler, was a mere puppet of the Company. The incongruity of a trading company, primarily interested in profits, exercising military and political power was tragically demonstrated on the morrow of the battle of Plassey. The new ruler of Bengal, creature of the Company, gave its officials in the province huge presents. These gifts, of a forced nature, ran into the hundreds of thousands of pounds sterling. Clive's share of what has been termed the booty of Plassey amounted to £234,000, and in addition he was given by the Nawab a quit-rent for certain lands amounting to £30,000 a year. Clive returned to England in 1760, and the historian Macaulay could well say of him, "No Englishman who started with nothing has ever, in any line of life, created such a fortune at the early age of thirty-four."[1]

What followed in Bengal after the departure of Clive is the sordid story of irresponsible and uncontrolled servants of the Company feathering their nests at the expense of the people. Unscrupulous adventurers were also at work elsewhere. In south India there was the scandal of the Nawab of Arcot's debts, which has been described by an English authority as "the organised exploitation of a ruler's extravagance by a group of British sharks."[2]

In Bengal, Indian rulers and officials were periodically turned out of office, and the new puppet incumbents expressed their gratitude to their creators by suitable gifts to personnel of the East India Company. In the field of business, weavers were forced to accept the terms offered by the officials. Passes giving exemption from local tolls and duties, and originally granted only to the Company, were sold to Indian traders. Some of these merchants did business under the British flag, put their servants in Company uniforms, and forced the population to sell cheap and buy dear. Sir Alfred Lyall, usually a defender of British rule in India, says in referring to this period of plunder that it was "the only period of Anglo-Indian history which throws grave and unpardonable discredit on the English name."[3] Macaulay in his *Essay on Clive*, while not always as restrained and objective as a historian should be, was substantially correct when he wrote:

The servants of the company obtained—not for their employers, but for themselves—a monopoly of almost the whole internal trade. . . . They covered with their protection a set of native dependents, who ranged through the provinces, spreading desolation and terror wherever they appeared. Every servant of a British factor was armed with all the power of his master, and his master was armed with all the power of the company. Enormous fortunes were thus rapidly accumulated at Calcutta, while thirty millions of human beings were reduced to the last extremity of wretchedness. They had been accustomed to live under tyranny, but never under tyranny like this.[4]

In this period India to most Englishmen was a fabulous El Dorado. They were adventurers, often taking great risks, and living in a kind of frontier society comparable to that of the United States in the early nineteenth century. "There is," writes Professor Furber, "the same omnipresence of danger, the same untrammeled scramble for wealth quickly acquired and often as quickly lost, the same atmosphere of building new careers in a new land after failure in the old . . ."[5]

After accumulating enormous fortunes the "nabobs"—as the Company officials were dubbed back home—returned to England. Here they usually tried to enter the ranks of the country gentry and to get a seat in Parliament. Frequently the nabobs were guilty of bad taste and of ostentatious expenditure. Well might Lord Chatham declare, "The riches of Asia have been poured in upon us, and have brought with them not only Asiatic luxury but, I fear, Asiatic principles of government."[6] The process of fortune-making in India was called "Shaking the Pagoda Tree," the pagoda being a gold coin current in southern India.

In the meantime, while Company officials were waxing rich in Bengal, the directors of this body in London witnessed the disastrous decline of revenues. In 1765 they sent Robert Clive out to Bengal for his second governorship. On his arrival he wrote that "such a scene of anarchy, confusion, bribery, corruption, and extortion was never seen or heard of in any country but Bengal." Realizing that the Company was the real power in the province and that it was destined to be responsible for the welfare of the people, he set about with a will to improve conditions and to curb those actions "which make the name of the English stink in the nostrils of a Hindu or a Mussulman."[7] He discouraged individual trading by Company officials, prohibited the acceptance of presents from Indian

[1]- *Quoted in Lord G. Elton, Imperial Commonwealth (New York: Reynal and Hitchcock, 1946), p. 215.*

[2]- *Sir Reginald Coupland,* India: A Restatement *(London: Oxford University Press, 1945), p. 42.*

[3]- *Sir Alfred Lyall,* The Rise and Expansion of the British Dominion in India *(London: John Murray, 1920), p. 143.*

[4]- *Quoted in Joan Beauchamp, British Imperialism in India (London: Martin Lawrence, Ltd., 1934), p. 20.*

[5] *Holden Furber,* John Company At Work *(Cambridge: Harvard University Press, 1948), p. 321.*

[6] *Quoted in Sir Reginald Coupland,* Britain and India, 1600-1945 *("Longman's Pamphlets on the British Commonwealth"; London: Longmans, Green and Company, revised ed., 1946), p. 18.*

[7] *Quoted in Ramsay Muir, ed., The Making of British India (Manchester: Manchester University Press, 1923), p. 76.*

Clive

8- *Kumar Goshal,* The People of India *(New York: Sheridan House, 1944), p. 104.*

9- *Furber, op. cit., p. 323.*

10- *Quoted in the* Cambridge History of the British Empire, *IV (Cambridge: Cambridge University Press, 1929), p. 182.*

11- *A. B. Keith,* A Constitutional History of India *(2d ed.; London: Methuen and Co., 1936), p. 11.*

12- *Coupland,* Britain and India, *p. 20.*

potentates, raised the atrociously low salaries paid by the Company, and dismissed corrupt officials.

Clive's most important act was to secure from the Mogul emperor the *diwani,* or right of collecting the revenue. Instead of the Company assuming the direct collection of revenue and the civil administration that went with it, the bulk of these duties were given to Indian officials, while the Company remained responsible for their actions.

Robert Clive left India for the last time in 1767. After his departure the scramble for wealth recommenced, and in 1767 a terrible famine broke out which was due in part to or at least aggravated by the financial abuses prevalent in the administration. Clive had left behind him a kind of double government, in which the Company received and expended revenue collected by Indian officials who were often corrupt or who were coerced and corrupted by servants of the Company.

The story of the first impact of British rule in India is a melancholy one. One school of writers, using arguments advanced by Brooks Adams in his *The Law of Civilization and Decay,* has maintained that the plunder taken from Bengal after Plassey provided England with the necessary capital to initiate and carry through her Industrial Revolution. "Thus the wealth drained from India was a major contributing factor in the industrialization of England. Some of the ingredients that went into the building of modern England were the 'blood, sweat and tears' of the Indian peasantry and artisans."[8]

However, in a thorough analysis of this question, another authority has pointed out that a drain of wealth could have taken place only if India exported more than she imported, that is, if England took more than India received. The conclusion is made that, although there was a drain of moderate proportions, about £1,800,000 annually from 1783 to 1793, "Nothing in these pages gives the slightest warrant for thinking that Brooks Adams' hypothesis as to the all-important role played by Indian wealth and Plassey Plunder in stimulating the industrial revolution should continue to be viewed with anything but skepticism."[9]

The Rise of British Responsibility

The years from 1772 to 1786 have been called the formative period of British Indian history. During this time Indian affairs were constantly debated in Parliament and became enmeshed in the party politics and rivalries of the day. At the outset the East India Company was enjoying power and profit without responsibility; at the end of the period it had been definitely subordinated to the British government and made in essence a kind of department of the state.

There were important reasons for this momentous change. In the first place, it had become evident that bad government in India meant poor profits or none for the shareholders of the Company. Secondly, the Company was establishing an *imperium in imperio* in India. As Edmund Burke declared, "The East India Company did not seem to be merely a Company formed for the extension of the British commerce, but in reality a delegation of the whole power and sovereignty of this kingdom sent into the East."[10] As far back as 1683, although by charter the Company was given the power to declare war and make peace, the British Crown reserved "the sovereign right, powers, and dominion over all the forts, places, and plantations" of the Company. Professor A. B. Keith points out, "We have here expressed in unmistakable fashion the essential rule that the acquisition of sovereignty by subjects of the Crown is on behalf of the Crown and not in their own right."[11] While the Company, then, in its political actions was ultimately responsible to the British Parliament in London, no machinery had been worked out that would insure a constant and effective check and control over the actions of its agents in India.

In the third place, there was a rising moral reaction against the excesses of the Company in India. This force sprang largely from the humanitarian movement which was such a factor in British politics and life in the late eighteenth and early nineteenth centuries and which was responsible for the successful fight for the abolition of slavery, for prison reform, for the humanizing of the brutal criminal code, and for the improvement of working conditions in the factories of England. Professor Coupland writes:

The appeal of India to the humanitarian spirit was different, but no less cogent. Indian peasants were not being torn away from their homes like the Africans to a life of slavery beyond the ocean, but they were the victims of gross mismanagement and all the misery it meant in lands where Britain had the power, if she had the will, to govern.[12]

In 1772 the storm broke in Parliament, and a Select and Secret Committee was set up to investigate Indian affairs. Back of this action there were mingled motives—humanitarianism, an element of party politics, and downright personal hatred in some instances against Clive. Robert Clive was cross-examined thoroughly and the sordid details of Plassey were aired. Clive bitterly resented the examination and complained he was being treated like a mere sheep-stealer. After a stormy debate in the House of Commons, Clive was exonerated but was reproved by indirection. Brooding over the case, the victor of Plassey committed suicide in 1774.

As a result of the debates and inquiries, Parliament in 1773 passed the Regulating Act, which was an attempt to separate the Company's trading activities from its governing policies. By this Act the head of the government of Bengal was made Governor-General of all British India. This official was to be assisted by a Council, named in the first instance in the Act, with subsequent appointments to be made by the Company. All correspondence of the Company had to be submitted to the British government, which could disallow its policy.

The Regulating Act did not function satisfactorily. During its operation Warren Hastings was Governor-General, and, lacking effective power, he was constantly at logger-heads with his Council. At the same time, Hastings—as we have seen in the previous chapter—was fighting for the very life of the Company in India against a hostile coalition of Mysore, Hyderabad, and the Mahrattas. His administration was further complicated by the fact that the home country was fighting the French and Spanish and was confronted with the American Revolution. In coping with these adverse circumstances, Hastings resorted to some rather high-handed methods, especially in extorting money from unwilling Indian allies for military purposes.

The result, as hostilities closed in 1783, was another hue and cry in Parliament in which Warren Hastings was fiercely attacked. In 1781 two more India Committees had been set up, and in 1783 a bill was introduced into the House of Commons that would in effect have transferred all of the Company's responsibilities to the Crown. Edmund Burke took a leading part in the debates and clearly enunciated a doctrine that later became known as "Trusteeship" in the realm of British

imperial affairs. "All political power," declared Burke, "which is set over men . . . ought to be some way or other exercised ultimately for their benefit."[13]

In 1784, Prime Minister William Pitt sponsored a new bill for the government of India which was enacted into law. The Regulating Act had proved to be an utter failure, for under it no one could say whether the Crown or the Company was responsible for conditions in the Indian provinces. It was said of the Act, "It had neither given the State a definite control over the Company nor the Directors a definite control over their servants, nor the Governor-General a definite control over his Council."[14] Pitt's India Act sought to rectify these weaknesses. By it a Board of Control was set up to supervise all civil, military, and revenue matters. This body was made up of a Secretary of State, who had a place in the British cabinet; the Chancellor of the Exchequer; and four privy councillors. The Governor-General was the servant of the British government and was appointed by it. All patronage and trading activities were kept by the Company.

Instead of abolishing all political responsibilities of the Company, the British government had in a sense made it its partner. The Company still traded, and its servants and soldiers continued to govern and fight in India, but it acted as the carefully supervised agent of the British government.

A by-product of the parliamentary investigations into Indian affairs from 1781 to 1784 was the impeachment of Warren Hastings in 1788. This former Governor-General was accused of the violation of treaties with the native rulers, interference in the affairs of independent States, and the acceptance of bribes and presents. The trial dragged on until 1795, when the accused was acquitted. While the charges against Hastings were greatly exaggerated and on the whole most unfair, the trial gave warning to all that the British Parliament was holding all of its servants in India responsible for their actions.

Lord Cornwallis, with the memory of his surrender to the Americans at Yorktown quite fresh, arrived in India as the first Governor-General under the Act of 1784. This official was to have better success in India than in America. He was a man of absolute honesty who plunged with vigor into the arduous labor of improving the administration of the Company. Private trading by Com-

13- *Quoted in* Cambridge History of the British Empire, IV, p. 197.

14- *R. C. Majumdar, H. C. Raychaudhuri, and K. Datta,* An Advanced History of India *(London: The Macmillan Company, 1946), p. 785.*

pany officials was eliminated, corrupt officials were dismissed, and an elaborate hierarchy of civil courts was set up. The double system of government instituted by Clive, with its two sets of officials, British and Indian, was abolished, and servants of the Company now took over all the important posts. Cornwallis made the district the unit of administration and a Code of Regulations was issued defining the duties of all officers. It can be said of Cornwallis that his work did much to retrieve the British reputation in India, so sullied in the 1760's and 1770's, and that his system of administration became the model and basis for that gradually built up in India early in the nineteenth century.

With the relationship of the British government to the Company settled by the Act of 1784 and the danger of unfriendly Indian powers and chronic political disorder lessened by the victories of the Company's armies, the great question in India at the opening of the nineteenth century was what should be the aims of British rule. One of the Company's best informed officials, Sir Thomas Munro, who was governor of Madras from 1820 to 1827, raised the issue of the ultimate future of British rule when he said:

> There is one great question to which we should look in all our arrangements: What is to be their final result on the character of the people? Is it to be raised, or is it to be lowered? Are we to be satisfied with merely securing our power and protecting the inhabitants, leaving them to sink gradually in character lower than at present; or are we to endeavor to raise their character, and to render them worthy of filling higher situations in the management of their country, and of devising plans for its improvement?[15]

The answer to the questions raised by Munro and other like-minded officials was the development of a strong and liberal reform movement in Indian government. In 1813, when the charter of the Company was renewed by Parliament, it was laid down as the duty of Britain to promote the interest and happiness of the inhabitants of British India. A strong parliamentary committee was created in 1833 to review Indian affairs. In its report it urged that the Company cease as a profit-making organization and that its primary concern be the welfare of the Indians, not the dividends of shareholders.

The report of this Committee was the basis for the Act of 1833, which renewed the charter of the Company for a period of twenty years. By this Act the commercial side of the East India Company was closed down, its debts became a charge on Indian revenues, and its shareholders received an annuity of £630,000, also charged out of the territorial revenues of India. Provision was also made for the repayment of the Company's capital in forty years or earlier if it ceased to operate in India. Other provisions in this landmark of British rule called for the creation of a Law Commission to study the courts of justice and the police establishments and for proper training of the Company's civil servants. And the Charter Act expressly provided:

> No Native of the said [Indian] Territories, nor any natural-born subject of His Majesty resident therein, shall, by reason only of his religion, place of birth, descent, colour, or any of them be disabled from holding any Place, Office, or Employment under the said Company.[16]

The Charter Act was passed during the governor-generalship of Lord William Bentinck (1828-1835), who was perhaps the earliest such official to make reform and the uplift of the Indian people the first charge of his administration. Bentinck was interested, as he expressed it, in founding "British Greatness upon Indian Happiness."[17] There followed much administrative reform, especially in the direction of opening up positions in the subordinate grades of the government service to qualified Indians. Attention was also given to cutting the costs of government. Supervision of the Native States, bound to the British Crown by treaty, was also made more strict. In the case of the state of Coorg, the raja was deposed for cruelty, and in the great state of Mysore the Indian government took over the complete administration of the state owing to the evils and excesses of the ruling raja.

Most famous of Bentinck's reforms was his abolition of the practice of suttee (or *suti*), i.e., widow-burning. English missionaries had long been denouncing its inhumanity, and some reform groups in Indian circles likewise were asking the government to interfere. Suttee was a custom of great antiquity in which the widow placed herself on the funeral pyre of her late husband. This was considered to express the highest idealism of Hindu womanhood. The practice was especially prevalent in Bengal, where the average annual number of

15- *Quoted in Muir, op. cit., p. 283.*

16- Ibid., *p. 304.*

17- Ibid., *p. 283.*

suttees reported from 1818 to 1826 was six hundred. Against some warnings from his officials that the British government dare not interfere with Hindu custom and religion, Bentinck in the famous Regulation XVII of 1829 declared the practice of suttee to be illegal; the ruling made it murder if the act were involuntary and culpable homicide if otherwise. In the Native States outside British India it was more difficult to get the practice abolished, and as late as 1844 we read of one Sikh chief's funeral in which ten wives and three hundred concubines were burned to death.

Another outstanding accomplishment of Bentinck was the suppression of thuggee (or *thagi*), ritual strangling. The thugs were worshipers of the goddess Kali, to whom their victims were dedicated. Gangs of these murderers lurked around the main highways, where they waylaid their victims, murdered them with a noose, and buried the corpses so they could not be traced. The task of hunting down the thugs was given to a capable officer, Major-General Sleeman, and in a few years the secrets of the terror society were discovered, many of the murderers were hanged, and the organization was disbanded. An account of these events may be found in Meadows Taylor's novel, *Confessions of a Thug*, published in 1836.

Bentinck and the Governors-General who succeeded him also gave attention to the problem of infanticide. Many girl babies were killed because of the economic burden of securing marriage for them. Often families could not afford to provide the necessary dowries, and, as unmarried women were considered a disgrace, ruthless steps were taken to insure the limitation of girls in the family. British officials gradually eliminated female infanticide by giving large presents to tribes that kept their daughters, and also by obtaining funds to supply dowries for marriageable girls.

All of these reforms were outstanding in their own right, but probably the most important of Bentinck's acts, in terms of its influence upon modern India, was his selection of English as the medium of Indian education. The argument for the use of English was presented to the Governor-General by his brilliant Legal Member of the Indian Council, Thomas Macaulay, who put forward his case so effectively that Bentinck in 1835 announced that the object of the government should be the promotion of European science and literature in India, to be taught in the English language.

The administration of Lord Bentinck was concerned almost exclusively with the affairs of peace; accent was on reform. He has been called the first of the modern rulers of India, and there are few, either in India or Britain, who would find fault with the inscription on his statue in Calcutta: "He abolished cruel rites; he effaced humiliating distinctions; he gave liberty to the expression of public opinion; his constant study was to elevate the intellectual and moral character of the nations committed to his charge."[18]

The program of reform and modernization initiated by Bentinck reached its climax in the governor-generalship of Lord Dalhousie (1848-1856), who had been trained in public affairs under Peel and Gladstone at home and was outstanding for his great ability and energy. Every aspect and department of government was galvanized and improved by his statesmanship. A Public Works Department was set up; great roads such as the Grand Trunk highway from Peshawar to Calcutta were constructed; new harbors were built; telegraph lines were laid and a postal service introduced; and impressive progress was made in irrigation. Ably supported by the Board of Control in London, Dalhousie began to build the foundations of a national system of education.

Dalhousie had little use for the system of Subsidiary Alliances introduced by Wellesley, whereby the British government guaranteed the native rulers the enjoyment of their thrones without, at the same time, demanding from them suitable guarantees to provide decent and just government for their subjects. In the old pre-British days, at least the people had in the last resort the right of revolution. Under the alliance existing between the Company and the native rulers this was taken away. Dalhousie firmly believed that direct British rule would be a great improvement over raja rule, and he was determined on every occasion to annex states governed by Indian dynasties. His weapon at hand was the Doctrine of Lapse. Whenever the direct line of succession died out in a state he refused to accept the Hindu practice of adoption of an heir, but added the state to the British holdings. The great states of Nagpur and Oudh were accordingly annexed, together with a number of small states such as Sattara and Jhansi. In the case of Oudh, the ruler had been warned on several occasions that, unless his scandalous misrule ceased, the Company on behalf of the Brit-

- Quoted in Howard Robinson, The Development of the British Empire (Boston: Houghton Mifflin Company, rev. ., 1936), pp. 199-200.

British India in 1856

19- *Quoted in H. G. Rawlinson, The British Achievement in India (London: William Hodge and Co., 1948), p. 151.*

20- *Quoted in Guy Wint and Sir George Schuster*, India and Democracy *(London: The Macmillan Co., 1941), p. 78.*

21- *Quoted in Rawlinson*, The British Achievement in India, *p. 92.*

22- *L. S. S. O'Malley*, Modern India and the West *(New York: Oxford University Press, 1941), p. 78.*

ish government would be forced to act. Altogether about 150,000 square miles of territory, heretofore under the rule of Indian potentates and rajas, were annexed to British India.

The conclusion of Dalhousie's administration in 1858 was in a sense the terminal point of a distinct period in Anglo-Indian history characterized by liberalism and reform and by the belief, even the wish, on the part of many eminent British administrators that India some day would ask for self-government. Referring to this possibility, the Governor-General Marquis of Hastings declared, "In that hour it will be her greatest boast that she [England] has used her sovereignty towards enlightening her subjects, so as to enable the native communities to walk alone in the paths of justice."[19] And Macaulay, referring to this possibility, announced, "Whenever it comes, it will be the proudest day in English history."[20]

The Indian Mutiny and Its Legacy

Lord Canning, son of the famous prime minister, was appointed Governor-General of India in 1855 and arrived in the country he was to govern in the spring of the following year. Before leaving London he had warned the directors of the Company that, though he hoped for peace, yet, "In the sky of India, serene as it is, a small cloud may arise, at first no bigger than a man's hand but which, growing larger and larger, may at last threaten to burst and overwhelm us with ruin."[21] These words were prophetic, for a terrible mutiny broke out in the spring of 1857.

The causes of the Indian Mutiny are numerous and complex. Together they can be described as a "revulsion against western influence."[22] For a century India had been figuratively turned inside out and stood on its head as it experienced the impact of western civilization at the hands of the British. This impact had reached its greatest intensity during the administration of Dalhousie, when this reforming Governor-General tried to transform the pattern of Indian culture.

Specific causes of the Mutiny can be singled out, however. Politically, there was the anger and discontent created among some Indian princes by the Doctrine of Lapse. Economically, British rule in certain areas had led to the loss of land by property holders as the government carefully scrutinized land titles. Then there was the whole complex of causes clustered around fear for religion and caste. There was a widespread rumor that Canning had been sent out to India to convert the Hindus to Christianity. In some instances, the missionaries had been too zealous in their disparagement of Hinduism, and certain British officials, such as Macaulay, had decried Hindu culture. To some rock-bound Indian conservatives the prohibition of suttee and infanticide and the enactment of laws enabling widows to remarry were anathema.

The strongest single force, and one that took advantage of the prevailing discontent in certain quarters, was unrest in the Bengal Sepoy Army. In these regiments there was a large percentage of men of high castes who resented being sent outside the borders of India to fight, since such a journey involved loss of caste. Troops had been sent to Afghanistan in the late 1830's, and there was a possibility that there would be more foreign service for the Sepoys as Great Britain became involved in controversies with Persia, China, and Burma. This prospect was confirmed by a law passed in 1856 requiring all Indians enlisting in the army to serve anywhere.

The Indian soldiers, furthermore, no longer believed in the invincibility of British troops, who had received a terrible mauling in the disastrous Afghan War of 1839-1842. The Sepoys often had little respect for their British officers, who, because of the seniority system, were too old. The average age of generals was seventy, colonels sixty, and captains fifty. There was also the tendency to take the best officers and switch them into civil administration, the army thus losing its most capable personnel. Finally, there was a growing disparity in numbers between British troops and the Indian Sepoys, the figures when Dalhousie left being respectively 45,000 and 233,000.

There had been a number of revolts in the Indian Army beginning as early as 1766 when a Bengal Sepoy regiment had mutinied. Other revolts had occurred in 1806, in 1824, and in 1844, and at least three mutinous incidents took place from 1849 to 1852. The immediate cause precipitating the Mutiny of 1857 was the incident of the "greased cartridges." The British had issued the new Enfield rifle, which required the Sepoys to bite off the end of every cartridge as it was loaded. The rumor quickly circulated in January 1857 that the cartridges were greased with cow's fat and hog's lard, the first sacrilegious to the Hindu and the second defilement to the Muslim. Apparently this story was true, for beef-fat was being used in a munitions factory in England. The practice was stopped following Indian complaints, but the damage had already been done. British officers were ignorant of the facts, and the Sepoys regarded their denials about the use of fat on the cartridges as deliberate falsehood.[23]

The initial outbreak of the Mutiny occurred May 10, 1857, at Meerut, an important military post not far from Delhi. Here a Sepoy cavalry regiment had refused to handle the cartridges and in consequence had been court-martialed and sentenced to ten years in prison. The following day three native regiments revolted, shot their officers, and made off to Delhi. Entering the ancient imperial city, the mutineers dragged the old Mogul Emperor from his retirement and proclaimed the restoration of his dynasty to the throne. All Europeans in Delhi, numbering some fifty, were massacred.

The story of the next twelve months is a chronicle of the most savage fighting, in which terrible atrocities were committed by both sides.

One of the most horrible incidents was the massacre of the entire garrison of Cawnpore, both soldiers and their families, by the Indian leader the Nana Sahib. British troops entered the city two days after the massacre, and one of the soldiers wrote of his experience, "Had any Christian bishop visited that scene of butchery when I saw it, I verily believe that he would have buckled on his sword."[24] On the other hand, the British troops committed equally bloody deeds, as can be judged by this extract from a British historian: "The city [i.e., Delhi after its recapture] was sacked as ruthlessly as had been Cawnpore in July. Most of the male population, which had not already fled, were slaughtered, though many were known to have been friendly to the British cause, and few can have actively helped the rebel force."[25]

Although minor guerilla warfare was carried on until the end of 1858, the Mutiny was to all intents crushed by the spring of that year. On the Indian side there had been few outstanding leaders, the most determined and colorful being the Mahratta princess, the Rani of Jhansi, who had died at the head of her troops and who was called by her British adversary "the bravest of the brave."

After little more than a year British arms had restored order. The reasons for this success are several. (1) The revolt was fundamentally a local one, with India south of the Narbada River generally tranquil, Sind and the Rajput states remaining loyal. (2) Practically all of the great feudal princes remained aloof from the revolt. (3) Indian leadership was poor, and the Mutiny showed little careful planning on their part. (4) The British leaders who came to the fore were men of exceptional courage and audacity who, though greatly outnumbered, stood off the first attacks and then passed to the offensive.

What was the character of the Indian uprising of 1857? Can it be regarded as a war of national independence? The tendency among many Indian historians is to label it as just that. Nehru writes, "It was much more than a military mutiny, and it spread rapidly and assumed the character of a popular rebellion and a war of independence."[26] Another quotation serves to show how the Mutiny has been interpreted in the light of the development of a nationalistic mystique:

It is not easy for an Indian to write about the Rebellion of 1857, of its blood and tears, its sufferings,

23- E. L. Woodward, The Age of Reform, 1815-1870, Oxford History of England, *Vol. XIII* *(London: Oxford University Press, 1938), p. 415.*

24- *Quoted in* ibid., *p. 419.*

25- Edward J. Thompson and G. T. Garratt, Rise and Fulfilment of British Rule in India *London: The Macmillan Company, 1934), p. 455.*

26- *Jawaharlal Nehru, The Discovery of India (New York: John Day Co., 1946), p. 324.*

heroism and humiliations. Until India regains her freedom the writing will never be free from emotional overtones. "1857" strikes a flint on his heart and sparks fly.... With an obstinate silence we have rejected and passed by the spate of literature on the Mutiny that has come from British writers. It, however, continues to stalk through our memory—an unavenged and unappeased ghost.[27]

Historical objectivity, however, would seem to indicate that the Indian Mutiny cannot be correctly interpreted as an organized national movement. It is hardly a compliment to Indian capacity to imply that a full-scale national movement could have failed so miserably as it did in 1857. The truth is that, as we will see in the next chapter, there was practically no nationalistic movement as we think of it today in existence in India until at least the 1870's.

The most obvious result of the Mutiny was the end of the East India Company. Despite a powerful memorandum prepared by John Stuart Mill and presented to Parliament, an "Act for the Better Government of India" was passed in August 1858, whereby the government of this great dependency was transferred to the British Crown. It should be remembered, however, that "... the taking over of the Company's powers by the Crown in 1858 was less a revolution than a formal and explicit recognition of facts already existing."[28] The Court of Directors had their last meeting in September 1858, but the Company survived as a corporation until 1874, as the Charter Act of 1833 had guaranteed an annuity to the stockholders for forty years.

There are some British historians who see in the Mutiny a beneficial influence abolishing, in their opinion, a pampered Indian army, sweeping away the anomalous Company machinery of government, and generally clearing the way for a modern regime. Perhaps there are elements of truth in this view, but certainly any benefits that may be attached to the Mutiny are greatly discounted by its evil consequences. The reprisals of British soldiers and the ruthless mopping-up process left among Indians a feeling of bitterness and resentment for many years. In referring to this bitter legacy two British historians quote from Thomas Hardy's *The Dynasts:*

> Nought remains
> But vindictiveness here amid the strong,
> And there amid the weak an impotent rage.[29]

Up to the time of the Mutiny, as we have seen, there was a strong liberal and humanitarian outlook among British Indian administrators, especially after the 1820's. After 1857, however, much of this liberalism evaporated. The optimistic view that Indian customs and traditions would be transformed by the impact of western ideas had been rudely shaken by the horrors of the Mutiny. It logically follows that British policy in India became much more conservative in spirit. There was more caution about reforms, more concern in maintaining the *status quo* than zeal in improving and transforming it. The new conservatism was plainly evidenced in a Royal Proclamation issued by Queen Victoria in November 1858. This message declared:

> We hereby announce to the native princes of India, that all treaties and engagements made with them ... will be scrupulously maintained. ...
> We desire no extension of our present territorial possessions....
> Firmly relying ourselves on the truth of Christianity, ... we disclaim alike the right and the desire to impose our convictions on any of our subjects ... and we do strictly charge and enjoin all those who may be in authority under us that they abstain from all interference with the religious belief or worship of any of our subjects on pain of our highest displeasure.[30]

This proclamation was a far cry from Dalhousie's Doctrine of Lapse, and while its effect politically was to freeze and petrify the India of 1858 in the field of social and religious custom, its consequence was a "hands off" policy on the part of the British government.

The British Framework of Control

Following the end of Company rule a governmental system was established for India that was to last until after the First World War. It was a vast hierarchy with its base in India but its official apex in London in the person of the Secretary of State for India. This official, of course, was a member of the British cabinet, and his term of office depended upon the fortunes of party politics. This post was usually given to men of outstanding ability who stood in the front rank of their party. Some of the important secretaries from 1858 to 1914 were Sir Charles Wood (later Lord Halifax), Lord Salisbury, Lord Hartington,

27- *Asoka Mehta, 1857: The Great Rebellion (Bombay: Hind Kitabs, Ltd., 1946), p. 7.*

28- Cambridge History of India, *IV (Cambridge: Cambridge University Press, 1927), p. 181.*

29- *Quoted in Thompson and Garratt, op. cit., p. 458.*

30- *Panchanandas Mukherji, ed.,* Indian Constitutional Documents *(Calcutta: Thacker and Spink, 1915), pp. 356-357.*

The Background of
India and Pakistan:
First Picture Section

IN THE *following pages a brief visual
survey of Indian history shows particularly the art and architecture of
its three great religions, Buddhism,
Hinduism, and Mohammedanism,
and then illustrates some features of
the era of British rule up to 1947.*
THE BUDDHIST *religion branched off
from Hinduism about 500* B.C., *and
flourished until after 500* A.D., *when
it was destroyed in India by a revival
of Hinduism. It left behind master-
pieces of architecture, sculpture, and
painting. Among the earliest and finest Buddhist monuments are the gateways to the Great Stupa (a stone
mound housing religious relics) at
Sanchi, made in the first century* B.C.
*and richly carved with narratives and
symbols of the life of Buddha. The
east gateway is shown here.*

India Office, London

THE LION *capital of the Pillar of Asoka at Sarnath is the earliest Buddhist sculpture still in existence. The lions, symbolizing Buddha, stand above the Wheel of the Law, which he is said to have set in motion. The two Buddhas shown on these pages are both from South India; the seated Buddha on the Lion Throne was made in the first century* A.D. *while the standing Buddha at Madura was carved from sandstone in the fifth century. A last example of Buddhist art is the fresco from Cave XVII, Ajanta, shown at the lower right of the opposite page. These remarkable paintings on Buddhist themes were executed between the first and the seventh centuries* A.D.

HINDUISM ALSO *produced a rich variety of artistic expression. Below is the Kailasa temple at Ellora, a monolith carved from solid rock between 600 and 850* A.D. *and dedicated to Mt. Kailasa, the Himalayan retreat of the god Shiva. Hindu temple architecture shows great variety.*

Govt. of India Information Services

Berlin Museum of Ethnology

Govt. of India Information Servi

THE SMALL *but perfectly designed Hindu temple at the right above is Kandarya Mahadeva, constructed between 950 and 1050 A.D. at Khajuraho. Designs and figures cover the building. Below are the figures of the god Vishnu, his wife Lakshmi, and their son Mammadon in symbolic postures.*

Shiva as Lord of the Dance is represented in the copper statue, left, and above is a Rajput painting of two hermits. This Hindu style flourished after 1500.

THE MOHAMMEDANS *brought to India a wholly new style of architecture, different in spirit and design from the indigenous product but of great beauty also. On the opposite page is shown the marble interior of the Pearl Mosque, built 1646-1653 at Agra. Less famous than the Taj Mahal but of exquisite detail is the tomb of Itmad-ud-Din, above, also at Agra. Mogul painting usually depicted the palace life of the Mogul emperors, showing court scenes and persons, hunts, and night landscapes. The seventeenth-century painting here shows a durbar, or daily audience, of the emperor Akbar (see p. 37 ff.).*

A DURBAR *of quite a different era is shown below. Queen Victoria was proclaimed Empress of India with elaborate ceremonial at Delhi in 1877. This contemporary woodcut shows the reading of the proclamation in the presence of the Viceroy.*

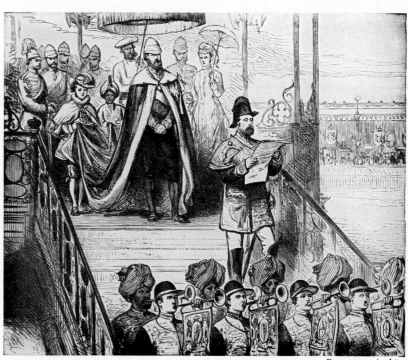

The development of self-government in British India

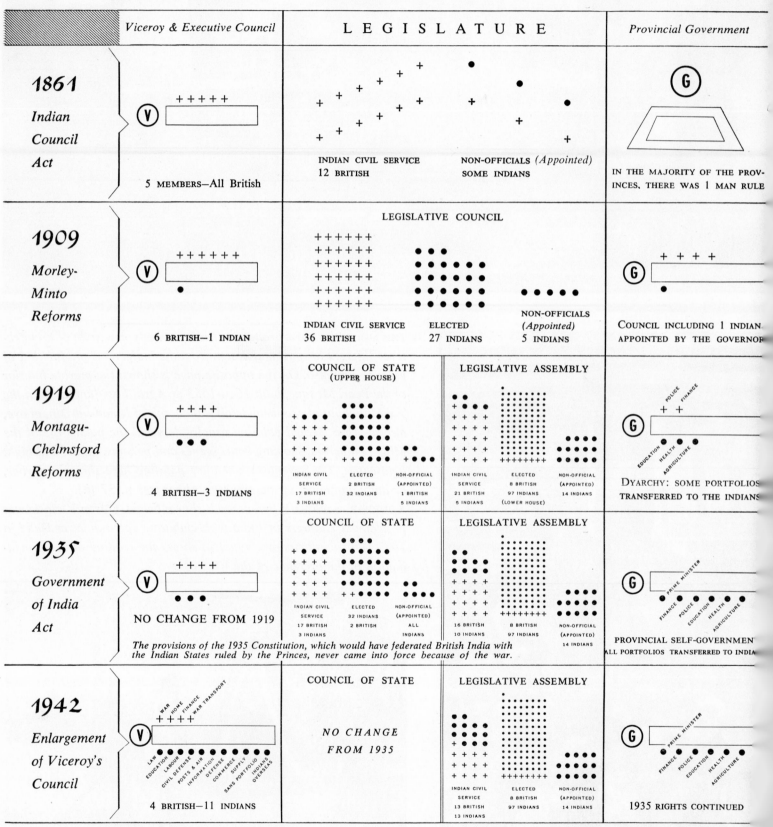

	Viceroy & Executive Council	LEGISLATURE	Provincial Government
1861 *Indian Council Act*	Ⓥ +++++ 5 MEMBERS—All British	INDIAN CIVIL SERVICE 12 BRITISH — NON-OFFICIALS (*Appointed*) SOME INDIANS	Ⓖ IN THE MAJORITY OF THE PROVINCES, THERE WAS 1 MAN RULE
1909 *Morley-Minto Reforms*	Ⓥ ++++++ • 6 BRITISH—1 INDIAN	LEGISLATIVE COUNCIL INDIAN CIVIL SERVICE 36 BRITISH — ELECTED 27 INDIANS — NON-OFFICIALS (*Appointed*) 5 INDIANS	Ⓖ ++++ • COUNCIL INCLUDING 1 INDIAN APPOINTED BY THE GOVERNOR
1919 *Montagu-Chelmsford Reforms*	Ⓥ ++++ ••• 4 BRITISH—3 INDIANS	COUNCIL OF STATE (UPPER HOUSE) INDIAN CIVIL SERVICE 17 BRITISH 3 INDIANS — ELECTED 2 BRITISH 32 INDIANS — NON-OFFICIAL (APPOINTED) 1 BRITISH 5 INDIANS LEGISLATIVE ASSEMBLY INDIAN CIVIL SERVICE 21 BRITISH 5 INDIANS — ELECTED 8 BRITISH 97 INDIANS (LOWER HOUSE) — NON-OFFICIAL (APPOINTED) 14 INDIANS	Ⓖ ++ POLICE FINANCE / EDUCATION HEALTH AGRICULTURE DYARCHY: SOME PORTFOLIOS TRANSFERRED TO THE INDIANS
1935 *Government of India Act*	Ⓥ ++++ ••• NO CHANGE FROM 1919	COUNCIL OF STATE INDIAN CIVIL SERVICE 17 BRITISH 3 INDIANS — ELECTED 32 INDIANS 2 BRITISH — NON-OFFICIAL (APPOINTED) ALL INDIANS LEGISLATIVE ASSEMBLY INDIAN CIVIL SERVICE 16 BRITISH 10 INDIANS — ELECTED 8 BRITISH 97 INDIANS — NON-OFFICIAL (APPOINTED) 14 INDIANS	Ⓖ PRIME MINISTER FINANCE POLICE EDUCATION HEALTH AGRICULTURE PROVINCIAL SELF-GOVERNMENT ALL PORTFOLIOS TRANSFERRED TO INDIA
1942 *Enlargement of Viceroy's Council*	Ⓥ WAR HOME FINANCE WAR TRANSPORT ++++ LAW EDUCATION LABOUR CIVIL DEFENSE POSTS & AIR INFORMATION DEFENSE COMMERCE SUPPLY SANS PORTFOLIO INDIANS OVERSEAS 4 BRITISH—11 INDIANS	COUNCIL OF STATE NO CHANGE FROM 1935 LEGISLATIVE ASSEMBLY INDIAN CIVIL SERVICE 13 BRITISH 13 INDIANS — ELECTED 8 BRITISH 97 INDIANS — NON-OFFICIAL (APPOINTED) 14 INDIANS	Ⓖ PRIME MINISTER FINANCE POLICE EDUCATION HEALTH AGRICULTURE 1935 RIGHTS CONTINUED

The provisions of the 1935 Constitution, which would have federated British India with the Indian States ruled by the Princes, never came into force because of the war.

Adapted from a chart prepared by the British Information Services.

Acme Photo

Acme Photo

Acme Photo

Life

THE NEW *states of India and Pakistan emerged from a long series of conferences, negotiations, and often bitter arguments, as a reading of Chapters VII to IX will reveal. On this page some of the most important participants in the final events leading to independence are shown actively engaged in threshing out the multiple problems involved.*

AT THE *top Lord Mountbatten is shown in the June 1947 meeting with Congress and Muslim League leaders in New Delhi. Jawaharlal Nehru and Sardar Patel are shown among Congress leaders at Mountbatten's right while at his left Mohammed Ali Jinnah and Liaquat Ali Khan represent the League. Below this group is an interesting study of Gandhi conferring with Nehru while at the right Sir Stafford Cripps is shown with Jinnah in April 1946. Finally, the photograph at the left seems to symbolize Gandhi's departure after the achievement of independence with all its hopes and problems.*

Alice Schalek from Three Lions

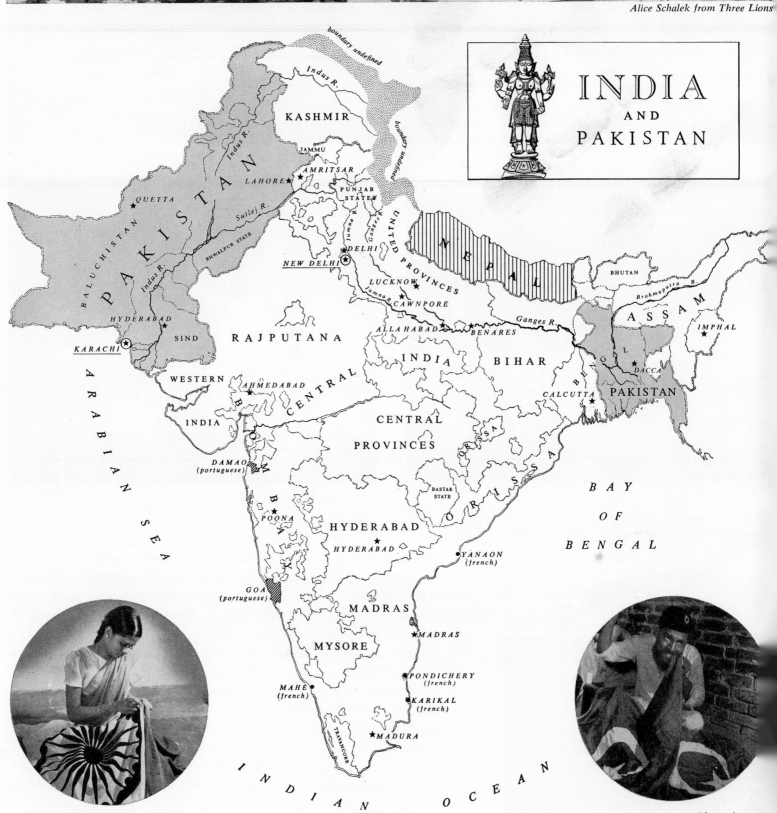

INDIA
AND
PAKISTAN

Photos from

Lord Randolph Churchill (father of Winston Churchill), and Lord Morley.

The Council of India, originally consisting of fifteen members, nine of whom must have lived at least ten years in India, was established in London to advise the secretary; but, although it was originally designed to wield considerable power, its influence waned after 1870. In fact the position of the Secretary of State for India tended to become more and more dominant in relation to other elements in the government of India. Parliament, embroiled in Irish problems, foreign affairs, and domestic issues, had little interest in Indian affairs and generally gave the secretary a free hand. Moreover, the large degree of initiative and independence that was exercised before the Mutiny in India by the Governor-General steadily declined after 1858. One of the most important reasons for this development was the improvement of communications between India and England. In the old days wars could be fought and territories annexed without the East India Company directors in London learning of the events until months after they had happened. After the Mutiny a telegraph line was built via Basra and Baghdad, and in 1870 a direct submarine cable was laid down by way of the Red Sea. No longer was the Governor-General able to present the home government with *faits accomplis*.

In the old offices of the East India Company in Leadenhall Street, London, there must have been an air of comfortable leisureliness, as witness a poet's description of a day in its confines:

Ten to eleven, have breakfast for seven.
Eleven to noon, think you've come too soon.
Twelve to one, wonder what's to be done.
One to two, find nothing to do.
Two to three, begin to see
'Twill be a great bore to stay till four.[31]

Under government by the Crown, however, more efficient and less leisurely conditions prevailed. The India Office was established as the central administrative agency. Much of the responsibility for the details, and even policy, of Indian affairs was taken care of by the Permanent Undersecretary for India. This official was usually of very high caliber, an outstanding administrator, and often a scholar and authority on Indian affairs as well. A case in point was Sir Thomas Holderness, Permanent Undersecretary from 1912 to

1920, whose small volume, *Peoples and Problems of India,* was very widely read.

The head of the British government in India was the Governor-General, styled the Viceroy when acting as the direct representative of the Crown, and usually appointed for a term of five years. This official was assisted by an Executive Council of five members, none of them Indian until 1909. This Council, for the purposes of lawmaking, was expanded by the addition of not less than six nor more than twelve members, at least half of whom were to be non-officials. Although not expressly provided by law, two Indians were appointed to this Legislative Council.

While the powers of this lawmaking body were very limited and at all times subject to the assent of the Governor-General, its creation constituted a landmark in the political development of modern India. It was the first step toward parliamentary government. In addition to these Councils of the central government, there were similar bodies in the provinces, all of which were completely subordinated to the control of the center.

For administrative purposes British India was broken up into units called provinces, each under a Governor or a Lieutenant-Governor. These political units in turn were broken into Divisions and these in turn into Districts. The District was the basic administrative unit in the British scheme of government. Altogether there were 250 of these Districts, averaging a little less than 4000 square miles with a population, in the 1890's, of 875,000. The key figure in Indian administration was the District Officer, called the Magistrate and Collector in some provinces and in others merely the Collector. This official had to maintain the peace, dispense justice, and collect the revenue. His activities were numerous and varied, as can be judged from the words of a British Indian official:

Police, jails, education, municipalities, roads, sanitation, dispensaries, the local taxation, and the imperial revenues of his district are to him matters of daily concern. He is expected to make himself acquainted with every phase of the social life of the natives, and with each natural aspect of the country. He should be a lawyer, an accountant, a financier, and a ready writer of state papers. He ought also to possess no mean knowledge of agriculture, political economy, and engineering.[32]

By no means a desk man, the District Officer spent much of his time touring the countryside,

Quoted in Sir Malcolm C. C. on, The India Office *(London: P. Putnam's Sons, 1926),* '78.

Sir William Hunter, The ian Empire *(London: Smith, er and Co., 1892),* 513-514.

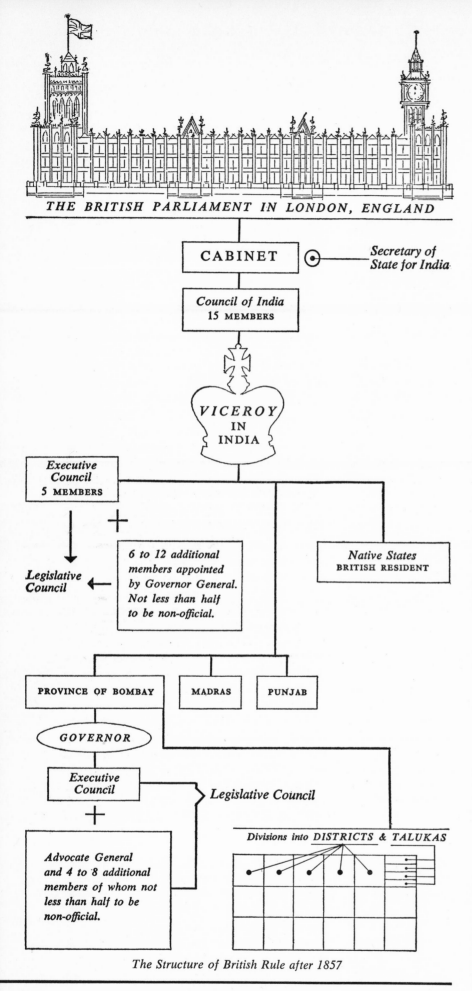

THE BRITISH PARLIAMENT IN LONDON, ENGLAND

CABINET — Secretary of State for India

Council of India
15 MEMBERS

VICEROY IN INDIA

Executive Council
5 MEMBERS

6 to 12 additional members appointed by Governor General. Not less than half to be non-official.

Legislative Council

Native States
BRITISH RESIDENT

PROVINCE OF BOMBAY   MADRAS   PUNJAB

GOVERNOR

Executive Council

Legislative Council

Advocate General and 4 to 8 additional members of whom not less than half to be non-official.

Divisions into DISTRICTS & TALUKAS

The Structure of British Rule after 1857

33- Sir John Strachey, India (London: Kegan Paul, Trench, Trubner and Co., 1894), p. 63.

34- Coupland, India: A Restatement, p. 46.

checking the crops, investigating crime, helping to fight plague, and always meeting the people.

From 1860 to 1885 the post-Mutiny governmental structure was planned, established, and completed. Old government departments were expanded and new ones introduced. By 1885 a number of highly centralized departments, dealing with education, public works, public health, railways, irrigation, and forests, were in operation.

To run the administrative machine in India the British operated with a small force; there was never the host of minor European officials one found in the French colonies. Writing in the latter part of the nineteenth century, Sir John Strachey pointed out that less than 1000 Englishmen were employed in the civil government of 221 million people and in the partial government of 67 million in the Native States.[33] Another authority, referring to the situation about 1900, says that, counting all types of administrative personnel, excluding the military, there were 4000 British in contrast to 500,000 Indian.[34] The great majority of the latter were of course in subordinate positions. The creation of a Provincial and a Subordinate Service in 1891 by the British opened up more administrative posts of an intermediate rank to Indians, but the upper echelons of the Indian government were almost exclusively reserved for Britons.

The heart and sinew of the British administration in India was the I.C.S. (Indian Civil Service). This body of men is considered to be one of the oldest civil services in the world; and this term "civil service," first used by the East India Company to designate its civilian employees, had become current by 1765. As early as 1800 Lord Wellesley established a college at Calcutta to train the Company's civil servants, and in 1805 a college was set up at Haileybury, in England, for the same purpose. After 1853 appointments for the service were taken from the Company and opened to public competition.

The I.C.S. has been well described as a *corps d'élite;* its high standards of admission, excellent remuneration and generous pension allowance, and opportunities for advancement always attracted some of the most capable and brilliant young men in Great Britain. The I.C.S. in 1892 consisted of only 939 officials. Entering the service at an initial salary of £320, they could look forward in twenty-five years to a salary of £2350, with a few top positions paying from four to six thousand pounds. Retirement came at a relatively early age, after thirty-five years of service, which usually meant around the age of fifty-five. All officials, regardless of rank, received a pension of £1000. There was, undoubtedly, room for much argument on the ultimate justification of British rule in India; but few would deny that the I.C.S., within the pattern of day-to-day administration carried on by the average official, was a remarkable body of conscientious, hard-working, and incorruptible men.

In the minds of most British Indian officials, the Mutiny was primarily a revolt of the Bengal Sepoy Army. It was natural, therefore, that after 1857 there should be fundamental changes in military organization. There was a drastic reduction in the strength of Indian personnel; artillery and the most important weapons were placed exclusively in British hands; and care was taken to recruit troops from tribes and peoples who could be trusted to maintain the government's authority. The new policy was succinctly expressed in a *Report* of the Indian Army Commission of 1879 thus:

> On the reorganization of the army, after the mutiny was quelled, it was decided that the proportion of Native and European troops in India should never greatly exceed two to one, and that the field and other artillery should be exclusively, or almost exclusively, manned by Europeans. . . . All the fortresses in the country are now served by British artillery. All the heavy batteries and all the batteries of field artillery are manned by Europeans. The lessons taught by the Mutiny have thus led to the maintenance of the two great principles of retaining in the country an irresistible force of British troops, and of keeping the artillery in the hands of Europeans.[35]

By 1863, British troops numbered 65,000 and the number of Indian troops had been reduced to 140,000. In 1910 the numbers were 69,000 and 130,000 respectively. It should also be noted that the Indian army was not a "national" force, in the sense of including fairly equal proportions from each section of the country. The army came mainly from the north-west and consisted in great part of Pathans, Sikhs, Punjabi Muslims, and Gurkhas. The military arm of the government, therefore, was a professional rather than a national force. The leadership of this army, as can be expected, was British. No Indian could hold the King's Commission. He might become a *Risaldar* or *Subadar* but "he was junior to the youngest [British] subaltern."[36]

Another important factor in the British framework of control was the group of Native States, already described in Chapter I. After the Mutiny, the Queen's proclamation made it evident that Great Britain would show a new solicitude toward the states and that Lord Dalhousie's Doctrine of Lapse was repudiated. In the 1860's, "Sanads of Adoption" were signed with the various native rulers, guaranteeing their thrones and admitting the right to adopt heirs when necessary. Most Indian historians make the point that this post-Mutiny policy toward the Native States was, in effect, an alliance of Britain with the conservative, even reactionary, forces in India.

The attitude of Britain toward the princes of India is summed up in the following statement:

> The rulers of the Native States are very loyal to their British connection. . . . Their affection and loyalty are important assets for Britain in the present troubles and in the readjustments which must come. . . . The situation of these feudatory states, checkerboarding all India as they do, are [sic] a great safeguard. It is like establishing a vast network of friendly fortresses in debatable territory. It would be difficult for a general rebellion against the British to sweep India because of this network of powerful loyal Native States.[37]

It should also be pointed out that British concern for the Native States was not to be explained exclusively by reference to self-survival but that there was also another important factor of a less selfish nature. Many British administrators sincerely believed it was desirable to perpetuate the traditional monarchical systems of the Native States as a kind of stabilizing factor, one that would be a bulwark against too rapid changes and insure a proper balance between the old and the new in India.

While the Native States were supposedly sovereign in their domestic affairs, the British exercise of what was known as the principle of Paramountcy meant that there was considerable limitation of their powers. No State could participate in foreign relations, for this was the prerogative of the Paramount Power. Furthermore, all matters between one State and another had to pass through the channels of the Viceroy acting for the British government. It was also understood that no State should concern itself with the affairs of British India.

35- *Quoted in Strachey, op. cit., pp. 343-344.*

36- *Thompson and Garratt, op. cit., p. 539.*

37- *Quoted in Goshal, op. cit., p. 131.*

The Paramount Power, for its part, pledged itself to protect and support the government of the Native States but reserved to itself the right to intervene in cases of maladministration and gross injustice. In referring to the Sanads of Adoption, which guaranteed the perpetuation of the native dynasties, Lord Canning in 1860 wrote:

The proposed measure will not debar the Government of India from stepping in to set right such serious abuses in a native Government as may threaten any part of the country with anarchy or disturbance, nor from assuming temporary charge of a native State when there shall be sufficient reason to do so.[38]

On several occasions the Viceroy intervened in the affairs of a Native State and went so far as to depose the ruler when this was considered necessary. One of the most important instances was the case of the Gaekwar (ruler) of Baroda, who, on coming to the throne in 1870, produced confusion and disorganization in his state during the first three years of his rule. A British commission warned him to mend his ways, which he refused to do. He was accordingly deposed and a new Gaekwar was selected.

While democracy, industrialism, western education, and urbanization throughout the nineteenth century increasingly modified the pattern of life in British India, the Native States in many ways remained isolated from this modernizing impact. Some of the States remained entirely untouched by the spirit of progress. A British Indian official has referred to them as "museum pieces, their political institutions being those of Mogul times."[39]

In describing the backwardness of these States, an American journalist wrote in 1939: "In some States newspapers are forbidden; in most the ruler has life and death powers over his subjects; in some, the people may be bought and sold like serfs. In most States the ruler, who may be recklessly extravagant, commands the entire State income."[40] Power over life and death is largely a vestigial theory, but in most of the States educational facilities were quite inadequate; there was too frequently no separation of the monies which the prince might use for himself and those to be employed for the benefit of his subjects; and in many instances the judicial and executive departments were not separated, as the courts were under the personal domination of the ruler.

In the 1920's the political situation in the 108 most important States was reported as follows: Thirty had legislative councils, mainly consultative in nature; fifty-six had a privy purse separated from public funds; and forty had High Courts patterned after those in British India.[41] There was evidence, however, that the Native States did not have to be medieval backwaters. Some of the large States, especially Mysore, Cochin, Baroda, Travancore, and Gwalior, were further advanced than British India in such matters as education, public health, and advancement of women. While politically the Native States were in too many instances seventeenth-century remnants, anachronisms in modern times, yet from the standpoint of Indian culture they were at the same time valuable preservers of much that was distinctive and autochthonous, including many of the beautiful handicrafts of the past, picturesque festivals, colorful costumes, and the pageantry of court *durbars*.

The Golden Age of the British Raj

The four decades following the Indian Mutiny may be thought of as the golden age of the British bureaucratic machine in India. The comparatively easy defeat of the uprising of 1857 was taken by most Britishers as a justification for their rule. In the 1870's and 1880's came the influence of the new imperialism and with it the halcyon days of the White Man's Burden, a term which implied the conviction that it was the right and the responsibility of Europeans in general, and the British in particular, to extend their rule and culture to the four corners of the earth. Benjamin Disraeli was the prophet of imperialism in Britain in the 1870's, urging Englishmen to "be a great country, an imperial country where your sons, when they rise, rise to paramount positions, and obtain not merely the esteem of their countrymen, but command the respect of the world."[42] It was Disraeli who as Prime Minister carried through an Act in the British Parliament in 1877 proclaiming Victoria Queen Empress of India. This announcement of the imperial title symbolized the rising tide of imperialism in Britain.

The British bureaucracy in India naturally was imbued with this pride of empire. In justification of their rule the members of the Indian Civil Service could point to a number of indisputable achievements. With British ascendancy had emerged peace for all of India. In the wake of

38- *Quoted in Sir Geoffrey de Montmorency,* The Indian States and Indian Federation *(London: Cambridge University Press, 1942), p. 61.*

39- *Quoted in Wint and Schuster, op. cit., p. 130.*

40- *John Gunther,* Inside Asia *(New York: Harper and Brothers, 1939), p. 444.*

41- Report of the Indian States Committee *(London: His Majesty's Stationery Office, 1929), p. 12.*

42- *Quoted in W. F. Moneypenny and G. E. Buckle,* The Life of Benjamin Disraeli *(London: John Murray, rev. ed., 1929), II, p. 536.*

the Mogul Empire's disintegration had come law-lessness and banditry. Millions of adventurers were on the loose, out for all they could get by the sword, and restrained by none. It has been esti-mated that at the close of the eighteenth century there were two million mercenaries in India. Lacking protection of effective government, the people obtained arms for themselves and defended their lives and property as well as they could; one authority estimates that as late as 1851 every third man possessed arms. The extirpation of the Pindaris, the freebooters, and the bandits, together with the establishment of law courts backed with adequate force, introduced a new era of peace throughout India. To Indians of the first half of the nineteenth century this was a great boon. Later generations, however, born amid conditions of tranquillity, tended to take the rule of law for granted.

Much could be claimed by the British Indian civil servant for the new system of law accom-panying his rule. The old indigenous systems—both Hindu and Muslim—were well developed in the law of family relations, but otherwise there were serious gaps. "There was no definite law of procedure, criminal or civil, no law of torts, no pub-lic and constitutional law."[43] The British brought into India a new structure of law, outside Hindu and Muslim personal law, yet based on careful regard to the customs and feelings of the people. The most important legal contribution undoubtedly was the Indian Penal Code. The result of three years' work, it was written in the concise and beautiful prose of Macaulay, who acted as presi-dent of a commission to inquire into the juris-diction of British India from 1834 to 1837. This draft was not put into effect until 1862, but sub-sequently it has been widely accepted as almost a model criminal code. While the British system of justice as it has worked in India has had its weak-ness, it nevertheless brought into the country the great legal principle of equality under the law of all individuals, regardless of their caste status.

Closely connected with the development of a modern judiciary and impartial justice under Brit-ish auspices was the elimination of slavery. The slave trade was forbidden by Cornwallis as early as 1789. In 1833 the Governor-General was em-powered to take steps leading to the abolition of slavery, a task involving the emancipation of some nine million persons. In 1843 the courts were

instructed to refuse to recognize the status of slave, and the final act in 1860 decreed that the keeping of slaves was a criminal offense.

By the end of the nineteenth century another achievement that could be rightly claimed by British rule in India was the introduction of the first steps toward representative government. Such institutions on a national scale had heretofore been entirely unknown in Asia. The first advance in self-government in local units was the work of Lord Ripon, Governor-General from 1880 to 1884. This official has been likened to Bentinck for his interest in social and political reform; he was a real liberal of the Gladstonian type. In sponsoring an advance in local self-government, he issued an important resolution in 1882 in which it was stated: ". . . it is not primarily with a view to improvement in administration that this measure is brought forward. It is chiefly desirable as a measure of political and popular education."[44]

Following this lead, acts were passed in the provinces whereby local elected boards were to be set up beginning with the smallest administrative units and including municipal boards for cities. In addition to this attempt to foster local self-government, there was also a slight liberalization at the highest level in the Legislative Councils of the various provinces and in the Council of the Governor-General. After much discussion in the British Parliament, the Indian Councils Act was passed in 1892. This measure enlarged the non-official membership of the provincial Councils and provided that they should be nominated by mem-bers chosen by such local bodies as district boards, municipal corporations, and universities. In the Governor-General's Legislative Council the non-officials were appointed from the four pro-vincial councils, and one was selected by the Cal-cutta chamber of commerce. Thus in a very roundabout manner the principle of election was admitted, and these new Councils were also granted the new power to discuss budgets and to interpel-late the executive officers of government on mat-ters of public policy. While the Act of 1892 fell far short of introducing real representative gov-ernment into India, it was a transition from the purely bureaucratic and paternal government that had prevailed during most of the nineteenth century to the increasingly representative sys-tem that was to develop during the first decades of the twentieth. While the advance in 1892 was

O'Malley, op. cit., p. 110.

Quoted in Cambridge His-*y of the British Empire,* *(Cambridge: Cambridge* *iversity Press, 1932),* *521.*

admittedly small, it "did bring a breath of life and reality into the proceedings of the councils, and quite definitely marked a stage in the development of popular government in India."[45]

Throughout the long history of India famine has been a constant menace, bringing death and suffering to millions of people. Rainfall over much of the land depends upon the south-west winds, the monsoons, and their failure spells catastrophe. After his service in India as Governor-General and his return to England, Lord Curzon in speaking of famine said:

> You have your sunshine and storms, your droughts and floods, in this country, but you do not know the awful possibilities that are summed up in the single word "monsoon," and which spell the difference in India between life and death to areas in any one of which the whole of the United Kingdom might be swallowed up.[46]

Records indicate there were fourteen major famines between 1660 and 1750. In the writings of such European travelers as Van Twist, the Dutch merchant, we have vivid pictures of the misery and death resulting from these famines. This eye-witness observed of a famine that took place in 1630 and 1631:

> As the famine increased, men abandoned towns and villages and wandered helplessly. It was easy to recognize their condition: eyes sunk deep in the head; lips pale and covered with slime; the skin hard, with the bones showing through; the belly nothing but a pouch hanging down empty; knuckles and knee-caps showing prominently. One would cry and howl for hunger, while another lay on the ground dying in misery. Wherever you went, you saw nothing but corpses.[47]

Witnessing another famine in 1670, the Dutch traveler van Graaf wrote, "We saw nothing but poverty and misery . . . The people died in heaps and their corpses remained extended on the roads, streets, and market-places. . . ."[48]

It was not until the 1860's that the British government began to study the problem of famine systematically. In 1866-1867 a catastrophe took place in the area of Orissa. The crops failed and the lack of transport facilities prevented the authorities from sending grain and supplies into the stricken districts. As much as one quarter of the population may have perished; the death toll was estimated at more than one million.

This Orissa catastrophe marked the turning point in famine administration. A start was made in creating machinery that would go into action as soon as famine threatened in any district. In 1876-1877 an unusually terrible famine raged in south and central India and, although more than eleven millions were spent in relief measures, five million people lost their lives. Following this holocaust a famine commission was set up under Sir John Strachey. The recommendations of this Commission, which were reported in 1880, formed the basis for the Famine Code adopted in 1883 by the Indian government.

This Code, which was continually improved and expanded, was based on the principle that government must provide adequate relief to the needy during times of crop failures. Schemes for employment on public works were prepared and a regular sum was set aside by the government for famine insurance. A chain of "protective railways" was built to insure the delivery of adequate stocks of food in any part of the country that might be threatened by famine. Great irrigation projects were also completed, so that by 1900 India could claim to have the greatest irrigation system in the world, serving some fourteen million acres.

A heavy strain was placed on famine-prevention machinery during the four years' drought that affected India from 1896 to 1900. Despite herculean efforts and the saving of millions of lives, the loss of life was still heavy. Improvements, therefore, continued to be made in the Famine Code, and in the next major emergency in 1907-1908 the relief measures proved to be very effective.

It is this progressive improvement of famine-prevention machinery, together with the elimination of civil wars and banditry, that accounts for the rapid increase of the Indian population. In the seventeenth century the population has been estimated at 100 million; in 1850 the figure was 150 million; in 1881, 250 million; and in 1901, 283 million. In the first half of the twentieth century the increase was maintained and even accelerated, so that by 1945 the population was 400 million.

The establishment of peace and equality under the law, the elimination of slavery, the introduction of semi-representative government, and the first systematic attack against the age-old problem of

45- Sir John Cumming, ed., Political India (London: Oxford University Press, 1932), p. 170.

46- Lord Curzon, Lord Curzon in India (London: The Macmillan Company, 1906), p. 38.

47- Quoted in H. G. Rawlinson, India: A Short Cultural History (New York: D. Appleton-Century, 1938), p. 338.

48- Quoted in O'Malley, op. cit., p. 13.

famine were important accomplishments of British rule; the most significant, however, was the realization of political unity for India. In the past the country had enjoyed a common socio-religious way of life and culture. "But political activities meant little to the Hindu; dynasties came into power and fell from power, empires arose and broke up, yet history leaves them unrecorded and they never affected India's real life and her profounder unity."[49]

For the first time in its history, India under British rule was unified under the same government, since the Native States in the last analysis were subordinate to the Paramount Power—Britain. Furthermore, as we shall see in the next chapter, under British auspices the country was drawn together by a network of modern transportation and communication facilities and, in the upper levels, by a common form of education given in the English language. In ancient and medieval India, even in the days of the Guptas or those of the Mogul Empire, there had been no administrative unity in all the country by which an integrated and continuous chain of allegiance and authority proceeded from the king or emperor down to the lowliest ryot. In consequence of British rule this lack was filled. "The Indian people, for the first time," writes an Indian historian, "found a substantial sector of their economic and social life coming under the governance of a universally and equally operating system of law."[50]

In summary, under the new dispensation of the British raj the individual enjoyed liberty—if not self-government—under a unified government whose law offered him the enjoyment of freedom of religion, freedom from arbitrary arrest, and much freedom of speech.

Britain's Border Problems in India

The period from 1858 to 1876 was one of peace in India. As far as internal conditions were concerned, there were few clouds in the sky, no subversive movements of any consequence, and no outstanding leaders to challenge British rule. After 1876, however, wars and rumors of wars confronted the Indian government, and the defense of the great dependency became the primary concern of British officials.

The question of the security of India arose mainly from the remarkable expansion of Russia southward in Central Asia toward Persia, Afghanistan, and the frontiers of northern India. In the path of the forces of the Tsar lay the colorful tribes of the Turcomans, Kazaks, and Uzbeks, organized in their little Islamic states of Bokhara, Khiva, and Kokand. Beginning in the 1830's, Russia began to drive south, extending her authority over the loosely organized people of the Khanates, and by 1885 the process of assimilation had been completed.

This rapid Russian advance was alarming to the Indian government, which at times had visions of Afghanistan becoming a puppet state of the Tsar and pictured Russian troops ready to advance through the mountain passes on to the plains of northern India. As a result of the Russo-Persian War of 1826-1828, Persia had fallen under the control of the Tsar's government, and at the same time Russian agents were received at Kabul, the capital of Afghanistan. Palmerston, the British Foreign Secretary, was intensely anti-Russian in his point of view, and indoctrinated with this outlook Lord Auckland, who went to India in 1835 as the new Governor-General. Spurred on by this Russophobia, the Governor-General decided that a pro-British Amir must be installed by British arms in Kabul. This decision led to the First Afghan War. British troops invaded Afghanistan in 1839, placed a new Amir on the throne, and installed a British Resident in the capital.

Retribution for this rash policy of Lord Auckland's soon followed. Toward the end of 1841 the Afghans rebelled and murdered the British Resident. During terrible winter conditions the British army sought to retreat to the Indian frontier in January 1842. Trying to fight their way back to safety, an entire British army of four thousand men, together with twelve thousand camp followers, was destroyed by the Afghans, and only one survivor reached a British force at Jallalabad.

The upshot of this disaster was the recall of Lord Auckland and the dispatch of a new expedition to Afghanistan to retrieve British prestige and rescue some prisoners held at Kabul. The Afghan forces were defeated, some fortresses destroyed, and the prisoners released. However, the Amir, Dost Mahomed, who had been judged pro-Russian and who had been dethroned by the first British expedition, was allowed to return. Nothing, in fact, had been gained by intervening in Afghanistan.

- *Hans Kohn,* A History of ationalism in the East *(London: orge Routledge, 1929), p. 350.*

- *A. R. Desai,* Social Background of Indian Nationalism ombay: Oxford University ess, 1949), p. 154

"Russophobe ministers in Downing Street had scorned the advice of Indian experts and humiliating disasters had resulted therefrom. Britain mourned and India paid."[51]

The Afghanistan drama was not yet played out. In 1867 the new province of Russian Turkestan was created and the armies of the Tsar quickened their operations against the Khanates. At the same time Russia began to exert pressure in an ominous manner against Turkey, with the objective of controlling the Straits and much of the Balkan peninsula. Russophobia was kindled anew in both Britain and India. The "Russian Danger" became the primary problem, and the general attitude of most Indian officials was well expressed by Sir John Strachey when he remarked, "It has thrown into the minds of men uncertainties and hopes and fears regarding the future; it has seriously disturbed the finances, it has retarded the progress of works essential to the prosperity of the country, and has checked improvement in administration."[52] In the twentieth century authorities have been inclined to doubt the ability of Russia to invade or in any serious way menace the security of India. But in the 1870's and 1880's there is no doubt that British fear was genuine, and northern India, close to the frontier, often seethed with rumors about imminent Russian moves against India.

From 1864 to 1868 the usual story of disputed succession to the Afghan throne recommenced. After five years of struggle among twelve brothers, one—Sher Ali—vanquished all opposition. The new Amir was inclined to welcome the protection of Great Britain, but the latter for her part, while not desiring the Afghan ruler to depend on the friendship of Russia, refused to give him an unequivocal pledge of support. A small state wedged between two great powers cannot alienate both of her neighbors, so the Amir began to court Russian support. While this diplomatic shadow-boxing was going on, Disraeli, the ardent imperialist, became Prime Minister (1874), and the natural consequence was the adoption of a stiffer Russian policy. The government of India asked the Afghan Amir to accept a permanent British Resident, and Lord Lytton was sent out to India by Disraeli in 1876 to carry through a "forward policy."

All efforts of the new Governor-General to pin Sher Ali down to a definite agreement failed, and, while negotiations were being carried on, the Russo-Turkish War broke out in 1877 in Europe. Russia's victories and her plans to dominate the Balkans precipitated a diplomatic crisis in Europe and led to the convening of the Congress of Berlin in 1878. While Anglo-Russian tension mounted in Europe, a Russian mission, apparently against the wishes of the Amir, entered Afghanistan. The Tsar's agent persuaded the Afghan ruler to stand firm against any British demands. Relying on Russian support, the Amir refused to admit an English envoy into his country.

Meanwhile, in Europe the Congress of Berlin had removed the threat of war between Russia and Britain and the agent of the former country was advised from St. Petersburg to leave Afghanistan. In short, Russia, after encouraging the Amir to defy Britain, left this hapless ruler to stand alone. There was apparently no need for British intervention in Afghanistan, but the impetuous Governor-General, Lord Lytton, was determined to teach the Amir a lesson. In November 1878 British armies invaded Afghanistan by three separate mountain passes. Afghan resistance was easily brushed aside and the Amir fled to Russian territory, where he died shortly.

The Treaty of Gandamak, signed by a new Amir, granted certain strategic border districts to Britain; promised to follow the advice of the British Viceroy in Afghan foreign relations; and accepted a permanent British Resident at Kabul. Lord Lytton's policy of intervention thus far had been a notable success, but in less than six months his achievement was brushed aside by a terrible disaster. In September 1879 the Afghan army rose up against the British, murdering Lytton's agent and his staff. Hostilities were thereupon reopened, and, after heavy loss of life and the expenditure of much money, British armies again decisively defeated the Afghans.

It was now obvious to the Indian government, after two wars and the expenditure of more than twenty million pounds, that interference in Afghan affairs was a costly and ineffectual business. Lord Roberts, the famous English general who had taken a prominent part in the hostilities, said:

It may not be very flattering to our *amour propre*, but I feel sure I am right when I say that the less the Afghans see of us, the less they will dislike us. Should Russia in future years attempt to conquer Afghanistan or invade India through it, we should have a better chance of attaching the Afghans to our

51- *Paul Knaplund,* The British Empire, 1815-1939 *(New York: Harper and Brothers, 1941), p. 146.*

52- *Strachey, op. cit., p. 341.*

interest if we avoid interference with them in the meantime.[53]

The Indian government followed this line of reasoning. A new Amir, popular with his people and the puppet of neither Britain nor Russia, came to the throne. An agreement was made whereby the Indian government promised an annual subsidy to the Afghan ruler, retained two strategic districts taken from Afghanistan, and secured the right of handling the foreign affairs of the Amir's government. The new ruler proved to be a friendly, if independent, neighbor until his death in 1901, and Afghanistan during this span ceased to be a problem.

There were other areas, however, along the land frontiers, that witnessed armed intervention by the Indian government. Two wars had already been fought with Burma, and in the 1880's relations again became strained. The cruelty of King Thibaw in clubbing to death eighty members of the royal family when he came to the throne in 1879 contributed to the breach. There were also disputes and clashes along the Indo-Burman frontier and complaints against the Burmese government by British firms engaged in the teak trade. But the most potent factor in bringing about the Third Burmese War was the expansion of French influence into Burma. At this time there was bad blood between Britain and France over their rival claims in Africa. France, having consolidated her hold on Indochina, began to expand her influence in Burma. Britain had no intention of standing idly by and seeing a European power assume the same dominant role in Burma as Russia had aspired to in Afghanistan. An ultimatum therefore was dispatched to the Burmese government demanding the admission of a British envoy at Mandalay, the capital, and the acceptance of British advice on foreign policy. This ultimatum was rejected, and war followed in 1885. The conflict lasted only two weeks; what was left of independent Burma was annexed and administered as part of India.

Anglo-Russian rivalry led to intervention in yet another region, Tibet. During the governor-generalship of Lord Curzon news was received in India that the government of the Dalai Lama was entering into close relations with Russia. This fact alarmed Curzon, who in 1904 received permission of the home government to send an expedition under Colonel Younghusband to Tibet. The Tibetans would not treat with the mission, and the British troops, after some fighting, forced their way into the capital of Lhasa, where a treaty was exacted. This agreement in its final form authorized British trade marts in Tibet. It pledged the Tibetans not to admit any foreign agents, and any economic concession given to a foreign power was to be granted also to Britain.

All the diplomatic and military activities described thus far have concerned the defense strategy of land frontiers; but there was also the problem of the sea approaches to India. In a fundamental sense, as has already been indicated, command of the seas in the waters leading to and adjacent to India enabled Britain to hold this great dependency. By means of sea power Britain was able to bring troops and supplies more effectively than any land power could transport them through the mountain passes.

The cornerstone of British naval supremacy in the Indian Ocean was control of all approaches into the Arabian Sea by means of the Persian Gulf and the Red Sea. This meant effective control of the entire coastline from Aden to Baluchistan. In the latter part of the nineteenth century Britain blocked all attempts by rival powers to secure a foothold in this area. France in 1898 was prevented from getting a coaling base from the Sultan of Oman, and two years later a similar design by Russia was also frustrated. A more serious threat from the British point of view came from the plans of Germany and Turkey to construct a Berlin to Baghdad railroad that would have its terminus at the Persian Gulf. In 1899 Britain made an agreement with the ruler of the small state of Kuwait that no concessions were to be given to a foreign power. The following year Kuwait, supported by Britain, refused Germany's request for permission to build the terminus of the Berlin-Baghdad railroad. Three years later, Lord Lansdowne, the Foreign Secretary, announced what has been referred to as the British Monroe Doctrine of the Middle East. Speaking in the House of Lords in 1903 this statesman declared: "I say it without hesitation, we should regard the establishment of a naval base or of a fortified port in the Persian Gulf by any other power as a very grave menace to British interests, and we should certainly resist it by all the means at our disposal."[54]

- *Quoted in Rawlinson,* **The** *itish Achievement in India,* *143.*

- *Quoted in N. D. Harris,* *rope and the East (Boston:* *ughton Mifflin Co.,* *26), p. 285.*

Less weighted with international complications but equally important to the defense of India was the North-West Frontier area. Located on the southern slopes of the Hindu Kush mountains, and populated by warlike Pathan tribes who were constantly fighting each other or raiding Indian territory, this North-West region was a perpetual source of anxiety to the military authorities in India. It has been estimated that fifty-four British expeditions had to be sent into this area from 1848 to 1898 to punish the mountaineers for their looting expeditions. This practice of going in and burning the Pathan villages and then retreating was called the policy of "butcher and bolt."

In 1893, by an agreement with the Amir of Afghanistan, the Durand Line was laid down to indicate the political boundary, while some thirty miles to the east was the administrative line of British India. Close control ended at the latter, leaving a sort of no man's land between it and the Durand Line. It was the policy of Lord Curzon to pay subsidies to the tribes in this buffer "unorganized area." In addition, the government of India supported tribal forces called Khassadars who were paid to support some semblance of law and order. No British troops were stationed west of the administrative boundary. The frontier system of Lord Curzon was, on the whole, an improvement over the policy that preceded it, but tribal raids were not eliminated. No matter what group governs India, whether the alien British or the native Indians, the existence on its borders of a people forced, without raiding and looting, to scrape a bare pittance from the barren mountains, usually occupied with blood-feuds, and always ready to listen to the voice of the mullah (holy man) calling them to a jihad (holy war), will constantly be a source of danger to the more wealthy and less martial people living on the plains at the foot of the mountains. This problem of the North-West Frontier will be referred to again in the discussion of political developments in India after Britain's withdrawal in 1947.

There was another positive achievement of British rule that should be mentioned. India for the first time in her history no longer suffered from continual incursions through the northern mountain passes. The Indian Ocean was a British lake and the land frontiers were held as effectively as were those of Rome when her legions were at the height of their power. Mistakes, of course, were made by the Indian government. Looking back, it would seem that Britain was unduly alarmed over the Russian menace and that both Afghan wars were unnecessary. Curzon's Tibetan expedition also would come in this category. Despite these errors, however, India enjoyed such a peace as had never been known before in its history.

British Rule Evaluated

British rule, as we have seen, had its positive side, but at the same time there were a number of serious defects. In this chapter reference will be made only to the political shortcomings, while the economic results will be analyzed in the following chapter and referred to again briefly later.

Three defects may be commented upon. In the early days of Company rule there had been close contact between the ruler and the ruled. There was no rigid machine of administration with rules to cover all exigencies, but rather improvisation and individual responsibility on the part of the Indian civil servant were expected to get his day's work done in a satisfactory manner. After the Mutiny, however, a rigid administrative machine was built up in which there was too much routine and too much departmentalism. An English historian has written: "For these reasons the system of Indian government was becoming not merely more efficient and punctiliously exact, it was becoming gradually more mechanical, more formal, and more impersonal."[55]

This official machine that was built up after the Mutiny was in some ways more efficient than the system of administration in the days of the Company; ironically enough, however, the new bureaucracy grew steadily more aloof and more out of touch with the Indian people. Early in the nineteenth century communications and transportation between India and England were very poor, and British officials in consequence came to regard India as a second home. Relations between Company employees and Indians were usually cordial and often intimate. The absence of European women also inclined the civil servants to mix socially with Indians. But the improvement of transportation brought important changes. It meant that British officials could return more frequently to England and could also have their wives and families with them in India. The official British community, therefore, set itself apart and

55- *Ramsay Muir,* A Short History of the British Commonwealth *(New York: World Book Company, 1923), II, p. 557.*

lived in a kind of exclusive caste, detached and remote from the people whose problems and attitudes they were supposed to understand.

The gulf between Indians and the British was widened further after the Mutiny. The expansion of business enterprise in India brought out increasing numbers of Englishmen to run the plantations, banks, and factories. These newcomers had been inflamed by the Mutiny and, as an English historian admits, "They came out to India ready to suspect, and sometimes to despise, all things Indian, and with a sense of racial cleavage and racial superiority."[56]

Perhaps there is some justification in the statement of Professor Coupland that the aloofness of the British official was not caused so much by racial arrogance but "was a sort of defensive mechanism"[57] by which he clung to his way of life with its clubs, teas, and sports. Whatever the explanation, there is no doubt that a gulf of racial estrangement increasingly divided the British community from the people of India.

The impersonal nature of the official machine and its lack of contact with the people it ruled was a serious weakness of the post-Mutiny British bureaucracy. Another, and a closely allied defect, was that British administrators had little concern with the ultimate results, goals, or purposes of their rule in India. Day-to-day efficiency rather than the preparation of the people of India for some objective, such as self-rule, was the hallmark of the Indian Civil Service. This was completely unlike the liberal attitude expressed in the 1820's and 1830's by British Indian officials, who gave much thought to why Britain was in India and what, in the long run, she should make of her responsibility. The following statement well describes the attitude of British officials in the second half of the nineteenth century: "In India . . . during the greater part of this period they are merely governing. Their rule, if often aloof and unimaginative, is superbly incorruptible and highly efficient and it achieves many prodigious results, yet does not seem to contain within it . . . the impulse of organic growth."[58]

In keeping with the day-to-day philosophy of the British Indian bureaucracy and its disregard of the ultimate aims of administration, there existed opposition to reforms in government and a strong reluctance to open the upper brackets of public service to Indians. There had been too little prog-

ress made in alleviating the attitudes which as early as 1818 had caused Sir Thomas Munro to remark: "Foreign conquerors have treated the native with violence and often with great cruelty, but none have treated them with so much scorn as we; none has stigmatized the whole people as unworthy of trust, as incapable of honesty, and as fit to be employed only where we cannot do without them."[59]

There was a lack of sympathy of British officials with the scheme for local self-government introduced by Lord Ripon, and two English historians of India assert that the rural boards were allowed by the officials to "function in an almost farcical manner."[60] This explanation, however, was not the whole story, as other authorities have pointed out that Indian politicians tended to disdain the humble apprenticeship of local government and that the peasants were often apathetic.

Less open to debate than this question of the failure of the plan to develop local self-government was the determination of the British officials to monopolize the highest posts and not to share with Indians the formulation of public policy. The appointment of Indians to the highest posts had been legalized in the Charter Act of 1833 and in Queen Victoria's proclamation in 1858, in which it was promised ". . . that, as far as may be, our subjects, of whatever race or creed, be freely and impartially admitted to office in our service."[61] This promise, however, was not carried out. Examinations for the Indian Civil Service, which monopolized all high positions, were held in England, and Indians were practically debarred from the I.C.S. when the maximum age for taking the examination was reduced from twenty-one to nineteen. In 1870 there were only seven Indian candidates and in 1880 only two. By 1892, out of 939 members in the I.C.S. only 21 were Indians; and in 1913 out of 2501 administrative officers with salaries of 800 rupees ($266) a month or more, only 242, less than 10 per cent, were Indians. Among the educated Indians who were ambitious to rise in the ranks of the public service there was naturally much resentment against the I.C.S., "the practical owners of India, irremovable, irresponsible, and amenable to no authority but that of their fellow members."[62] The passage of the Indian Councils Act of 1892, with its hesitant acceptance of the principle of election, marked the end of bureaucratic paternalism.

Lord Elton, op. cit., p. 461.

Coupland, Britain and ia, p. 40.

Lord Elton, op. cit., p. 459.

G. R. Gleig, The Life of Sir omas Munro, I, pp. 518-519; ted in Raleigh Parkin, India day (New York: John Day ., rev. ed., 1946), p. 178.

Thompson and Garratt, cit., p. 536.

A Collection of Extracts m Royal Proclamations, Offi- Reports and Speeches w Delhi: Government of ia Printing Office, no date), 7.

W. S. Blunt, India Under on (London: T. F. Unwin, 9), p. 313.

On the eve of British conquest Indian civilization had reached a low ebb. While strong and centralized monarchies developed in much of western Europe, in India the fatal weakness of political fragmentation and instability brought turmoil and widespread disorder to the unhappy land. While the western Europeans were rapidly forging ahead with the development of modern science, seeking to discover and control the secrets of nature for the happiness of man, and beginning at the same time to interest themselves in the problems of government and economics, the Indians exhibited little creative thought, contenting themselves with a culture that had become both stagnant and esoteric.

AS WE *have seen in the previous chapter, British rule brought about a revolution in India in the realm of law and government. It was also the vehicle for the impact of western culture, causing significant economic and intellectual changes in the pattern of Indian life. This impact of the West largely explains the all-important Hindu revival, or recovery, that got well under way shortly after the mid-point of the nineteenth century.*

FURTHERMORE, WHILE *the status of the great mass of the people in the villages was changed with the commercialization of agriculture and the passing of a subsistence economy, in the cities a relatively new class— the bourgeoisie—emerged. Along with the economic influences came new intellectual forces. The city people were exposed to western science and nineteenth-century liberal thought. And western education, established by the British, exposed the eager Indian students to the democratic and nationalistic currents that were agitating the stream of European history. Out of this western impact, with all its complexities and ramifications, came the Hindu revival and the genesis of modern nationalism in India as both a reaction to and an emulation of the West.*

The Hindu revival and the growth of nationalism

chapter 5

1- *Sir Reginald Coupland,* India: A Restatement (*London: Oxford University Press, 1945), p. 56.*

2- *Kate Mitchell,* India Without Fable (*New York: Alfred A. Knopf, 1942), p. 121.*

AN ECONOMIC transformation, more thorough and basic than any that had taken place in India in its entire history, followed upon the conquest of the country by Great Britain. In the early days of its activities the English East India Company was interested mainly in securing cheap Indian goods for export, chiefly to England and the Continent. This trade, especially in cotton and silk goods, reached its height about the year 1700. In the following decades, as English manufacturing began to grow, especially in the field of textiles, there was a demand for protection against Indian goods. And in accordance with the mercantilistic philosophy of the day, which foolishly preferred to have many exports and few imports, various duties and prohibitions were placed against imported goods from India. The East India Company, however, managed to sell a large volume of them as re-exports from England to the Continent. This re-export trade suffered severely during the Napoleonic wars when the European market practically ceased to exist. In 1813 the Company lost its monopoly of trade in India and the field was opened to all comers. After this date, because of the rapid development of the Industrial Revolution in England, most businessmen desired to sell their manufactured wares in the Indian market. No longer able to compete against the machine-made fabrics of England, the native textile industry declined, and a large number of weavers and other workers lost their traditional employment. At the same time, however, India greatly increased her export trade, for she still enjoyed a comparative economic advantage in the production of certain raw materials, such as indigo, cotton, tea, jute, wheat, oilseeds, hides, and linseed oil.

After the mid-point of the nineteenth century, when British control was completely established, India had a very moderate tariff based on the free-trade principle. In 1882 the small 5 per cent duty on manufactured cotton goods was abolished. Twelve years later, however, this rate was imposed on all imported goods. This action aroused the hostility of the English Manchester cotton interests, who succeeded in obtaining a countervailing excise on domestic cottons manufactured in India. After 1894 there was a general tariff rate of 5 per cent. Imported cotton goods, however, paid the lower rate of 3½ per cent, a rate which also had to be paid by the Indian manu-

facturers of domestic cotton cloth, whose factories had begun to be important in the 1880's. Outside of the imposition of this cotton excise tax, no preferential treatment was enjoyed by British goods, at the expense of either Indian producers or Britain's foreign competitors for the Indian market. The cotton excise is generally admitted by the present generation of British historians of imperial affairs to have been a serious mistake; one of them comments, "It was a short-sighted policy, for it did more than anything else to strengthen Indian distrust of British motives and impair the goodwill on which in the long run all trade depends."[1]

Nearly all the socio-economic evils from which modern India suffers today are attributed by most Indian historians to the decline of native industry. Nehru charges that as a result of British policy "India became progressively ruralized." He points out that there was an exodus from the urban centers to the countryside as industry declined. Land became overpopulated and the rents paid by the peasants steadily mounted in consequence. An American writer supporting this view states: "India was thus rapidly transformed from a country of combined agriculture and handicrafts into a purely agricultural colony of British industry, resulting in the severe overpressure on agriculture which has remained one of the most critical problems of modern India."[2]

Accompanying the decline of industry came fundamental changes in the status of the Indian village. For hundreds of years, while dynasty succeeded dynasty in India, the village had remained changeless. It was little affected by the outside world and was practically self-sufficient. Its members had a primitive form of self-rule and usually land was held as communal property. The impact of the new economic forces that entered India with British rule upset this ancient village way of life.

Early in the nineteenth century railroads were built and began to criss-cross the countryside. The old roads were also improved and made usable through the rainy season. These changes gradually opened up the villages to the outside world. Cash could be obtained by the peasants from the sale of their produce in the nearby markets. Agriculture consequently became commercialized. Before the British conquest farm products had to be sold in each local area. A good crop meant

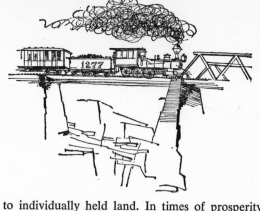

only a local glut, as the surplus could not be transported elsewhere. There were also wide variations in prices, which would be low in one area and excessively high in another. The opening of the village now brought it into contact with the Indian market, and, in the case of certain products such as wheat or tea, with the world market.

Cash crops meant that the villager could buy the enticing English manufactured goods. As a result, many of the village handicrafts declined. The introduction of enameled ironware hurt the village potter. The village oil man felt the competition of the new kerosene, and, as carcasses went now to the tanning industry, the village tanner had less call for his services. Another change in the village was the increased mobility of its members. Although the great majority of Indian villagers still are born and die in the same rural area, the advent of better communications gave the more ambitious the chance to "try their luck elsewhere," sometimes in a less densely populated district or perhaps in a large city.

New concepts of property also exerted their influence in village life. From time immemorial the rulers of India had obtained the bulk of their revenue from the land. In an attempt to regularize the system in Bengal, just acquired by the East India Company, Governor-General Lord Cornwallis in 1790 made what is known as the Permanent Revenue Settlement. By this action the old tax collectors, the zamindars of the Mogul Empire, were recognized as private landlords. These landholders were expected to turn over to the government a permanent annual sum, taken from the rents they collected. Unfortunately, as land values increased, the government by its own arrangement got no part of the increased rents. The peasants, in spite of efforts made to protect them in the late nineteenth century, were increasingly overcharged and exploited.

In large parts of Bombay and Madras a different approach was made to the land-revenue problem. Here the government dealt directly with the peasants, collecting the rent, or taxes, from the villagers. Unlike those under the zamindari system of Bengal, the cultivators in the ryotwari settlement were recognized as the owners of the land, endowed with the rights of private property and privileged to sell, lease, or mortgage their land. Unfortunately, the peasants were not adequately prepared for this transfer from village ownership

to individually held land. In times of prosperity they tended to be extravagant, and "improvident borrowing and unscrupulous lending"[3] became all too common. When the monsoon failed and crops were nonexistent, the peasants were unable to pay off their debts to the moneylender. The result was heavier and heavier indebtedness.

In explaining what has become a major agrarian problem of modern India, rural indebtedness, some writers tend to stress what they believe is the heavy and inelastic land taxation in relation to peasant income. Other authorities point out the effect of certain social and religious customs, such as the high expense of marriage. It is charged that moneylenders (the banias) and the Brahmans all too frequently conspired in insisting upon expensive purifications after certain diseases. In *The Home and the World*, Rabindranath Tagore explains, "Panchu's wife had just died of a lingering consumption. Panchu must undergo purification to cleanse himself of sin and to propitiate the community. The community has calculated and informed him that it will cost one hundred and twenty-three rupees."[4]

Thus the village was swept into the stream of world economic forces and, as the villager was not prepared to stand alone and take care of his property, the results in all too many instances were tragic. It can be argued, however, that the change from self-subsistence and isolation was necessary before India could begin to approach a modern economy. The important question involved is whether the economic status of the village could have been transformed with less human dislocation and suffering. It seems that economic changes, whether they have been technological unemployment in an advanced nation such as the United States, or the impact of a money economy upon the tribal structure in tropical Africa, usually have just happened instead of being planned in orderly fashion; the transformation of the village in India has been no exception.

In commenting on this situation an Indian economic historian has observed:

But the fact remains that the village life was poor in cultural quality, on a narrow village scale, unprogressive, and passive. If the Indian people were to advance to higher forms of social existence such as nationhood, economic unity and intellectual progress, the self-sufficient village had to leave the stage of history.[5]

3- Edward J. Thompson and G. T. Garratt, Rise and Fulfilment of British Rule in India *(London: The Macmillan Company, 1934), p. 485.*

4- *Quoted in* ibid., *p. 489.*

5- A. R. Desai, Social Background of Indian Nationalism *(Bombay: Oxford University Press, 1949), p. 39.*

The negative aspects of the economic impact of the West were in some instances counterbalanced by compensatory effects. While some classes suffered economically, others prospered and gained materially in wealth. One of the most important results of the new economics in India was the rise of a well-educated, dynamic, and ambitious middle class numerically small in proportion to the total population (perhaps totaling five million) but influential. Opportunities for expanding trade and better protection for property brought about the development of a wealthy banking and commercial class. To its ranks were added the new professional men, especially the educators, journalists, and lawyers. Under the Moguls the middle class had been insignificant and inconsequential; now, for the first time, a bourgeois element emerged which was to have a major role in shaping the new India.

Continuing the discussion of the positive effects of British economic influence, special attention should be paid to the creation of a modern business structure in India, mainly by foreign capital. The period from 1858 to 1900 may be called the "opening up period" of Indian economic history. It was during this time that India received her railroads, posts and telegraphs, modern roads, banks, and harbors. Before the British period only a few roads existed, connecting the main centers of population, and these were only fair-weather arteries.

The first railroad dates from 1853; by 1869, there were 4000 miles of road open to traffic; and by the 1890's the mileage had reached 24,000. "Railways," wrote Sir Edward Arnold, "may do for India what dynasties have never done . . . they may make India a nation."[6] The consequences of the new railroads were manifold. They helped materially in combating famine; they made easier religious pilgrimages from one part of the country to the other and thus assisted the movement—discussed later in this chapter—for the revival of Hinduism. Finally, they helped to open up areas of land heretofore inaccessible. In this last case the underdeveloped section of Assam is a good example.

Following the Mutiny, British capital flowed into India in huge amounts, financing the railroads and the plantations producing indigo, jute, and tea. By 1911 these investments were in the neighborhood of four billion dollars. India's foreign trade

6- Quoted in L. S. S. O'Malley, *Modern India and the West* *(New York: Oxford University Press, 1941)*, p. 241.

7- Holden Furber, *John Company at Work* *(Cambridge: Harvard University Press, 1948)*, p. 311.

reflected the modernization of her economic structure:

	Exports (in millions of pounds)	Imports (in millions of pounds)
1834	8	4.5
1870	53	33.5
1910	137	86

While the natural center of gravity for this trade was Great Britain, foreign countries were not unimportant, as can be seen from the following figures:

	United Kingdom	Other Parts of British Empire	Foreign Nations
Exports from India, 1910, to:	26%	17%	57%
Imports into India, from:	61%	8%	31%

There was little rapid development of industry in the nineteenth century. Only three kinds of industrial activity were of any importance: cotton mills, which increased from 58 in 1880 to 264 in 1914; jute mills, which increased in number from 22 to 64 in the same period; and coal mines, which increased their yield from 1,294,000 tons in 1885 to 15,738,000 tons in 1914.

Only the more obvious results of the economic impact of British control of India have been indicated. It is difficult to strike a judicious balance, not only because the problem is so complex but because much more research will have to be done to secure the necessary facts. Professor Furber had this in mind when he wrote:

It is quite apparent that the process of European expansion in India cannot be thought of simply in terms of the "exploitation" of millions of impoverished peasants and artisans by ambitious conquerors. During the last half of the eighteenth century, European enterprise acted as a powerful catalyst on the economic life of the East. Under its auspices, commercial revolutions took place . . . within the vast fabric of Indian society. . . . It brought about closer economic ties between all regions of India which must be carefully studied before the European influence can be universally condemned as harmful. European activity unquestionably fostered social change. It brought prosperity to some groups within Indian society and depressed the economic status of others.[7]

This quotation refers particularly to the consequences of British economic influence in the closing decades of the eighteenth century, but it holds generally for the nineteenth as well.

On this matter of the pros and cons of the economic consequences of alien rule in India, the fundamental question is whether she would have been any better off without foreign control. In such an event, political stability would have been an essential prerequisite for the attainment of economic well-being, and no one can hazard how long it would have taken India to build up an effective system of government, law, and order on the debris of the Mogul Empire. And even if one grants the possible rapid achievement of political stability, would India have been able to create a modern structure of business? Above all, would she have been able to build up her own industries? Certainly the task would have been extremely difficult, for India in the nineteenth century lacked the necessary technological knowledge. Furthermore, she lacked capital, a condition explained by the age-old propensity of her people to hoard precious metals instead of using them for productive purposes. There would have been not only the difficulty of procuring capital, but also the problem of interesting most of the upper-class Indians in business enterprise. As an American economist has observed, "Anything that savored of material productivity or of trading for gain was strictly tabooed by these 'twice born.' "[8]

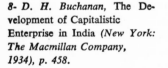

8- *D. H. Buchanan,* The Development of Capitalistic Enterprise in India *(New York: The Macmillan Company, 1934), p. 458.*

The Intellectual Impact of the West

The introduction of western thought and education was as significant for India as the economic transformation. The missionaries were the pioneers in introducing European culture into India. First the Portuguese in the sixteenth century, then Italians in the seventeenth, and Danes in the early eighteenth century set up their missions. These early missionaries carried on important linguistic studies and prepared grammars in various native languages. British missionaries were at first excluded by the East India Company, but managed to establish themselves on Danish territory not far from Calcutta. Here at Serampore in 1801 William Carey, a Baptist missionary, and his colleagues set up a printing press and began the publication of books in the Indian vernaculars, grammars and dictionaries, and works in the English language.

Up to this time, with the exception of the printing presses brought in by European trading companies and used for official purposes, no presses existed in India, and only the very wealthy possessed written works in their libraries in the form of manuscripts. The Serampore press soon had many imitators, and by 1838 printing was a widespread industry. The first Indian newspaper was issued in 1816, followed by another published at Serampore two years later. By 1823 there were four Indian newspapers in Calcutta alone. The product of these presses brought out a flood of new ideas which were eagerly absorbed by the small but influential group of literate Indians.

In the early days of the English East India Company most of the officials were pro-Orientalists, that is, they favored the encouragement of the classical languages, Persian and Sanskrit, used by the governing class and the scholars. At this time the vernacular languages were in low esteem, lacking grammars and models of good literary style. Thus it was that Warren Hastings sponsored a Muslim college in 1780, and in 1792 Lord Cornwallis set up a comparable college for the study of Sanskrit at Benares.

Early in the nineteenth century both Indian intellectuals and Englishmen began to look favorably on the establishment of western education in India. In 1817 the Hindu College for the study of English was set up at Calcutta through the efforts of David Hare, an English watchmaker in Calcutta, and Ram Mohan Roy, an Indian admirer of European culture. The following year saw a Mission College started by William Carey at Serampore. In the Charter Act of 1813 the Company was authorized to make an annual grant of £10,000 for education, to be used for the teaching of Arabic and Sanskrit. Meanwhile, however, the ranks of the Anglicists, as they were called, were increasing, and the government of India in 1829 announced its intention of making English the official language.

Thomas Babington Macaulay, member of the Governor-General's Executive Council, issued his famous *Education Minute* in February 1835. In it he showed a lack of appreciation of Hindu culture and a cocksure confidence in the superiority of European thought. "I have never found one [of the Orientalists]," declared Macaulay, "who would deny that a single shelf of a good European library was worth the whole native literature of

India and Arabia."[9] Such rhetoric was unnecessary; but Macaulay's basic recommendation, that English be the medium and English literature and science the material of instruction in the advanced schools, was cogently argued, and was accepted not only by the Indian government but by many influential Indians. The decision to base higher education in India upon the English language and on western culture was announced by Bentinck in March 1835. Behind the *Minute* was the belief of English officials that western education was the best medium for "modernizing" India, the recognition that Britain needed a western-educated class to help in the administration of the country, and also the understanding that western education *might* lead to the demand for Indian self-government. But such a possibility did not worry the liberally-inclined British administrators of the early nineteenth century. It was only after the Mutiny of 1857 and the consequent growth of the imperialistic spirit that British officials failed to see the inconsistency of teaching Indians western history and ideals and at the same time scoffing at their desire to rule themselves.

The British Parliament in 1853 for the first time thoroughly investigated Indian education. In consequence a famous dispatch was issued in 1854 by Sir Charles Wood, who stated that its aim should be the extension of European knowledge among all classes in India. In accordance with the instructions of the dispatch, the Governor-General, Lord Dalhousie, in the 1850's began laying the foundation of a national system of education. The dispatch called for the setting up of universities, establishing training colleges for teachers, expanding the government colleges and high schools, and the extension of vernacular elementary schools designed for the masses.

By 1885 this educational system was well established; the number of students in colleges and universities increased between 1885 and 1900 from 11,000 to 23,000, and those in secondary schools from 429,000 to 633,000. It was this system of education that was the vehicle of western culture and brought about a veritable revolution in the thought-climate of India.

The new western learning dispensed in the English high schools and colleges exerted tremendous influence. By it the Indian recovery, soon to be traced, became possible; by it India became part of a world community, sharing in the rich legacy of science and rational thought that was the product of the nineteenth century. A new generation of Indian intellectuals was produced who looked to Europe for their inspiration. The number of these western-educated Indians has never been large; in the 1920's it was estimated that two and a half million persons were literate in English. One Englishman wrote:

Familiarly acquainted with us by means of our literature, the Indian youth almost cease to regard us as foreigners. They speak of our great men with the same enthusiasm as we do. Educated in the same way, interested in the same subjects, engaged in the same pursuits with ourselves, they become more English than Hindus, just as the Roman provincials became more Roman than Gauls or Italians.[10]

Nehru in describing them has written: "The British had created a new caste or class in India, the English-educated class, which lived in a world of its own, cut off from the mass of the population, and looked always, even when protesting, toward their rulers."[11] This evaluation is hardly tenable, since traditionally the upper classes throughout Indian history have shown little interest in and solicitude for the masses, while, in fact, it has been among these very western-educated Indians, trained in liberal and rationalist thought, that the main reform movements for uplifting the masses have arisen. Nehru himself is an outstanding example!

The best early example of the product of western education was Ram Mohan Roy (1772-1833). A member of a Brahman family in Bengal, he broke with his parents over the spectacle of his sister's torture on the funeral pyre of her husband. Ram Mohan Roy then traveled widely in India and entered the service of the British government. Learning English, studying Greek and Hebrew, he became fascinated by western thought and deeply interested in all religions. He translated some of the *Upanishads* into English and also published a book of extracts from and commentaries on the New Testament, called *The Precepts of Jesus, A Guide to Peace and Happiness.* As a reformer he supported the introduction of English education and the elimination of barbarous customs, such as suttee. While championing reform and admiring European thought, he was nevertheless interested in preserving the best in Hindu culture.

In 1828 Ram Mohan Roy founded his society, the Brahma Samaj, which sought to purge Hindu-

9- Quoted in Ramsay Muir, ed., The Making of British India, 1756-1858 (Manchester: Manchester University Press, 1923), p. 299.

10- Quoted in O'Malley, op. cit., p. 92.

11- Jawaharlal Nehru, The Discovery of India (New York: John Day Co., 1946), p. 412.

ism of such practices as purdah and child marriage. The society also rejected polytheism and image-worship. While Hindu in its orientation, the Brahma Samaj contained Christian and humanistic elements. It was open to all comers regardless of creed or race, and was strongly reminiscent of the credo of the European Deists of the eighteenth century.

The Society never reached the masses, but it had widespread influence among the middle-class intelligentsia. Of its founder a fellow countryman has well said:

> The chief value of the Raja's labours . . . seems to lie in his fight against the forces of medievalism in India, and it is for this reason that we claim for him the honour of being the Father of the present Indian renaissance. . . . The objective of all the many-sided activities of Raja Ram Mohan Roy was to free the country from this fatal incubus of medieval abstraction.[12]

The Origin of Nationalism and the Founding of Congress

Modern nationalism was imported into India from Europe. Most authorities agree that there is nothing to indicate the existence of any genuine nationalist sentiment until at least two decades after the Mutiny of 1857. Before India could be truly nationalistic it had to be united; and, furthermore, it needed the inspiration so abundantly provided by the various nationalistic movements that sprinkled the pages of European history from 1500. The story of the national unification of France and England, the patriotic crusade of subjugated Europeans against the imperialistic tyranny of Napoleon, the struggle of the Greeks against the Turks for their national independence, and the achievements of Bismarck and Cavour in creating united and independent motherlands for their peoples—all these helped to kindle the nationalistic fire in India. In addition to the political unification brought about by the British conquest, the use of English as the lingua franca made it possible for men all over the country to exchange views and compare opinions. Cheap postage and the printing press were indispensable agencies working for a sense of unity that had never existed before in India. The railroads also assisted in the process, mainly by facilitating travel all over the country.

The education provided in the schools was a rich well from which young middle-class Indians drank deeply. They read of the political philosophy of John Locke, of his social contract theory justifying revolution. They studied the lives of Charles Stewart Parnell, the Irish patriot; Giuseppe Mazzini, the inspirer of Italian youth; and Louis Kossuth, fighter for a lost cause in Hungary. This type of instruction inevitably caused Indians to consider their own case and claim the liberties and rights which had been acquired by other peoples, including the English who ruled them. This first generation of Indian nationalists followed the tradition of Ram Mohan Roy. They were liberals and had an abiding faith in parliamentary institutions; and, while awakening to the thrill of nationhood, they were in no sense anti-English, for they confidently expected the "Mother of Parliaments" to grant them self-government without too much delay.

In addition to the stimulating shock of western ideas, Indian nationalism was also nourished by the recovery of India's past, which, before the opening of the nineteenth century, was almost a blank page as far as the pre-Mogul period is concerned. A number of enthusiastic Europeans, many of them scholar-administrators, carried out historical, archeological, and linguistic researches of inestimable value. Societies like the Asiatic Society of Bengal did much to recover the glories of India's past. India owes a great debt to such scholars as Charles Wilkins, Sir William Jones, Henry Thomas Colebrooke, James Prinsep, and Alexander Cunningham. This debt is thus graciously recognized by an Indian historian: "Today when we talk of the Mauryas, the Guptas, the Chalukyas and the Pallavas, let it be remembered that the story of these great ages of Indian history was recovered to us by the devoted labours of European scholars in the service of the British Government in India."[13]

A sense of nationalism hesitatingly made itself evident in the 1860's, but in the next decade, during the viceroyalty of Lord Lytton (1876-1880), it grew rapidly. This British official was the spokesman for the rising tide of jingoism and imperialism that was sweeping Britain under the leadership of Prime Minister Benjamin Disraeli. It was the flood of this new spirit, fortified by the fear complex engendered by the Mutiny, that completely inundated the liberal and reformist

12- Bepin Chandra Pal, The New Spirit *(Calcutta: Sinha, Sarvadhikari Publishers, 1907), pp. 52, 54.*

13- K. M. Panikkar, A Survey of Indian History *(London: Meridian Books, Ltd., 1948), pp. 264-265.*

attitude so characteristic of British Indian officials from 1820 to 1850. During Lytton's administration, therefore, little concern was manifested for the national susceptibilities of Her Majesty's Indian subjects. A vernacular press act was passed, giving the government better control over Indian newspapers. People were also restricted from carrying firearms by the enactment of an arms act. Another action, this time by the government in London, aroused much resentment. Official statements and royal proclamations had been made, promising Indians equal opportunities in the government service. Yet the I.C.S., the top-level branch of the administration, was kept practically a closed preserve to Indians. Whatever feeble intentions the home government might have entertained in the direction of widening the opportunities in the administrative services were stymied by the opposition of the British bureaucracy in India. One of its members, Sir John Strachey, frankly wrote: ". . . let there be no hypocrisy about our intention to keep in the hands of our own people those executive posts . . . on which, and on our political and military power, our actual hold of the country depends."[14]

In 1877 the age over which candidates for the I.C.S. could not sit for the examinations in England was reduced from twenty-one to nineteen years. This act stirred up considerable indignation in India. An Indian eyewitness of these reactions wrote, "Throughout India, this was regarded as a deliberate attempt to blast the prospect of Indian candidates for the Indian Civil Service."[15] Even when Indians were successful in the examinations, they experienced difficulty in securing posts in the I.C.S. This was true in the case of Surendranath Banerjea, who was finally admitted only to be dismissed from the I.C.S. on a minor charge.

Frustrated in his ambition for a government career, Banerjea turned to politics, and in 1876 founded the Indian Association of Calcutta with branches in the main cities of north India. This organization was definitely nationalistic in inspiration and had as its objective a united India strong enough to secure concessions from Great Britain. In 1877, following the reduction in age for the I.C.S. examinations, Banerjea used the Indian Association for a whirlwind campaign against the action of the British government. As a result an All-India Memorial was sent with-

out success to the British House of Commons, asking that the examination age be raised. There can be no doubt that this civil service agitation played an important part in the story of the origin of nationalism in India.

Another factor that helped to bring nationalistic feelings to a head was the widening gulf in race relations between the British and Indians. English writers point out the unfortunate consequences of the influx into India in the 1860's of a stream of British planters and businessmen who were inclined to be raucous and superior and who looked down upon, and sometimes despised, all Indians. Undoubtedly the Mutiny had much to do with this feeling. In India this group constantly exacerbated relations between Europeans and Indians by their noisy determination to uphold the prestige and superiority of the "white man."

Lord Ripon, the Governor-General following Lytton, was a Victorian liberal, and during his administration (1880-1884) sincere attempts were made to liberalize the government. One of the measures was the Ilbert Bill, introduced in 1883 and designed to remove the privilege heretofore enjoyed by Europeans by which they were guaranteed a British judge in case of trial. As Indians were now moving up into the higher brackets of the judiciary, Ripon saw no reason why these well qualified public servants could not preside at any trial regardless of the birthplace of the defendant. This Ilbert Bill, however, provoked a tempestuous explosion among the members of the European community, who started a Defence Association and carried on a noisy and violent agitation against the measure. Consequently the bill was emasculated and toned down. The European community had won its point, but, at the same time, it had given Indians a good object lesson in the value of organization and agitation. The European explosion over the Ilbert Bill also exposed to sensitive Indian nationalists the racial arrogance of many Englishmen in their country. Indian vernacular newspapers assumed a new tone in attacking the government and the press had by this time become an influential factor in molding public opinion, as there were twenty newspapers published in English and some two hundred in Indian languages.

It was during the agitation over the Ilbert Bill that Indian spokesmen for the nationalist movement responded by organizing the Indian National

14- *Sir John Strachey*, India (London: Kegan Paul, Trench, Trubner and Co., 1894), p. 390.

15- *Sir Surendranath Banerjea, Nation in the Making* (London: H. Milford Co., 1925), p. 44.

Conference. Led by Surendranath Banerjea, it met in Calcutta in 1883 with representatives from all parts of India. The following year the growing national spirit was reflected in a meeting held at Madras under the aegis of the Theosophical Society, whose importance will be shortly discussed.

Meanwhile, the initiative was taken by Allan Octavian Hume, a retired civil servant, who, after thirty years in the Indian government, occupied himself in studying the country's problems. Hume believed that British rule had given the land he had come to love peace and political stability, but that much more had to be done to raise the standard of living of the people. Hume believed too that the British bureaucracy was out of touch with the people and maintained it was "of paramount importance to find an overt and constitutional channel for discharge of the increasing ferment which had resulted from western ideas and education."[16]

Acting upon this belief, Hume sent out in 1883 a letter to the graduates of Calcutta University urging them to form an association for the mental, moral, and political regeneration of India. Following a meeting held at Madras in December 1884, attended by such representative Indians as S. S. Iyer, Surendranath Banerjea, and Dadabhai Naoroji, a circular was sent out the following March inviting attendance at a meeting to be held in Poona, December 25 to 31, 1885. The objective of the meeting was outlined thus: "Indirectly this Conference will form the germ of a Native Parliament and . . . will constitute in a few years an unanswerable reply to the assertion that India is still wholly unfit for any form of representative institutions."[17]

The first meeting of what came to be known as the Indian National Congress duly convened in December at Poona. There were seventy delegates, mostly Hindu lawyers, educators, and journalists, with only two Muslims among them. The Congress carried on its deliberations in English and the tone was loyal and moderate. In the first presidential address by W. C. Bonerji, parliamentary government was declared to be the goal, but it was claimed that this was in no way incompatible with loyalty to England. The President further declared:

I ask whether in the most glorious days of Hindu rule you could imagine the possibility of a meeting of this kind. . . . Would it have been possible even in the days of Akbar for a meeting like this to assemble, composed of all classes and communities, all speaking one language. . . .? It is under the civilizing rule of the Queen and the people of England that we meet here together, hindered by none, freely allowed to speak our minds without the least fear or hesitation. Such a thing is possible under British rule, and under British rule only.[18]

Resolutions were passed asking for a Royal Commission to investigate the workings of Indian administration; for the abolition of the India Council in London; for the right to have the government budgets presented to the Legislative Councils for examination; and for the creation of a Standing Committee in the British House of Commons to consider formal protests from the Indian members of the Legislative Councils.

Each year following 1885 the National Congress met in December in a different city of India. In 1888 the Congress carried out extensive publicity, distributing thousands of pamphlets and arranging for hundreds of lectures. In 1894, at Madras, the ranks of the annual Congress meeting swelled to fifteen hundred delegates and three thousand visitors. The delegates in the annual meetings discussed various problems connected with British rule and passed resolutions urging the spread of education, the reduction of military expenditures, wider government employment for Indians, the improvement of the status of Indian nationals in South Africa, and the abolition of the countervailing excise of 3¼ per cent on domestic cotton goods.

The Indian National Congress during this period was controlled and directed by what we may refer to as the first generation of nationalists—men like G. K. Gokhale, Surendranath Banerjea, Pherozeshah Mehta, and Dadabhai Naoroji. These leaders championed a western and a liberal view. They admired Great Britain and were apostles of co-operation. Gokhale was the outstanding Indian political leader up to the First World War. Born a Brahman in Bombay Presidency, he received an excellent education and became a professor of law at Ferguson College. Entering politics in 1899, he became a member of the Bombay Legislative Council and from 1902 to 1915 was a member of the Indian Imperial Legislative Council. Gokhale served as President of the National Congress in 1905. As an orator and debater he had no superiors in India, and in his speeches he advocated

16- Quoted in Sir H. Verney Lovett, A History of the Indian Nationalist Movement (London: John Murray, 1920), p. 34.

17- Quoted in Annie Besant, How India Wrought for Freedom (Adyar, India: Theosophical Publishing House, 1915), p. 4.

18- Quoted in Coupland, op. cit., p. 89.

self-government for India within the Empire and compulsory education. In 1905 Gokhale founded the Servants of India Society, an idea derived from the Jesuit Order. Its purpose was "to train men prepared to devote their lives to the cause of the country."[19] The members had to spend five years as initiates, during which time they could not marry and were not supposed to earn more than £4 a month. The Society interested itself in social reform, such questions as improving the status of women and raising the level of the Depressed Classes (i.e., the Untouchables).

As we have already mentioned, there were other great moderate leaders, but Gokhale towers above them all. "Gokhale was perhaps the finest character that India has produced," wrote one English observer, "blending accurate knowledge of Western history and Western thought with a profound understanding of the Indian mentality and of the ancient civilization that has moulded it."[20]

And what of the attitude of British officials to the Congress? At first the government of India was friendly to the new movement. Officials attended the Congress, and governors in the various provinces arranged official receptions and garden parties for the members. This sympathy, however, soon waned, and the Viceroy, Lord Dufferin (1884-1888), rather contemptuously referred to Congress membership as a "microscopic minority." In common with the usual European derogatory attitude toward the political aspirations of "native people," British officials during this heyday of Kiplingesque imperialism refused to take the Congress seriously. Most Europeans discerned no merit in the Congress. For example, in 1909 one French student of Indian affairs lambasted the Congress as a group of middle-class, doctrinaire intellectuals. He declared:

It is, in essence, a party of theorists—arm-chair politicians, who, I fear, shrink in reality from the open air and a life of action. Writers and orators, proud of their knowledge and their caste, disdainful, and perhaps even ignorant, of the lower classes, aloof from the mass of the people, they have little more knowledge of that mass than they can derive from the documents brought together and published by the Anglo-Indian Government which they tax with selfishness, oppression, and ignorance.[21]

There was some truth in this allegation, but the National Congress was much more than this observer and many British officials suspected, and

it is unfortunate that this fact should not have been recognized when the Congress was in a pliant and conciliatory mood.

Denied recognition from officialdom, the National Congress received valuable support from unofficial British circles. Allan Hume was known as the "Father of Congress," and until 1907 he was—at times with others—in charge of the general Congress Secretariat. Visiting England, Hume solicited and secured the support of John Bright and Charles Bradlaugh. Before the First World War, Britishers were frequently elected Presidents of the Congress. Sir William Wedderburn received this honor in 1889 and 1910, Sir Henry Cotton in 1904, and David Yule in 1888. A group friendly to the cause of Congress also carried on work in England. Known as the British Committee for Representative Government, founded in 1888, this agency published a journal and subsidized the distribution of pamphlets and the giving of lectures. Each annual Congress expressed its "thanks to the British Committee."

The Hindu Renaissance

The first reaction to the impact of the West in India had been the growth of an influential class of liberals who looked to Europe as an intellectual home. They were critical of many elements in their own culture pattern, and their ideal was the rationalization and modernization of Indian life, to be best achieved by a harmonious blend between East and West. This sometimes uncritical admiration and imitation of things European came to be challenged by a new movement that emerged in the 1870's and reached full tide in the closing years of the century. Often referred to as the Hindu Renaissance or Recovery, this movement regarded western culture as soulless and materialistic. At the same time, the culture and the past of India were idealized, some thinkers going so far as to assert that all modern inventions could be found in germ in the ancient Vedas. There was a poetic and emotional glow in the references to India's past Golden Age.

We had corn in our granaries; our tanks supplied us with fish; and the eye was soothed and refreshed with the limpid blue of the sky and green foliage of the trees. All day long the peasant toiled in the field; and at eve, returning to his lamp-lit home, he sang the song of his heart.[22]

19- Hans Kohn, A History of Nationalism in the East (London: George Routledge, 1929), p. 369.

20- Sir Valentine Chirol, India (London: Ernest Benn, Ltd., 1926), p. 108.

21- Joseph Chailley, Administrative Problems of British India (London: The Macmillan Company, 1910), p. 163.

22- Earl of Ronaldshay, The Heart of Aryavarta (London: Constable and Co., 1925), p. 93.

Above all, the Hindu Renaissance, as a new manifestation of nationalism, was suffused with religion. Nationalism was deified as the manifestation and voice of God. This idea was made possible by the fact that Hinduism had long taught that God reincarnates himself from time to time for the saving of the world, and now God had appeared in the form of Mother India. An Indian newspaper in 1919 asserted:

This motherland . . . is the symbol of our nation-idea . . . the Divine Idea, the Logos, which has been revealing itself through the entire course of our past historic evolution. The Motherland is really the synthesis of all the goddesses that have been, and are still being, worshipped by Hindus.[23]

The religious motivation of the Hindu Renaissance gave it a fervor and an emotional strength comparable to what religion gave to Elizabethan England in its struggle against Spain. But this religious tinge to nationalism meant that the movement was to lose some of its early catholicity; that the Indian revival was going to be prevented from being truly national. As a European observer pointed out in the early 1900's, "The National party really replaces true Indian patriotism by a Hindu nationalism, in which Musalmans and Buddhists could not join without very considerable reserves."[24]

Swami Dayanand Saraswati is usually regarded as the founder of the new nationalism and the Hindu Recovery. Although his family was well-to-do, Saraswati eschewed an English education, left home, and became a homeless ascetic. In 1860 he began his teaching. To his mind everything foreign was bad. Attacking modern Hinduism as corrupt, he exhorted the people to go back to the Vedas, in which there was no justification for caste, images, or polytheism. In 1875 this teacher established the Arya Samaj, the antithesis of the previously founded liberal-rational Brahma Samaj. The Arya Samaj was intensely nationalistic, opposing both Islam and Christianity. Its motto could be said to be "India for the Hindus." While it preached a primitive and purified form of Hinduism, the Society was not unmindful of the evils in contemporary Hindu life. It therefore opposed child marriage, proposed reforms in the caste system, and carried on extensive educational operations. The Arya Samaj became very influential in the Punjab.

Another apostle of the superiority and self-sufficiency of Hindu culture was the Swami Vivekananda, of whom it has been said, "The call to reform, restore and revive India, to help India in every way possible for human effort, was essentially Vivekananda's call, and of all the makers of modern India, his was the most classless and purely patriotic voice."[25] Born into a high-caste Bengali family, Vivekananda received a thorough education, impressing his English teachers by his brilliance and his remarkable memory. Becoming interested in spiritual problems, he turned in 1882 to the teacher Ramakrishna, a famous ascetic. After the death of his *guru* (teacher) in 1886, Vivekananda carried out various pilgrimages and in 1893 was sent by his supporters and friends to the Parliament of Religions, meeting in Chicago.

On September 11, 1893, Vivekananda made before the Parliament a famous speech which created a tremendous impression. The young Hindu declared he spoke for "the Mother of Religions, a religion which has taught the world both tolerance and universal acceptance." Disclaiming any narrow denominationalism, however, he went on to proclaim the basic oneness and universality of all religions, using as his text the following lines from an ancient Vedic hymn:

As the different streams having their sources in different places all mingle their water in the sea, so, O Lord, the different paths which men take through different tendencies, various though they appear, crooked or straight, all lead to Thee.[26]

He became famous, not only in the United States, but all over the world, and for three years he remained in America and Europe lecturing and founding his missions. In January 1897, Vivekananda returned to India and was welcomed as a national hero, for he was the first Indian in modern times to become a world figure. To this teacher all religions were true and good, but the most venerable and noblest was Hinduism. His was the voice of militant nationalism blending political aspirations with religious exhortation. After his return from abroad he gave this message to the Hindus:

Once more the world must be conquered by India. This is the great ideal before us. Let them come and flood the land with their armies, never mind. Up, India, and conquer the world with your spirituality!

23- *Quoted in Ramsay Mac-Donald,* The Awakening of India *(London: Hodder and Stoughton, 1910), p. 187.*

24- *Quoted in Chailley, op. cit., p. 164.*

25- *Vincent Sheean,* Lead, Kindly Light *(New York: Random House, 1949), p. 354.*

26- *Quoted in ibid., pp. 341-342.*

Spirituality must conquer the West. Where are the men ready to go out to every country in the world with the messages of the great sages of India? There is no other alternative, we must do it or die. The only condition of national life, once more vigorous national life, is the conquest of the world by Indian thought.[27]

Vivekananda founded his Ramakrishna Order to propagate his beliefs, and it continued after his death in 1902 to do valiant work in the regeneration of Indian life. Today there are some three dozen monasteries and sixty-six missions run by the Ramakrishna Order, plus a number of schools and colleges.

There were other manifestations of the Hindu Revival, chief of which was the work of the Theosophical Society. Founded by Madam H. P. Blavatsky and Colonel H. S. Olcott in New York in 1875, the organization came to India in 1879 and established its headquarters at Adyar in Madras. The distinctive features of the Society were its championship of Hindu ideals and practices, its acceptance of the doctrines of Karma and transmigration, and the idealization of India's past. The Society also evinced a critical attitude toward Christianity.

The importance of the Theosophical Society really began with the leadership of Annie Besant, a remarkable woman whose career was varied and tempestuous. Born in 1847 the daughter of a London doctor, Mrs. Besant married early in her life, her chosen husband being a minister. She soon left him, however, after repudiating Christianity, and for some years was a follower of Charles Bradlaugh, the English free thinker and reformer. Mrs. Besant championed such un-Victorian causes as birth control and atheism; in the mid-1880's she came under the spell of Bernard Shaw and was converted to socialism. In 1889 she became a Theosophist and four years later went to India, where she became the spokesman of the Theosophical Society. In 1898, with Olcott and others, she founded the Central Hindu College, which ultimately became the Hindu University at Benares. From the beginning of her sojourn in India, Mrs. Besant allied herself with the Hindu Renaissance. In her autobiography she wrote:

The Indian work is, first of all, the revival, strengthening, and uplifting of the ancient religions. This act

brought with it a new self-respect, a pride in the past, a belief in the future, and, as an inevitable result, a great wave of patriotic life, the beginning of the rebuilding of a nation.[28]

The Muslim Reaction

In contrast to the stirrings that activated the Hindu community after the Mutiny, the Muslims lacked any animation. The British conquest of the Mogul Empire had removed the upper-class Muslims from the status of the elite governing class. After the Mutiny the Muslim community passed under a dark cloud, as it was saddled with most of the responsibility for the outbreak of 1857. While many Hindus took advantage of the commercial opportunities that came in the nineteenth century with the growth of trade in India, the Muslims lagged behind economically, showing little aptitude for business. Furthermore, their Koran forbade them the practice of usury. And while the new schools were filled to capacity with Hindu youths eager for the new western learning, the leaders of the Muslim community urged their people to have nothing to do with it. In consequence, the professions of law, medicine, teaching, and journalism were closed to the Muslims, and, most important, they could not compete with the Hindu candidates for positions in the government service.

While Bengali Hindu, Madrasis, and Marathas inspired by the arts and sciences of Europe were experiencing an intellectual and moral renaissance, the Muslims all over India were falling into a state of material indigence and intellectual decay.[29]

It was from this melancholy state that the Muslims were elevated through the vision of a remarkable leader, Sir Seyed Ahmad Khan (1817-1898). Born in Delhi of an old Muslim family, Sir Seyed entered the service of the British government in India at the age of twenty-one. During the Mutiny he supported the cause of the British, and after its conclusion concentrated on two objectives: (1) to achieve better understanding between his coreligionists and the Viceroy's government and (2) to arouse his fellow Muslims from the torpor and stagnation that had been retarding their progress.

In the 1860's Sir Seyed Ahmad Khan busied himself with these two tasks; a visit to Europe in 1869 convinced him that his community must

27- *Quoted in J. F. C. Fuller,* India in Revolt *(London: Eyre and Spottiswoode, 1931), p. 76.*

28- *Quoted in R. C. Majumdar, H. C. Raychaudhuri, and K. Datta,* An Advanced History of India *(London: The Macmillan Company, 1946), p. 886.*

29- *Sir John Cumming, ed.,* Political India *(London: Oxford University Press, 1932), p. 87.*

adopt certain aspects of western culture. His letters written in Europe are full of astonishment and admiration for the wonders he encountered on his tour. He was especially impressed with what he saw in England, and in referring to the differences between conditions in Great Britain and India he wrote:

I am not thinking about those things in which, owing to the specialities of our respective countries, we and the English differ. I only remark on politeness, knowledge, good faith, cleanliness, skilled workmanship, accomplishments, and thoroughness, which are the results of education and civilization. All good things, spiritual and worldly, which should be found in man, have been bestowed by the Almighty on Europe, and especially on England.[30]

The message of Sir Seyed to his fellow Muslims was to lay aside their old superstitions and bigotries. He argued that the Muslim way of life must be regenerated, and that this end could only be achieved through western education. Such a course was not contrary to the teachings of Islam, and Sir Seyed reminded his people of the Prophet's words, "Go even to the walls of China for the sake of learning." As a result of this reformer's efforts the Aligarh Anglo-Oriental College was founded in 1877. This institution was pro-British and was modeled after Oxford and Cambridge. The opening Prospectus declared its object was "to establish a College in which Musalmans may acquire an English education without prejudice to their religion." The college at Aligarh, later to become a university, became the heart of the Muslim reform movement, winning a considerable body of Sir Seyed Ahmad Khan's community to western education and ideas.

From the very inception of the National Congress Sir Seyed perceived in it a potential danger to the Muslims. He was bitterly opposed to the extension of the representative principle because he saw in it the device which would relegate the Muslims into the status of a permanent minority. In 1883 Sir Seyed made this quite clear when he said:

For socio-political purposes the whole of the population of England forms but one community. It is obvious that the same cannot be said of India. The system of representation by election means the representation of the views and interests of the majority of the population, and in countries where the population is composed of one race and one creed, it is, no

doubt, the best system that can be adopted. But in a country like India, where caste distinctions still flourish, where there is no fusion of the various races, where religious distinctions are still violent, where education in its modern sense has not made an equal or proportionate progress among all sections of the population . . . the system of election, pure and simple, cannot safely be adopted. The larger community would totally override the interests of the smaller community.[31]

If Sir Seyed was concerned about the ultimate results of the program outlined by the Indian liberals who initiated the Congress movement, he was, with his followers, more and more alarmed over the Hindu bias of the new wave of nationalism that obtained its inspiration from Vivekananda and Saraswati. And in the late 1890's, as we will note shortly, new militant nationalists, such as B. G. Tilak, sponsored "cow protection societies" definitely aimed against the Muslims. Tilak referred to the Muslims as foreigners and glorified the famous Hindu patriot, Sivaji, for his exploits in the seventeenth century against Muslim oppressors. As a result of Sir Seyed Ahmad Khan's influence, the Muslims had little to do with the National Congress. In 1885 only two Muslim delegates attended the first meeting of Congress; the next year there were 33 out of a total attendance of 440; in 1890 there were 156 Muslims out of a total of 702. After this date there was a rapid decline, and in 1905 only 17 Muslim delegates attended out of a Congress membership of 756.

In 1906, the Muslims launched their own All-India Muslim League, mainly through the activities of the Aga Khan and the two brothers, Mohammed and Shaukat Ali, who had assumed the direction of the Muslim movement after the death of Sir Seyed Ahmad Khan. The first meeting of the League was held at Dacca; in 1907 it met at Karachi and in 1908 at Aligarh.

Much has been written to the effect that it was the British authorities who originated this artificial Muslim-Hindu dichotomy in Indian politics. Undoubtedly, when its existence was presented to them, the British understandably welcomed the Muslim League as a make-weight against the Congress. In this stage of Muslim-Hindu relations the dominant factor was not the policy of the British government but rather the Hindu bias of the Congress movement. This fact is supported by the statement of R. P. Dutt, who wrote:

30- Quoted in Raja Rao and Iqbal Singh, ed., Changing India (London: George Allen and Unwin, 1939), pp. 51-52.

31- From "Proceedings of the Council of the Governor-General of India, 1883," quoted in Coupland, India: A Restatement, p. 93.

The insistence on orthodox religion as the heart of the national movement, and the proclamation of the supposed spiritual superiority of the ancient Hindu civilization to modern "Western" civilization . . . inevitably retarded and weakened the real advance of the national movement and of political consciousness, while the emphasis on Hinduism must bear a share of the responsibility for the alienation of wide sections of Moslem opinion from the national movement. . . .[32]

The same author went on to say that it was the militant Indian national leaders who "sought to build on a basis of Hindu religion for their agitation and to identify the national awakening with a revival of Hinduism. By this act they cut off the Moslem masses from the national movement and opened the way to the Government's astute counter-move with the formation of the Moslem League in 1906."[33] Rather than the British officials, it was the Indians themselves who held the initiative, when the situation was still fluid in the formative period of Indian nationalism, in determining the nature of the movement. While recourse to religion, that is, Hinduism, is understandable, it is apparent that the Hindu leaders did not appreciate the implications of transforming the nationalist movement from a purely secular to a politico-religious one. And, when there was the inevitable Muslim reaction, most members of the Congress made a serious error in refusing to admit the existence and validity of Muslim nationalism.

Lord Curzon and the End of an Epoch

There was a basic change in the Indian situation after 1890. The epoch of complacency on the part of the British bureaucracy came to a slow end, and, at the same time, the heretofore liberal and constitutional Indian nationalist movement was challenged by a militant wing of nationalists who sought their inspiration in the ancient Vedas rather than in European thought and who condoned and even supported the use of violence in attaining their ends.

By 1895 what came to be known as "the Indian problem" had emerged. The stars in their courses seemed to conspire against British authority in India as plague, drought, famine, unrest along the North-West Frontier, and political terrorism descended on the land. "The Government of India," two British historians wrote, "never regained the aloofness, conscious rectitude, and con-

fidence of the 'eighties and early 'nineties."[34] It was ironic that this revolutionary change should have coincided with the Viceroyalty of Lord Curzon (1899-1905), who was an ardent believer in British imperialism and the classic prototype of an English proconsul.

The transformation to militant nationalism was mainly the work of Bal Gangadhar Tilak (1856-1920), who is referred to by British historians as the "father of Indian unrest." Tilak came from the Mahratta country, where his father was a school inspector at Poona. An excellent student, Tilak not only received a good western education but seriously studied both Sanskrit and Marathi. At the age of twenty he received a college degree with honors and until 1890 taught law at Ferguson College, which he had helped to establish.

In 1880 Tilak began the publication of two newspapers, one in English and one, the *Kesari* (the *Lion*), in the vernacular. Becoming editor of these publications in 1890, he at once initiated a campaign of militant nationalism. The secular counterpart of Saraswati and Vivekananda, Tilak stoutly defended Hindu orthodoxy. In 1890, for example, he entered politics by roundly condemning the Age of Consent Bill, by which the government hoped to lessen the evil of child marriage. To Tilak everything indigenous was sacred. A fierce opponent of western culture, he denounced the Brahma Samaj and had little use for moderates, like Gokhale, who admired European institutions. Tilak sought to resurrect what he believed was the former martial prowess and manliness of a past Hindu age, symbolized by the courage of the great Mahratta leader Sivaji, who had assassinated a Muslim general. Gymnastic societies were founded by Tilak, especially from the ranks of college students. Sivaji was revered as a great hero, and festivals were held in honor of Ganesh, the elephant-headed god of the Hindus. Tilak's nationalism was exclusively Hindu and in this connection he founded a Cow Protection Society that was aimed against the Muslims.

In June 1897 Tilak in his *Kesari* justified the use of force in defense of national ideals and used Sivaji's deed as an example. Shortly afterwards two British officials who had been active in plague-prevention measures, such as the disinfection and evacuation of houses, were murdered by youthful nationalists. As Tilak had accused the Plague Commissioner and his assist-

32- *Quoted in Desai, op. cit., p. 303.*

33- *Quoted in* ibid., *p. 304.*

34- *Thompson and Garratt, op. cit., p. 527.*

ants of tyranny in carrying out their prevention measures, he was sentenced to prison for one year.

While Tilak was beating the drums of militant nationalism, other factors were helping to strengthen his cause. There is little doubt that the India Councils Act, passed in 1892, disappointed many moderate nationalists. It was too cautious an advance toward representative government, and one wonders what might have been the course of politics in India had British statesmen been more courageous in their constitutional reforms.

Famine and plague in the 1890's caused much suffering and added to the general sense of grievance in India. Plague was first detected in Bombay in 1896, and within two years the recorded deaths from this scourge reached 173,000. The monsoon was deficient in 1895 and almost failed in 1896, and the rains failed again in 1899. This brought about the worst drought in two hundred years. The total area affected was 475,000 square miles with a population of 60 millions. Six million people were placed on government relief and 25 million dollars were spent in relief measures. Despite all this, the death toll was tremendous.

Outside of India the trend of events also worked to strengthen the cause of nationalism. Heretofore, European supremacy had been unchallenged. At the end of the nineteenth century, however, a number of happenings seemed to indicate that this uncontested leadership was waning. In 1896 an Italian army was completely defeated in Abyssinia by the African warriors of King Menelik. The Indians were also amazed at the stout resistance of the Boer farmers, as they inflicted resounding defeats upon the best soldiers Britain could send to South Africa. While ultimately victorious, British arms lost much of their luster in the Boer War (1899-1902). Above all, the rise of Japan electrified the Indian nationalists, who in 1905 witnessed this Asiatic power, so small compared to her opponent, defeat the Russian Empire, which had so long been described by British officials as a dread and powerful foe of their Empire. Describing the effect of the Japanese victory, Mr. C. F. Andrews wrote:

A stir of excitement passed over the North of India. Even the remote villages talked over the victories of Japan as they sat in their circles and passed round the *huqqa* at night. A Turkish consul of long experience in Western Asia told me "that in the interior you could see everywhere the most ignorant peasants tingling with the news." Asia was moved from one end to the other, and the sleep of the centuries was finally broken.[35]

The slogan of "Asia for the Asiatics" now became the rallying cry of young nationalists in China, Burma, and the Dutch East Indies as well as in India.

It was an unkind trick of fate from the British point of view that the period which witnessed such an increase in nationalistic fervor should also coincide with the viceroyalty of Lord Curzon, who—while desiring to rule the country with what he considered to be the best traditions of enlightened bureaucratic despotism—would brook no criticism of his policies and had little regard for the likes or dislikes of his Indian subjects. His one aim was to rule India efficiently, and he felt that the government of India, of which he was the head, was alone qualified to decide how best this should be done.

No Viceroy had ever been so well prepared for his duties. A product of Eton and of Balliol College, Oxford, he had been elected to the House of Commons in 1886; he had been appointed Undersecretary of State for India in 1891 and Undersecretary for Foreign Affairs in 1895. At the same time he was an inveterate traveler, and during the period 1883 to 1895, with the exception of one year, he visited some foreign country annually. Persia, Central Asia, India, and the Far East were of greatest interest to him. Before he was made Viceroy in 1899 he had visited India four times and was personally acquainted with such rulers as the Amir of Afghanistan, the Shah of Persia, the Emperor of Annam, and most of the Indian princes. In addition to his travels, Curzon had written several scholarly books on such subjects as Persia, Japan and Korea, and Russia in Central Asia; furthermore, he had received the gold medal of the Royal Geographical Society for discovering the source of the Oxus River.

As for the character of Curzon, this indefatigable student and globe trotter was thoroughly honest and unusually hard-working and competent. He was also, be it said, completely convinced of his own unusual powers, and one member of the House of Commons once remarked, "When I say that Mr. Curzon is about one-tenth as clever as he thinks himself I am paying him a very high compliment indeed."[36] Closely tied in with this

35- *Quoted in Fuller, op. cit., p. 91.*

36- *Quoted in Lord Ronaldshay, The Life of Lord Curzon (London: Benn and Co., 1928), I, p. 187.*

self-confidence, which some might label simple egotism, was a certain aloofness and hauteur that seriously detracted from his other great qualities.

Immediately upon his arrival in India, Curzon set about with feverish energy to tackle the country's problems. It is difficult to catalog all of his activities or credit him with all of his achievements. He strove to make the land revenue system more elastic and equitable and to protect the peasant from the moneylender. He initiated rural banks and the system of cooperative credit for the farmers. Under his direction the agricultural department was reorganized and scientific research undertaken. Fresh impetus was given to railroad building and to irrigation projects. An ardent student of Indian history and a keen admirer of her ancient culture and monuments, Curzon was instrumental in passing the Ancient Monuments Act of 1904. No man has done more to preserve and also to unearth the precious relics of early India. He also introduced a new policy along the North-West Frontier, and waged an energetic foreign policy in defense of British imperial interests in the Persian Gulf, Tibet, and Central Asia.

In the early years of his Viceroyalty Curzon was popular with the Indian people. On several occasions he took severe measures against British soldiers who had abused Indians yet had been protected by army authorities. After three years, however, his popularity waned; then it completely disappeared and was superseded by hostility and even hatred. Curzon's fundamental lack of sympathy with Indian aspirations alienated even the moderate leaders like Gokhale. "The Congress," wrote the Viceroy, "is tottering to its fall, and one of my great ambitions while in India is to assist it to a peaceful demise."[37]

While failing to appreciate the growing national sentiment, Curzon also initiated two reforms that did more to arouse hostility and misunderstanding against the British regime in India than perhaps any act of a previous Viceroy. The first measure concerned the reform of education, which was in an unsatisfactory condition. While elementary education was neglected, the universities were overcrowded. Bengal had as many college students as Great Britain with perhaps one-tenth of the opportunities for employment. In many educational institutions the discipline was poor and the teachers inefficient, and the main effort was in drilling the students to pass examinations. Of these institutions

Curzon wrote that they constituted "a huge system of active but often misdirected effort, over which, like some evil phantom, seemed to hover the monstrous and maleficent spirit of Cram."[38] After two years of investigation the Universities Act of 1904 was passed. By this Act, which sought to eliminate the more serious abuses, government control was made much more effective and the examination system was revised.

The Act kindled the wrath of Indian leaders, who saw in it the desire of the government to curb and even throttle higher education; an Indian observer wrote of the *Report* of the Universities Commission upon which the Act was based that it "convulsed educated India from one end of the country to another."[39] While this reform was justified from many angles, it had been imposed in such a fashion as to infuriate the very people whom it was designed to benefit.

The second Curzon measure to intensify Indian nationalism was the partition of Bengal. This province covered a huge area of 189,000 square miles with a population of 78 million. Because of this huge mass of people the provincial administration was overburdened, and, in particular, the area of the province east of the Ganges was neglected. While Indian writers usually saddle Curzon with all the responsibility for the partition measure, in reality the Viceroy himself did not originate it. For more than one year the partition was discussed by various officials without Curzon's knowledge. Finally, the file of correspondence reached the Viceroy. In commenting upon the cumbersome methods of the British bureaucratic machine in India, and upon this episode in particular, Curzon, in a much-quoted memorandum, sardonically wrote:

Departmentalism is not a moral delinquency. It is an intellectual hiatus—the complete absence of thought or apprehension of anything outside the purely departmental aspects of the matter under discussion. For fourteen months it never occurred to a single human being in the department to mention the matter, or to suggest that it should be mentioned. Round and round like the diurnal revolution of the earth went the file, stately, solemn, sure, and slow; and now, in due season, it has completed its orbit, and I am invited to register the concluding stage.[40]

Having once studied the partition proposal, Curzon was completely convinced of its worth. It would lighten the burden of administration in

37- Lord Ronaldshay, The Life of Lord Curzon, II, p. 33.

38- Quoted in O'Malley, op. cit., p. 167.

39- Banerjea, op. cit., p. 175.

40- Quoted in A. Lovat Fraser, India Under Curzon and After (London: William Heinemann, Ltd., 1911), pp. 378-379.

West Bengal, would help to rectify the previous neglect of East Bengal, and would give Assam a much-needed seaport. The partition was administratively justified, and that was sufficient for the Viceroy, who could not appreciate the fact that Bengal more than any other section of India had developed a local patriotism. Here the Hindu Renaissance of which we have already spoken had been particularly active, not only in a religious revival, but in the development of a rich literature using the Bengali language as the medium of expression. The Hindu Bengalis thought of themselves as one nation, and many interpreted the proposed partition as a British plot to enfeeble their nationalistic movement. There were other motives, too, less ingenuous. Lawyers in Calcutta feared the competition of the new law courts to be set up in Dacca, and businessmen also disliked the prospect of competition from new enterprises that might spring up in the new province.

Despite widespread opposition among the Hindus of Bengal—not the Muslims—the scheme was passed in June 1905. East Bengal was created a province inhabited by eighteen million Muslims and twelve million Hindus and with a new capital at Dacca, while the new West Bengal contained forty-two million Hindus and twelve million Muslims with the capital at Calcutta. After the passage of this partition act Hindu resentment reached unprecedented heights. On August 7, 1905, a vast multitude congregated in Calcutta to protest against the partition. An annual day of mourning was planned, and at the same time the Swadeshi movement, a boycott against English goods and later to be such a feature of Gandhi's program, was initiated for the first time. The vernacular press created a wide feeling of emotional excitement among the public. A feature of the rising nationalistic fervor was the resurrection of an old folk song, *Bande Mataram (Hail to thee, My Mother)* "as the Marseillaise that was to carry young Bengal to the storming of the British Bastile."[41]

While anti-partition agitation raged, Curzon resigned following a disagreement with Lord Kitchener, the military commander-in-chief in India. In spite of his herculean efforts, Curzon was a failure in India because, with all his many accomplishments, he failed in the most important task—the true appreciation of the temper of the Indian people.

Lovat Fraser, one of Lord Curzon's biographers, argues the point that the rapid advance of intransigent nationalism during his term of office was basically the result of world-wide forces beyond his control and as such could have been little altered, no matter what policies the Viceroy followed. Fraser writes:

. . . unrest and its accompaniment of violence would have appeared in India at this juncture, and would have spread with almost as much incendiary rapidity, if the universities had been left alone, if Bengal had remained one and indivisible, if indeed Lord Curzon had never been born. The times were ripe for it; all Asia was astir; and it was only a chronological coincidence which led short-sighted observers to attribute its appearance to an educational reform and a rearrangement of administrative boundaries . . .[42]

There is much to be said for this view, but it would seem unduly to minimize the influence that can be wielded by dominant personalities upon the historical trends of their times. The Indian national movement might have been something different from what it was in the first decade of the twentieth century had Curzon been more sympathetic and tactful. Rabindranath Tagore has said the last word about this Viceroy's efficient and impersonal administration when, likening it to the claim of a new-fangled bakery in Calcutta, he declared it was "untouched by hand."[43]

Bombs and Boons, 1905 to 1914

As Lord Curzon departed, he left behind him an indignant and vociferous national movement that demanded more self-government than that afforded by the cautious constitutional reform of 1892. Lord Minto, the new Governor-General who arrived in India in November 1905, soon admitted, "The Government of India cannot shut our eyes to present conditions. The political atmosphere is full of change; questions are before us which we cannot afford to ignore, and which we must attempt to answer."[44]

For some time the moderate leaders of the National Congress had been dissatisfied at the lack of response of the British government to their suggestions for a constitutional advance. Various schemes had been offered, such as the one in 1895 proposing the inclusion of six Indian representatives in the House of Commons so that this body could be kept informed of Indian public opinion.

41- Chirol, op. cit., p. 118.

42- Fraser, op. cit., pp. 32-33.

43- Quoted in H. C. E. Zacharias, Renascent India (London: George Allen and Unwin, 1933), p. 132.

44- Report on Indian Constitutional Reforms (The Montagu-Chelmsford Report), Cd. 9109 (London: His Majesty's Stationery Office, 1918), p. 63.

In 1905 the National Congress adopted a more uncompromising tone. Referring to the partition of Bengal, the moderate leader Gokhale indicted the government for "its utter contempt of public opinion, its reckless disregard of the most cherished feelings of the people."[45] And for the first time the Congress came out for self-government (*swaraj*) in a form similar to that existing in the self-governing colonies of the British Empire, such as Canada.

While the tone of moderate nationalists was hardening, Bengal had become the center of a militant movement elements of which were quite ready to use violence to achieve their ends. Getting under way in 1902, and strongly influenced by the tactics of Tilak in Bombay, the extremists (that is, the wing of the national movement whose ideas were "extreme" compared to those of the moderates) borrowed many techniques and objectives from abroad. They studied the use of the boycott by the Irish nationalists, and the operations of the Nihilists in Russia were carefully followed. At the same time, the story of the Italian *Risorgimento* and the work of Louis Kossuth in Hungary were studied. Turning to America's past, the extremists borrowed the term "War of Independence."

This Bengal movement was suffused with religion. Indian nationalism was personified in the form of a goddess. B. C. Chatterji, in a famous novel written in 1882, had interpreted the motherland by using the goddess Kali as a national symbol. This Black Goddess was the deity of destruction and death, and was worshiped as the symbol of creative power by her monks, who sang the sacred hymn *Bande Mataram* in a temple near Calcutta (from "Kalighat"). Kali now became the religious token for Bengali nationalism. The ultra-nationalist newspaper, *Yugantar (New Era)*, advocated that young men be trained in secret bands, that weapons be made, and that money for the cause be obtained by any method. In one of its issues of May 1908, this paper declared, "The mother is thirsty and is pointing out to her sons the only thing that can quench that thirst. Nothing less than human blood and decapitated heads will satisfy her . . ."[46]

The party of direct action in Bengal first inaugurated a policy of terrorism through the use of bombs in 1906. On December 6, 1907, a train carrying the Lieutenant-Governor of Bengal was bombed and derailed. The first bombs used were not very effective, and the revolutionary party sent one of its number to Paris to learn the intricacies of bomb making. Returning in 1908, this post-graduate in explosives helped to set up a bomb factory in the suburbs of Calcutta. Several serious outrages followed. In one of these a bomb was thrown into the wrong carriage, and two Englishwomen were killed. A few days later the bomb factory was raided and a large number of suspects arrested. The desperate nature of violent nationalism in Bengal is seen in the reprisals inflicted upon persons connected with this case. A member of the group who turned informer was shot in prison; later an Indian police officer was killed in the streets of Calcutta, and another who had taken a prominent role in investigating the case was actually shot and killed in the High Court of Calcutta.

While popular unrest, of both a constitutional and a terroristic nature, was mounting in Bengal, the same phenomenon appeared in the Punjab. Sporadic violence broke out, numerous arrests were made, and two leaders—Lala Lajpat Rai and Ajit Singh—were deported. The former was one of the most influential nationalists in India at this time. He was an ardent member of the militant Arya Samaj and helped found the important Anglo-Vedic College at Lahore. Lajpat Rai went to the United States just before the First World War, and while there carried on ceaseless work for the cause of Indian freedom and wrote the important work *Young India*. He was the author of many books and exerted tremendous influence because of his attainments as an orator and an author and because of his simple, austere life.

It is interesting that much of the pre-1914 revolutionary movement in India and many of the instances of terrorism were stimulated and directed from centers outside the country, notably in London, Paris, and San Francisco. A group of enthusiastic young nationalists was established at "India House" in London in 1905 and carried on active propaganda in the newspaper, the *Indian Sociologist*. The intrigues of India House unfortunately culminated in the outrage of July 1, 1909, when one of its members slipped into a gala reception being held at the Imperial Institute and shot to death Dr. Lalkaka and Sir William Curzon Wyllie. The latter had been an official at the India Office and had been active in the welfare of young Indian students in London.

5- Report of the Twenty-first Indian National Congress, *1906*, . 8.

Quoted in Cumming, ed., litical India, pp. 228-229.

There were other foreign centers of undercover movements, notably San Francisco and Paris. The former will be discussed in connection with World War I in the following chapter when the famous Ghadr Conspiracy will be related. In Paris the schemes of a nationalistic group were under the direction of Madame Cama, a Parsi who edited the paper *Bande Mataram*. This group assisted in smuggling arms into India before the First World War.

While the extremist wing of the Indian national movement was becoming active, and in Bengal alone, between 1906 and 1917, was responsible for 168 outrages which took the lives of 61 persons, the moderates led by Gokhale denounced terrorism and believed in resort only to constitutional methods. Denouncing the extremist faction, Gokhale declared its aim was "to stir up disorder and have recourse to every practicable form of violence because it regards any disorder or misery, or even anarchy itself, as preferable to the presence of the foreigner in the land."[47]

The alarming growth of terrorism and the rising dissatisfaction of even the moderate majority in the National Congress convinced the British government that some advance would have to be made to satisfy Indian national aspirations. The time was propitious, because at the end of 1905 in Britain the Conservative party had fallen from power and had been succeeded by a Liberal Cabinet much more inclined to be sympathetic to the cause of Indian reform. Visiting London at the end of 1905, representatives of the Congress reported that "narrow and aggressive imperialism" was declining and that the new Liberal government was definitely friendly. In particular Indian nationalists expected much from the Liberals because of their new Secretary of State for India, John Morley. Famous as a historian and the biographer of William Gladstone, editor of the *Fortnightly Review,* a lifelong liberal and champion of freedom, Lord Morley was looked to by India with hope and expectancy as a British official who would be likely to concede a generous advance in the direction of self-government.

Between the years 1907 and 1909, therefore, Morley and the Governor-General in India, Lord Minto, sought to satisfy the growing demands of Indian nationalism by liberalizing what had been up to this time an almost completely bureaucratic system of government. In 1907 two Indian representatives were appointed to the advisory India Council in London. During this same year Lord Minto canvassed many sections of public opinion in India to determine views on constitutional reform. The Muslim community made it plain that they feared the introduction of the representative principle, which could only mean their relegation to the position of a permanent and impotent minority. The Muslims pointed out that heretofore in one area, the United Provinces, with 14 per cent of the population, they had not secured a single representative in the Provincial Council.

On November 1, 1908, the fiftieth anniversary of the assumption of direct responsibility for the government of India by the British Crown, a message from the King-Emperor to the people of India announced the extension of representative government. The details of the new scheme, commonly known as the Morley-Minto Reforms, were made known shortly afterwards and were enacted into law in 1909 by the British Parliament.

The Indian Councils Act increased the membership of the provincial legislative councils and also provided for a majority of non-official members in contrast to the official members, who represented and were nominated by the British government and who, in turn, were bound to support its decisions and measures on all occasions. Election to these Provincial Councils was voted by certain bodies, such as district and municipal boards, landowners, chambers of commerce, universities, and the Muslim community. Voters representing these agencies were very few, the largest constituency numbering less than seven hundred. In the central legislature the membership was raised to sixty, twenty-seven of whom were elected—seven by landowners, five by Muslims, two by chambers of commerce, and the remainder by legislatures in the provinces. Another important feature of the Morley-Minto Reforms was the appointment of an Indian member to the Executive Council of the governors in both Bombay and Madras and, most important, to the Executive Council of the Viceroy. For the first time an Indian had been admitted to the inner sanctum of the Central Government of India where fundamental decisions were made and policies discussed.

The Indian members of the new Councils were given much greater latitude in criticizing the policies of the government. On all matters of

47- *Quoted in O'Malley,* op. cit., *p. 96.*

public interest—save those affecting the Native States—discussion was allowed and resolutions could be made.

A study of the Morley-Minto Reforms makes it apparent that they in no sense introduced responsible government into India. In the last analysis, even where an unofficial majority existed, as in the Provincial Councils, the British Governor was fully prepared to override any opposition. In essence, therefore, in the words of a famous British report on Indian affairs, "They [the reforms] were based on the fundamental principle that the executive government should retain the final decision on all questions, although some degree of popular control over legislation was established in the provinces by providing small non-official majorities."[48] The desire of the British government to introduce an element of representative government while, at the same time, maintaining complete control over all policy made the reforms a contradiction within themselves. They attempted to blend the past autocracy of traditional Hindu monarchy and that of the Mogul emperors with the representative principle derived from Great Britain. The result was a kind of "constitutional autocracy."

The most controversial feature of the reforms was that providing communal electorates for the Muslim community. By this feature the Muslims were guaranteed a certain number of seats in the new Councils, and these representatives could be elected only by voters on the Muslim Communal Roll. Furthermore, Muslim representation was weighted, that is, their numbers were in excess of those that would be computed if only the exact proportion of Muslims to the entire Indian community was taken into consideration. Apparently Lord Morley was against the idea of separate electorates for the Muslims, but reluctantly gave up his opposition after hearing the arguments of a deputation sent to England by the Muslim League. It is also asserted by the Muslims that the eminent Hindu nationalist, Gokhale, supported their claim. Mohammed Ali Jinnah, the leader of Muslim separatism in the 1930's and 1940's and founder of Pakistan, maintained in one of his speeches that in 1907 Gokhale had declared:

Confronted by an overwhelming Hindu majority, Muslims are naturally afraid that release from the British yoke might in their case mean enslavement to the Hindus. Were the Hindus similarly situated as

are the Muslims in regard to numbers . . . we would undoubtedly have felt the same fear and adopted the identical policy which the Muslims are adopting to-day.[49]

When the Muslim-Hindu feud began to mount to serious proportions in the late 1920's, most Hindu publicists took the view that the gulf between the two communities was a result of British *divide et impera* technique initiated by the foreign ruler in 1909 with the policy of Communal Electorates. British authorities indignantly deny this charge, maintaining that the policy of separate electorates for the Muslim community was only the expression in the field of government of the fundamental facts already existing in the socio-religious sphere. On this whole moot question, Mohammed Ali, a prominent Muslim leader, declared: "It is the old maxim of 'divide and rule' but there is a division of labour here. We divide and you rule."[50]

During the gestation and enactment of the Morley-Minto Reforms, important events had been taking place in the National Congress. In its annual meeting in 1906 at Calcutta, the left-wing group led by Tilak, forming what we might think of as the New Party, clashed headlong and bitterly with the Moderates led by Gokhale. Some semblance of harmony was retained only through the mediating efforts of the venerable leader, Dadabhai Naoroji, India's "Grand Old Man." The showdown occurred the following year when the National Congress convened at Surat. The left-wing element tried to secure the presidency for Lala Lajpat Rai, the Punjab nationalist leader recently deported by the government. When a motion of Tilak's, designed to pave the way for this result, was declared out of order by the presiding officer, delegates swinging *lathis* (i.e., weighted clubs) stormed the platform and the meeting broke up in a riot. An eyewitness who was present has described the scene for us:

Chairs flew through the air, like shells discharged at a venture. Long sticks clashed and shivered. Blood flowed from broken heads. It was a confused and difficult conflict—ten thousand men crowded together among ten thousand chairs; no uniform, no distinction, nothing to mark off Extremist from Moderate except the facial expression of temperament.[51]

The following day the Moderates met and a new constitution for the Congress was drawn up. Ar-

48- Report on Indian Constitutional Reforms, *Cd. 9109, p. 7.*

49- Jamil-ud-Din Ahmad, ed., *Some Recent Speeches . . . of Mr. Jinnah (Lahore, Pakistan: Muhammad Ashraf, 1943), I, p. 455-456.*

- Quoted in Sir Reginald Coupland, The Indian Problem (London: Oxford University Press, 1944) Part I, 36.*

- Quoted in Edward Thompson, Reconstructing India New York: The Dial Press, 30), p. 97.*

ticle 1 of this document called for a system of government for India similar to that existing in the self-governing members of the British Empire, such as Canada, and declared that this object was to be achieved by constitutional means through the process of steady reform. As for the Extremists, they remained outside the fold of Congress, a faction without much following until 1916.

Following the announcement of the Morley-Minto Reforms, Congress, dominated in 1908 by the Moderates, expressed "its deep and general satisfaction at the Reform proposals." Gokhale and his followers, however, had hoped for more than had been received from Lord Morley, who had not lived up to his reputation as a progressive liberal. Nevertheless, Congress accepted the Reforms while hoping for further advances in the not too distant future.

Between 1910 and 1914 a more tranquil spirit seemed to pervade the Indian political atmosphere. For one thing, the more militant extremists were either imprisoned or deported, and the government passed new acts controlling seditious meetings, the purchase of explosives, and the use of the press, all of which restricted the more militant variety of nationalism. In 1911 the British government decided to "play the king and take the trick." For the first time the King and Queen, George V and Mary, were crowned in a Grand Durbar at Delhi. This ceremony, with its pomp and circumstance, sought to strengthen the ties between the British Crown and the Indian people. Under a resplendent canopy surrounded by Native Princes and with a great concourse of India's crack regiments, the King-Emperor in a royal message announced the imminence of a number of boons for his Indian subjects. As later announced by the Governor-General, these included: (1) the annulment of the unpopular partition of Bengal, a gesture to Hindu sentiment; (2) transfer of the capital of India from Calcutta to the ancient seat of Mogul power at Delhi, a concession to Muslim feeling; (3) the release of certain political prisoners; and (4) the setting aside of a substantial sum of money for the advancement of education.

Despite these coronation boons and the Morley-Minto Reforms, political extremism continued to exist as an undercover movement. In December 1912, Lord Hardinge, the Viceroy, was seriously wounded by a bomb while making a state entrance into Delhi. And scattered incidents of violence occurred in various parts of the country.

The National Congress, however, controlled by such Moderates as Gokhale, Malaviya, Mehta, and S. Banerjea, was convinced that constitutional and evolutionary methods formed the only appropriate path leading to self-government for Indians to take. In a famous speech delivered at Poona in July 1909, Gokhale summed up the philosophy of the Indian Moderate's creed, declaring:

Our public life was based on frank and loyal acceptance of British rule, due to a recognition of the fact that it alone could secure to the country the peace and order which were necessary for slowly evolving a nation out of the heterogeneous elements of which India was composed. . . . We have to realise that British rule, in spite of its inevitable drawbacks as a foreign rule, has been on the whole a great instrument of progress for our people. Its continuance means the continuance of that peace and order which it alone can maintain. . . . Our rulers stand pledged to extend to us equality of treatment with themselves. This equality is to be sought in two fields: equality for individual Indians with individual Englishmen and equality in regard to the form of government which Englishmen enjoy in other parts of the Empire.[52]

Jawaharlal Nehru in his autobiography, *Toward Freedom,* has no word of praise for Gokhale and the dominance of the Moderates in the national movement. In 1912 Nehru attended the National Congress meeting in which Gokhale was the outstanding leader, and he described it as very much "an English-knowing upper-class affair where morning coats and well-pressed trousers were greatly in evidence." As to politics, Nehru found them very boring and wrote, "Toward the end of 1912 India was, politically, very dull. Tilak was in jail, the Extremists had been sat upon and were lying low without any effective leadership."[53]

With the year 1914, the first great phase in the history of modern Indian nationalism was coming to an end. The new sense of the unity of India and the desire for representative institutions had come, as we have seen, mainly from the impact of the west through the medium of British rule. During the period from 1880 to 1914 both the Hindu and Muslim communities had experienced a revival comparable to the *Risorgimento* in nineteenth-century Italy. While this new nationalism expressed itself in certain quarters by acts of violence, in the main it was a constitutional movement guided by Moderates who were essentially

52- *Quoted in* Cambridge History of the British Empire, V *(Cambridge: Cambridge University Press, 1932), pp. 557-558.*

53- *Jawaharlal Nehru,* Toward Freedom *(New York: John Day Co., 1942), p. 39.*

nineteenth-century liberals who admired British institutions and had faith in British intentions.

In the quarter of a century since its establishment in 1885, the National Congress had grown until its membership covered all parts of British India. It was, however, almost exclusively a middle-class movement dominated by lawyers, journalists, and merchants, who were concerned only with political freedom and had little appreciation of the economic misery of the masses. These politically ambitious members of the Indian bourgeoisie conducted their proceedings in English and sprinkled their speeches with references to Magna Carta, Milton, Gibbon, Spencer, and Darwin. Congress before 1914 was definitely a minority urban movement. The great masses of people were little affected by its gospel except when some specific and tangible grievance—as the partition of Bengal—could be exploited and dramatized. Congress did not become a mass movement until after World War I and the appearance of Mohandas K. Gandhi.

Not long after Big Ben, the Empire's symbolic timepiece in London, had struck midnight on August 4, 1914, and given notice that a state of war existed between Great Britain and Germany, many eyes were turned in the direction of India. Now that Britain and her Empire were engaged in a desperate struggle, what would be the course of events in this great dependency? Would India, especially its more militant and revolutionary nationalists, see in 1914 a golden opportunity to throw off the yoke of the British raj?

SUCH A course had been predicted by many writers, mainly German, such as Count von Reventlow and the Prussian general and military author, Friedrich von Bernhardi. The newspaper Berliner Tageblatt *in March 1914 discussed in detail the various secret subversive organizations in India and explained how they were being directed by radical leaders outside the country, particularly in California.*

THIS CHAPTER will describe various German-inspired plots against British rule in India, showing how they were foiled and how the great bulk of Indians supported the Allied cause. We will see that Indian troops fought in many theaters all over the world, in Europe, the Near East, Africa, and in Asia. Even more important than the military repercussions was the impact of the war upon Indian nationalism. Aspirations for self-government were accelerated, but, unfortunately, Britain did not appreciate the strength of the new nationalism. Out of this failure plus the frustrations and tensions of the postwar period, when the Indian masses felt the shock of high prices, scarcity of goods, and the ravages of a deadly epidemic, there emerged the figure of Mohandas K. Gandhi, the leader who was to take his people into their promised land and who was to dominate the course of Indian politics for three decades.

World War and the advent

of the Mahatma

chapter 6

1- India and the War, *a collection of documents, introduction by Lord Sydenham (London: Hodder and Stoughton, 1915), pp. 51-52.*

2- *Ibid., p. 56.*

WHEN THE British Empire went to war against the Central Powers led by Germany, in August 1914, Britain feared and her foes hoped that a period of unprecedented turmoil and disorder would follow in India. To the world's astonishment, the Indian people—including moderate and extremist nationalists—in both British India and the states of the Indian princes immediately pledged their full support in the struggle against Germany. There were some revolutionary conspiracies and intrigues with German agents; but, considering the extent of the unrest of prewar days, these outbursts were few and were easily controlled. India remained loyal because the Moderates, still in control of the Congress, believed that self-government would soon be granted by Britain. Furthermore, there is little question that the invasion of Belgium by German armies shocked liberal opinion in India and led it to believe that Britain was defending the cause of justice. As for the Native Princes, their support of Britain came primarily from self-interest. These native potentates regarded Britain as the guardian of their thrones and as an ally to be assisted against its enemies, even in distant Europe.

Many of the Native Princes immediately volunteered for active duty. One, the Regent of Jodhpur, was seventy years of age, yet he insisted upon going with his young ward, the sixteen-year-old Maharaja, to the battle front in France. The twenty-seven larger Native States, which maintained forces known as the Imperial Service Troops, placed them at the disposal of the Indian government; and from twelve other states the Viceroy accepted contingents of infantry and cavalry. On September 9, 1914, the Secretary of State for India, speaking in the House of Commons, paid tribute to the loyalty and support of the Crown's Indian subjects. At this time mention was made of the gift of a hospital ship by a number of Princes; of the Maharaja of Mysore's gift of $1,600,000 to help defray the expenses of the Indian expeditionary force; of the large donations of horses and camels from many Princes; and of the little mountain state of Nepal placing all its troops at the government's disposal. Somewhat later came the gift of £400,000 from the Nizam of Hyderabad together with an offer to pay the entire expense of two of his regiments while they were fighting overseas.

In British India the Legislative Council, meeting in Simla on September 8, 1914, passed a resolution which expressed the members' "feelings of unswerving loyalty and enthusiastic devotion to the King-Emperor and an assurance of their unflinching support to the British Government. They desire at the same time to express the opinion that the people of India, in addition to the military assistance now being afforded by India to the Empire, would wish to share in the heavy financial burden now imposed on the United Kingdom."[1] Letters and telegrams pledging loyalty streamed into the offices of the provincial governments and were also received by the Viceroy.

Not to be outdone by the patriotic manifestations of the Indian Legislative Council and by the Princes of the Native States, the Indian press was almost unanimous in its declarations of support. The *Bengalee* declared:

We may have our differences with the Government —and what people have not?—but in the presence of a common enemy, be it Germany or any other power, we sink our differences, we forget our little quarrels and close our ranks, and offer all that we possess in defense of the Great Empire, to which we are all so proud to belong, and with which the future prosperity and advancement of our people are bound up.[2]

India was remote from the main theaters of the conflict, and her masses had little idea of what was taking place. The wildest rumors were spread. At night planets were mistaken for German airships; German battleships were reported off the coast; and the raids of the cruiser *Emden* in the Bay of Bengal, and especially its bombardment of Madras, created widespread alarm. There were also considerable disturbance of trade and fluctuation in prices in the first months of the war. Money became scarce and heavy withdrawals from the banks took place. After a few months, however, confidence returned, trade improved, and there was considerable expansion in industry.

From the standpoint of trained men, India in 1914 was far better prepared than any other part of the Empire. The Indian army was designed to take care of two responsibilities: defense of the frontier and the maintenance of internal order. In 1913, a committee appointed to study the status of the army officially reported that

. . . while India should provide for her own defense against local aggression and, if necessary, for an attack on the Indian Empire by a great power until reinforcements can come from home, she is not called upon to maintain troops for the specific purpose of placing them at the disposal of the Home Government for wars outside the Indian sphere.[3]

Notwithstanding this agreed policy, the situation in France in the early months of the war was so serious and the demand for reinforcements so urgent that the British government felt it had no alternative but to utilize the Indian army for service overseas. Therefore, in the early days of September 1914, within a few weeks after the outbreak of war, an expeditionary force was organized and sent from Bombay and Karachi. The country was practically denuded of troops. For a few weeks, before British territorial troops arrived to take the place of the departed regulars, there were only 15,000 British troops in all India. It was what one writer has called India's "rare chivalry" in not taking advantage of the Empire's danger that permitted the withdrawal of so many British regiments.[4]

The Indian expeditionary force sent to France under the command of General Sir James Willcocks consisted of 44,000 men from all parts of India in two divisions. These Indian divisions were hurriedly sent to Flanders, where they distinguished themselves in the first battle of Ypres. According to General Willcocks they "arrived in the very nick of time and took their place in the sadly reduced battle line."[5] During the difficult winter of 1914-1915 the Indian expeditionary force helped hold the Allied line in Flanders. The cold was intense and many of the troops, accustomed only to subtropical weather, suffered severely. The losses of the Indian Corps in France in killed, wounded, and prisoners were 34,250. Recognition for their services was generously given by Britain.

Apart from the invaluable aid of the Indian expeditionary force in France, in November 1914 a contingent from India was sent to German East Africa. During October and November two divisions of Indian infantry and one brigade of cavalry were sent to Egypt; and in November 1914 Indian troops assisted Japanese forces in capturing the great German fortress of Kiaochow on the Shantung peninsula, in China. It is estimated that, in the first few months of the First World War, 80,000 British and 210,000 Indian troops were sent overseas from India. Well might a German writer in *Der Tag* early in the war ruefully admit: "We have been mistaken in so many

of our calculations! We expected that the whole of India would revolt at the first sound of the guns in Europe; but, behold, thousands and tens of thousands of Indians are fighting with the British against us."[6]

Within a few months after the outbreak of war, in order to relieve the serious shortage of munitions, India from her own supplies furnished to England seventy million rounds of ammunition, sixty thousand modern rifles, and five hundred pieces of artillery. During the course of the First World War Indian troops fought in France, Belgium, Gallipoli, Salonika, Palestine, Egypt, the Cameroons, German East Africa, Persia, Kurdistan, North China, Mesopotamia, and the North-West Frontier in India.

Participation on so many fronts was made possible only by the strenuous mobilization of manpower in India. During the more than four years of the First World War, over 800,000 soldiers and more than 400,000 noncombatants were recruited. The greatest war effort was made by the province of the Punjab, the home of the Sikhs, which provided half of all the soldiers recruited in India. The war memorial arch at Delhi and monuments at Gallipoli, in Palestine, Persia, East Africa, and in France are reminders that more than 26,000 Indians were killed and 70,000 wounded in World War I. Commenting on this fact an English historian muses: ". . . it must be the first time in the world's history that so many thousands from a subject race willingly offered themselves, in a war dreadful beyond all precedent and to support a quarrel which was none of their bringing about and cannot have seemed any of their business."[7]

The invaluable service of the Indian people to Great Britain and the Allied cause did not end with the recruiting of thousands of men. Almost as significant was the achievement of supplying the Allied war effort with badly needed strategic materials and foodstuffs. In 1917 the Indian Munitions Board was established to develop local industries and to centralize their direction so that India could become, in large measure, the arsenal for the Allies in the Near East. This Board had under its direction munition works; the tanning of hides; the supply of railway track; the production of textiles, clothing, boots, tents, and jute goods; and the shipping of timber. Under its direction India contributed vast supplies of war material. The wolfram mines were developed until

3- Cambridge History of the British Empire, V (Cambridge: Cambridge University Press, 1932), p. 342.

4- H. N. Brailsford, "Indian Question," Encyclopedia of the Social Sciences, VII (New York: The Macmillan Company, 1932), p. 667.

5- "The Indian Army Corps in France," Blackwoods, CCII (July 1917), p. 8.

6- Quoted in A. L. Cross, A Shorter History of England and Greater Britain (3rd ed.; New York: The Macmillan Company, 1939), p. 798.

7- Edward Thompson, Reconstructing India (New York: The Dial Press, 1930), p. 116.

they produced one-third of the world's supply, and the Tata Iron and Steel Works, established a few years before the outbreak of war, supplied the steel rails so essential for the transport of troops and equipment in Mesopotamia, Egypt, Palestine, and East Africa. India's cotton and jute mills turned out enormous quantities of material, and immense supplies of petroleum, mica, rubber, and tea—to mention only a few commodities—were shipped abroad. It is estimated that the total value of materials exported overseas to troops dependent on India for supplies reached the sum of £34,408,000. Finally, India supplied the British wheat pool with some five million tons of this cereal.

The creation of large armies and the production of huge quantities of war materials obviously necessitate the expenditure of large sums of money. India, therefore, made heavy financial sacrifices during the war years. The government was compelled to raise a great deal of money in spite of the fact that India is a relatively poor country and cannot stand a high rate of taxation. Normally, when Indian troops served abroad, it was understood that the British imperial exchequer would defray their expenses; but during the First World War, at the suggestion of the Indian government, India undertook to pay the cost of maintaining her troops regardless of the place of service. This obligation cost between twenty and thirty million pounds sterling a year at a time when the total revenue of the central government was only £100,000,000. In September 1918 it was voted in the Indian Legislative Council that India would defray the cost of an additional 100,000 troops. India's greatest single financial contribution was a free gift of £100,000,000, a sum that added 30 per cent to its national debt. As a result of these extraordinary financial efforts, India experienced grave difficulties with its currency system, which in 1917-1918 nearly collapsed. Even when India sold goods to Great Britain, it had to act as the latter's banker. Although payment was made in London, owing to the difficulty of transferring funds to Delhi, payment had first to be made in India. This placed a staggering burden upon the monetary reserves of the country.

Wartime Plots and Conspiracies

It must not be thought, of course, that India was perfectly tranquil under British rule during the period 1914-1918. Naturally, attempts were made by German agents to enlist the help of Indian nationalists in the war against Britain. On the whole, however, the plots were remarkably few. The most serious was the so-called *Ghadr* conspiracy, which had two centers, one in the Punjab and the other in the western United States and Canada. The founder was Har Dayal, a former native of Delhi who had been granted a government scholarship to Oxford and had made a brilliant record at this university. On his return from England Dayal came in contact with such nationalists as Lajpat Rai, prominent in the Arya Samaj, and henceforth became an ardent advocate of Indian independence.

The year 1914 found Har Dayal in Berkeley, California, where he carried on an active anti-British campaign among the students attending the state university. Contact was also made with many Indians, chiefly Sikhs, who had settled in British Columbia and in western states of the United States. Several anti-British newspapers were set up and distributed up and down the coast, the most important being the *Ghadr* (*Mutiny*), established in San Francisco by Har Dayal in November 1913. In a mock advertisement this newspaper in its first issue announced: "Wanted: Brave soldiers to stir up *Ghadr* in India; Pay—death; prize—martyrdom; pension—liberty; field of battle—India."[8]

Har Dayal for a time served as a lecturer on Indian philosophy at Stanford University, but was discharged from this post because of his propagandist activities. Under his direction the *Ghadr* group in the San Francisco Bay region was very active. Pamphlets were distributed and many meetings held. In December 1912 a jubilation meeting was called to celebrate the attack on the life of the Viceroy, Lord Hardinge; and in December 1913, in a meeting at Sacramento, Har Dayal told his audience "it was time to get ready to go to India for the coming revolution."[9]

It became more and more evident that the United States was being utilized as a base for stirring up revolution in India, and in March 1914 the United States government arrested Har Dayal as an undesirable alien. Released on bail, which he forfeited, he made his way to Geneva, Switzerland, leaving a trusted lieutenant in the United States to continue the *Ghadr*. It is probable that all this time Har Dayal was in contact with German

8- Quoted in William Roy Smith, Nationalism and Reform in India *(New Haven: Yale University Press, 1938), p. 78.*

9- Sir Michael O'Dwyer, India As I Knew It, 1885-1925 *(London: Constable and Company, 1925), p. 187.*

agents. At any rate, we know that when the First World War broke out he and a group of Indian revolutionists were in Berlin. Har Dayal and his colleagues were attached to the Indian section of the German General Staff, and assigned the work of fomenting revolt in India. Aiding in this was the German Oriental Bureau, which translated into Indian languages pamphlets that were distributed among the Indian prisoners of war and letters that were smuggled into India.

In the early months of 1914, the British secret police had notified the Indian government that thousands of Indians, mainly Sikhs, were planning on returning to India to spearhead a revolution against British authority. In January 1914 a large meeting of the *Ghadr* group had met in Stockton, California, and volunteers enrolled for the prospective mutiny. To meet this situation, the government in India passed an emergency act regulating the entry of suspicious Indians from abroad. About this time occurred the *Komagata Maru* incident, which added further fuel to the *Ghadr* movement. This Japanese vessel was chartered by a Sikh to collect several hundred Indians from various parts of the Far East and to convey them to Vancouver. When the steamer arrived in port the Canadian authorities refused to admit them. Returning to the Far East, the *Komagata Maru* was not permitted to land its passengers at either Shanghai or Hongkong, but had to proceed to Calcutta. Here, on September 27, 1914, the Indians were disembarked and, as most of them came from the Punjab, trains were waiting to return them, under police supervision, to their homes. Apparently the majority of these Indians had been indoctrinated with *Ghadr* ideology. Only a few consented to enter the trains, and over three hundred started to march in the direction of Calcutta, where they were met by a force of soldiers. Shots were fired on both sides, and the Indian rioters fled and scattered over the countryside. In a few days, however, most of them had been rounded up.

Meanwhile, ship after ship began to return Indians at such ports as Madras, Calcutta, and Colombo. Machinery for supervising their entry was at this time entirely inadequate, and many hundreds of ardent revolutionists, members of the *Ghadr* movement, slipped into the interior. It is estimated that as many as eight thousand Indians returned to India as a result of *Ghadr* propaganda.

As a great majority were Sikhs, they made their way to the Punjab, where they launched a widespread revolutionary movement that called for a revolt during February 1915. Fortunately for the British, the plot was uncovered, the revolutionary headquarters in Lahore were raided, and by the summer of 1915 the conspiracy was completely quashed.

Back in the United States the successors of Har Dayal were busily engaged in various conspiracies that read now like a cloak and dagger mystery with such elements as codes, an underground movement, the smuggling of arms, and the secret rendezvous. By using large sums of money provided by German agents an underground movement was built by which converts to revolution were sent to Shanghai, thence to Swatow, and finally to Siam, from which country the Indians were smuggled into India. The most ambitious plot concocted by the *Ghadr* group in the United States was a plan to land enough arms and ammunition on the Indian coast to equip a revolutionary army of ten thousand men. Active in this conspiracy was Captain Franz von Papen, the German military attaché in Washington. Sixteen carloads of arms were obtained and paid for by German agents and sent to San Diego, California. From this port two vessels were to be used to carry the arms through the British blockade to India.

This plot did not succeed, and during the months of March and April, 1917, numerous arrests of Indian agents were carried out in the United States. The trial of the main Indian leaders and their accomplices in a federal court in San Francisco aroused much interest in the American press. As if to supply the newspapers with a smashing climax, on the last day of the trial one of the Indian defendants, apparently suspicious of his leader, Ram Chandra, shot him dead in the court room with a pistol he had managed to conceal on his person. While spectators dashed for cover, a United States marshal shot and killed the murderer.

From time to time, as the war progressed, other plots were unearthed in India and sporadic outrages continued, but these were minor compared to the *Ghadr* conspiracy. One serious outbreak did take place at Singapore in February 1915, when an Indian regiment, the Fifth Bengali Light Infantry, revolted and terrorized the city. Marines from anchored war craft in the harbor quelled the uprising, but not before some fifty persons had been killed.

Apart from the *Ghadr* conspiracy the most serious menace to British authority during the war emanated from the area of the North-West Frontier, inhabited by fanatical Muslim hill tribes. A Pan-Islamic movement on the part of certain Mohammedan groups in India, designed to bring about closer cooperation with Turkey and the weakening of British rule, was already under way before 1914. The entrance of Turkey on the side of Germany accelerated this movement, for it seemed that Britain had now become the enemy of the Sultan, who was the Caliph and as such the head of Islam and the Protector of all Mohammedan Holy Places. In February 1915 a number of young Muslims left college at Lahore and crossed the border into the chaotic territory of the North-West Frontier. Here they joined with fanatical tribesmen who were intent on launching a jihad (a holy war) against the British in India. The persistent hostility of these frontier tribesmen made it necessary for the British to send several expeditions against them. That more serious revolts did not take place along the border was due largely to the rôle played by the Amir Habibullah of Afghanistan, who "despite all difficulties and dangers, kept his turbulent people to strict neutrality and threw the whole of his great influence into the task of tranquillising the border."[10] An interesting episode along the North-West Frontier was the mission of Mahendra Pratap. This Indian at the outset of the war made his way to Switzerland and then to Berlin. An interview was obtained with the Kaiser, and as a result a Turco-German Mission, with Pratap as one of the leaders, was sent to Afghanistan, but it was unable to dissuade the Amir from his position of benevolent neutrality toward Great Britain.[11]

Nationalist Politics Revive

For almost two years following the outbreak of war there was little hint of political unrest. In the imperial Legislative Council, the appeal of the Viceroy to cease controversy of any sort was heeded and no attempt was made to harass the government. In the late months of 1914, the radical nationalist Tilak, who had been expelled from the ranks of Congress in 1907, was released from prison and then tried to re-enter the Congress in

order to obstruct the government in any manner possible within the law, so that Great Britain would be forced to grant *swaraj* (home rule). But Tilak's trumpet call fell mainly upon deaf ears, for the moderates were still in control of the Indian nationalist movement.

Throughout the year 1915 politics in India continued serene. The only disquieting event was the untimely death of G. K. Gokhale, who in the decade before the war had been both the heart and the spirit of the Indian National Congress. So long as he lived it followed the path of conciliation and moderation. The Congress held its annual meeting in Bombay in December 1915, and was presided over by the Moderate and colleague of Gokhale, Mr. S. P. Sinha, who delivered a momentous presidential address. He argued in this message that Britain should announce a definite goal or objective for India in order to satisfy the rising generation of young Indians and thus check anarchistic tendencies kindled by frustration. It was also stressed by Sinha that this goal, which should be democracy pure and simple, could only be achieved by gradual advances, for India was not as yet prepared for full self-government. He paid tribute to the spirit and work of the British government in India, but he insisted firmly that good government was no substitute for self-government.

In his closing remarks, Sinha tried to arouse interest in the idea that social and economic reconstruction and reform were at least as important as political agitation for constitutional advances:

I believe in the doctrine of self-help as much as, probably more than, any of you here. I ask, therefore, that, not content with these oratorical feasts for three days in the year, we should have a continuous programme of work—work not political in the sense of public meetings, but work in the sense of trying to uplift the low and weak . . . remedying the evils that there are in our daily lives—ignorance, poverty, and disease.[12]

Sinha also declared that the fullest Indian patriotism could be reconciled with the idea of remaining part of the British Empire. Although there was little evidence at this Congress meeting of 1915 to indicate the almost complete transformation that was to take place in the Indian nationalist movement during the next two years, it was prophetic that changes were made in the rules of

10- Cambridge History of the British Empire, *V, p. 485.*

11- See Mohendra Pratap, *"My German Mission to High Asia,"* Asia, *XXV (May 1925).*

12- Quoted in Sir Verney Lovett, A History of the Indian Nationalist Movement *(London: John Murray, 1920), pp. 100-101.*

the Congress that would permit the return of ousted extremists like Tilak. Looking back, it can be seen that Sinha's address constituted the swan song of the old Liberal and Moderate leaders. A new generation was about to take over.

During the course of the year 1916 it became apparent that the war was quickening and sharpening Indian nationalism. A new group of young Nationalists was just coming of age. They were excited at the news of the Irish Revolt of 1916 and read with intense interest accounts of the eloquent speech made by its leader, Sir Roger Casement, at his trial. Speaking of the Nationalist revival, Nehru writes in his autobiography, "The atmosphere became electric, and most of us young men felt exhilarated and expected big things in the near future."[13]

These young nationalists noted that for two years Britain and her Allies had been continually reiterating the idea that they were fighting for the principle of the self-determination of nations. Later this aim was given even more advertisement by President Woodrow Wilson's Fourteen Points. Wide publicity was also given in India in the early months of the war to speeches made by British officials in which they promised generous measures of constitutional reform for India. In particular, Prime Minister Asquith had declared: "Henceforth Indian questions would have to be approached from a different angle of vision."[14]

Apart from the effect of the Allies' war aims and the promises of British statesmen, another factor explaining the rapid advance of Indian nationalism in 1916 was the failure of Great Britain to utilize adequately the loyalty and support for the war manifested by all classes in 1914 and 1915. After being assured that there was little danger of serious revolt, the Indian government went its own way. Consequently, somewhat rebuffed and with little to do, the educated classes turned back to politics.

By the middle of 1916 there was a definite undercurrent of unrest. Nothing had been done about the pledges of reform. The British government was too preoccupied with the problems of the war, and maintained an enigmatic silence on the question of Indian constitutional reform. Furthermore, war weariness began to manifest itself in India as in other parts of the world. The war was too long. Many Indians could not understand why the powerful British armies could not secure speedy victory. Casualty lists, return of the wounded, and rumors of bad management at the battle fronts all helped to spread the spirit of disillusionment. In the spring of 1916 came the surprising news of a British disaster when Turkish forces compelled the surrender of General Townshend's army at Kut-El-Amara.

In this atmosphere of disillusionment and mounting political consciousness, Mrs. Annie Besant and Lokamanya Tilak stepped forward to lead a vigorous campaign for Home Rule for India. Somewhat repulsed by the extremes of Bengali nationalism in the anti-partition controversy of Lord Curzon's day, Mrs. Besant had stood aside until 1913, when she actively entered politics. In 1914 she started two newspapers to publicize her ideas and was recognized as one of the leaders of the National Congress. Early in the war Mrs. Besant began her campaign for Home Rule, and at the same time Tilak began a similar movement. In the Congress meeting of December 1915, Mrs. Besant tried unsuccessfully to enlist its support for her movement. Thereupon she carried out a whirlwind campaign, formally establishing her Home Rule League in September 1916 and setting up some fifty branches of the organization in different parts of the country. September 14 was celebrated by these branches as Home Rule Day.

In October 1916 an important memorandum was presented to the government by nineteen elected members of the Imperial Legislative Council. This document was the work of balanced and moderate nationalist leaders, who declared that India's loyalty entitled her to a position of comradeship, not subordination. In essence the document asked for responsible government for India, and it made this plea:

What is wanted is not merely good government or efficient administration, but a government acceptable to the people, because responsible to them. This is what India understands would constitute a new angle of vision. If after the War the position of India remains practically what it was before, the beneficent effects of participation in common danger overcome by common effort will leave nothing behind, save the painful memory of unrealized expectation.[15]

Momentous developments in the Indian national movement took place in the closing months of 1916. Hindu-Muslim enmity had been an unfortunate but nevertheless basic feature of Indian history for many years, and the Muslim League

13- Jawaharlal Nehru, Toward Freedom *(New York: John Day Company, 1941), p. 44.*

14- *Quoted in Sir Valentine Chirol, India (London: Ernest Benn, Ltd., 1926), p. 160.*

15- *Quoted in H. C. E. Zacharias,* Renascent India *(London: George Allen and Unwin, 1933), p. 168.*

since its establishment in 1906 had consistently maintained an attitude of both aloofness and suspicion toward the National Congress. In November 1916, however, representatives of the Congress and the League met in Calcutta. Differences were patched up and both agreed to support Mrs. Besant's Home Rule League. This *rapprochement* between Hindu and Muslim was hailed as signifying the end of controversy between these two great religious groups and the birth of an undivided nation.

This amicable Congress-League agreement is explained largely by a few significant developments. First, the younger intellectuals in both the Muslim community and Congress were becoming much more nationalistic than their older leaders. In 1913 the Muslim League for the first time came out definitely for the goal of Indian self-government while maintaining its continued loyalty to the British Crown. This statement caused much controversy in the ranks of the League and led the Aga Khan, who tended to be conservative and very pro-British, to resign his presidency of the League. Second, a considerable section of the Muslim community became anti-British because of Great Britain's policy toward Turkey. Active war was waged by Britain against this Mohammedan power, and further, as in the case of the revolt of Sharif Hussein of Mecca, leader of the Arabs, the British subsidized the enemies of the Sultan and seemed bent on the destruction of his spiritual authority in the Mohammedan world. The unhappy position of many Muslims was underlined by a resolution passed at the League's session in 1915, at which time it was stated: "It is a sore point with us that the Government of our Caliph should be at war with the Government of our King-Emperor."[16] The predominantly Hindu Congress had always maintained that this body was truly national and secular. As the majority group in India, the Hindus had nothing to fear and everything to gain by accepting the support of the Muslim minority.

The Congress and the League both held their annual meetings in Lucknow the last week of December 1916. Leaders of both organizations came out for Home Rule and joined in supporting the recommendations of the "Memorandum of the Nineteen," which they made the basis for the so-called Congress-League Plan. This scheme demanded that India be granted immediately the status of a self-governing entity within the British Empire. While under the Congress-League Plan the British government would have control of military matters and foreign affairs, Indian members of the government would have fairly complete control over legislation as far as the central government was concerned and full control over all matters in the provincial governments. As part of this scheme, Muslims and Hindus joined in the Lucknow Pact, in which it was agreed that the members of the former community were to elect their representatives by means of special Muslim electorates—as had been granted in the Morley-Minto Reforms—and were to be guaranteed a specific number of representatives in both the provincial and central legislatures.

The Congress-League Plan is a landmark in Indian history, and equally important were the developments within the ranks of the National Congress. Since 1907 the so-called Extremists had been debarred from membership, but a change in the rules made in 1915 allowed the prodigal radicals to re-enter the fold. This they did, and when Tilak mounted the platform he was given a tumultuous ovation. Not only were the Extremists permitted to rejoin the Congress, but it was evident that they had actually won over most of its members to their militant views.

An enthusiastic campaign soliciting support for the Congress-League scheme was carried out during the first six months of 1917. Mrs. Besant was in the van of this movement, and her articles in the newspaper *New India* spread the gospel of Home Rule. In June the Indian government ordered the internment of Mrs. Besant, prohibiting her from speaking in public or writing for publication. This action resulted in an angry volume of protests from all over India. It became increasingly clear that some positive action should be taken in order to appease Indian national sentiments. Yet no move was made by the British government in London, "until the Government of India implored it to put war-maps aside for a moment and make some definite pronouncement that should stem the rising tide of political unrest in India."[17]

Britain Turns to Reform

The British government, which on the surface seemed oblivious to the rising chorus of discon-

16- *Lovett*, op. cit., *p. 101.*

17- *Chirol*, India, *p. 163.*

tent in India, had not been wholly idle. Shortly after Lord Chelmsford had become the new Viceroy in April 1916, this official presented two basic questions at the first meeting of his Executive Council. These were: "What is the goal of British rule in India and what are the steps on the road to that goal?"[18] In 1917 Chelmsford in a dispatch to London recommended a greater measure of Indian self-government. It was made clear that the government of India was not committed to any definite scheme. All that was suggested was that the Indian people should be progressively granted a larger measure of control, the ultimate result of which would be a form of self-government consistent with the traditions and unique circumstances existing in India.

These proposals were given careful study by the British government. It was realized that questions relating to methods of procedure were secondary to the matter of fundamental policy. The paramount and pressing problem, therefore, was the question of what should be Britain's conception of India's constitutional future. And just at this juncture an event took place which helped to crystallize the problem of Indian constitutional reform. This was the report on the Mesopotamian fiasco of 1916, already referred to in this chapter.

In the first year of the war, a British expeditionary force had been sent to the Persian Gulf to defend a strategic oil pipe line. Following this action a force of 4500 British and 12,000 Indian troops, under the command of General Townshend, pushed its way to Kut-El-Amara, 300 miles from the Gulf. Kut was captured, and thus far the expedition had been a brilliant success. This good fortune, however, turned to tragic disaster. Moving toward the next objective, Baghdad, 150 miles away, the British army suffered a complete defeat at the hands of the Turks at Ctesiphon. Retreat was made to Kut-El-Amara, where Townshend was completely surrounded by the Turks on December 7, 1915.

The beleaguered army had been promised relief, but week followed week with no sign of aid from the south. The rainy season made rescue doubly difficult, and the evacuation of Gallipoli by the British army released large Turkish reinforcements for action in Mesopotamia. Within Kut-El-Amara food and medical supplies ran low, the heat was terrible, and the hospital was filled to overflowing. Townshend finally gave up hope of relief, and after

a defense of 147 days he capitulated to the Turkish army.

This Mesopotamian disaster to British arms has been emphasized because of its effect upon the growing demand for Indian constitutional reform. The surrender was a grievous blow to British prestige. Ugly rumors and biting criticism spread concerning the management of the campaign, and public opinion in Britain demanded that the matter be investigated. A special Commission, therefore, was appointed in August 1916 to investigate the Mesopotamian campaign.

Its report accused the government of India, which had directed the venture, of fatal inaction and lack of vision. The bureaucratic system in India was castigated in such phrases as "intense isolation and centralization," and "cumbrous and inept."[19] One of the Commissioners in a minority report declared: "My last recommendation is that we should no longer deny to Indians the full privileges of citizenship, but should allow them a large share in the government of their own country and in the control of that Bureaucracy which in this War, uncontrolled by public opinion, has failed to rise to British standards."[20] The Mesopotamian Report, submitted in June 1917, was vigorously debated in Parliament. In spite of the plea of Austen Chamberlain, the Secretary of State for India, that only injury could come from mixing up a debate over alleged military mismanagement with the question of the political future of India, the discussion resolved itself into an attack upon the bureaucratic and outmoded structure of Indian administration.

Mr. Samuel Montagu, a former Undersecretary of State for India, was foremost in criticism. Speaking in the House of Commons, July 11, 1917, he characterized the existing Indian system of government as "too wooden, too iron, too inelastic, too antideluvian to be of any use for modern purposes." He further demanded that the whole system of Indian government be explored in the light of the Mesopotamian Report.[21]

One result of these debates was that Sir Austen Chamberlain resigned, but more important was the fact that while Indian nationalists were demanding governmental reform, coincidentally a similar demand was being made in the British Parliament. Meanwhile, Mr. Montagu had become the new Secretary of State for India and immediately set to work formulating a pronouncement clearly

18- Cambridge History of the British Empire, V, p. 587.

19- Zacharias, op. cit., p. 171.

20- Ibid., p. 172.

21- Quoted in Nihal Singh, "Constitutional Reforms for British India," Fortnightly Review, CIII (1918), p. 775.

stating the direction and goal of Indian constitutional evolution. As we have already noted, the British government and the Viceroy had been paving the way for such action as far back as the spring of 1916. A draft was prepared by Montagu, submitted to the British cabinet, and reshaped, mainly at the hands of the former Viceroy, Lord Curzon. It was a fateful and dramatic moment in British imperial history when Samuel Montagu on August 20, 1917, announced in the House of Commons Britain's long-term objective in India. The announcement in part declared:

> The policy of His Majesty's Government, with which the Government of India are in complete accord, is that of the increasing association of Indians in every branch of the administration and the gradual development of self-governing institutions with a view to the progressive realisation of responsible government as an integral part of the British Empire.
>
> . . . .
>
> I would add that progress in this policy can only be achieved by successive stages. The British Government and the Government of India, on whom the responsibility lies for the welfare and advancement of the Indian peoples, must be judges of the time and measure of each advance, and they must be guided by the co-operation received from those upon whom new opportunities of service will thus be conferred and by the extent to which it is found that confidence can be reposed in their sense of responsibility.[22]

While making his historic announcement in the House of Commons, Montagu also stated that substantial steps toward more self-government in India should be taken as soon as possible and that he was proceeding shortly to India to confer with the Viceroy, Lord Chelmsford, and to study conditions at first hand. The Secretary of State for India and his deputation arrived in India in November 1917 and at once began their investigations. Preliminary conferences were held with the Viceroy and the heads of the provincial governments. Then, accompanied by Lord Chelmsford, the deputation visited Calcutta, Madras, and Bombay. Mr. Montagu's tour attracted wide interest. Everyone felt that the old order of things was doomed, and all were anxious to present arguments before the investigators. At every place visited by the Secretary, members of Congress, Muslims, Sikhs, Eurasians, Untouchables, and others appeared to press their claims.

The investigation was completed by the end of April 1918, and the deputation returned to England to formulate its report, published on July 8. Signed by both the Viceroy and the Secretary of State for India, this document is usually referred to as the Montagu-Chelmsford Report. At the time it was written it undoubtedly was one of the most penetrating and valuable studies of constitutional problems in India, and it has been called "the first authoritative survey of the state of India since the Mutiny."[23]

The Montagu-Chelmsford Report was liberal in its approach and sympathetic to Indian aspirations. Montagu, in particular, was occasionally irked by the attitude of British civil servants in India and in *An Indian Diary* he wrote, "I wish I could get the damned Bureaucracy to realize that we are sitting on an earthquake."[24] The Report made it quite plain that the Morley-Minto scheme of government no longer met the needs of the times, that the World War had accelerated political aspirations in India, and that the desire for self-government was the natural outcome of British rule and the impact of liberal western thought.

The nature and functioning of the scheme of government established in India in 1919, and based on the Montagu-Chelmsford proposals, will be discussed in the next chapter and is shown on the chart in the first picture section. It may be noted that the changes proposed constituted a great advance over the system set up before the war by the Morley-Minto reforms. In short, the bloc of British officials constituting a majority was abolished in the central legislature at Delhi, although in emergencies the Governor-General was given power to override the Indian majority. As for the provincial governments, the first elements of responsible government were introduced and Indian ministers were given complete charge of such departments as education and public works.

These reform proposals received wide publicity, and liberals all over the world regarded them as a valuable contribution to the problem of colonial self-government. Opinion in India, however, was sharply divided. Nationalist leaders like Tilak and Mrs. Besant considered the Report a sham and in no way a fulfillment of the pledge made in the House of Commons in August 1917. Mrs. Besant in her newspaper, *New India*, declared: "The scheme is unworthy to be offered by England or to be accepted by India."[25] And at a special session of the Madras Provincial Congress she char-

2- *Quoted in* Report of the Indian Statutory Commission, *I*, *Cmd. 3568 (London: His Majesty's Stationery Office, 1930), p. 2.*

3- *Sir Valentine Chirol*, India Old and New (*New York: The Macmillan Co., 1921), p. 151.*

4- *Quoted in* Zacharias, op. cit., p. 173.*

5- *Sir Surendranath Banerjea*, Nation in the Making *(London: H. Milford Co., 1925), 305.*

acterized the reforms as "leading to a line beyond which its authors cannot go—a perpetual slavery which can only be broken by revolution."[26] Dr. J. T. Sunderland, a leading exponent of the Indian militant nationalist view in the United States, declared:

The real objects of the scheme seemed to be two, namely, to quiet the growing unrest of the Indian people by making them think they were getting something important (when they were not), and to produce a favorable impression upon the public opinion of the world by spreading the idea that the British were generous to India and were leading her as fast as seemed wise toward her desired goal of freedom and self-rule.[27]

The most important immediate result of the projected reforms was a schism between the moderate and radical elements in the Indian National Congress. In contrast to the intransigence of the radicals, the so-called moderate nationalists, though disappointed that no major reforms were to be made in the Indian central government, regarded the Montagu-Chelmsford Report as a substantial advance toward Indian autonomy and were prepared to pledge their support. This moderate faction believed that the difference between itself and the militant group—which had completely dominated the Congress in 1917—was fundamental, and therefore absented itself from the special session of the National Congress held in August 1918. In the following November the secessionists met at Bombay and organized the Liberal party. Immediately after this conference came the news of the Armistice, and the First World War came to an end.

The Aftermath of War

During the last six months of the war, despite the dissatisfaction on the part of the Indian Congress with the Montagu-Chelmsford Report and the agitation of the Home Rule League, India was at the height of its war effort. In March 1918 had come word of the disastrous British reverses in France, and, following an urgent appeal from the British prime minister, a great war conference was held in Delhi, in April, to determine what could be done to provide additional assistance in men, money, and supplies. The majority of the delegates expressed willingness to cooperate

wholeheartedly in bringing the war to a successful termination. The only hint of dissent was an attempt by one delegate to introduce a resolution into the conference requesting the British government immediately to bring before Parliament a bill "meeting the demands of the people to establish a responsible government in India within a reasonable and specified period."[28] In contrast, it is interesting to note that on April 29 another member of the conference, Mohandas Karamchand Gandhi, spoke eloquently in support of a resolution requesting the Viceroy to dispatch a message to the King-Emperor pledging India's full support and loyalty in the prosecution of the war.

The Armistice, then, found the politically-minded classes in India united in their war efforts but split into contending factions on the merits of the Montagu-Chelmsford reforms. Purged of its moderate members, the Congress held its annual meeting at Delhi in December 1918. It was the feeling of many of its members that India had contributed generously to victory and Great Britain, therefore, should immediately demonstrate her appreciation by instituting sweeping reforms. In this spirit the Congress assembled and demanded the application of the principle of national self-determination to India, the release of political prisoners, and the introduction of complete self-government in the provinces. It was also stated that the Montagu declaration of August 1917 was cautious and cold and that the proposed reforms were inadequate. The Congress further branded the recommendations of the Rowlatt Sedition Committee, shortly to be discussed, a violation of the basic liberties of the people. Coincidentally the Muslim League also met and passed resolutions (1) urging Britain not to interfere with the Sultan of Turkey as the true Khalifa (Protector, Caliph) of the Muslim Holy Places and (2) supporting the goal of self-determination.

Leaving for the moment the constitutional demands of the politically conscious Indians, what was the temper of the people when peace again returned to their land? Peace was acclaimed not so much with relief as with expectancy. A widespread publicity campaign had spread roseate accounts of the war aims of Britain and her Allies. The masses had been willing to endure high prices, aggressive recruiting campaigns, stringent restrictions upon personal liberty, and other abnormal conditions because it was believed that the inau-

26- *Quoted in Lovett, op. cit.,* p. 168.

27- *J. T. Sunderland,* India in Bondage *(New York: Lewis Copeland Co., 1929), p. 416.*

28- *Quoted in Lovett, op. cit.,* p. 153.

guration of a golden age, almost a Utopia, was bound up with the victory of the Allies. The "war to end wars" had created similar hopes among the masses in Europe, particularly in Italy.

However, the months after the Armistice brought no surcease from the existing hardships and restraints, but rather accentuated them. Following the failure of the monsoon in 1918, famine conditions existed in many parts of India. A serious bubonic plague had ravaged the country in 1917, but this was nothing compared to the horrors of the influenza epidemic of 1918-1919, which caused the deaths of thirteen million people—more than the number who had died on the battlefields of the late war. Prices showed no decline. The cost of living was still mounting in 1919, "and the few cotton rags worn by a peasant became almost un-purchasable."[29] Transportation and railway service were still disorganized as a result of war demands and contributed to the general chaos. And, although the war had brought great riches to a few, the rural population had suffered severely. Such conditions were especially onerous in view of the visions of an era of plenty that had been expected to follow the victory of Great Britain. Widespread dissatisfaction grew into active discontent and resentment.

This Indian discontent was directionless in itself, but was to achieve much under a leader, Mohandas K. Gandhi, who stimulated and directed it into a constructive channel of protest of his own creation. He created a movement to throw off the foreign yoke combined with an attempt to regenerate the social, economic, and religious elements of Indian society. It was one of those unusual coincidences of history that there was available at the crucial moment a man like Gandhi, who blended in his makeup the traits of a religious saint, a Mahatma, which gave him irresistible power over the masses, and the shrewdness of a practical politician, which enabled him to use his great influence to embarrass and weaken the authority of British rule.

The Emergence of Gandhi

As Gandhi's entrance into the Indian limelight was precipitated largely by the government's enactment of the Rowlatt Acts, it will be necessary to discuss their origin and purpose before taking up the career of this great Indian nationalist.

Revolutionary terrorist crime, frequently in the form of assassinations, had, as we have seen, first begun in India in 1897; but it was in 1906 that there began a long series of outrages which were deplored by the moderate leaders of the National Congress but with which the government seemed powerless to cope. The ordinary machinery of justice could do little in the face of various kinds of intimidation, and even murder, practiced on witnesses or jurors who aided the government in the prosecution of terrorism.

No changes, however, were made in legal procedure until the First World War, when, as a counterpart to the Defence of the Realm Act in Great Britain, the Defence of India Act was passed by the Indian Legislature. This Act, by means of special tribunals and special wartime powers, enabled the executive branch of the government to curb espionage and revolutionary activities.

The Act was destined to come to an end six months after the end of the war, and British officials began to consider what, if anything, should take its place when the struggle ended. Their perturbation was increased at the prospect of the release of many Indian extremists, regarded as dangerous revolutionists from the English point of view, who were being held in prison under the terms of the Defence of India Act.

Sir Sidney Rowlatt, judge of the Court of the King's Bench in England, was, therefore, sent to India to preside over a Committee appointed in December 1917 to study this situation. In addition to the President, there were four other members on the Rowlatt Sedition Committee, two of whom were Indian. Holding sessions in Calcutta and Lahore, the Committee examined a large number of witnesses and handed in its unanimous report to the government in April 1918. A large part of this document describes the propaganda and terrorist methods used by what it refers to as the Indian revolutionists and traces in detail the bomb outrages, gang hold-ups, and shootings that almost paralyzed certain parts of India before 1914. According to the Rowlatt Report, because witnesses were intimidated and therefore afraid to testify few of the perpetrators of terrorist acts were punished. For example, during the period from 1906 to 1917 the police had information indicating the complicity of more than one thousand offenders in various kinds of terrorist activity in Bengal, but

29- *Chirol,* India, *p. 184.*

only eighty-four were brought into court and convicted. And further, from January 1915 to June 1916 there had been fourteen murders, eight victims being police officers, and no single terrorist had been apprehended and placed on trial.

The Rowlatt Committee members were of the opinion that ordinary legal procedure, with open trials, witnesses, and juries, had proved entirely ineffectual in dealing with terrorist outrages, and that, following the lapse of the special war powers conferred by the Defence of India Act, it was likely another serious wave of crimes would occur. It was recommended, therefore, that the government should not wait for a revival of these outrages, but should proceed to enact special legislation. Two bills were recommended for this purpose. One entailed certain minor changes of a permanent nature in the criminal law, and the other, only to be invoked by order of the Governor-General in case of an emergency, provided for the trial of seditious crime by three judges of the highest grade, without juries or witnesses. Provincial governments were also given the authority to intern dangerous suspects.

The proposals of the Rowlatt Sedition Committee were discussed in the Legislative Council at Delhi during the September session. At this time, the Indian members did not appear unduly alarmed over the Committee's recommendations. On January 2, 1919, the provisions of the two proposed bills were published by the government, and immediately a storm of protest followed on the part of the Home Rule League, the Congress, and even the Moderates. An active press campaign and a series of meetings were launched to stir up opposition to the bills. Word was passed around that they were "a monstrous engine of tyranny and oppression," and "an attempt to invent crimes." An orator declared that "when the bills become law, life will be impossible for a single day." Another affirmed that the measures "would divide husband from wife, tear away innocent children from the bosom of the father, would break the ties of friendship and extinguish the flame of love."[30] Many unfounded rumors were disseminated to the effect that property would be confiscated by the government, that there would be excessive fees for marriage, and that all assemblies of five people would be prohibited.

In February 1919, the Viceroy in his opening speech to the Legislative Council strongly urged the passage of the two Rowlatt Bills. So strong was the opposition, however, that the government dropped one of the bills and only proceeded with the main emergency one. Hoping to placate opposition, the government proposed that the Act would operate for only three years. Further, to help reassure the Indian public that the Act was not designed to threaten the liberties of the mass of people, it was officially described as a measure "to cope with anarchical and revolutionary crime." In the legislature one British member stated that the criminals against whom this act would apply were "enemies of civilisation, enemies of progress, and enemies of any form of organised government, whether European or Indian."[31] Such arguments did nothing to mollify the opposition of the Indian members of the Legislative Council, but, finally, the Act was passed despite their negative votes.

In view of the fateful repercussions following the enactment of the Rowlatt Bill, one is naturally led to inquire into the justification of the government's action and to ask whether the nationalist denunciation was deserved. As is the case with so many of the issues of history, arguments and testimony can be secured in about equal volume for both sides. The late Professor Claude H. Van Tyne, noted American historian, following a tour of investigation in India during 1921-1922, intimated that a mountain was made out of a molehill. The Act, according to this observer, "has always had a fictitious value in the argumentative battle between the Indians and the British."[32] On the other hand, one gets the impression from another American historian, Professor W. P. Hall, that the Act, while not as bad as painted, was an unnecessary provocation to the Indian people. Upon one point, however, there can be no argument, and that is about the widespread campaign, not so much of mere resistance, but of absolute distortion and misrepresentation that was carried out against the bills. This fact, however, does not answer the question as to what tactics are fair under the circumstances in which Indian nationalism operated. Certainly much distortion of the fact is usually found in most of the elections in Europe and in the United States.

The answer that may be given is that the government did not intend the Rowlatt Acts to serve any despotic purpose, but only to act as a legitimate safeguard against anticipated terrorist and subversive activities. And, in understanding the In-

30- *J. E. Woolacott,* India on Trial *(London: The Macmillan Company, 1929), pp. 90-91.*

31- *Ibid., p. 90.*

32- *Claude H. Van Tyne,* India in Ferment *(New York: D. Appleton & Co., 1923), p. 140.*

dian reaction to the bills, it should be kept in mind that Indian national pride and sensitivity—as well as aspirations for the future—had been greatly heightened by the war. India in 1919 was not thinking in terms of any abridgement of her liberties but rather of their rapid expansion.

"The Rowlatt Act," says Sir Surendranath Banerjea, "was the parent of the Non-Co-Operation Movement."[33] It was this Act more than anything else which brought Mahatma Gandhi to the center of the Indian political scene. It is a truism that no adequate explanation of modern India can be made without reference to the influence, activities, and ideals of this enigmatic leader about whom have raged such storms of controversy. To some a "supreme humbug," a "madman," a "half-naked fakir," a "self-deluded visionary," to others Gandhi has been the Holy One, and to Rabindranath Tagore, who by no means agreed with all of his teachings, he was not only the greatest man in India, but the greatest on earth.

The fascinating story of Gandhi's life may be read in his remarkable autobiography, *The Story of My Experiments with Truth,* which was dictated by Gandhi to one of his fellow-prisoners during a period of imprisonment in the years 1922-1924. Originally published in two large volumes in India, both in Gujarati and in English, the work was published in abridged form by C. F. Andrews, an English missionary and long the friend and intimate confidant of Gandhi. This story has been likened to the *Confessions* of St. Augustine and of Rousseau. It is above all self-revealing in its frankness, for Gandhi does not spare himself as he digs into his past and describes his sins, mistakes, and frailties of character.

Born in 1869 at Porbandar, the capital of an Indian Native State situated in the Kathiawar peninsula north-west of Bombay, Mohandas Gandhi was the son of respectable middle-class parents. The family belonged to the Vaisya caste and was very religious, especially the mother, who followed the dictates of the strictest Hindu orthodoxy. The future Mahatma was reared according to the Hindu traditions of his parents. It is not surprising that, although he did not exhibit unusual intellectual prowess in the classroom, Gandhi from the very first manifested a tendency to introspection, a love of truth, and a sensitive conscience. The *Autobiography* relates, almost as if it were a heinous crime, how the young boy be-

came the friend of a youth who had no compunctions about breaking the Hindu code. Gandhi's acquaintance quoted the following doggerel:

> Behold the mighty Englishman;
> He rules the Indian small,
> Because being a meat-eater
> He is five cubits tall.

This persuaded Gandhi to eat meat, but he was overcome with remorse and confessed the deception to his father with great sorrow.

The first great decision in his life, and one that was to have momentous effects upon his destiny, was that made at a family conference following his father's death to send Gandhi to London to study law. There was some fear expressed that the young student might fall prey to the wicked practices of the foreign city. Thereupon a friend of the family advised that the boy should take three vows. "He administered the oath and I vowed to live a celibate life in England and never to touch wine or meat. This done, my mother gave her permission and her blessing."[34]

London in 1888 proved to be very strange and disquieting to the bewildered youth. Ignorance of English customs constantly proved a source of embarrassment to his sensitive nature. One of his new-found Indian friends ridiculed his determination to abstain from meat, and for a time he nearly starved amid an abundance of good English beef, until one day by chance he ran across a good vegetarian restaurant. "There I had my first hearty meal since my arrival. God had come to my aid."[35] For a few months Gandhi tried to emulate the sophisticated young Englishmen he met, taking elocution and dancing lessons and wearing clothes of the most rakish cut. This phase soon passed, however, and the young student settled down to live frugally and to concentrate on his legal studies.

In the second year of his sojourn in London he made several contacts that helped to stimulate and shape his philosophical bent and his religious point of view. Two members of the Theosophical Society interested him in the *Bhagavad-Gita,* the great Hindu epic poem, and also Sir Edward Arnold's *The Light of Asia.* About this time he purchased a Bible from a Christian friend and was especially delighted with the message of the New Testament, which "went straight to my heart."[36]

The law examinations were finally taken and passed, and in 1891 the young lawyer, proud of

33- Banerjea, op. cit., p. 300.

34- C. F. Andrews, ed., *Mahatma Gandhi: His Own Story (London: George Allen and Unwin, 1930),* pp. 77-78.

- Ibid., p. 83.

- Ibid., p. 93.

his success, sailed for home. These three years in London had brought him into contact with the forces of nationalism, democracy, and Christianity, while his study of the *Gita,* the New Testament, and other similar books had kindled within him the fire of ascetic self-renunciation and service.

In 1893, after little success in India in the practice of law, Gandhi accepted a commission to represent a large Indian firm involved in an important legal suit in Pretoria, South Africa. This was the beginning of a career in which Gandhi first achieved great success, building up a practice paying as much as £3000 a year. This was to be followed by a period of self-renunciation in which he courageously and unselfishly fought for the removal of inhuman legal disabilities imposed by the South African government upon his countrymen. It was in this struggle that he was imprisoned four times, beaten by a mob, and once left for dead.

Gandhi soon became the champion of the thousands of Hindus who had been brought out to South Africa as indentured laborers. In the courts he was a constant defender of their rights and was also instrumental in starting a newspaper to publicize the wrongs of the Indians. At this time the Indian "coolies," as they were called, were treated with equal injustice in both the Boer Republics and the English South African colonies. But when the Boer War broke out in 1899, Gandhi persuaded his countrymen to offer their services to England. The war offered the despised "coolies" an opportunity to show their loyalty as British subjects, to render good for evil. Perhaps after the victory of British arms, thought Gandhi, something might be done for the Indian cause. An ambulance corps was therefore organized, whose members received official commendation for their bravery under fire.

Victory for Great Britain did little, however, to ease the disabilities of the Indians. In fact, after the Boer and the English population came together to form the Union of South Africa, the burdens of the Indians became heavier. Especially galling was the Asiatic Registration Act of 1906, which finger-printed Indians; the $15 poll tax on Indians in the province of Natal; and the decision of the Cape province that all marriages performed under Hindu rites were illegal. And in addition to these and other legal disabilities there was a whole pattern of Jim Crowism that placed the South African Indians in a subordinate status, somewhere midway between the European at the top and the black Kafirs at the bottom.

For eight years, from 1906 to 1914, Gandhi carried on the fight, rousing to action the Indian laborers and instilling into them the precepts and techniques of non-violence. From the time of his early days in London, Gandhi had been studying and familiarizing himself with the traditional Hindu belief of *Ahimsa,* or non-violence, and the possibility of using it as a technique to rectify injustice. This idea was not entirely unknown to the western world in the form of passive resistance, but Gandhi preferred to coin a new term for his weapon against injustice, which he named *Satyagraha,* or Truth Force. Without violence the object was to win over your opponent by "sympathy, patience, and self-suffering."[37] Resorting to *Satyagraha,* no force should be used, but this fact, according to Gandhi, did not imply weakness or cowardliness but rather the positive and courageous action of moral character. "I cultivate," said Gandhi, "the quiet courage of dying without killing."[38]

Under the leadership of Gandhi a series of hunger strikes, public demonstrations, strikes in mines, and mass marches of protest followed. Arrest was welcomed, martyrdom gloried in, and prison embraced by thousands. The courage of the "passive resisters" under all kinds of physical intimidation aroused public opinion in both India and Great Britain. Lord Hardinge, the British Viceroy, openly criticized the South African authorities, who, it must be remembered, were enjoying self-government from Britain after 1909. In a speech given at Madras in November 1913, Hardinge expressed "the sympathy of India, deep and burning, and not only of India but of all lovers of India like myself for their compatriots in South Africa in their resistance to insidious and unjust laws."[39] This protest carried much weight and was supported by pressure exerted by London. The result was the enactment of legislation in South Africa in the summer of 1914 that removed the most vexatious legal injustices.

The victory now won, Gandhi left South Africa in the summer of 1914 for a visit to England, arriving in London on August 6, just two days after Britain had declared war against Germany. Gandhi immediately urged all Indians in England to render all possible service to the Empire. His

37- *R. R. Diwakar,* Satyagraha, The Power of Truth *(Hinsdale, Illinois: Henry Regnery Co., 1948),* p. 5.

38- Ibid., *p. 26.*

39- *Chirol,* India, p. 202.

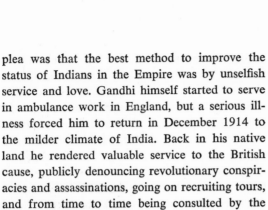

- *Quoted in Sir John Cumming, ed.,* Modern India *(London: Oxford University Press, 1932), p. 49.*

- *Report of the Disorders Inquiry Commission (*The Hunter Report*) (London: His Majesty's Stationery Office, 1920), p. 61.*

plea was that the best method to improve the status of Indians in the Empire was by unselfish service and love. Gandhi himself started to serve in ambulance work in England, but a serious illness forced him to return in December 1914 to the milder climate of India. Back in his native land he rendered valuable service to the British cause, publicly denouncing revolutionary conspiracies and assassinations, going on recruiting tours, and from time to time being consulted by the Viceroy on important problems. Not long after his return to India, Gandhi was given the Kaiser-i-Hind Gold Medal by the government of India for distinguished humanitarian service in the empire.

Gandhi was forty-five when the triumph of non-violent passive resistance in South Africa made him the Mahatma, the Holy One or Great Teacher, in India, and earned him respect and admiration throughout the British Empire. In May 1915, he established his Ashram, or seminary, with twenty-five of his disciples from South Africa, near Ahmadabad in order to teach his ideas to the Indian masses. Even at this time, because of his work in South Africa, the Indian crowds reverently paid him homage when they caught a glimpse of his slight figure passing by. Gandhi had promised G. K. Gokhale, the noted Indian leader, not to enter politics for a year after his return while he became acquainted with conditions in India. The returned native son, however, was eager to use *Satyagraha* for the redress of injustice in India should the need arise. The opportunity was soon to come.

In addition to his war services from 1915 to 1918 in India, Gandhi felt constrained to intervene as the champion of justice on several occasions. There was his investigation of the exploitation of the peasants of North Bihar by the indigo planters, and the encouragement of the peasants in the Kaira district of Gujarat to take up passive resistance against the government in response to unjust taxation. Gandhi intervened in several other instances where he believed injustice was being committed. Most of these affairs were not of any great significance, and were settled merely by the threat of a *Satyagraha*. These tentative beginnings of passive resistance in India, however, were given much publicity by the nationalist press and thus educated public opinion for the more ambitious program of *Satyagraha* later to be undertaken by Gandhi.

Gandhi's First Challenge

There may be differences of opinion as to the degree of provocation presented to Indians by the Rowlatt Act, but it is a plain fact that, justified or not, this was the first of several actions of the Indian government that changed Gandhi from a friend to a foe of British rule. Up to 1918 he believed in the basic justice of Britain, but "The first shock," wrote Gandhi, "came with the Rowlatt Act, a law designed to rob the people of all freedom."[40] While the Rowlatt Bill was being debated in the Indian Legislature, Gandhi urged the Viceroy to drop the measure, and warned that if the government proceeded there was no other course left except resort to *Satyagraha*.

On February 23, 1919, a meeting of the Ahmadabad branch of the Home Rule League was held to protest against the Rowlatt Act. This event may be regarded as the beginning of Gandhi's first nation-wide campaign against British rule in India. The following day a similar meeting was held at Gandhi's Ashram and was attended by nationalist leaders from Bombay. At this time a manifesto was drawn up inaugurating passive resistance if the Rowlatt Act became law. In part this declaration announced: "We shall refuse civilly to obey these laws and such other laws as a committee to be hereafter appointed may think fit, and we further affirm that in this struggle we will faithfully follow truth and refrain from violence to life, person, or property."[41]

Upon receiving the news of the passage of one of the Rowlatt Acts, Gandhi appealed dramatically to his countrymen to observe a hartal, a day of national humiliation and prayer. This was to be a time of self-purification, the inauguration of *Satyagraha*, a sacred fight. All the people, therefore, were to close their shops, cease their work, and observe the day by means of fasting and prayer. The day of the hartal was first set for March 30 and then changed to April 6. Word did not reach Delhi of the change in date until too late, and on Sunday, March 30, Gandhi's non-violent hartal was observed. It soon ceased to be non-violent, however, when vendors of food at the railway station refused to close their shops in deference to the hartal. A large mob stormed the station. Police were called to disperse the throng, and, finally, troops had to be called in to restore order, which they succeeded in doing only after they fired on the rioters, killing eight and wounding many more. Minor disturbances continued in Delhi for the next two weeks.

In the meantime, Gandhi had decided to visit Delhi and Amritsar in the Punjab. Fearing the spread of rioting, the British authorities arrested Gandhi and returned him to Bombay, where he was shortly released. The news of the arrest was the signal for serious riots in Bombay, Ahmadabad, and all over the Punjab. At Virmagam, in Gujarat, an Indian magistrate who opposed a mob was seized and beaten; kerosene oil was poured over him, and he was burned to death. A British troop train was also derailed, but no lives were lost in the accident.

Deeply crushed by the failure of his followers to maintain their campaign on a non-violent plane, Gandhi in a great public meeting at Ahmadabad bitterly reproached them for using force.

The disturbances thus far were nothing compared to the terrible holocaust which broke out in the Punjab and had its main storm center at Amritsar, a city of some 150,000. For some weeks there had been rumblings of revolt. Those killed at Delhi in the rioting had been glorified as martyrs, and posters had mysteriously appeared warning the Government that there would be a great *Ghadr*. The British authorities tried to counteract the agitation by spreading thousands of leaflets explaining the purposes of the Rowlatt Act. The unrest, however, mounted, and the news of Gandhi's arrest and the deportation of two militant nationalists from the Punjab precipitated the most bloody incidents since the Mutiny of 1857.

Rioting began in Amritsar the morning of April 9, and troops were called out to fire on the milling crowds. Outbreaks occurred all over the city. Several Europeans were murdered and banks, churches, and railway stations were burned. Meanwhile, in the city of Lahore, in the Punjab, the European residential section was barely saved from attack by the arrival of a detachment of troops. On April 12 a serious riot took place at Kasur, forty miles from Amritsar, in which two British officers were taken from their train compartment and beaten to death. There were numerous other scattered incidents of violence, and all telegraph connection between Amritsar and the outside world was cut off.

The situation in this city was still serious when a British officer, General Dyer, arrived with a force of about one thousand soldiers. On April 12 he arrested some men regarded as the leaders of the outbreaks and the next morning issued a proclamation, by beat of the drum, warning that no public meetings were henceforth to be held and that if this order were disobeyed the troops would use their rifles.

On the following day word was received by Dyer that a great crowd was collecting in the Jallianwalla Bagh, a low cleared space enclosed on all sides by mud walls with a few narrow entrances. What followed was a terrible and excessive retribution for the recent acts of violence of the Indian mobs. General Dyer marched about fifty Gurkha soldiers to the Bagh, where he saw a large throng of people, most of them listening to speeches. Without warning, he opened fire and did not cease until the ammunition was nearly exhausted. The crowd was in a *cul-de-sac* and vainly tried to escape, but did not succeed before some four hundred had been killed and more than one thousand wounded.

For a week after this terrible scene isolated outrages continued. Trains were derailed, telegraph lines were cut, and the movement of railway freight was practically paralyzed. Sir Michael O'Dwyer, then Governor of the Punjab, maintains that news of General Dyer's stern action spread rapidly and was responsible for the prevention of further serious outbreaks. Whether or not the disorders would have gradually died down in the face of less stringent measures was an issue which later led to bitter controversy. By the end of April the Punjab was tranquil again. A new threat, however, materialized from Afghanistan, where a new Amir, bitterly hostile to Britain, began moving his troops to the attack and actually attempted in May an invasion of northern India. The Afghans proved to be no match for the British Indian army. Airplanes bombed the Afghan capital and by June 2 the Amir's forces had been badly beaten. Peace was signed in August, but the North-West Frontier continued to prove troublesome, and for a year expeditions had to be sent to subdue various marauding tribes.

Gandhi, the mystic and idealist, was shocked over the blood shed by both the British authorities and by his followers. After Amritsar and the riots in other parts of India he suspended passive resistance. In a speech the Mahatma declared that his followers had not been sufficiently educated and disciplined to carry out *Satyagraha,* and that resort to what he had hoped would be non-violence was a "Himalayan miscalculation."

And so Gandhi's first campaign against British authority came to what seemed to be a sorry and inconclusive end. As for his future plans, the Mahatma in the summer of 1919 said little and seemed to be following a policy of "wait and see." There were some indications, however, that Gandhi might still assume a more or less co-operative role with the government in trying out the new postwar governmental reforms—based on the Montagu-Chelmsford Report—recently passed by the British Parliament.

India in the 1920's experienced little tranquillity, while the world watched with keen interest the growing intransigence of Indian nationalism and the increasing discomfiture of British rule, as it sought to convince the people of its good intentions and of the urgent necessity of co-operation between them and the British in progressing toward self-government. As this chapter will show, there was much of the element of the unreal and make-believe in the Indian scene in this decade. The machinery of administration was ostensibly designed to give experience in the art of self-government, but the dominant national party, led by Gandhi, would not co-operate. This attitude ruled out any possibility of evolutionary and harmonious development toward freedom. As we will see, Britain temporized, cajoled, and reflected upon new schemes of government. In essence, however, she had only two alternatives: either to get out of India or to govern the country in her own way and according to her own principles. What actually happened? Britain followed neither course but hopelessly confused the situation by following a line made up of elements taken simultaneously from both alternatives. And, meanwhile, the Indian nationalists became more frustrated and irresponsible, glossing over basic problems inherent in their society and blaming all ills upon the alien ruler. The inevitable result is pictured in Chapter IX, when independence was not achieved as a result of any ordered and planned procedure but improvised in hurry, confusion, and desperation.

THERE WERE *in the 1920's many observers in the United States and Europe who believed Gandhi was justified in embarking upon the road of complete defiance and non-co-operation. At the same time, there are those in the 1950's who wish that both Gandhi and the British had pursued a more consistent and positive policy.*

Toward

self-government

chapter 7

WHILE INDIA seethed with indignation over the Rowlatt Acts and the tragedy of Amritsar, the British government proceeded with the task of carrying out the recommendations of the Montagu-Chelmsford Report. The problem was turned over to a Joint Select Committee of both houses of Parliament. This body had its first meeting on July 16, 1919, and sat continuously, hearing evidence, for a period of six months. All shades of British and Indian opinion were heard, and its report was finally presented to Parliament on November 17, 1919. The Joint Committee made a few minor amendments to the India Bill that had been prepared by the government. These were accepted by the coalition ministry of Lloyd George, and the bill became law, December 23, 1919.

During the debate in the House of Commons, the Secretary of State for India, Edwin Samuel Montagu, was eloquent and convincing in his defense of the reforms. Outlining the goal of a free India, Montagu declared:

I implore this House to show to India to-day that Parliament is receptive of the case for self-government and only seeks an opportunity of completing it by the demonstrable realisation of the success of its stages. . . . Here is a country desirous of achieving nationality. . . . Let us pass this Bill and start it, under the aegis of the British flag, on the road which we ourselves have travelled.[1]

Other supporters of the India Bill, especially Lord Sinha, who was an outstanding Indian nationalist, an ex-president of the Congress, and a leader of the Indian Moderates, cogently argued that the Bill was not aimed at setting up a final constitution for India. It was intended to provide a bridge of transition whereby India could pass from a bureaucratic form of control to a government in which she would determine her own destinies.

The Indian Governmental Reforms of 1919

The new Act had a twofold purpose: to initiate the first step in the direction of self-government and, at the same time, to give to Indians the opportunity of responsibility and experience in democratic government. The field primarily selected for this opportunity was in the provincial governments. Here, in the provinces, an ingenious device or mechanism in self-government was pro-

vided. Each province was to be allowed a legislature in which 70 per cent of the members were elected by voters in urban and rural constituencies. The governmental administration of the province was to be of a dual nature, in which the departments were classified as either "reserved" or "transferred." In the former category were such departments as justice, famine relief, irrigation, police, and prisons. These were under the exclusive control of a British Governor, assisted by a small Executive Council, and acting independently of the will of the provincial legislature.

The transferred departments, such as education, local government, sanitation, health, and agriculture, were turned over to Indian ministers, who in turn were responsible to the provincial legislature. While unchecked by the legislature in the field of reserved powers, the Provincial Governor was expected to accept the advice of his ministers in the area of transferred government. This bifurcation of governmental administration into two halves—one responsible and the other bureaucratic—was termed Dyarchy.

The Act of 1919 for the first time divided the functions of government in India between the provinces and the central government. To the latter went such powers as customs, military and foreign affairs, and relations with the Indian States; to the former (i.e., the provinces) went such functions as police, justice, education, and public works. The old unitary form of government was thus discarded, and in effect a quasi-federal system was established. This action was taken in the belief that the ultimate form of government in India, one uniting both the British provinces and the Native States into one integrated political pattern, must be some type of federation.

In the central government of British India, the Act of 1919 established a bicameral legislature, consisting of the Council of State and the Assembly, in which the unofficial element (that is, elected members) were in a majority over those official members who were expected to support the views of the British government. Voters on a restricted franchise selected their representatives for the Central Legislature, while the official members were designated by a section in the Indian constitution. In the last analysis, however, the Governor-General could override the will of the elected majority by the power of "certification." The Governor-General was able to certify any bill

1- *Quoted in Sir George E. Schuster and Guy Wint,* India and Democracy *(London: The Macmillan Company, 1941), p. 79.*

which in his opinion might endanger the general safety and tranquillity of the country, and thus prevent its enactment. He could also certify a bill as essential, and thus enact it into law without the consent of the legislature. Also, in the budget of the central government a number of items, relating to salaries of officials, to the military establishment, and other matters, were not votable. The Governors in the provinces were also endowed with the certifying power, and were able to block legislation even in the transferred field of government if the British executive thought it essential.

Despite the certifying power possessed by both Governor-General and the Provincial Governors, the Act of 1919 constituted a major constitutional advance toward ultimate Indian self-government. Before 1919 the franchise was enjoyed by a microscopic minority, only 33,000 voters, but after the Act the vote was given to 5,179,000 males. The usual requirement for the franchise was the payment of a small amount of land tax or municipal rates. All who paid income tax and all former soldiers in the Indian army were also given the vote. Even with what might be thought to be a very moderate extension of the franchise, many of the voters were illiterate, and special devices at the polls were necessary to facilitate elections. On the ballots, for example, candidates were given symbols rather than names, such devices as the tiger, elephant, flag, and sword being used. Women did not receive the right to vote in 1919. The various legislatures, however, were given power to confer female franchise. Madras led the way in 1921, and by 1928 practically all constituencies had women voters. Also, in seven out of the nine provinces of British India and in the Assembly of the Central Legislature women could be members by 1928.

A feature quite distinct from customary democratic practice was the provision of communal electorates in the voting machinery set up in India in 1919. Apparently the Montagu-Chelmsford investigators held an adverse opinion of the system as it had been first applied by the Morley-Minto Reforms, but the various minorities—especially the Muslims—demanded guaranteed representation in separate or communal electorates, and Mr. Montagu was reluctantly forced to concur. In voting for the Central Legislature, therefore, separate electorates were set up for the Muslims, Sikhs, and Landholders, and for Indian Commerce as well

as the electorate termed Non-Muslim, which presumably would be overwhelmingly Hindu. In the voting for the Provincial Legislatures additional electorates were created to represent Anglo-Indians, Indian Christians, and representatives of universities.

The Indian National Congress has frequently castigated the British for introducing communal, or separate, electorates. That there were, at least, two sides to this question is shown by the testimony of Claude Van Tyne, late professor of history at the University of Michigan, who after visiting India in the early 1920's wrote:

And one who imagines that India is ready for our democratic ideas of rule by a majority should read the addresses presented to the Montagu Commission by the farmers of the Deccan, by the zamindars or great landholders, by the depressed classes, the Europeans, by the Mohammedans, by the Indian Christians, and by interests of various kinds, pleading that in a new representative system to be set up they should not be left to the mercy of any mere numerical majority. It is as if the Christian Scientists, the Scandinavians, the Jews, the tobacco-growers, the Greek shoeblacks of the United States should protest against their minority interests being left to a majority decision in the American Congress.[2]

Such was the system of government introduced in India by the Act of 1919, which was opposed both by the National Congress in India and by the imperialistic diehards in Britain. From many quarters came criticism and skepticism concerning the practicality of Dyarchy, or Divided Government. The Calcutta *Statesman*, for example, asserted that the new-fangled device of Dyarchy "can result only in an irritating form of association and a profitless semblance of responsibility."[3] A diehard British newspaper, the *Morning Post*, satirized the origin of Dyarchy in a conversation between Montagu and Chelmsford. "The latter says, 'How can we ever come to an agreement since I believe in a Trinity and you believe in a Unity?' Montagu replies, 'Let us split the difference,' and the worship of the great God Dyarchy is forthwith inaugurated."[4]

Despite a heavy volume of censure, however, the Indian Moderate party, which had bolted the Congress, and most liberal opinion in Great Britain stuck to their guns in defense of the new scheme of political reform. And in February 1921 the reforms were officially initiated when the Duke

2- *C. H. Van Tyne*, India in Ferment *(New York: D. Appleton and Co., 1923), p. 22.*

3- *Quoted in* Literary Digest, *LXVIII (December 20, 1919), p. 23.*

4- *Quoted in H. E. A. Cotton, "Constitution-making for India,"* Contemporary Review, *CXVII (1920), p. 69.*

of Connaught formally presided at the opening of the new Indian Legislature at Delhi. The ceremony was impressive, with troops in full-dress uniform, and the Native Princes attending in their colorful costumes. A message of good-will was read from the King-Emperor, who sent his assurances that Indians on this day were witnessing the beginnings of self-government within the Empire.

Undoubtedly with Amritsar in his mind, the Duke of Connaught made a strong appeal for co-operation in making Dyarchy work. Said he:

> My experience tells me that misunderstanding usually means mistakes on either side. As an old friend of India, I appeal to you all—British and Indians—to bury along with the dead past the mistakes and misunderstandings of the past, to forgive where you have to forgive, and to join hands and to work together to realise the hopes that arise from to-day.[5]

The inauguration of the new scheme of Indian government, however, coincided with a great mass movement of Hindus and Muslims, led by Mohandas Gandhi, in which the declared object was the boycotting of the reforms and the achievement of complete self-government, *swaraj,* for India.

Non-co-operation and the Khilafat Movement

In order to understand how this mass boycott of British rule came to be launched, it is necessary to retrace our steps a little, back to the closing months of 1919. At this time Gandhi, notwithstanding the Amritsar incident, was apparently inclined to cooperate with the government in working the reformed Indian constitution. In his newspaper *Young India* he wrote, "Our duty is not to subject the Reforms to carping criticism, but to settle down quietly to work so as to make them a success."[6] The Congress met at Amritsar in December 1919, and here the Mahatma urged the gathering to give the reforms a fair trial. This 1919 conclave may be regarded as the first Gandhi Congress. Gandhi was rapidly becoming the idol of the young nationalists and a veritable god to the masses. From now on in the Congress the cry "Mahatma Gandhi Ki jai," was heard more and more frequently.

Only six months after the Amritsar Congress, Gandhi was spurning the reforms and calling for a mass movement against a government he termed

"Satanic." Said the Mahatma, "It is better to die in the way of God than to live in the way of Satan. Therefore, whoever is satisfied that this Government represents the activity of Satan has no choice left to him but to dissociate himself from it."[7]

Why this Gandhian *volte-face?* The answer is easily found in what the Mahatma maintained were the broken pledges and insincerity of the British government manifested in the "whitewashing" of the culprits of Amritsar and in another injustice imposed upon Indian Muslims, the Khilafat grievance.

As the facts of the disturbances in the Punjab, and especially the details of the Amritsar outbreak, became fully known in the late spring and summer of 1919, Indian public opinion loosed a storm of denunciation against the ruthless tactics of the British officials involved. Seeking to mollify aroused Indian sentiment, the British Governor-General appointed a special Committee under the chairmanship of Lord Hunter to investigate the disturbances in Bombay, Delhi, and the Punjab. Coincidentally, the Congress had appointed its own special Committee to secure the facts on the "Punjab wrong."

In March 1920 the Congress Committee *Report* was published, and it contained a scathing attack against the measures resorted to by British officials in coping with the Punjab disturbances of the spring of 1919. The official Hunter Commission in the meantime heard evidence in four Indian cities. In defending his actions, General Dyer maintained that law and order had been menaced and were in the balance at Amritsar, and said that if this challenge had not been met, open and bloody rebellion would have broken out. Said Dyer, "It only struck me at the time it was my duty to do this [i.e., fire on the assembled crowd], and that it was a horrible duty."[8] Nevertheless, the Commission in its Report published in May 1919 censured Dyer for firing without notice and continuing to fire after it was evident that the situation was well in hand. A minority Report, signed by the three Indian members of the Commission, went much further than the majority Report (signed by the five British members) in condemning the brutality and inhuman treatment meted out to Indians at Amritsar. On receipt of the Hunter Report the government of India, summing up its final view, declared that Dyer's action was "dictated by a stern though misconceived sense of

5- India in 1920 (*Calcutta: Superintendent Government Printing, 1921*), p. 21.

6- Quoted in Kate Mitchell, *India Without Fable (New York: Alfred A. Knopf, 1942*), p. 160.

7- Quoted in Glorney Bolton, *The Tragedy of Gandhi (London: George Allen and Unwin, 1934*), p. 156.

8- Quoted in H. G. Rawlinson, *The British Achievement in India (London: William Hodge, 1948*), p. 202.

duty. . . ." It added, "We can arrive at no other conclusion than that General Dyer acted beyond the necessity of the case, beyond what any reasonable man could have thought to be necessary, and that he did not act with as much humanity as the case permitted."[9]

Accordingly, Dyer was deprived of his command and censured, actions that were fully discussed and approved in a decisive debate carried on in the House of Commons. So far so good, from the Indian standpoint, but the conciliatory gestures of the Indian government and the Commons were undone by the action of the House of Lords, which dissented from the lower House and vigorously supported Dyer. At the same time, the British diehard press launched a shrill campaign in favor of Dyer, a campaign which included sponsoring a fund for the aggrieved officer.

These events opened up anew the Amritsar wound. Tagore, the great Indian poet, astounded by some of the speeches in Parliament in defense of Dyer, wrote that "The unashamed condonation of brutality expressed in their speeches . . . is ugly in its frightfulness."[10] Anti-imperialists in other parts of the world joined in the chorus of denunciation. In rebuttal British writers pointed out that the very torrent of criticism against what had happened in the Punjab was evidence that such occurrences were rare under British rule, and that nothing like Amritsar had happened since the days of the Indian Mutiny in 1857.

While the Report of the Hunter Commission and the debates on Amritsar in the British Parliament were adding fuel to the fires of nationalism in India, the Khilafat (or caliphate) controversy was alienating many Indian Muslims against British rule. All Mohammedans in India looked to Turkey as the greatest Muslim power. Furthermore, the Turkish Sultan was the Caliph of Islam and as such the spiritual head of Mohammedanism. During the First World War it was a source of great embarrassment to Britain that she was at war with Turkey, a state whose ruler was revered by so many millions of her subjects in India. In January 1918 the British Prime Minister, Lloyd George, had declared that Turkey was not to be deprived of its capital or the lands of Thrace and Asia Minor, which were predominantly Turkish. At the conclusion of the war, however, there were rumors of secret treaties made by Britain and France for the division of the Ottoman Empire.

Constantinople was seized by Allied troops, and in the spring of 1919 Greek forces landed in Smyrna with the encouragement of the British government.

In May 1920 the draft treaty of Sèvres was published. This document imposed a severe peace upon Turkey, internationalizing the Straits; depriving her of all rights in Egypt, Tripolitania, Morocco, and Tunisia; and taking away the territories of Arabia, Palestine, Mesopotamia, and Syria. In addition, Greece was temporarily to administer Smyrna and southwestern Asia Minor, and to add Eastern Thrace to her realm.

Such terms were regarded by Muslims, especially in India, as unnecessarily severe, and the cry of "Islam is in danger" was raised. In vain did British statesmen try to point out that Britain herself could not undo the Treaty of Sèvres, that Britain had commitments to France, that the Allied world supported the design of a Zionist National Home in Palestine, and that a soft peace for Turkey—after the long history of Turkish misrule and atrocities—was out of the question.

Despite these arguments, Indian Muslims proceeded to organize their Khilafat movement to force the British government to amend the Sèvres Treaty on the side of leniency. In November 1919 a Khilafat conference was held in Delhi. Gandhi attended and suggested the possibility of all Indians, Muslim and Hindu, joining in a boycott of the government. In the spring of 1920 the Khilafat movement rapidly gained momentum. In March a Muslim delegation was sent to London to demand revision of the Sèvres Treaty, and March 19 was proclaimed as a national day of fast for Turkey by Indian Muslims.

At this juncture Gandhi stepped forward as the Khilafat champion. He warned the government that if justice were not done to Turkey he would launch a great Hindu-Muslim non-co-operation movement. In his *Open Letter to All Englishmen in India,* Gandhi accused Lloyd George of treachery and declared that the Khilafat wrong and the British whitewashing of Amritsar had completely shattered his faith in the good intentions of Britain. In August Gandhi returned to the Viceroy various medals and decorations he had received from the British government for his services during the Boer War and the First World War. Following this action, the leaders of the Khilafat movement, Mohammed Ali and his brother Shaukat Ali, pro-

9- India in 1920, *p. 238.*

10- *Quoted in Van Tyne, op. cit., p. 144.*

claimed a Hindu-Muslim entente and toured India with Gandhi appealing for support.

The National Congress convened in special session at Calcutta in September 1920. This meeting was dominated by Gandhi, who made a powerful speech in favor of "progressive non-violent non-co-operation" to be used as a weapon in support of the Khilafat movement and also to force the British government to grant India self-rule "within the British Empire if possible, without if necessary."[11] The Congress accepted Gandhi's non-co-operation program, which called for the following measures: (1) the surrender of all British titles; (2) refusal to attend any government functions; (3) the withdrawal of all students from schools and colleges; (4) the boycott of courts; (5) no service by Indians in the British army in Iraq; and (6) absolutely no co-operation with the new governmental reforms, either as candidates for office or as voters in elections. A few months later, the regular annual session of the Congress, meeting at Nagpur, enthusiastically endorsed the non-co-operation movement. And so it was that Gandhi completely repudiated his position, taken just a year before in 1919 at the Amritsar Congress, in support of the new governmental reforms.

This *volte-face* was a decisive event destined to shape the course of India's history from 1920 through the next two decades. Gandhi was not perhaps greatly motivated by an appreciation of any deep injustice to his Muslim colleagues inflicted by the Sèvres Treaty or even by the "condoning" of Amritsar, but rather by the fact that an unusual opportunity had been offered him of uniting all Indians—Muslim and Hindu—and thus of accelerating the pace toward national independence. As Gandhi declared, it was "such an opportunity of uniting Hindus and Mohammedans as would not arise in a hundred years."[12] Yet there was something incongruous in this union of soul-force and militant Islam. Perhaps Gandhi had rationalized his advocacy of the Khilafat cause until he came to believe in its inherent justice, but actually it would seem that this alliance sprang primarily from political expediency.

In initiating his non-co-operation movement, Gandhi was not concerned exclusively with the rectification of the Khilafat injustice or the realization of self-rule *(swaraj)*. His campaign also became the vehicle for spreading his way of life,

for securing certain moral and social objectives. To Gandhi's mind western civilization, with its science, industry, and cities, was a soul-destroying curse. Gandhi, Rousseau-like, espoused the simple and the uncluttered life. In his view:

India's salvation consists in unlearning what she has learned during the last fifty years. The railways, telegraphs, hospitals, lawyers, doctors and suchlike have all to go; and the so-called upper classes have to learn consciously, religiously, and deliberately the simple peasant life. . . . Every time I get into a railway car or use a motor bus I know that I am doing violence to my sense of what is right.[13]

To Gandhi, wherever the curse of modern civilization had not reached India was happy and free. The simple and unspoiled village life, therefore, must be resurrected. As part of his non-co-operation movement Gandhi consequently preached the boycott of all foreign manufactured goods, especially cloth. He urged the use of the spinning wheel, the charkha, for the production of homespun cloth, khaddar. To cleanse India of another evil excrescence of modern civilization, Gandhi also championed the temperance movement. He detested liquor as a root cause of poverty and moral depravity. Liquor shops were boycotted and the American prohibition leader "Pussyfoot" Johnson was invited from the United States to give advice to Gandhi and his Congress leaders.

The non-co-operation campaign reached a climax in 1921. Symbolic burnings of foreign cloth were carried out, some of which were attended by multitudes of more than 100,000 people. An eyewitness of one of these burnings of a great pyramid of cloth gives the following vivid description: "The Mahatma lighted the heap of foreign clothing. The sight was extremely impressive; the vast audience, the burning clothes, and the passionate speakers, under God's sky in the growing night."[14] It should be kept in mind that this attack on foreign goods was an expression of nationalist demands for economic independence as well as political *swaraj*.

In parts of India college and secondary education was seriously disrupted. Calcutta University reported that four thousand students had dropped out of Bengal's colleges, and the loss of students in this province's secondary schools ran to about 40 per cent.

While Gandhi exhorted his followers to practice

11- *Post Wheeler,* India Against the Storm *(New York: E. P. Dutton, 1944), p. 177.*

12- *Edward J. Thompson,* Reconstructing India *(New York: Dial Press, 1930), p. 127.*

13- *Quoted in Jawaharlal Nehru,* Toward Freedom *(New York: John Day Company, 1942), p. 314.*

14- *Gertrude Emerson, "Non-Violent Non-Cooperation in India," Asia, XXII (August 1922), p. 610.*

non-violence scrupulously, his movement became increasingly marred by incidents of bloodshed and force. Strikes, riots, and raids on property became more and more common. The Khilafat movement was also getting out of hand. Aroused by religious fanaticism, many Muslims had preached a *Hijrat,* that is, a mass exodus, enabling true believers to escape from the pollution of British rule. Accordingly, a great mass emigration got under way in the latter part of 1920, and at one time some eighteen thousand people were on the move through the Khyber Pass en route to Afghanistan. This country at first gave the Muslim pilgrims a friendly asylum but later closed the frontier. Thousands of emigrants were stranded, and the road from Kabul to Peshawar became dotted with the graves of homeless refugees.

Along the Malabar coast of India in the province of Madras a group of Muslim people, the Moplahs, inflamed by the Khilafat propaganda, rose in rebellion and turned against their Hindu neighbors. Hundreds of Hindus were murdered and their temples defaced. At least two thousand Moplahs were killed by troops striving to restore order, and martial law was in force for seven months. It was this bloody outbreak that terminated the brief Hindu-Muslim entente, and the president of the All-India Muslim League announced the withdrawal of his organization from the Congress campaign of non-co-operation. A year later events took place in Turkey which completely shattered the Khilafat agitation. In 1922 the Sultanate was abolished. Mohammed VI was deposed but remained as the Caliph; however, in 1923, when the Turkish Republic was proclaimed, steps were taken to abolish completely the institution of the Caliphate, which was ended in March 1924.

Despite these setbacks, Congress and its leader were still confident of success. Perhaps the surrender of Lloyd George to the demands of the Irish Sinn Fein leaders, Michael Collins and David Griffiths, with the consequent creation of a self-governing Irish Free State, was a straw in the wind indicating Great Britain's growing willingness to admit the validity of nationalistic aspirations in her empire. Accordingly, at the Ahmadabad Congress in December 1922, Gandhi asked for and was given authority to initiate a campaign of mass civil disobedience. Heretofore, non-co-operation of schools, political offices, and courts had only touched the upper classes; now Gandhi was about to appeal to the common people to refuse to pay taxes and to "non-co-operate" against the government in every possible manner. On February 1, 1922, Gandhi addressed to the Viceroy, Lord Reading, a letter demanding a complete change of heart on the part of the government within the space of a week. If Congress demands were not met by this time, civil disobedience would be introduced in the district of Bardoli, in Gujarat.

Three days later, however, a mob of Congress volunteers attacked a police station at Chauri Chaura, set it afire, and burned twenty-one policemen to death. Following the receipt of this news, Gandhi with his Congress Working Committee suddenly suspended his whole program of non-co-operation and civil disobedience. Gandhi deplored the bloodshed at Chauri Chaura; insisted that all defiance of authority should cease; declared that the withholding of taxes and rent payments was contrary to the interests of Congress; and, most significantly perhaps, assured the landlords that the Congress movement in no way intended to attack the rights of private property.

The news of the suspension of non-co-operation was received with dismay by many members of Congress. Nehru, a young and ardent nationalist destined for leadership, observed:

Suddenly, early in February 1922, the whole scene shifted, and we in prison learned, to our amazement and consternation, that Gandhiji had stopped the aggressive aspects of our struggle, that he had suspended civil resistance. . . . We were angry when we learned of this stoppage of our struggle at a time when we seemed to be consolidating our position and advancing on all fronts.[15]

There has been much conjecture about the motive behind this cancellation of the Congress campaign against British authority. Was it because Gandhi, as a pacifist and a believer in non-violence, refused any longer to tolerate bloodshed? Undoubtedly this explanation has relevance, but there are some authorities who find the solution in the bourgeois character of the Congress. The middle-class leaders of the nationalist movement, including wealthy landowners and industrialists, were fearful of a genuine popular movement that might become an attack on all property, privilege, and power—Indian as well as British. More and more in the 1920's funds flowed from Indian capitalists into the coffers of Congress. Apart from

15- *Nehru,* Toward Freedom, *p. 79.*

purely patriotic motives, the millionaires could hardly be blamed for trying to hurry the day when their own national government would adjust Indian tariffs to suit their interests.

After the Bardoli retreat, Gandhi's bolt seemed to have been shot. His promise of *swaraj* "within a year" had not been realized, and a growing number of critics questioned the utility of non-co-operation and boycott of the new legislatures. Mrs. Besant had assailed Gandhi's tactics and had taken refuge in the ranks of the Liberal party, a group that had bolted from the Congress. Even Tagore, ardent nationalist that he was, averred:

> The idea of non-co-operation is political asceticism. Our students (kept out of colleges) are bringing their offerings of sacrifices to what? Not to a fuller education, but to a non-education. It has at its back a fierce joy of annihilation which at its best is asceticism, and at its worst is that orgy of frightfulness in which the human nature . . . finds a disinterested delight in an unmeaning devastation. The anarchy of mere emptiness never tempts me.[16]

Gandhi was arrested on March 10, 1922, and brought to trial by the British authorities. The court room proceedings made excellent copy in the newspapers of the world. Mrs. Sarojini Naidu, poetess and nationalist, likened the trial to that of Jesus, with the British magistrate cast in the role of Pontius Pilate. Gandhi and his judge outdid themselves in trying to be polite. The former declared he was here "to invite and submit cheerfully to the highest penalty,"[17] and the latter, after sentencing the prisoner to six years, added that no one would be more pleased than he if circumstances in India might make it possible for the government later to reduce the period of imprisonment.

On the surface the non-co-operation campaign seemingly failed, but Gandhi had succeeded in making an all-important contribution to the Indian nationalist movement. He was the first national leader not only to secure the support of the Indian intelligentsia and the middle classes, but also to stir and attract the loyalty of the untold masses in the countless villages of India. No better evaluation of Gandhi's significance in the 1920's can be found than the following passage written by an eyewitness of non-co-operation just a few months after the Bardoli surrender:

> Gandhi has, I believe, done his work. He has made India self-conscious. He has given India a new sense

of self-respect. His program has been characterized by many negative features. . . . It has never put forward even a suggestive outline of the government it would substitute for the one it would tear down. . . . But Gandhi has given a moral basis and a spiritual standing to India's revolution.[18]

Politics in the Uneasy 1920's

At the end of 1920, when Gandhi and the Congress had decided to inaugurate "non-violent non-co-operation," elections had just been held for the first time under the new Government of India Act. Because of the Congress boycott only 30 per cent of the voters went to the polls in the provincial elections, and for the lower house of the central government, the Assembly, only 182,000 voted out of a possible one million. Out of a total of 747 seats in all legislatures, however, only 6 in all were unfilled because of no candidate.

In February 1921 the legislatures convened. The great majority of representatives belonged to the Liberal or Moderate party, whose members had forsaken what they thought to be the unnecessary extremism of Gandhi and the Congress. These moderates were anxious to get parliamentary government initiated, and in most of the legislatures they acted with good faith, with responsibility, in helping to make the new system of government work. In the lower house of the central government, the President, Sir Frederick Whyte, presided with dignity and impartiality and at the same time "drilled and disciplined this embryo parliament in the best traditions of the House of Commons."[19]

To this first legislature under the new constitution must be given credit for a number of significant accomplishments. A fiscal commission was created which recommended a protective policy for India. Such action had been made possible by the declaration of the Joint Select Committee on Indian Reforms, which, as we have seen, in 1919 paved the way for the enactment of Dyarchy in India. This declaration stated that "whatever be the right fiscal policy for India, it is quite clear that she should have the same liberty to consider her interests as Great Britain, Australia, New Zealand, Canada and South Africa."[20] From 1921, therefore, protection was the accepted policy of the Indian government, and the cotton industry was given a protective tariff on piece goods that rose to a figure of 25 per cent against British cloth

16- *Quoted in Van Tyne*, op. cit., pp. 134-135.

17- *Quoted in Roy Walker,* Sword of Gold *(London: Indian Independence Union, 1945), p. 88.*

18- *Emerson*, op. cit., p. 674.

19- *Van Tyne*, op. cit., p. 38.

20- Report of the Joint Select Committee on the Government of India Bill *(London: His Majesty's Stationery Office, 1919), p. 11.*

in the early 1930's. As for steel, the famous Tata Iron Works was assisted by a 33 per cent duty and for a time by bounties. The importance of the Fiscal Convention, as it is called, can be seen by the following figures: In the five years preceding 1914 India imported annually goods worth an average of £61 million from the United Kingdom and exports averaged £37.5 million. In 1938-1939, however, the corresponding figures were £34.8 million and £43.5 million.

In addition to tariff enactments, the Legislature repealed what it thought to be an obnoxious press act and also the much-discussed Rowlatt Act, which had helped to set off the disturbances of 1919. The same body adopted a program of retrenchment in the public services, planned the nationalization of all railways, and agitated for the more rapid "Indianization" of the civil services and the initiation of the same policy in the army. Other important pieces of legislation were the Indian Factories Amendment Act and the Workman's Compensation Act. The Indian representatives in the Assembly were on the whole co-operative, but they also pricked and pushed the government for more reforms. On several occasions there was strong criticism expressed over the heavy military expenditures and much controversy when the Governor-General, Lord Reading, in 1923 used his power of certification to double the salt tax. In the Act of 1919 it was laid down by the British Parliament that after a period of ten years the reform scheme should be studied and its operation assessed. The Assembly in September 1921 passed a resolution urging a re-examination of the Constitution, as, in its view, an immediate and more democratic revision was warranted.

In the provincial legislatures Indian representatives were getting valuable experience in law-making and in administrative responsibility in the field of the "transferred powers." Considerable attention was given by the legislators to an attempt to strengthen the units of local self-government. Local village boards were given power to try petty civil suits and to expand taxation for such purposes as sanitation. A serious obstacle, however, was the traditional reluctance of the villager to agree to additional taxation. Much attention was paid to education in the provincial legislatures, and in every province compulsory elementary education was adopted for certain areas. In the field of agriculture and rural reconstruction,

the provincial governments encouraged the work of the rural co-operatives, which built new roads, opened dispensaries and schools, and, with the aid of the department of agriculture, taught better methods of farming. Other features of rural reforms were the beginnings of consolidation of small, fragmented holdings; co-operative banking for the villages; and the initiation of irrigation projects. In themselves these reforms were admirable, yet taken as a whole they were pitifully meager when compared with the needs of the country.

By the middle of 1923, when the first Indian Legislature came to an end, there occurred a revolt against the leadership and policy of Mohandas Gandhi, who was in prison. Two outstanding members of the Congress, C. R. Das and Pandit Motilal Nehru, defeated Gandhi's policy of non-co-operation. These leaders believed the Congress party must contest elections and enter the legislatures. The object, however, was not co-operation but rather the tactic of "wrecking the reforms from within." In September 1923 Das finally secured the approval of Congress to participate in the fall elections. The result was a striking decline in the strength of the Liberals and a major success for Das's Swaraj party in the Legislatures. Following the election, the Swaraj group dominated two Provincial Councils and had a powerful block of forty-five representatives in the Central Assembly.

With the advent of the Congress-sponsored Swaraj party, the era of good feeling disappeared in the Central Legislature at Delhi. The aim of most of the representatives now was "uniform, continuous, and sustained obstruction with a view to making government through the Assembly and the Councils impossible."[21] The debates became more bitter; demands were made for full responsible government to take the place of the makeshift system of Dyarchy; and the atmosphere in the Legislature was frequently enlivened by "scenes," such as the symbolic withdrawal of the Swaraj party on one occasion in 1925.

Increasingly in 1926, in newspapers and on the public platform, one read or heard caustic criticisms against the system of government. As Lord Reading left India in the spring to make way for a new Viceroy, Lord Irwin, it was quite evident that Dyarchy and the reforms of 1919 were breaking down. In 1925, C. R. Das, at that time the outstanding Congress leader, had intimated the possibility of reconciliation with Britain. In a speech Das had praised Dominion status, asserting, " . . . it affords complete protection to each constituent composing the great Commonwealth of Nations called the British Empire, secures to each the right to realise itself . . . and therefore it expresses and implies all the elements of Swaraj which I have mentioned."[22] Whatever promise of partnership between the British raj and Indian nationalism there might have been in these words, it had no chance of realization, for Das died a few short weeks after the speech was given. Intransigent nationalism continued to mount, accompanied by a disturbing revival of Hindu-Muslim antipathy. Many elections in 1926 were fought on a straight Mohammedan-versus-Hindu ticket and, from 1926 to 1927, at least 300 people were killed and 2500 injured in communal riotings.

It was in this atmosphere of tension and mounting unrest that Lord Irwin arrived in the spring of 1926 as the new head of the Indian government. Before his appointment as Viceroy, Irwin was little known in British public life, his first important post being that of minister of agriculture under British Prime Minister Stanley Baldwin. A man of simple tastes, a good farmer, Irwin was scrupulously honest and a deeply religious Anglo-Catholic.

Nationalism continued to advance with seven-league boots throughout 1927. A bitter dispute took place in the Assembly over a currency bill, a measure that did much to line up the mill owners and Indian monied interests back of the Congress. The publication of *Mother India* by the American writer Katherine Mayo also stirred up intense resentment in India. This book, a scornful indictment of Hinduism and its way of life, was written in a completely unsympathetic mood without recognition of the many admirable features of the Hindu way of life. While *Mother India* did expose many evils demanding amelioration, it was completely one-sided. It was charged by some Indian nationalists that the British government had subsidized and encouraged the publication of the book. Gandhi very sensibly summed up the matter when he said that it was "a drain inspector's report, a book for Englishmen to forget and Indians to remember."[23]

Another factor exacerbating Indian nationalism was the unfair treatment meted out to Indians in several parts of the British Empire. In a previous chapter we have already noted the discriminations imposed upon the Indian community in South

Africa and their partial removal on the eve of World War I, due to the efforts of Gandhi. The problem reappeared, however, in 1925, when a bill was drafted designed to legalize the segregation of all Indians in the South African province of Natal, both for residence and business purposes. The same difficulty emerged in the British East African colony of Kenya. In this area British settlers had established a thriving European plantation economy in the highlands and were determined to exclude Indian immigrants. In 1919 the European settlers in Kenya succeeded in having a Commission, which had been appointed by the local government, report adversely on Indian interests. Indians were to be excluded from owning lands in the highlands, were to be segregated in the towns, and were not to have the same political privileges as the Europeans.

In the early 1920's this unfair treatment infuriated Indian nationalists. The National Congress in a special meeting held in 1923 violently attacked the policy of the British government in Kenya, and in 1925, at the Congress meeting at Cawnpore, Gandhi severely condemned the South African government for the injustices imposed on the Indian nationals. At this Congress, a delegate from South Africa in an impassioned speech declared: "If you had some battle-ships today, if you had your army, a little handful of the so-called whites who were vomited forth on the shores of Africa from the slums of Europe would not have dared do what they are doing today."[24]

Debates on the currency bill, resentment over *Mother India*, and anger over the discriminations suffered by Indians in East and South Africa were only small faggots in the fire of Indian nationalism; the real fuel was provided by the appointment of the Simon Commission. By the end of 1926 the British government had come to the conclusion that the date for the inquiry into Dyarchy, set by the Act of 1919 for the year 1929, would have to be chosen and a Parliamentary Commission appointed for this purpose immediately. Accordingly, such a body was appointed in November 1927. It was composed of Sir John Simon, the chairman, and six other members representing the three British political parties. The personnel of the Commission was entirely British, a fact that roused a storm of protest in India and showed lack of tact. Sir John Simon tried to rectify the blunder by asking that six selected members of

22- Quoted in J. Coatman, Years of Destiny; India, 1926-1932 (London: Jonathan Cape, 1932), pp. 25-26.

23- Quoted in Bolton, op. cit., p. 195.

24- Charlotte V. Wiser, "Madame President in the Chair in India," Asia, XXVI (July 1926), p. 635.

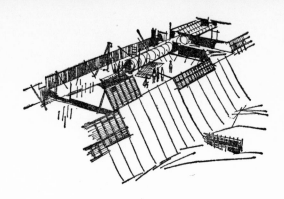

the central Indian Legislature and also representatives of the provincial legislatures should be included in this investigation of India's "fitness for self-government." But the initial slight claimed by most Indians was not rectified. The members of the Indian Legislative Assembly repudiated the Simon Commission by declaring that the Assembly would have nothing to do with the Commission at any time. Subsequently, as the Simon Commission toured India, it was boycotted in every phase of its work by the Congress party.

Buoying up and supporting the rapid advance of Indian nationalism in 1926 and 1927 was a new generation of young nationalists more dynamic and radical than their elders. Gandhi had been imprisoned in 1922 and remained in jail until early in 1924, when he was released by the government. For the next four years he remained out of the field of political agitation, contenting himself with working for the removal of untouchability, better relations between the Hindu and Muslim communities, and the development of his handspinning program. During this interregnum, first Das and then Motilal Nehru had assumed leadership of the nationalists. A new group of more ardent and radical nationalists, however, was emerging, including Jawaharlal Nehru, the son of Motilal, and Subhas Chandra Bose.

Up to this time the Congress movement had been mainly bourgeois and upper class in its leadership and policies. By 1925 it began to reflect the growth of socialist and workers' groups in India. The first socialist weekly had been founded in 1923 and the first Workers' and Peasants' party set up in Bengal in 1926, while a Communist movement was also growing. Thus it was that there developed in Congress a left wing whose members sponsored a Student and Youth Movement and an All-India Independence League. The objective of the latter was not only the complete cutting of the painter connecting India with the British ship of state, but also the amelioration of the masses, the liquidation of the parasitic zamindars (landlords), and the introduction of a socialist state. Jawaharlal Nehru was the president of this League, and its appearance signalized the fact that in addition to political independence there was crystallizing another objective—a complete socio-economic revolution.

Nehru, the leader destined to take his country eventually into the promised land of independence,

25- *Nehru,* Toward Freedom, p. 353.

came from a Brahman family of ancient lineage which had migrated from the state of Kashmir. His father, Motilal Nehru, first a prominent and wealthy lawyer and a lukewarm nationalist, had after 1919 thrown himself wholeheartedly behind Gandhi and had even adopted his ascetic way of life. The son, Jawaharlal, had all the advantages of wealth. He was sent to the English public school of Harrow and later to Trinity College, Cambridge, where he obtained his B.A. in 1910; he was admitted to the Bar in 1912.

Upon his return to India, Nehru showed little interest in the law and gradually became interested and then completely absorbed in his country's fight for freedom. While a great admirer of Gandhi, Nehru could not agree with the Mahatma's asceticism and mysticism, or with his antagonism against western industrialism. At heart this Brahman is a rationalist, a believer in science and a foe of all supernaturalism. Above all, he is a blend of the cultures of both the East and West, with the latter perhaps predominating. As he himself has said: "I have become a queer mixture of the East and the West, out of place everywhere, at home nowhere. Perhaps my thoughts and approach to life are more akin to what is called Western than Eastern, but India clings to me."[25] As a rationalist, a humanitarian, and an implacable foe of the exploitation of his fellow men, Nehru found it logical to support socialism, which he believed could be made compatible with democratic political freedoms.

By the end of 1927 the tide of nationalism was rapidly mounting. At the annual meeting of Congress held at Madras, Nehru—just recently returned from a visit to Europe, including Russia—persuaded the meeting to pass a resolution declaring complete independence to be India's goal.

Some response to this challenge had to be fashioned by the Viceroy, Lord Irwin, who, ever since the day he arrived in India, while sympathizing with nationalistic aspirations, had sought to divert them into constitutional and evolutionary channels. As we will see in the next chapter, the Viceroy made every attempt to encourage Hindu-Muslim amity. But anti-British feeling grew rather than diminished. The Liberal party continued to lose followers, while the more radical Congress became more impatient in its demands and also more popular and influential.

The year 1928 was a turbulent one. When the

Simon Commission landed in Bombay in February it was greeted by a huge hostile demonstration displaying the slogan, "Go back, Simon!" A fierce debate on whether the Simon Commission should be boycotted took place in the Legislative Assembly, and this body more and more, under the leadership of its President, V. J. Patel (brother of the late Sardar Vallabhbhai Patel), sought to obstruct the transaction of business. Outside the Legislature there was more than the usual unrest, with strikes on the railways, in the jute mills, and the Tata Iron Works. While taking part in a demonstration against the Simon Commission the popular nationalist leader, Lajpat Rai, was hurt in a scuffle with the police. His death not long after from a heart attack was blamed upon the British authorities, and the young police officer who was on duty at the time was later murdered.

Lord Birkenhead, the Secretary of State for India, who was not too sympathetic with Indian nationalism, introduced another complication into Indian politics when he more or less challenged the various Indian parties to get together and produce a scheme of government agreeable to all. The various groups, Congress, Muslim League, and Liberals, proceeded to set up a committee for this purpose under the chairmanship of Motilal Nehru. In August 1928 the Nehru Report was published. This document (discussed more fully in the next chapter) was in some ways a courageous attempt to draft a new constitution granting dominion status and one that would satisfy the various political groupings. The net result, however, was violent disagreement between the Muslim League and the Congress.

Meanwhile, Congress was rent with personal rivalries and divided by exponents of differing programs of action. Only one man could get it out of this impasse, and this was Gandhi, who returned to active political life in December 1928. At Calcutta the Mahatma succeeded in getting the Congress to accept a compromise which satisfied both the most radical and the more conservative wings. A resolution was passed demanding that Britain should accept the Nehru Report; and, as one British historian has pointed out with much justification, the Congress "ordered Government to accept what they could not persuade their own communities to accept."[26] This acceptance, moreover, was to be an accomplished fact within one year. If it were not forthcoming, a campaign of

non-violent non-co-operation would be initiated against the government.

Events were now rapidly moving in the direction of a decisive showdown. Angry scenes and stalemates were the order of the day in the Indian legislatures. The Central Legislative Assembly carried on its deliberations with the nerves of its members taut and not improved by the blazing sun. On April 8, 1929, a bomb was thrown from the public gallery into the benches of the government officials, but no one was seriously injured.

The very next month the Conservatives under Stanley Baldwin were turned out of office in Britain; their successors were the representatives of the Labour party under Ramsay MacDonald. The British Labour party since its inception had consistently attacked imperialism and expressed its impatience at the slow pace of democratization in India. In 1928 MacDonald had stated at the British Commonwealth Labour Conference, "I hope that within a period of months rather than years there will be a new Dominion added to the Commonwealth of our Nations, a Dominion of another race, a Dominion which will find self-respect as an equal with the Commonwealth. I refer to India."[27] In keeping with this view, the new Secretary of State at the India Office was Captain Wedgwood Benn, a warm friend of Indian aspirations.

In June 1929 Lord Irwin returned to England to discuss the serious deterioration of affairs in India, and he and Benn, supported by the Labour government, decided that the time had come for a bold gesture in Indian affairs. On October 25 the Viceroy returned to Delhi and six days later issued his momentous statement on Indian affairs. In part this statement declared:

In view of the doubts which have been expressed both in Great Britain and India regarding the interpretation to be placed on the intentions of the British Government in enacting the Statute of 1919, I am authorized on behalf of his Majesty's Government to state clearly that in their judgment it is implicit in the declaration of 1917 that the natural issue of India's constitutional progress . . . is the attainment of Dominion status.[28]

Furthermore, it was also announced that as soon as possible a Round Table Conference, with British and Indian representatives, would be called to take up the Indian problem—presumably to draft a new constitution.

26- Thompson, op. cit., p. 164.

27- Quoted in Edward J. Thompson and G. T. Garratt, Rise and Fulfilment of British Rule in India (London: The Macmillan Company, 1934), p. 633.

28- India in 1929-1930 (Calcutta: Superintendent Government Printing, 1931), p. 468.

The period from 1930 to 1939 was a fateful
decade in Indian history. During this
ten years India more than ever before was
placed in the limelight, with the press of
the world giving lengthy coverage to its
problems, its leaders, and its intermittent
crises. There was much for the journalists
to describe. Gandhi launched a great
civil disobedience movement designed to
achieve complete independence for his
homeland. London witnessed the coming
and going of many dignitaries, both British
and Indian, as constitutional reform was
debated in three separate Round Table
Conferences. And in the British Parliament
for many months both houses engaged in
long and often acrimonious debates over the
political future of India. Finally, in
August 1935, a new act designed to carry
India toward the goal of Dominion status
became law.

INDIA AT the beginning of the 1930's was
essentially in a fluid situation. British
statesmen and Indian patriots could in
large measure determine what the course of
events was to be. As one looks back on this
decade, however, it is apparent that something went wrong, that neither the British
nor the Indian leaders measured up
to their grave responsibilities and
opportunities. Some of the blame necessarily rests upon British shoulders. The
Labour government which conducted the
First Round Table Conference was quite
sensitive and sympathetic to Indian nationalistic aspirations. The coalition
government that followed, however,
dominated by the Conservative party, erred
in its insistence upon an unduly cautious
and watered-down program of constitutional
reform.

IN LARGE degree Indian leaders, particularly
Gandhi, representing the National Congress,
must bear responsibility for the hardening
of the British government following the
fall of the Labour ministry in the fall of
1931. Indian nationalism, represented by
its strongest spokesman, the Congress, had a
great opportunity to win friends and secure
concessions at the Round Table Conferences.
Instead it completely boycotted two of the
Conferences and at the most important,
the second, which it attended, its representative, Gandhi, lacking faith in the
Conference, followed a policy of obstruction.

Round Tables
and the shadow of partition

125

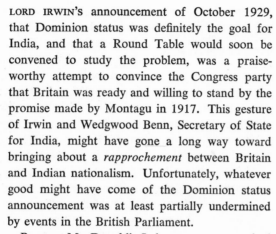

chapter 8

LORD IRWIN's announcement of October 1929, that Dominion status was definitely the goal for India, and that a Round Table would soon be convened to study the problem, was a praiseworthy attempt to convince the Congress party that Britain was ready and willing to stand by the promise made by Montagu in 1917. This gesture of Irwin and Wedgwood Benn, Secretary of State for India, might have gone a long way toward bringing about a *rapprochement* between Britain and Indian nationalism. Unfortunately, whatever good might have come of the Dominion status announcement was at least partially undermined by events in the British Parliament.

Ramsay MacDonald's Labour government had come into power in the spring of 1929. It was sympathetic with Indian national aspirations, but it did not command a majority in the House of Commons, since it was dependent upon the support of the small Liberal party representation to keep in office. The debate in Parliament began on November 5, with Lord Reading attacking the Irwin announcement in the House of Lords. Lord Birkenhead followed and declared that members of the Simon Commission, who were bringing their investigations to a close, should regard the Viceroy's statement as irrelevant. Discussion in the Commons was equally critical. Stanley Baldwin, the Conservative leader, was evasive. His speech was "wrapped round in ponderous rhetoric, simple thoughts, and resounding generalities,"[1] while Lloyd George, the leader of the Liberal party, implied that the Dominion status declaration was a form of unnecessary appeasement. Only members of the Labour party gave unqualified support to Lord Irwin.

There is no doubt that behind this debate lurked the exigencies of party politics in Britain, but the remarks made in Parliament were read in Delhi, Calcutta, and Bombay as well as in London. The first reaction to the Viceroy's invitation to a Round Table Conference had been encouraging. A group of Indian leaders, representing all parties, accepted with some reservations. But after the debate in Parliament the Congress attitude hardened, and Gandhi, in a meeting with the Viceroy, announced that the Congress would not attend the Round Table Conference unless it should be clearly understood that its purpose was the drawing up of a scheme of full Dominion status, to be put into effect immediately.

This meeting was attended by representatives of the Indian Liberal party and the Muslim League, who were keenly disappointed that Congress would not accept the Round Table invitation. Shortly afterwards, the Indian Liberals in annual conference at Madras passed a resolution calling for Dominion status in as short a time as possible, but accepting the offer of the Round Table meeting.

The Congress met at the close of 1929 in an intransigent and confident mood. A great city of tents was set up for the delegates at Lahore for their annual meeting, which has been described as "part gipsy encampment, part football match, part parish bazaar."[2] There was much excitement and activity, with great parades, the adulation of Gandhi, and the hoisting of the flag of independence. And everywhere there were correspondents, Indian, British, and especially American, for India had become front page news.

An unsuccessful attempt had been made to assassinate Lord Irwin just before the Congress met, and one of its first acts—on the insistence of Gandhi—was the adoption of a resolution congratulating him on his escape; this passed, after much debate, by a vote of 935 to 897. Within the higher circles of the Congress there was an inside struggle on the issue of whether Irwin's offer of a Round Table should be accepted. Gandhi, supported by the two Nehrus, had his way, and on December 31, 1929, Congress adopted his pledge of complete independence, which was to be taken by all Congress members on the following January 26, a date to be observed as Independence Day. This pledge undoubtedly obtained much inspiration from some of the great revolutionary declarations of the past, especially the French Declaration of the Rights of Man and the American Declaration of Independence. In part it read:

We believe that it is the inalienable right of the Indian people, as of any other people, to have freedom and to enjoy the fruits of their toil and have the necessities of life, so that they may have full opportunities of growth. We believe also that if any government deprives a people of these rights and oppresses them the people have a further right to alter it or abolish it. The British Government in India has not only deprived the Indian people of their freedom but has based itself on the exploitation of the masses, and has ruined India economically, politically, culturally, and spiritually. We believe, therefore, that India must sever the British connection and attain Purna Swaraj, or

1- Alan Campbell Johnson, Viscount Halifax *(New York: Ives Washburn, Inc., 1941), p. 229.*

2- Guy Wint and Sir George E. Schuster, India and Democracy *(London: The Macmillan Company, 1941), p. 166.*

complete independence. . . . We will therefore prepare ourselves by withdrawing, so far as we can, all voluntary association from the British Government, and will prepare for civil disobedience, including non-payment of taxes.[3]

In other words, the one-year period of grace granted to the British at Calcutta to accept the Nehru Report had lapsed. Gandhi was empowered to initiate civil disobedience at his own discretion, and, as a preliminary move, Congress declared a boycott on all the legislatures and directed its followers who were members of them to resign immediately. On January 26, 1930, thousands of people signed the pledge of independence and witnessed the raising of the Congress tricolor flag.

For a few months after the Lahore Congress there was some sparring between Gandhi and Lord Irwin. The former presented the Viceroy with a number of demands which, if met, would mean the cancellation of the forthcoming civil disobedience movement. Among the demands were: (1) total prohibition, (2) halving the land tax, (3) abolition of the salt tax, (4) a 50 per cent cut in the military budget, (5) the scaling down of the salaries of the higher officials, (6) an amnesty for political prisoners, and (7) the reservation of coastal shipping for Indians. Certain of these demands, notably the first four, were drastic ones, and it is debatable whether any independent Indian government could have carried them out. Irwin accordingly turned them down and on March 2 received a letter from Gandhi, addressed to "Dear Friend," announcing that civil disobedience would begin on March 12 and would be initiated by a pilgrimage to defy the salt tax.

On March 12 Gandhi was given a great ovation by thousands of his followers and, with 79 disciples, commenced a hike to the sea, 170 miles away. The march lasted three weeks and made headlines in most of the newspapers of the world. On April 6 Gandhi reached the sea at Dandi on the Gujarat coast and waded into the surf as his followers cried, "Hail, Deliverer." Sea water was then dipped up and placed on a fire, and the symbolic act of manufacturing salt was carried out in defiance of the government's monopoly. The defiance of the salt laws was a shrewd move by Gandhi, because this tax fell on every family and was universally disliked.

The salt march was the signal for full-fledged civil disobedience. Officials resigned, tax collec-

tion was resisted, railway employees quit, liquor shops and foreign businesses were boycotted. The full weight of the Congress was thrown into the fight to paralyze the government. The mounting effects of the world depression had done much to increase unemployment and lower the already atrociously debased Indian standard of living. In 1930 India lost nearly one fourth of its foreign trade. Congress, therefore, in its civil disobedience campaign received the support of a mass of disgruntled and often hungry workers and peasants; and, at the other economic extreme, the Congress received the enthusiastic support of Indian business, especially the cotton mill owners, who saw in the boycott of foreign goods an excellent opportunity to drive out their British and Japanese competitors. It has been estimated that several lakhs of rupees were donated every month to Congress by Indian business. This financial support enabled the nationalist organization to enroll large numbers of Congress volunteers and give them food and a daily wage. As the civil disobedience movement got under way, its exponents were motivated by a complex pattern of profits, patriotism, and piety. An American professor reported:

No generalization seemed justified except that India has been hard hit by the world depression. It is impossible to separate economic and political motives in resistance to tax-gatherers in the villages, strikes and riots in the cities and even in Gandhi's campaign of civil disobedience. Nationalism and the profit motive clashed in the boycotts of foreign cloth and in the attempts to make salt, with piety added in the case of the pickets at the liquor shops.[4]

In the spring of 1930 the flags and colors of the Congress were everywhere. Large crowds of youths paraded the streets of the main cities singing and shouting nationalist slogans. For the first time women were enlisted in large numbers in the Congress ranks. The nationalists had their own uniformed volunteers who patroled the bazaars allowing no carts to proceed without the driver presenting his certificate of "No British goods." Many European businessmen were ruined, and imports of Lancashire cotton cloth declined precipitously. At the same time tax strikes reduced Indian government revenues. Salaries of civil servants, budgets, and social services all had to be cut, and on several occasions loans had to be raised in London to meet deficits. While ostensibly non-

3- Quoted in Jawaharlal Nehru, Toward Freedom (New York: John Day Company, 1941), pp. 388-389.

4- J. Bartlet Brebner, "The British Empire," Current History, XXXIII (March 1931), p. 935.

violent, civil disobedience soon resulted in widespread disorders in which officials were murdered and salt depots of the government raided. Rioting broke out in the large cities.

In April 1930 an armory was raided and six government employees killed; riots took place in Peshawar, where the mob had control of the city for several days, and serious disturbances took place in Madras, Karachi, and Calcutta. There were also tensions between Muslims and Hindus, as the former refused to support the Congress campaign. It was natural that mass demonstrations, business boycotts, and from time to time outright terrorism should lead to clashes between the police and soldiery, on the one hand, and the followers of civil disobedience on the other. Frequently the police dispersed crowds or pickets by *lathi* charges, the *lathi* being a long, weighted club. Indian nationalists have heatedly charged the police with excessive brutality, and undoubtedly, in the confusion and turmoil of the moment, the police were unnecessarily severe. On the other hand, there is much evidence to show that soldiers and police acted with great patience and forbearance during the long months of the civil disobedience when nerves and tempers were at the breaking point.

Lord Irwin during these hectic days held out the olive branch to Congress, welcoming its participation in the Round Table Conference scheduled to be held in London in November, but demanding that civil disobedience cease and that laws be obeyed. Declaring that civil disobedience had degenerated into violent rebellion, Irwin had a number of special ordinances passed to strengthen the hand of the government. In May Gandhi was arrested and imprisoned, and soon the jails were filled with thousands of prisoners. The disorders reached their climax in the mid-summer of 1930, when perhaps 60,000 members of Congress were in prison. Yet, at the height of civil disobedience Lord Irwin in a speech to European businessmen at Calcutta declared:

> We should, I am satisfied, make a profound mistake if we underestimate the genuine and powerful feeling of nationalism that is today animating much of Indian thought. And for this no simple, complete or permanent cure ever has been or ever will be found in strong action by Government.[5]

During the turmoil of civil disobedience the Simon Commission released its Report late in the spring of 1930. This document was out of date as soon as it fell from the government presses. In the main it was an ultra-cautious and conservative analysis of the Indian problem, and it stressed the difficulties and obstacles lying in the way of self-government. Above all, it did not give adequate recognition to the dynamic qualities and the strength of Indian nationalism. It recommended the abolition of Dyarchy and the introduction of self-rule, i.e., responsible government, in the provinces; but it did not suggest substantial changes in the central government. Most surprising, the Simon Report nowhere specifically mentioned the goal of Dominion status. No wonder all Indian opinion, moderate as well as Congress, joined in denouncing the document. No one took the Report too seriously anyway, because the future of India was to be threshed out at the forthcoming Round Table Conference.

During the summer of 1930 Lord Irwin encouraged the efforts of the Liberal party leaders to persuade the Nehrus and Gandhi to call off the civil disobedience campaign. Gandhi, however, refused to withdraw the demands he had served on the government just prior to launching civil disobedience. The peak of the movement was reached in August, and in September it began to subside. Meanwhile, delegates representing all views and parties in India, except the Congress, were assembling in London for the Round Table Conference which convened in November. This body, as will be shown shortly, made remarkable progress and continued in session until the middle of January 1931. Its activities and those of the Second Round Table will be analyzed together a little later (see p. 130 ff.). At the end of the Conference, the British Prime Minister, Ramsay MacDonald, announced an amnesty for all political prisoners in India, including Gandhi. It was the hope of both the Labour government and its Viceroy that Congress still might be induced to come into the fold of the Round Table discussions and that a new constitution might be devised, one which would enjoy the support of all Indian parties.

The release order for political prisoners was announced by Lord Irwin on January 25, 1931, and the leaders, including Gandhi, were set free immediately, with the rank and file to be released later. The country by this time was sick of civil disobedience. Business in many cities was at a

Quoted in Johnson, op. cit., *284.*

standstill and trade disrupted. Gandhi, because of urgent appeals by Indian representatives who had attended the Round Table Conference to open negotiations with the Viceroy, and because of the evident desire of Irwin for such a move, proceeded to Delhi to see the head of the government. Gandhi wrote to Irwin asking to see him "not as a Viceroy but as a man." The first personal meeting took place on February 17, and in the next four weeks eight additional conversations took place. There was much criticism of Irwin's conciliatory policy from diehard circles in Britain. Lord Rothermere in the *Daily Mail* attacked the Viceroy as a "weak and sentimental man," who has "humiliated himself and lowered the prestige of his country on which British rule in India entirely depends."[6] Churchill, doughty defender of the Empire, naturally was aroused at the news that the leader of civil disobedience had been received with courtesy by Irwin. Churchill was "nauseated," he declared, "to see Mr. Gandhi, an Inner Temple lawyer, now become a seditious fakir of a type well known in the East, striding half-naked up the steps of the Viceregal Palace while he was still organizing and conducting a defiant campaign of civil disobedience, to parley on equal terms with the representative of the King-Emperor."[7]

Notwithstanding attacks from extremists in both India and Britain, Irwin persevered in his conversations with Gandhi. Finally, an agreement was drawn up on March 5, known as the Delhi Pact, bringing an end to civil disobedience and providing for Congress participation in the next session of the Round Table Conference. Although the salt tax was not abolished, there were to be some concessions in areas where the people were especially poor. The boycott of foreign goods for political purposes was halted, but Irwin recognized the right of peaceful propaganda in behalf of domestic industries. All special ordinances of government aimed against civil disobedience were to be ended, and all persons in prison were to be released, unless they had committed crimes of violence.

In most circles, in India as well as in Britain, there was complete satisfaction when the news of the Delhi Pact was released. A month after the document had been initialed Lord Irwin left India and was succeeded by Lord Willingdon as Viceroy. Irwin, or Lord Halifax, to give him his later title, was to assume high office in the British cabinet

later in the 1930's. He was to serve as the Foreign Secretary during the lamentable days of appeasement under Neville Chamberlain, and thus his policies, both at home and abroad, were on occasion harshly criticized. For his Indian record, however, there was warm praise, and the verdict was that he was not only one of the greatest of Britain's Viceroys but, what was more important, one of the best loved by Indians. One great English liberal newspaper declared:

For a Viceroy to be attacked by the fanatic nationalists of both countries is not to his discredit. . . . He will be remembered in India not because he came there as the representative of a Great Power, but because in the discharge of his duties as a Viceroy he exemplified all that was best in the civilisation to which he belonged and in the religion he followed.[8]

The Argument over British Rule

In a sense, the high point of the Congress nationalist movement was reached in 1930. There was a buoyant spirit of optimism and confidence, oversimplification of the obstacles barring the path to independent nationhood, and a tendency to hold British rule responsible for all India's problems, which would somehow be removed almost automatically by the magic solvent of independence. During the next two decades, and particularly after the achievement of independence in 1947, a sobering realization of the complexity of India's situation gradually dawned upon the more realistic nationalist circles. In 1930, however, the nationalist indictment of British rule was unequivocal and uncluttered by any qualifications.

It was charged that the widespread poverty in India was primarily attributable to British policy. Sixty per cent of the Indian budget was spent on the army, allowing Britain to train thousands of her own troops and make India foot the bill. Besides this, the best positions in the Indian Civil Service were earmarked for Englishmen, who were paid unnecessarily high salaries. In addition, these favored alien bureaucrats were also given fat pensions on retirement. Every year, it was claimed, a large portion of India's wealth, usually referred to as the "drain," had to be sent to England in the form of pensions and interest payments on the huge amounts of British capital invested in India. The British capitalists got the profits but Indians did the work. Britain kept India a free trade

6- Quoted in ibid., p. 281.

7- *Great Britain, Parliamentary Debates (5th series), House of Commons, Vol. 247, column 755.*

8- Manchester Guardian, *April 24, 1931, p. 322.*

country, discouraging industrialization and thus maintaining it as a convenient market for British manufactured goods. Indians desired tariff protection. It was also charged that the Indian people, especially the impoverished peasants, were bowed down by a crushing burden of taxation imposed by the British regime.

In the political realm, it was asserted that Britain had followed a policy of divide and rule, supporting and coddling the medieval autocratic Native States and encouraging factionalism in India, especially in the case of the rivalry between the Hindus and Muslims. On this last point an Indian writer asserted in 1933:

The so-called Mohammedan leaders . . . are mere creatures of the government, without standing in India and without influence there except in the direction of working mischief. Hindus and Mohammedans could reach agreement tomorrow were it not for the continuous wire-pulling of those in authority who expect to benefit by keeping them divided.[9]

The neglect of health and medical services, as proved by the high death rate, and the prevailing mass illiteracy were also blamed on the British. Finally, the Indian indictment asserted that British rule was autocratic and would continue so, clumsily camouflaged by such devices as Dyarchy without real self-government and vague promises of ultimate Dominion status.

On the other side of the balance sheet, British publicists called attention to the safety afforded India by the British fleet, and pointed out that army expenditures for the defense of India were very reasonable compared with the burden carried by other nations. It was true that Englishmen in the Indian Civil Service were paid generously and retired handsomely, but the standards of admission were so high that only men of the highest caliber were selected, whose incorruptibility and efficiency had more than given back to India the value of their salaries. The argument of the "drain" was countered by the assertion that much of the money sent to Britain from Indian sources represented interest—and a very low rate usually—paid on capital which had helped build railroads, telegraphs, canals, and great irrigation projects. Furthermore, these modern facilities earned enough not only to pay the interest charges due in London but to leave a surplus besides.

British officials in India also pointed out, in answer to the charge of overtaxation, that the items most criticized, land and salt revenue, were taken over from the Mogul regime and that the amount collected under British rule was substantially less than it was under the Mogul emperors. Widespread poverty had little connection, the British claimed, with politics and the kind of government ruling India. Rather this condition was the result of factors within the Indian culture pattern: the caste system and its resultant social stratification, excessive spending on religious and marriage ceremonies, the despotism of the moneylender, and "the sacred cow, an undue regard for mere life as opposed to good life."[10] It was stressed that, because of the sanctity of all life in India, the ravages of rats alone cost each year more than the sum spent on the army and that the annual loss incurred by maintaining old cattle ran to 1,760,000,000 rupees, four times the land revenue obtained by the government.

Round Tables in London

In the last week of March 1931 a special meeting of the National Congress was called to approve the Delhi Pact and to give Gandhi a mandate to represent the organization at the Second Round Table Conference. A great throng of 30,000 filled a desert arena at Karachi to discuss the pact. The amphitheater was filled with delegates wearing their white Gandhi caps and to one journalist, "from the height on which I was sitting, it looked as if thousands of large snowflakes had fallen on the dark bare earth."[11] Extremists like Subhas Chandra Bose harangued the multitude, urging non-ratification, but Gandhi was the unchallenged leader and his agreement with Irwin was approved. Somewhat disturbing to British ears was the news that Gandhi had been directed to ask for "control over the Army, external affairs, finance, fiscal and economic policy, and to have scrutiny by an impartial tribunal of the financial transactions of the British Government."[12]

Gandhi's attendance at the Round Table was still uncertain, however, for he found the new Viceroy, Lord Willingdon, less patient and perhaps less sympathetic with Congress claims than his predecessors. The atmosphere in India seemed charged with unrest as news of Hindu-Muslim riots and criticisms against the government for failure to carry through the terms of the Delhi

9- D. N. Bannerjea, "India's Case for Independence," Current History, XXXVIII (May 1933), p. 173.

10- Vera Anstey, "Population, Poverty, and the Drain," in Modern India, ed. Sir John Cumming (London: Oxford University Press, 1932), p. 267.

1- Christian Science Monitor (Boston), March 31, 1931.

2- J. Coatman, Years of Destiny, India 1926-1932 (London: Jonathan Cape, 1932), p. 341.

Pact appeared in the press. Gandhi in August announced he would not go to London, but on the 27th of the same month he signed a new agreement with Lord Willingdon and was put on board a special train to enable him to catch at Bombay the steamer *Rajputana* en route to Marseilles.

Gandhi's steamer passed through the Suez Canal into the Mediterranean and headed toward the shores of France. It is well to point out here that Gandhi was not going to London to start negotiations with the British government on a new Indian constitution, for such a task had already been undertaken by the First Round Table, which must now be described.

The First Round Table Conference proper was in session from November 1930 to January 1931, and was made up of some of the foremost leaders in Indian public life. There were fifty-seven of them, representing various parties, including the Sikhs, Untouchables, Muslims, Christians, and the Liberal party in British India. In this group Dr. Ambedkhar represented the Untouchables, Mohammed Ali Jinnah and the Aga Khan the Muslims, and Sapru and Sastri the Liberals.

In his early days Jinnah had been a nationalist pure and simple, working with any Indian—Muslim or Hindu—for self-government. Thus it was that Nehru once wrote of Jinnah as "the ambassador of Hindu-Moslem unity," and the Indian poetess and patriot, Mrs. Sarojini Naidu, wrote a eulogistic biography of Jinnah in 1918. Born in Bombay in 1876, he had received a legal education in England, and on his return to India had built up a wide and extremely lucrative practice. Before World War I he was an outstanding member of Congress, but when the Gandhian period began, he resigned from the organization. In the 1920's Jinnah became increasingly antagonistic to what he regarded as the Hindu nationalistic tendency of Congress. In all aspects of his character Jinnah was a striking contrast to Gandhi. "He lived in stately mansions, was tall and elegantly groomed, with a distinguished presence and fastidious tastes. In his fast-greying hair a white lock stood aggressively like a plume."[13] Jinnah had none of the mysticism, pacifism, or philosophical subtleties of Gandhi. He was a fighter, believed himself to be a realist, and defended his position by cold, clear, lawyer-like logic.

Dr. Bhimrao Ramji Ambedkhar, the champion of the Untouchables, was a remarkable personality.

Coming from a poor Untouchable family, he attracted the attention of the ruler of the Native State of Baroda, who paid for his education in India and then sent him to the United States, where he received a Ph.D. from Columbia University in 1916. Postgraduate work was also done by the brilliant young scholar at the London School of Economics and at the University of Bonn in Germany. Returning to India in 1924, this promising intellectual soon found that "once an Untouchable always an Untouchable," and he came up squarely against the intolerance of high-caste Hinduism. Notwithstanding many obstacles, Ambedkhar set himself up as a lawyer in Bombay and became very successful. Not forgetting the many disabilities and insults heaped upon himself and his fellow Untouchables, he entered politics to advance their cause. "He preferred British raj to Hindu raj; he preferred Muslims to Hindus and once thought of leading the Untouchable community, as a body, into the Mohammedan church."[14]

From the Native States came sixteen representatives, including such well-known persons as the Nawab of Bhopal, the Maharaja of Patiala, and the Maharaja of Bikanir. There were sixteen members representing the three main British political parties, with the leading roles played by Ramsay MacDonald, Lord Sankey, Lord Reading, and Sir Samuel Hoare.

The First Round Table Conference started off with the usual series of speeches, and at the outset the representatives from British India and those speaking for the British government were surprised by the attitude expressed by the Native Princes. The spokesmen for these rulers let it be known they would support a federation for India, which form of government they were prepared to enter. This offer was contingent upon the grant of self-government to India and also upon the recognition of the right of the Princes themselves to negotiate with the government of British India. This gesture on the part of the Princes seemed to be motivated by a mixture of selfishness and patriotism. As Indians they naturally wanted an end of British rule, but as rulers of monarchical states—some progressive and benevolent, many hardly passable, and some downright bad—they naturally wished to protect their prerogatives. What better way than to get into a loosely organized federation and thus be in a position to shape the new constitution as a safeguard for their dynasties?

13- The Times *(London)*, *September 13, 1948, p. 7.*

14- *Louis Fischer,* The Life of Mahatma Gandhi *(New York: Harper and Brothers, 1950), p. 312.*

The Native Princes' support of the federal principle cleared the way for agreement on additional fundamental principles. (1) Dyarchy was to be abolished and self-government was to be conferred upon the provinces. (2) Dyarchy of a kind, however, was to be moved up to the proposed central federal government, for here defense and foreign affairs were to be in the hands of the Viceroy. (3) While granting a considerable extension of self-government, the Round Table members agreed that the Viceroy and the provincial governors should be endowed with certain special and emergency powers designed to insure the stability of the new government. (4) The important decision was made to separate the province of Burma from India. Essentially, therefore, the First Round Table Conference recommended federalism, responsible provincial government, and safeguards to be exercised both in the center and in the provinces.

After the general speechmaking had been done, the Round Table set up nine special committees to start the work of filling in the specific details on the rather bare constitutional blueprint that had been sketched in the first few days of deliberation. All of the committees made good progress except the one dealing with the rights of minorities. The minority groups, especially the Muslims, Sikhs, and Untouchables, made it clear that they wanted specific guarantees for the protection of their rights and also specific recognition of the principle of separate electorates. The Hindu delegates were little inclined to concur, and one of them stated, "Communal electorates are bad enough, but communal provinces would be the death-blow to Indian nationalism."[15] Speaking for the Muslims, a delegate let it be known that "we have at the same time made it perfectly clear . . . that our safeguards, our rights, the rights for which we have been fighting for years, must be preserved and guaranteed."[16] For the first time in modern Indian history the communal problem had been clearly exposed, not by British officials but by Indians themselves. Until the last hour of the Conference the Minorities Committee labored to reach some agreement, but just before adjournment on January 19 the members of the Committee joined their waiting colleagues with the disappointing news that no progress had been made.

There was one serious weakness in the delibera-

tions of the Conference. It voiced the interests and demands of all the various parties in India except the most important one, the Congress. While not a fair evaluation by any means, Nehru's contention that the Indian members of the Conference were an "assembly of vested interests—imperialist, feudal, financial, industrial, religious, communal,"[17] was believed by the followers of the most dynamic and popular nationalist organization in India. This was the reason why Lord Irwin tried so hard to bring the Congress back on the road of constitutionalism and why Gandhi found himself on the way to the Second Round Table Conference in August 1931.

There was much work waiting to be done at the Second Round Table Conference. It was necessary to determine the exact details of federation, including the composition of the central legislatures, the financial relations between the federal government and its component parts, the formulation of the safeguards asked for by Great Britain, the distribution of powers between the various legislatures, and the extent of the guarantees to the various minority groups. The Conference got under way on September 7, 1931, and was in session until December 1. On the whole, the expectations created at the first session were not realized, for the meeting served primarily to advertise the differences dividing the Indians themselves. Britain, unfortunately, was not as helpful as had been expected. Interest had turned from Indian affairs to a crisis much nearer home—the problem of escaping national bankruptcy. The world economic crisis had brought about the fall of the Labour government and the creation of a coalition National government under MacDonald. In October a national election was held in which Labour suffered a crushing defeat; to all intents the National government was now the agent of the Conservative party, although it still retained a thin camouflage of Labour members, including the Prime Minister, MacDonald.

While not repudiating the policy of Indian reform, the new National government and its Indian Secretary, Sir Samuel Hoare, were more cautious, less inclined to see the Indian point of view, and more interested in formulating safeguards for British interests in India. As for Gandhi, he had been given such sweeping demands by the Karachi Congress that even with the most conciliatory and friendly British delegation it would have been

15- *Quoted in Coatman, op. cit., p. 325.*

16- Proceedings of the Round Table Conference, *Cmd. 3778 (London: His Majesty's Stationery Office, 1931), p. 432.*

17- *Nehru,* Toward Freedom, *p. 208.*

impossible to secure agreement. Furthermore, he realized that there had been much opposition to the Delhi Pact from extremists in the Congress, and that unless he was able to secure a complete, that is, a Congress victory, at the Conference his leadership would be seriously challenged back home. Sensing a tightening rather than any liberalizing tendency on the part of Sir Samuel Hoare and his colleagues at the Conference, Gandhi apparently decided not to take the Conference seriously. In fact he obstructed it at every turn, preferring complete deadlock to a compromise settlement in which Congress would recognize the claims of other groups, particularly the Muslims led by Jinnah. As he told Bernard Shaw, "It requires more than the patience of a Job. The whole thing is a huge camouflage."[18]

Gandhi found much to do outside the Round Table deliberations, and he followed an amazing round of engagements with such notables as Lady Astor, Charlie Chaplin, Lloyd George, and General Jan Christian Smuts. In addition he spoke to the boys at Eton; was entertained at Balliol College, Oxford; and took a side trip to a mill town in Lancashire. No wonder some of the journalists wrote that Gandhi always seemed tired at the Conference.

Under such conditions little progress was made. Gandhi in effect told all the other delegates that he alone, the spokesman for Congress, represented India. He refused to agree to the claims of the minorities, especially those of the Muslims and Untouchables; and he demanded that in the new constitution defense and foreign policy be turned over to the Indian government. The Conference closed on a note of frustration, Gandhi declaring that it had been a complete failure. Sastri, the leader of the Liberals, bitterly reproached Gandhi in his concluding remarks, saying:

You cannot but have seen that there is some knowledge, some wisdom, some patriotism, even outside the ranks of the Congress you so worship! With you and your chosen associates we can fashion our constitution to great ends, and India will have cause to be truly thankful that you changed your plans and came here. . . . Dismiss Civil Disobedience from your mind and take up this work in a spirit of complete trust in us, and of faith in the British people, too.[19]

While the Second Round Table was in session, unrest and disorders had again broken out in

India. Terrorism was especially active in Bengal, and the Viceroy, Willingdon, had promulgated four stiff ordinances designed to control lawlessness. These emergency measures laid down severe penalties for anti-government propaganda in the press, for refusal to pay taxes, and for picketing and boycotting governmental agencies. On his return Gandhi found the Viceroy unwilling to discuss repeal of the drastic ordinances, and in consequence, on the last day of 1931, Gandhi and his Congress Working Committee revived civil disobedience. Willingdon reflected the viewpoint of the predominantly Conservative National government of Britain and his policy was more stern and unbending than had been Lord Irwin's. As the Delhi Pact had only resulted in stalemate in London, perhaps Willingdon was justified, but, as can be surmised, there are two very different sides to this question.

The revival of civil disobedience got nowhere in the face of Willingdon's "tough" policy. Again thousands were sent to prison, including Gandhi and other leaders, and by the end of March 1932 it was apparent that the government had control of the situation. Aside from the renewal of civil disobedience, the most interesting development in 1932 was MacDonald's Communal Award and Gandhi's reaction to it. At the conclusion of the Second Round Table Conference, the British Prime Minister had reiterated his government's object of a federal government for India, together with self-government tempered by British control of defense and foreign affairs at the center and with certain safeguards to be held in reserve by Britain. MacDonald expressed his disappointment that the minority question had not been settled by the Indians themselves, and added that, if no other alternative presented itself, the British government would be forced to work out a scheme of communal representation. On August 16, 1932, MacDonald issued his Communal Award, which laid down the scheme of representation of the various communities and interests in the provincial councils.

Special guaranteed constituencies were set up for women, Hindus, Muslims, Sikhs, Anglo-Indians, Indian-Christians, and the Depressed Classes or Untouchables. It was made clear that the terms of this Award could be changed at any time if the Indian groups could agree to the change among themselves. Gandhi objected violently to

18- Quoted in Roy Walker, Sword of Gold (London: Indian Independence Union, 1945), p. 128.

19- Quoted in Post Wheeler, India Against the Storm (New York: E. P. Dutton, 1944), p. 260.

the proposed separate electorates for the Depressed Classes, and announced he would fast unto death if this provision were not changed. He did not want the Depressed Classes separated politically from the main body of Hindus, thus weakening Hinduism in relation to the other distinct communal groups. Gandhi in his prison cell at Poona started his fast on September 20; seven days later it came to an end. By the Poona Pact, drawn up by the caste Hindus and the Depressed Classes and approved by MacDonald, the Depressed Classes were made part of the general Hindu constituencies, but by a rather complex arrangement these classes were given a large number of reserved seats in the legislatures. Dr. Ambedkhar was not too happy, but most irritated were the high-caste Hindus, who resented the liberal representation given to the Untouchables, albeit they were kept in the Hindu fold.

Amid civil disobedience and communal rivalries in India the Third Round Table Conference convened in London on November 17, 1932, and continued in session until December 24. The Congress was not represented, and neither was the British Labour party. The purpose of the meeting was to fill in the final details of the new Indian governmental structure. After the Conference had concluded, the British government took over its proposals and from them drafted a proposed constitution for India. This draft was the famous White Paper of March 1933.

With this document in hand Parliament in the spring of 1933 proceeded to set up a Joint Committee on Indian Constitutional Reform to study the White Paper and make its recommendations. Composed of thirty-one members, three of whom were ex-Viceroys and three former Secretaries of State for India, and representing the three political parties in Britain, the Joint Committee spoke with much authority. Its Report, issued in November 1934, was used as the basis for the British National government's India Bill, which was introduced into Parliament in January 1935.

The proposed legislation was keenly and at times bitterly debated in Parliament. The so-called diehards against the Bill were led by Winston Churchill in the Commons and by Lord Salisbury in the Lords. Equally opposed to the legislation were most members of the Labour party, led by Clement Attlee. This union between the diehards and the traditional foes of imperialism—the La-

bourites—was a singular event. Each party, however, was actuated by a different motive. Churchill saw Britain, the arbiter between warring castes and communities and the protector of the inarticulate and defenseless ryot, turning over its imperial responsibilities to an oligarchic political pressure group. Attlee wanted both a political and economic revolution in India. By the terms of the proposed bill, he felt that India was merely replacing one set of capitalists with another.

Notwithstanding opposition from these extremes, the India Bill had the support of a good majority in Parliament, and in the most crucial vote it carried 404 to 133 in the House of Commons and 236 to 55 in the Lords. On August 4, 1935, the Bill received the royal assent and thus became law. In the main, public opinion in Great Britain warmly commended the Act. The London *Times,* for example, commenting on the legislation, editorialized: "A great constructive measure, the greatest indeed that a British Government has taken in hand in this century, has passed from project to enactment."[20]

Laboratory of Freedom

The new constitution for India was a complex and voluminous document, running to 451 clauses and 323 printed pages. As far as territorial changes were concerned, it provided for the separation of Burma from India. With an area of 262,000 square miles and a population of 17 million, Burma had been part of India only by reason of the accident of conquest. Its people differed from those of India in race and culture and they had come to resent being tied to what they considered an alien country. During the 1920's Burmese nationalism kept pace with that in British India in demanding more self-government. Accordingly, while the Round Tables on India were being held in London, a separate Burma Round Table was convened in December 1931. The following year a general election was held by the Burmese in which they voted to separate from India.

In 1937 Burma was given a new government which made it more autonomous than any other British colonial area and placed it in status just below that of an independent British Dominion. While the British Governor still had control of defense, foreign relations, monetary policy, and also over the tribal areas where such non-Burmese

20- The Times *(London),* August 3, 1935.

as the Shans and Karens lived, the Burmese people had a substantial area of government in which they enjoyed complete autonomy.

In India's new constitution, the governor's provinces of British India, of which there were eleven, were given a new and separate legal status. Except under certain emergencies they were independent of the central government, and untrammeled in their exercise of those powers designated in the constitution as "provincial." The old form of divided government, or Dyarchy, disappeared, and responsible government took its place. All the departments of government in a province were now under the direction of Indian ministers, who, in turn, were responsible to the elected members of the provincial legislature. The British, however, had tempered responsible government with certain safeguards. Each provincial governor was endowed with seven special responsibilities over which he could exercise his individual judgment without reference to the will of the legislature. Two of the most important of these special powers were the safeguarding of the legitimate interests of minorities and the prevention of any grave menace to the peace or tranquillity of a province. In addition, in case of the breakdown of government, the governor could take over the administration of his province.

Within the provincial franchise a complex system of separate electorates was introduced, based on MacDonald's Communal Award as modified by the Poona Pact. Under this system of voting there were separate electorates for the Sikhs, Backward Tribes, Labor, the Universities, Landholders, Commerce and Industry, the Indian Christians, Europeans, and Muslims, and an electorate termed the General Population, which would usually be predominantly Hindu. And within this scheme seats were reserved for the Untouchables and for women. Altogether, the franchise was extended to some thirty million voters in British India.

The federal part of the Government of India Act established a bicameral legislature: the Council of States and the Assembly. The powers which these lawmaking bodies could exercise were carefully listed, together with those powers that came solely within the purview of the provincial legislatures. While Dyarchy had been eliminated in the provinces, it reappeared in the federal government, for here the Governor-General had full authority in the fields of defense and foreign affairs. In the other departments of government, the Governor-General normally was expected to defer to the wishes of the Indian ministers and the legislature. As to finance, such items as the salaries of judges and the Governor-General, the pay of the Indian Civil Service, and the cost of the two reserved departments were excluded from the vote of the legislature. The Governor-General was to be appointed by the British government, and, like the provincial governors, he was endowed with a number of special responsibilities, among them the power to prevent any discrimination of an economic nature against British subjects and goods. He could also suspend the Constitution, prorogue the Assembly, veto its acts, and certify legislation which it refused to pass.

The Constitution of 1935 provided for the union of both British India and the Native States into a federal structure. The exact terms on which a Native State was to come into the federation were to be matters of negotiation between Britain and each ruler concerned, who would indicate what powers he would be willing to turn over to the federal government. Federation was not to be established until rulers representing 50 per cent of the population of the States and half of the States' representation in the Council of State had signified their intention of joining. Pending agreement with this required number of Native States, the Central Government was to remain unchanged under the provisions laid down in the Act of 1919.

Most politically conscious Indians from all parties were disappointed with this new Constitution. The Liberal party, the most moderate and most inclined to follow the path of co-operation with Britain, was irked at the Act's failure specifically to mention Dominion status, and also it considered the safeguards too numerous. The Liberals, nevertheless, reluctantly decided to accept the Act. The Muslims and other minorities in British India also considered the Act as falling short of what had been promised in self-government in 1930. They were gratified, however, by the provision of separate electorates in both the provincial and the federal legislatures and by those safeguards designed to protect the interests of the minorities. Muslim opinion, therefore, was in the main ready to try the Act. Only the Congress turned the Act down as completely unacceptable. "The Government of India Act of 1935," wrote a Congress supporter, "is, from start to finish, inspired with the very narrow and selfish idea of safeguarding and protecting British interests in India—of perpetuating British domination with a view to exploiting the human and material resources of India for the advantage of Great Britain."[21]

Congress opinion leveled a number of specific charges against the Act, some of which carried much weight. (1) The Native Princes, symbols of reaction and medieval autocracy in most instances, were given undue representation in the federal legislature. Representing 40 per cent of the area of all India but with just under 25 per cent of its population, the Native States were given one-third of the representatives in the Assembly and 40 per cent of those in the Council of State. (2) In all the legislatures the Hindus were under-represented in comparison with other groups. (3) The suffrage was too limited, since it conferred the vote on only 10 per cent of the adult males and .06 per cent of the females. In consequence, it was claimed, the masses were to be delivered into the hands of industrial and landed privilege.

(4) Britain carefully masked the fact that she retained effective and substantial powers capable of safeguarding her economic interests in India. Congressmen cited Harold Laski's dictum that the Act "seems to me a supreme example of economic imperialism in action."[22] In particular the Governor-General's powers to interfere with the tariff, currency, and the central budget were singled out for denunciation. (5) In the case of the Native States, it was pointed out that in the federal legislature their representatives were to be chosen by the rulers themselves. The political rights of eighty million subjects in the States were thus to be ignored. (6) And, finally, the Constitution could be modified only by Parliament, and no provision was made for its periodic revision.

These were weighty charges, and in rebuttal the British made the following points: (1) The continued control by Britain of defense and foreign affairs and the retention of the special responsibilities by the governors and the Governor-General were essential in view of the facts of the Indian situation. It was stressed that democratic government is impossible if the minority is not willing to acquiesce in the decisions of the majority. This condition existed in India and necessitated the existence of some kind of potential arbitral and neutral force kept in the background but ready for use. Then, when traditions of cooperation had been established between the various groups, these safeguards could be removed; or, as has so frequently been the case in British constitutional development, they would have become dead letters by then.

(2) It was also argued that political weightage is often the price of federation, as witness the senatorial votes given to a state like Nevada in the American Constitution and those given to New York. (3) Above all it was contended that if the scheme were tried it would rapidly evolve into full Dominion status. The safeguards were unduly magnified. They were to be used only if an emergency should arise. It was pointed out that the Governor-General, with his power of certification under the Act of 1919, overrode the will of his Legislature only ten times from 1921 to 1937. And, as the stability of the Indian government increased and the necessary conventions and traditions of democracy became deep-rooted, complete self-government would become more and more *de facto,* notwithstanding the *de jure* provisions of the constitution. This was exactly what had happened in the case of the British Dominions, where the Statute of Westminster of 1931 recognized in law their national independence, which had been a fact for some time.

There is no doubt that the Act of 1935 was much more cautious and conservative than the scheme first envisaged at the First Round Table Conference in 1930 when the Labour party was in power. The fall of Labour and the growing influence of the Conservative party in the British National government; the unfortunate tactics of Gandhi at the Second Round Table; and the strength of the diehard group in Parliament—all these factors help to explain why there was such an emphasis upon safeguards and why the goal of Dominion status was not clearly defined.

While Britain was unnecessarily niggardly, the Congress made an equal error in magnifying only the rights and powers that were withheld without investigating and appreciating the political rights and opportunities conferred. Constitutionally, India had made substantial progress in twenty-five years and it was fairly apparent that, in view of the precedents of constitutional evolution in the British Dominions, Great Britain was only carrying out a rear-guard action in India. Taking into account the complexity of the Indian situa-

21- *Ramananda Chatterjee, "This New Imperialism,"* Asia, *XXXVII (January 1937), p. 12.*

22- *Harold J. Laski, "The Indian Report,"* Nation, *CXL (January 2, 1935), p. 15.*

tion, and especially the fears of the Muslims, there is a good case for the argument that Congress might have been wise to accept and work the reforms. Suppressed nationalism, however, at all times and in all lands has been long on militancy and short on patience. And so it was in India.

The political atmosphere in India was one of exhaustion and uncertainty. While the India Bill was passing through Parliament the civil disobedience movement faltered and then flickered out. The ranks of Congress declined to little more than half a million members; the people were tired and discouraged. Gandhi and other leaders were released from prison in 1933. Nehru writes of this period, "India was numbed by the violence and harshness of repression. The nervous energy of the nation as a whole was for the moment exhausted and it was not being recharged."[23] In May 1934, Congress called off the civil disobedience campaign and in the following months the Government's ban on this body was lifted. The failure of civil disobedience had cost Gandhi some of his popularity. There were questioning and uncertainty among the Congress leaders; finally, in the fall of the year, Gandhi announced that, because of the growing difference between himself and some Congressmen, he was retiring from politics and henceforth would occupy himself with social reform, working to aid the Untouchables and in support of the movement for village industries.

Congress quickly revived. In the elections of 1935, held under the old constitution of 1919, this party showed remarkable recuperative strength and the old Liberal party practically disappeared. Meanwhile, the Native Princes met in Bombay and raised a number of objections to the federal scheme as it was proposed in the India Act of 1935. Preparations, therefore, were made by the Viceroy for introducing responsible government only in the provinces of British India. In the spring of 1936, at a conference held at Lucknow, Congress decided to contest the forthcoming elections. The following August it issued an important manifesto assailing the new constitution, declaring its aim still to be complete independence, and asserting that entry into the legislatures was not to co-operate with the act "but to combat it and seek the end of it . . . . to carry out the Congress policy of the rejection of the Act and resist British imperialism."[24] A new orientation in policy is discernible in the manifesto, which laid stress upon social and economic reform, asserting the determination of Congress to reduce poverty and unemployment and to reform such institutions of exploitation as the privileged position of the landholders.

This growing concern of Congress with the economic amelioration of the masses as well as with political independence was primarily the achievement of Jawaharlal Nehru, who in the mid-1930's became the outspoken advocate of socialism. Eloquently he declared:

Socialism is thus for me not merely an economic doctrine which I favor; it is a vital creed which I hold with all my head and heart. I work for Indian independence because the nationalist in me cannot tolerate alien domination; I work for it even more because for me it is the inevitable step to social and economic change.[25]

Disregarding the pros and cons of the particular means advocated by Nehru, his realization that political independence was not enough, that there was much work of a socio-economic reformist nature that Indians must do for themselves, was a healthy sign.

In December 1936, at the Faizpur Congress, Nehru gave a stirring address in which he castigated imperialism and fascism and also urged the necessity of economic reforms. He referred to the new Act as a "new charter of slavery," and warned the British that Congress was not going to the legislatures to follow the path of constitutionalism. With enthusiasm and confidence the National Congress entered the elections for the new provincial legislatures, held early in 1937. During the past two decades of agitation this organization had built up a nation-wide system which, starting with the humble "four anna" members in the villages, had a disciplined hierarchy culminating in the All-India Congress Committee, and in the president of the Congress with his cabinet of fourteen, called the Working Committee.

Congress demonstrated its strength in the elections by winning 711 seats out of a total of 1585 in the provincial lower houses. In five of the eleven provinces Congress had a clear majority and in two others was the dominant party. "This general success," wrote a British correspondent, "was largely due to sentimental regard felt for a movement which has focussed and fostered the

23- Nehru, Toward Freedom, p. 224.

24- Quoted in the Round Table, London (December 1936), p. 142.

25- Nehru, Toward Freedom, p. 401.

national aims, to an intensive and thorough party organisation, and to the obvious dissatisfaction of the poorer voters and the unemployed."[26] Congress membership climbed steeply at this time. It was three million in 1937 and by 1939 had reached five million. This revitalization of Congress was aided materially by more interest in and dependence upon the masses. The party was losing its once almost exclusive middle-class character and turning more and more to workers and peasants.

Provincial responsible government came into force in April 1937. While Congress controlled seven provincial governments, it held to its pre-election promise not to co-operate with the new reforms. Nehru and what might be called the left wing of the Congress were against taking office and were for resorting to any kind of obstruction to discredit the new legislatures. A partial retreat from this extreme position was made when Congress offered to allow its members to take their offices and form provincial ministeries, if each British Governor would promise not to use his special powers. Some months of bargaining ensued. Interim governments were installed, however, in the provinces; and, finally, when the Viceroy, Lord Linlithgow, made a conciliatory gesture, Gandhi emerged from retirement and used his great prestige to avert the deadlock. The Viceroy gave assurances that only under the most extreme provocation would the safeguards be resorted to. Members of Congress then took office and formed ministries in seven provinces.

It was soon apparent that provincial self-government was a success. British civil servants carried out the policies of Indian ministers and the governors remained in the background, giving Indians a free field. In only four instances in all the provinces were bills passed by legislatures vetoed. The provincial governments, and especially those controlled by Congress, during the brief period from 1937 to 1939 made a commendable record in social reform. In two provinces attempts were made to lower the rents charged by the landholders. Acts were passed designed to reduce the power of the moneylenders and to help the peasants get out of debt. Measures were also enacted for better famine relief and for providing improved market facilities for the peasants. A bold attempt was made to carry through prohibition, but this reform involved such a huge

loss of revenue that it was made effective in only a few districts.

Some attention was given by the provincial governments to economic planning, and in the field of education substantial progress was made. The governments supported Gandhi's Wardha Scheme, which sponsored what was called "basic education." Children were "to make things," and to work in the fields as well as to be given training in the three R's, while the products they made and grew were to be sold to help support the new schools. There was also some attention given to the problem of mass illiteracy. Altogether, the expenditure on the social services increased 14 per cent from 1937 to 1939. These socio-economic reforms have been evaluated by a British historian thus: "All in all, the agrarian legislation of the Congress Ministries, boldly conceived and swiftly carried through, was a notable achievement."[27]

Congress participation in the new provincial legislatures was to last for only two years, from 1937 to 1939. During this brief period three significant trends deserve comment. The first was the fading away of the possibility of federation. During 1936-1937 Linlithgow as Viceroy had sent his emissaries to visit the Native States with the purpose of ironing out problems raised by the Princes. Nothing came of this attempt, however, and in June 1939 the Princes of the Native States definitely turned down federation. Had they but known, this action was a fateful decision and, from the point of view of the Princes' interests, an act of suicide. Had they entered the federation, the course of events in 1947-1948, which practically obliterated what had been the Native States, might have been different. From the point of view of national unity, however, the action of the Princes in turning down federation was extremely fortunate.

An important factor explaining the Native States' refusal to federate was the princes' growing fear and resentment of Congress. At first this body had followed a policy of noninterference in the States. In 1927 the States' Peoples Conference had been organized, with the aid of Congress, to carry on agitation for democratic government in the States. In the mid-thirties, however, Congress began to assume a bolder policy and in 1938 it declared: "The Purna Swaraj or complete independence which is the objective of Congress is for the whole of India, inclusive of

26- *The Sunday Times (London), April 30, 1937.*

27- *Sir Reginald Coupland, India: A Restatement (London: Oxford University Press, 1945), p. 159.*

the States."[28] Gandhi warned the rulers to cultivate friendly relations with Congress. Between 1937 and 1939 Congress intervened in several States, such as Mysore and Rajkot, and demanded political reforms. Its prestige and influence were such that it gained partial victories in both cases. Agitation was also carried on in Kashmir, Travancore, and Hyderabad. Nehru was particularly embittered by what he regarded as the medieval autocracy of the States, referring to them as "sinks of reaction and incompetence."[29]

The second trend to be commented upon was the rapid growth of the leftist wing in Congress and an increasing emphasis upon social revolution. This shift from the pure politics of national independence to social reform and, in some instances, even to the class war of Karl Marx, was illustrated by new interest on the part of Congress in such problems as rural indebtedness, agricultural debt and the moneylender, unsanitary conditions in factories, and mass illiteracy. At the same time, the threat of a schism between its right and left wings appeared in Congress. It was claimed by the latter wing that the Congress provincial governments were becoming increasingly conservative. Their reforms were considered too limited. Governmental responsibility had brought a sobering experience to Congress statesmen as they sought to restrain extremists, collect taxes, and discourage strikes. Labor troubles, lawlessness, and tax strikes were met by stern measures on the part of the ministries, who were acting, to all intents and purposes, just the same as British officials in the old days. Radicals of all kinds began to charge that the Congress governments were backsliding, that the sweet fruits of office were turning them into imitators of the British.

The spring of 1939 saw a serious crisis in Congress ranks. Subhas Chandra Bose, long a stormy petrel, a Socialist, and an uncompromising nationalist, had been elected Congress president in 1938. As election approached for the new president, Bose charged that the conservative elements had made a deal with Britain, and that they were selling out. Bose ran against a presidential candidate sponsored by Gandhi and was victorious by a narrow margin. There was now a serious split in the Congress membership, as Bose and his adherents believed Gandhi was an incurable medieval mystic. The latter was of a

mind that Bose was skirting close to revolution and could not be trusted. As in so many crises in the past in Congress, when Gandhi appealed for support, he received it, and the party closed its ranks. Bose was forced to resign and did so in high dudgeon, proceeding to organize his own party, which he called the Forward Bloc.

It is extremely important, in view of recent developments, to understand that both Gandhi and Nehru were now coming to be regarded as old-fashioned by the younger Congress leftist elements. Nehru, a Fabian or evolutionary socialist, eschewed violence and intemperate extremism. He criticized attempts to embarrass the provincial ministries by strikes and demonstrations; he criticized the rowdies who joined peasant and workers' parties the better to fill their own purses rather than aid their fellow men; and he attacked the forces of what he called "indiscipline and chaos."

If war had not broken out in 1939 it is probable that the feud in Congress between right and left might have exploded. The same trend could be observed in China. As we will see in a later chapter, war and the achievement of independence interrupted the growth of a schism along economic lines in Congress. A new phase in this economic rivalry was to begin just as soon as the British left India.

The third and last trend during the period of provincial self-government, 1937-1939, was the mounting tension between the Muslim and Hindu communities; or, to put it specifically, between the Muslim League and the National Congress. In those provinces controlled by Congress ministries there were 57 serious communal outbreaks in two years, with some 1700 persons injured and 130 killed. Communal strife was becoming a frightening menace; the dark shadow of partition—what Gandhi called "the vivisection of India"—was appearing over the land.

Portents of Partition

In explaining the division of India into two parts —one the predominantly Hindu Indian Union, the other strongly Mohammedan Pakistan—the American journalist Margaret Bourke-White points a dramatic finger at one man, as if he alone created the conditions and conjured up the forces essential for the bifurcation of India. She says, ". . . the decision was made in Bombay. It was a one-man

28- Kate Mitchell, India Without Fable *(New York: Alfred A. Knopf, 1942), p. 210.*

29- Jawaharlal Nehru, The Unity of India, *Collected Writings 1937-1940 (London: Lindsay Drummond, 1941), p. 30.*

30- *Margaret Bourke-White, Halfway to Freedom (New York: Simon & Schuster, 1949), p. 13.*

Coupland, India: A Restatement, p. 123.

decision, and the man who made it [Mohammed Ali Jinnah] was cool, calculating, unreligious. This determination to establish a separate Islamic state came not . . . . from some Muslim divine in archaic robes and flowing beard, but from a thoroughly Westernized, English-educated attorney-at-law with a clean-shaven face and razor-sharp mind."[30] The great-man theory of history is perhaps the easiest for most people to comprehend, for it conveniently concentrates a complex of historical forces in the soul and mind of a single individual. That Jinnah had much to do with the creation of Pakistan will be made clear in the following pages; that he only directed and took advantage of forces and ideals already in existence will be equally manifest.

In earlier chapters we have already seen how the Muslims were once a ruling caste in India but that they lagged behind the Hindus in commerce and education following the British conquest. We saw, however, that an Islamic revival took place under the leadership of Sir Seyed Ahmad Khan; and we noted how, as a result, the Muslims developed the University of Aligarh as a cultural center, revived in memory the glories of their past, and encouraged the flowering of Muslim thought in their language, Urdu. In consequence, the Muslims developed a new sense of their cultural distinctiveness and a feeling of destiny. Early in the twentieth century it became evident, in the face of the increasingly Hindu outlook of the Congress party, that this destiny must be political as well as religious and cultural. The growing self-identification of the Muslims as a group which should have a special political place in India led to the establishment of the All-India Muslim League in 1906. The League secured political recognition when the British government granted it separate electorates under the Morley-Minto Reforms of 1909.

During the First World War a Hindu-Muslim entente was realized in the Lucknow Pact of 1916, in which Congress recognized the League as the spokesman for the Muslim community and, in addition, accepted the principle of separate electorates. For the next five years both communities were actuated primarily by nationalism. The common foe was Britain, the one all-important objective self-government. In this phase of Hindu-Muslim relations apparently little concern was paid to the problem of what would happen after independence had been secured; how would the fruits of office and political power be distributed between

Muslims and Hindus? This all-important question seemed of little moment as Hindu and Muslim nationalists joined in the Khilafat movement and in non-violent non-co-operation. This entente, however, rested on insecure foundations and in 1922, following the horrors inflicted upon hundreds of Hindus in the Moplah outbreak, the alliance broke down completely.

A tragic feature of the history of the 1920's in India was the mounting incidence of violent outbreaks between the Muslim and Hindu communities. The first serious clash took place in the Punjab in the fall of 1922, and in the following year violence continued to rise. By 1924 it was apparent that Hindu-Muslim antipathy was assuming menacing proportions, for during this year there were eighteen serious outbreaks, the worst at Kohat, where 36 people were killed and 145 wounded. It was in protest against communal fanaticism that Gandhi undertook a famous three-week fast, and in consequence a Unity Conference of all creeds was called to discuss the problem. As a result of this action there was some improvement in 1925, but in 1926 communal tension again increased, with a total of thirty-six outbreaks and some two thousand casualties. The most serious occurred in Calcutta, where the shrill music of a Hindu procession disturbed and angered the Muslim worshipers in a mosque. The result was a total of fourteen hundred dead or injured, two hundred shops gutted, and twelve churches wrecked.

Now the question of what would happen after the exodus of the British was being raised. "Behind the façade of a united nationalist campaign against the British Raj, a struggle had already begun for the heritage of place and power it would some day leave behind it."[31] By 1927 the toll of victims in the preceding four years had reached five hundred dead and five thousand injured in communal violence. It was in this atmosphere of tension that Lord Irwin arrived in India in 1926 as Governor-General. This official made a commendable but fruitless effort to bring the Hindu and Muslim communities closer together.

In the mid-twenties several events took place which seriously exacerbated communal tension. In December 1926 a prominent Hindu of the Punjab, Swami Shaddhanand, who was active in the movement to reconvert former Hindus who had turned Muslim, was assassinated by a Muslim fanatic. Then there was the uproar over the *Rangila Rasa* case. A Hindu bookseller of Lahore published a book in 1924 titled *Rangila Rasa* (*The Debauched Prophet*), which was a scurrilous attack on Mohammed. The bookseller was prosecuted in court but was not convicted, much to the anger of the Muslims; a few years later, however, he was murdered in his shop. The founding of the Hindu Mahasabha must also be regarded as an important factor in the worsening of communal relations. This organization was set up in 1923 at Benares under the leadership of Pandit Malaviya, and soon became the agency of militant Hinduism. Among its purposes were the reconversion of Hindus who had become Muslims; the Shuddhi movement, the encouragement of physical fitness among young Hindus; and the protection of the rights of Hinduism in any controversy with other communal groups. Its slogan was said to be "India belongs to the Hindus and is nobody else's patrimony." The Muslim reaction to the militant Mahasabha is seen in the following statement:

A new ideology was evolved, namely that India was the Holy Land of the Hindus, that the Hindus were a nation in their own right in which Muslims, Christians, and Parsis had no place, and that the political goal of the Hindus was Hindu Raj.[32]

32- F. K. Khan Durrani, The Meaning of Pakistan *(Lahore, Pakistan: Sh. Muhammad Ashraf, 1944), p. 93.*

Some of the outstanding Hindus in Congress emphatically excoriated the Mahasabha for its intemperateness, but the damage was done. In response the Muslims became more anti-Hindu and organized their own Tanzim movement for the conversion of Hindus to Allah. And in 1924 the Muslim League, which had been moribund during the Khilafat period, was revived by a leader destined to become famous in Indian history, Mohammed Ali Jinnah.

In 1928 the so-called Nehru Report had decisive influence upon the communal problem. In May of this year an All-Parties Conference met in Bombay to try to agree upon some pattern of government for a self-governing India that would be acceptable to all, especially to Hindus and Muslims. A committee headed by Motilal Nehru was set up to draft such a document, and in three months a report was submitted. This plan called for the Muslims to give up separate electorates, and proposed a federal plan of government in which the provincial units would have little autonomy. The Muslim community reacted strongly;

and when the All-Parties Conference met at Calcutta, December 22, 1928, to discuss the Nehru Report, Mohammed Ali Jinnah and his supporters attended and proposed a number of amendments, which were voted down. There was bitter debate, during which the Muslims left the Conference.

For some time the Muslims had been divided politically into a number of factions. The Nehru Report, however, tended to throw them together, and in the last week of December 1928 a great unity meeting was held at Delhi under the chairmanship of the Aga Khan. This conclave was the most representative meeting the Muslims had held up to this time, and it drew up a number of demands which would have to be met in any new constitution. Among the more important were: (1) Provinces in any federation must have complete autonomy. (2) In any legislature, provincial or federal, all legislation affecting communal relations can be blocked by the opposition of three-quarters of the votes of a community. (3) There must be separate electorates. (4) Muslims must be given fair representation in all cabinets. (5) They shall be given an adequate share of posts in the governmental services. (6) Muslim culture is to receive its rightful share of public funds, so that its schools and other institutions are not neglected.

The upshot of the Nehru Report was that it intensified communalism. Muslims such as Mohammed Ali, who had been an enthusiastic coadjutor of Gandhi's from 1920 to 1922, now attacked the Congress and the Hindus with vehemence; and in the spring of 1929 twenty-three prominent Muslims issued a Manifesto against the Nehru Report and its supporters. From now on the Congress was for all purposes a Hindu organization. The Muslim community, however, found it difficult to present a united political front. Jinnah drafted a platform, later famous as his Fourteen Points and modeled somewhat upon that adopted at Delhi's Unity Meeting, which was designed to unite all Muslim groups. But this endeavor failed, and one faction of Muslims, led by A. K. Azad and Dr. Ansari, joined the Congress, maintaining it was a secular all-India party. And outside the Congress there were the All-India Muslim Conference and the All-India Muslim League. It was this last organization which was destined to unite the great majority of Muslims under the leadership of Jinnah.

The decade of the 1920's ended with Gandhi taking the Congress into civil disobedience. Although there were some outstanding Muslims in Congress, the majority held aloof and refused to have anything to do with Gandhi's campaign. This led to serious communal riots. At Cawnpore, in March 1931, members of Congress tried to enforce a day of mourning in commemoration of a young terrorist who had been executed for killing a British police officer. The Muslims would not close their shops, and fighting broke out. The most terrible atrocities occurred, and in the course of three days more than four hundred people were killed and hundreds wounded. The exact casualties will never be known, since many bodies were dumped into the city's drains. Again, in 1932, there was a serious communal outbreak at Bombay caused by the refusal of non-Congress members, especially Muslims, to honor the boycott of foreign goods.

Communal tension spread far to the north, to the remote state of Kashmir. This native state was ruled by a Hindu Maharaja and a small Hindu governing caste, but the population was nearly 80 per cent Muslim. The mass of people had long been discontented with their rulers and in 1931 communal feeling from other parts of India fed their smoldering resentment. There were outbreaks in the summer which were successfully controlled. The news of the severity of repression spread, and by the end of the year bands of Muslims were trying to cross the border into Kashmir to help their co-religionists. Only the existence of British troops saved the government and prevented civil war. Kashmir was to serve again in 1947 as the arena for communal strife, but this time for two nations—Pakistan and the Union of India.

The Round Table Conferences, held in London between 1930 and 1932, did little to minimize communal rivalries; on the contrary, they tended to inflame them. The Muslim League signified its intention of supporting the proposed federation of India, but only if adequate safeguards were granted to the Muslim community, and in June 1931 the President of the League declared, "Moslems would rather die fighting for preservation of their rights than to accept slavery at the hands of the infidels."[33] The communal problem overshadowed all other issues and difficulties at the Second Round Table Conference, where Gandhi refused to recognize the right of any party or group other than Congress to speak on Indian affairs. This claim was heatedly refuted by all

the minorities, especially by Dr. Ambedkhar, leader of the Untouchables, and by the leaders of the Muslim delegation. As we have noted above in this chapter, there was complete deadlock among the Indian representatives on whether, how, and how far the minorities were to be protected by special safeguards. The impasse was cleared away only by the Communal Award worked out by MacDonald and his advisers.

While the Muslim community, like the Congress, was disappointed by the limits on complete independence which were presented by the India Act of 1935, they were content and reassured by the special rights and protection which it vouchsafed to minorities by means of the safeguards. Because of this feeling of safety there were indications in 1936 that Jinnah, now president of the Muslim League, was willing to revive the Hindu-Muslim entente of 1916. Events from 1937 to 1939 completely shattered this promising prospect.

When provincial self-government was inaugurated in 1937, Congress members were able to form ministries in seven of the eleven provinces. Bitter feelings among the Muslims were quickly aroused when Congress refused to admit any Muslim into a provincial ministry unless he became a member of the Congress and gave up allegiance to the League. Resentment ran especially high in such provinces as Bihar and the United Provinces, where strong Muslim minorities existed. The Muslims were quick to call this action a breach of faith, pointing out that at the Round Table Conference it was agreed that cabinets should include representatives of minorities and that this principle had accordingly been included in the Instructions of each provincial governor. Ambedkhar, the scholarly leader of the Scheduled Classes, was quite forthright in his denunciation of Congress policy, and wrote that it was "indeed a covert attempt to break all other parties in the country and make the Congress the only political party. The demand for signing the Congress pledge can have no other intention. This attempt to establish a totalitarian state may be welcome to the Hindus. But it means the political death of the Muslims as a free people."[34]

During the next two years the gulf of misunderstanding and acrimony between the Congress and the League continued to widen. It soon appeared that the Congress cabinets were not responsible to their respective legislatures but rather to the

33- New York Times, *June 2, 1931.*

34- *Quoted in Durrani, op. cit., p. 128.*

high command in Congress. Nehru frankly declared that "the ministers were the spokesmen of a mighty national movement of India and were under the discipline of their party, and directly controlled by the Congress Working Committee."[35] It was as though in the United States the National Committee of the Republican party laid down all the policies to be followed by all state governors who were Republicans. The Muslims believed that Congress policy was authoritarian and rendered provincial autonomy quite illusory.

There were other aspects of the Congress governments in the provinces that irritated and alarmed the Muslims. When the new provincial governments came in, the Congress tricolor was raised over the public buildings, and when the legislatures convened they were opened by the singing of the Hindu nationalist song, *Bande Mataram*. Further, it was claimed that in appointments to public offices members of Congress obtained nearly all of the positions and that in the realm of education Congress governments were determined to make Hindi the legal language of the educated at the expense of other languages, such as the Muslim Urdu. Finally, Congress initiated a mass movement to wean Muslims away from their organizations and into the party of Nehru and Gandhi. As it turned out, these Congress policies were very ill advised, but at the time it was natural that the party should assume it was the only political group that really mattered. As yet the Muslims were divided, there being no single, all-inclusive, organization to represent their interests. The Muslim League as late as 1937 was not well organized or supported. Its finances were inadequate, and only one English daily espoused the League cause in India.

Division and weakness in Muslim ranks were more apparent than real, however, for in two short years they were superseded by a new strength and unity that violently challenged Congress policies. While there was a strong foundation, as we shall see shortly, upon which to build a dynamic Muslim nationalism, the one single person responsible for the transformation was Mohammed Ali Jinnah. Up to 1937 Jinnah was not especially popular in Muslim circles. He still bore the stigma of being too friendly to Congress, of not being quite fully dedicated to the cause of Islam. In less than a year, however, Jinnah began to forge to the front as the *Quaid-i-Azam,* the Leader, of united Mus-

lim community. A master of invective, he lashed out in a number of speeches against Congress. His main thesis he expressed as follows: "Since the inauguration of the new provincial constitutions, it has been established beyond doubt that the sole aim and object of the Congress is to annihilate every other organisation in the country, and to set itself up as a fascist and authoritarian organisation of the worst type."[36]

Jinnah's leadership soon produced results; all over India there was an upsurge of Muslim League strength. Between 1937 and 1943, sixty-one elections were held for Muslim seats in the legislatures, and of these the League won forty-seven, independent Muslim candidates ten, and the Muslims sponsored by Congress only four. As 1937 drew to a close, 170 new branches of the League were established and in one province alone 100,000 new members were recruited. At a League Conference held in October 1937, Jinnah declared that Muslims could not expect fair play under Congress government.

Meanwhile, Nehru and his colleagues were becoming genuinely concerned over the League revival and what they regarded as the intransigence of its tone. In consequence the Congress Working Committee passed a resolution assuring all minorities that their rights would be scrupulously respected. And in the spring of 1938 Jinnah and Nehru exchanged correspondence in which the former demanded that the League be recognized as the sole organization representing the Indian Muslim community. There was no agreement, however, and in December 1938, at the annual meeting of the League, Jinnah declared that all hope of communal peace had been wrecked "on the rocks of Congress Fascism."[37]

In order to strengthen its case the League published several reports enumerating and describing various grievances and even atrocities suffered by Muslims in the Congress-ruled provinces. These documents (the *Pirpur Report* and the *Shareef Report*) undoubtedly contained charges that were greatly exaggerated. There was really no Congress plot against Muslim rights as such, but the seven provincial governments controlled by Congress continually neglected to appreciate the sensitivities and fears of a cultural minority. And in many instances irresponsible persons who thought of themselves as the agents of Congress aroused the fears of Muslims. That there was a genuine anxiety as

35- *Nehru,* The Unity of India, *p. 429.*

36- Some Recent Speeches . . . of Mr. Jinnah, *collected and edited by Jamil-ud-Din Ahmad (Lahore: Sh. Muhammad Ashraf, 1943), p. 86.*

37- *Sir Reginald Coupland,* The Indian Problem *(London: Oxford University Press, 1944), Part II, p. 184.*

to the future of their distinctive culture is witnessed by the Report of the Kamal Yar Jung Education Committee, drafted by a group of outstanding Muslim educators. This Report lamented the low percentage of Muslim students in colleges and universities; underlined the lack of attention paid in university research to Muslim studies; and drew attention to the decline of separate Muslim schools on the elementary level. The upshot, according to the Report, was that the Muslim "hardly has any opportunity to know anything about his Prophet, the Caliphs, the saints, the scholars, the philosophers, the poets or the heroes of Islam."[38]

It was in this atmosphere of mounting Muslim fear and resentment that a fundamental change took place in the policy of the League. Originally this organization had supported the new Government of India Act of 1935, but by the end of 1938 Jinnah was declaring that no democratic system of government by merely counting heads could work in India, and that the new Act had failed to protect the legitimate interests of the Muslim minority. The Muslims were now beginning to think of Indian independence in terms of self-determination for their own community.

In December 1938, at the Patna meeting of the Muslim League, a special committee, headed by Jinnah, was created "to examine various schemes already propounded and those that may be submitted to the President." A movement had now begun the goal of which was to obtain some kind of territorial autonomy for Muslims. This was ultimately to result in a separate state for the followers of Mohammed, in the partition of India and the creation of Pakistan.

As one looks back on the all-important developments in Indian affairs from 1937 to 1939, when the Muslim-Hindu gulf was irreparably widened, it is valuable to reflect upon the fundamental factors that made this tragic situation possible. There are many observers who emphasize economics as the basic cause of Hindu-Muslim rivalry. Nehru once said that all communal claims go back to the contest for jobs, and to a large extent he was right.

Generally speaking, the Muslims were "have-nots" in comparison with the Hindus, who had the lead in education, the professions, the government service, and in finance. The Muslim in the village was usually the debtor, the Hindu the moneylender.

Economic rivalries, while important, were distinctly secondary to the fact that Muslim and Hindu cultures in many ways constituted two distinct, and frequently antagonistic, ways of life. This dichotomy was strikingly expressed by Jinnah in an interview with a French author and journalist, Eve Curie, in the following words:

> How can you even dream of Hindu-Moslem unity? Everything pulls us apart: We have no intermarriages. We have not the same calendar. The Moslems believe in a single God, and the Hindu are idolatrous. Like the Christians, the Moslems believe in an equalitarian society, whereas the Hindus maintain the iniquitous system of castes and leave heartlessly fifty million Untouchables to their tragic fate, at the bottom of the social ladder. Now again, the Hindus worship animals. They consider cows sacred. We, the Moslems, think it is nonsense. We want to kill the cows. We want to eat them. Another thing: no Hindu will take food from a Moslem. No orthodox Hindu will even touch Hindu food if the shadow of a Moslem or the shadow of a Hindu of a lower caste has polluted the bowl.[39]

What Hindu leaders in Congress apparently failed to understand was the strength of Muslim revivalism. Hindu publicists claimed that a religious group, such as the Muslims, did not constitute a political entity and there was really no such thing as a distinctive Muslim culture in India. It was true, nevertheless, that beginning late in the nineteenth century there had been the rediscovery of the greatness of the Muslim period, especially that of the Moguls, in Indian history. And following the First World War there had developed a feeling of self-identification, of participation in a Pan-Islamic movement with the renascent Muslim states—such as Turkey, Egypt, Iraq, and Iran—which were assuming new dignity and influence in the family of nations. The importance of these developments can hardly be exaggerated.

38- *Ibid., p. 192.*

39- *Eve Curie,* Journey Among Warriors *(New York: Doubleday, Doran, 1943), p. 462.*

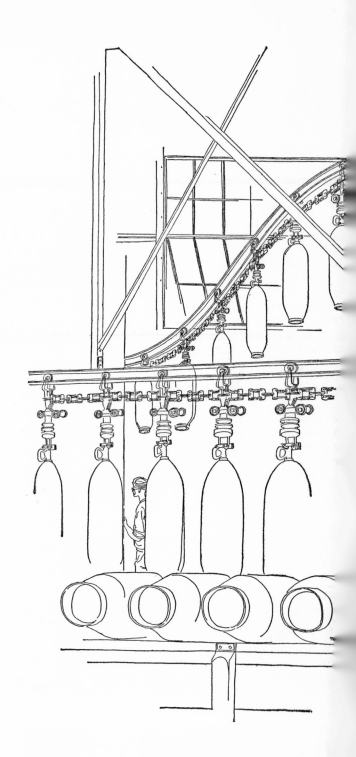

*The war that came to India in
1939 brought the same influences
as had the conflict of 1914 to
1919, only the intensity of its
impact was greater. In the Second
World War, European prestige declined to a new low throughout
Asia in general and India in
particular, as Britain, Holland,
and the United States were rocked
by disastrous defeats at Singapore
and Mandalay, Hongkong, Batavia,
and Bataan. At the same time,
nationalism, already aggressive and
self-confident at the outset of
this world war, took on renewed
strength and resolution from the
strong wave of idealism which existed
in the anti-Axis Grand Alliance
and championed freedom and self-
reliance.*

*THE ATLANTIC Charter played
much the same role in 1941
as Wilson's Fourteen Points
had played in 1918; and if the
First World War gave India the
beginning course on the banquet
table of self-determination, the
second global conflict added all
other items on the political
menu including the dessert of
absolute national autonomy. Instead
of one nation being created, however, freedom relinquished by the
British raj was to be shared by
two independent states, the Union
of India and Pakistan. Such a
settlement inevitably brought with
it new problems.*

*War, independence,
and partition*

1- Jawaharlal Nehru, The Unity of India: Collected Writings 1937-1940 *(London: Lindsay Drummond, 1941), p. 401.*

2- Quoted in Raleigh Parkin, India Today *(New York: John Day Co., 1946), p. 199.*

3- Sir Reginald Coupland, The Indian Problem *(London: Oxford University Press, 1944), Part II, p. 213.*

4- Quoted in Jawaharlal Nehru, Toward Freedom *(New York: John Day Co., 1941), p. 432.*

chapter 9

AS THE shadows of war began to lengthen in the spring of 1939, the National Congress warned that it would not fight in other people's wars and that, in its view, the present world tension was nothing more than a struggle between fascism and imperialism. As early as 1936, the Congress in an election manifesto had declared its implacable "opposition to the participation of India in an imperialist war."[1] During 1938, in the heyday of the Chamberlain appeasement, Congress leaders, and Nehru in particular, excoriated British foreign policy as a betrayal of democracy. In April 1939, Great Britain began to undertake precautionary military measures. Indian troops were sent to reinforce the garrison at Aden, and the British Parliament passed a bill giving the Governor-General and the central government in India complete power over the provincial administrations in case of a grave emergency. Replying to these British measures, the Congress charged that a war-dictatorship was in the making and Nehru again warned that "it was for the people of India to determine whether India would join a war or not, and any decision imposed on us by Britain would be resisted."[2] In the summer of 1939 additional Indian troops were sent to Singapore and Egypt, and Congress countered by ordering its members not to attend the Central Legislature.

On September 3 Great Britain declared war against the German Reich, and on the same day the Viceroy, Lord Linlithgow, proclaimed India to be at war with Germany. In the Central Legislature the Viceroy addressed the members, explaining the situation, and a Defence of India Bill was introduced and passed with no opposition. To be sure, Congress members were absent and thus were not able to express their opposition. While they and their colleagues bitterly protested against India's being dragged into the war, it should be noted that the provincial premiers of Bengal, Punjab, and Sind, representing ninety million people, pledged their support of the war effort. Furthermore, all political parties other than Congress took the same stand. The Liberals declared that this was no time for bargaining and that India should support the democratic powers. In the Native States the Princes promised "every possible assistance in men, money, and materials."[3] The Muslim League, interestingly enough, made its promise of support contingent upon Britain's guaranteeing the Muslims "justice and fair treatment in the Congress provinces," and promising not to make any constitutional changes in India without the consent of the League.

Two days after India became involved in the war, the Viceroy called Gandhi for a conference. After the meeting, the Mahatma announced in his newspaper *Harijan* that he had told Linlithgow he could not, as a pacifist, support the war, but his sympathies were with England and France "from the purely humanitarian viewpoint." Midway in September the Working Committee of the National Congress, led by Nehru, drafted a statement in which it was stressed that the "declared wishes of the Indian people . . . have been deliberately ignored by the British Government," and while the Committee "unhesitatingly condemn the latest aggression of the Nazi government in Germany against Poland . . . . the issue of war and peace for India must be decided by the Indian people."[4] The statement went on to denounce Britain for its past record of conniving at aggression in Manchuria and its acquiescence in Italian conquest in Abyssinia. Furthermore, the Committee let it be known that, if this war were really being fought against aggression and for democracy, India would fight with other free nations, but she must be free herself. And, it was averred, this freedom should be achieved by the Indian people's drafting their own constitution in a constituent assembly. The document closed by requesting Great Britain to declare in unequivocal terms its war aims "in regard to democracy and imperialism."

Meanwhile, the Viceroy had been interviewing all the important Indian leaders, some fifty in number, with the view of rallying public opinion to the side of Great Britain. On October 17 the Viceroy made an offer to the Indian people. His statement reiterated British aims of ultimate Dominion status for India; recognized that after the war the system of government laid down by the Government of India Act of 1935 would have to be reconsidered; and stated that the British government would be ready "to enter into consultation with representatives of the several communities" in order to frame a new scheme of government. It was made clear that the rights of minority groups, such as the Muslims, would be safeguarded in any new constitution. While the Viceroy offered at once to form a consultative group, made up of representatives of all parties, to associate public

India About 1940

British India

Native States

From that time to the end of the war the most powerful nationalist political organization in India refused to take office and boycotted the war effort. It was a complete stalemate and one that weakened the ability of the British Empire to stand up against the might of Hitlerite Germany. Opponents of Axis totalitarianism, not only in Britain and France, but all over the world, were deeply disappointed that the parties to the controversy, the British government and the Congress, had been unable to accommodate their different views. The Congress leaders continued to declare that the only solution was a constituent assembly called to draft a constitution for an independent India and that the mention by the British of minority interests in the October Declaration made by the Viceroy was completely irrelevant. Jinnah, the Muslim League leader, referred to the constituent assembly demanded by Congress as "a packed body, manoeuvred and managed by a Congress caucus."[6]

The position of British authority in India was a very delicate one as war broke out in 1939. Care had to be taken to avoid communal strife. Extensive concessions made to one group would only have alienated other elements in Indian public life. It also was an open question whether Britain, despite any concessions that might be made, could be sure, considering Gandhi's pacifism, that Congress could be rallied to the war effort. Even so, it does appear that the British government could have managed India's entrance into the war with more diplomacy and more appreciation of Indian nationalistic susceptibilities. As one British official has written:

In law, India was at war when Britain was at war; and, therefore, constitutionally speaking, no issue would arise . . . None the less, much more could have been done, and should have been done, to give India the opportunity of going to war by a political act of her own, performed by her existing representatives. It would have been feasible, tactical, and wise to have provided the Legislative Assembly and the Council of State with an opportunity to declare by resolution the hostility of India to the Axis.[7]

Furthermore, considering the importance of gaining the full measure of India's strength and good will in the conflict, it would seem that the Viceroy's declaration of October 1939 was a rather cold, jejune, and uninspired document.

For the first nine months most people in India

opinion with the conduct of the war, he curtly replied to the Congress demand for immediate self-government:

The situation must be faced in terms of world politics and of political realities in this country. . . . progress must be conditioned by practical considerations. . . . there is nothing to be gained by phrases which . . . contemplate a state of things which is unlikely at the present point of political development to stand the test of practical application. . . .[5]

Early in November the Viceroy's offer was further extended to include the temporary expansion of his Executive Council and thus to associate Indians more closely in the management of the war effort.

The Congress reaction was completely hostile. Gandhi let it be known it was his view that the government might just as well have made no declaration, while the Working Committee condemned the declaration outright and called upon its Congress ministries in the provinces to resign. Consequently, on November 8 the eight Congress governments gave up their authority. In response Jinnah called upon Indian Muslims to celebrate December 22 as "Deliverance Day" from Congress rule.

5- Quoted in Parkin, op. cit., p. 204.

6- The News Chronicle (London), December 11, 1939.

7- Sir Frederick Whyte, India: A Bird's-Eye View (New York: Oxford University Press, 1943), p. 31.

gave little thought to the conflict. During this period of the "phony war" India breathed easily behind the guard and shield of British sea power. As in 1914 the Indian army, consisting of some 160,000 Indian and 50,000 British troops, constituted a valuable pool of trained and seasoned soldiers. In the first months of the war some 60,000 were sent overseas, to Malaya, Aden, and to the Army of the Middle East. No one as yet had any notion of the terrible crisis that lay ahead for British arms, from both the German and the Japanese armies. The program of recruiting in India, therefore, was taken quite casually during the early stages of the war. Recruits were taken in at the rate of from ten to fifteen thousand per month and by May 1940 some 53,000 men had been recruited for the Indian army.

In the months following the outbreak of the Second World War, the Muslim League under the leadership of Mohammed Ali Jinnah became more aggressive, more the single representative of Muslim public opinion, and more determined to challenge the claims of the National Congress to speak for all elements and creeds in India. In particular, as a Muslim author has said, it was at this time that "Mohamad Ali Jinnah became the living symbol of Muslim Unity."[8] It will be recalled that, following the controversy between the League and Congress over the Nehru Report in 1928, the Muslim League under the leadership of Jinnah had formulated the famous Fourteen Points (see p. 140). They were the irreducible safeguards demanded by the Muslim League in any new constitution and for a decade formed the political platform around which the Muslims increasingly rallied. But just before the outbreak of war and immediately afterward, a more radical and ambitious program began to crystallize, the plan for Pakistan.

In the spring of 1939 a special committee headed by Jinnah was set up by the Muslim League to examine various schemes that had already been advanced to insure the rights of the Muslim minority in India. One of the first of these had been tentatively sketched by the great Muslim poet, Sir Muhammad Iqbal, in his presidential address before the League in 1930. He advocated a single Muslim state in north-west India, a state to be endowed with extensive autonomy but forming one of the constituent elements of a greater all-India federation. The next development was much more

ambitious. In 1933 a group of young Indian Muslims, led by Chaudhuri Rahmat Ali at Cambridge University in England, circulated a four-page leaflet calling for the creation of a new state in India, to be called Pakistan. The authors declared that "India is not the name of one single country, nor the home of one single nation," and called for the establishment of a Muslim national state in north-west India. To form the name of this new state, *P* was taken from Punjab; *A* from Afghan, a term representing the North-West Frontier Province; *K* from Kashmir; *S* from Sind; and *Tan* from the last syllable of Baluchistan.

Several alternatives to Pakistan were subsequently brought forward. For example, Dr. Syed Abdul Latif in 1938-1939 advanced in various publications his Culture Zone Plan. He argued that India was not a single nation, that the crude imposition of "Hindu nationalism" upon the subcontinent would inevitably result in war, but that the solution was not to be found in Pakistan, or partition. A free India should consist of a number of autonomous nationalities, each in its geographical home, and each forming part of a loose federal government. There were to be four Muslim and eleven Hindu zones, and the Native States were gradually to attach themselves to appropriate zones. Other similar plans were formulated, all endeavoring to recognize the cultural distinctiveness of the Muslims and to give them a wide area of complete political autonomy and yet, at the same time, to dovetail the Muslim zones or states into some kind of larger Indian federation. Thus the unity of India would be preserved.

The response of the National Congress was not sympathetic—in fact it was derisive. This body refused to admit the existence of a distinct Muslim nation and held to the program of calling a National Constitutional Assembly that would frame a constitution for all India. In the face of this attitude, and particularly during the period of the Congress ministries from 1937 to 1939, the policy of the Muslim League hardened. In September 1939, the Working Committee of the League stated that Muslim India was "irrevocably opposed to any federal objective which must necessarily result in a majority-community rule under the guise of democracy and a parliamentary system of government."[9] In the spring of 1940 Jinnah told the press that the Muslims were not a minority but a distinct nation. Jinnah asserted:

8- *Matlubul Hasan, M. A. Jinnah: A Political Study* (Lahore: Sh. Muhammad Ashraf, no date), p. 679.

9- The Indian Annual Register, 1939 (Calcutta: The Annual Register Office, no date), II, 351.

We are a nation of a hundred million, and what is more we are a nation with our own distinctive culture and civilization, language, literature, art and architecture . . . legal laws and moral codes, customs and calendar, history and tradition, aptitudes and ambitions. In short we have our own distinctive outlook on life and of life.[10]

It was in a mood of expectancy and excitement that the Muslim League met at Lahore in March 1940 to hear Mr. Jinnah declare in his presidential address that Muslims "must have their homelands, their territory and their State."[11] The following day a historic resolution was passed calling for the creation of autonomous and sovereign Muslim states in areas "in which the Muslims are numerically in the majority, as in the north-western and eastern zones of India."[12] Although this declaration was couched in vague terms, it seemed that the League did not view the new Muslim states as belonging to any larger political grouping, such as a federation. Partition could not be reconciled with the political unity of India.

Not long after these deliberations at Lahore the full fury of the Nazi blitzkrieg was unleashed in western Europe. Norway and Denmark were overrun in April 1940, Belgium and Holland in May. France surrendered to Hitler on June 22. As the news of the French debacle reached India, there came with it a recognition of the serious state of Great Britain, and the Congress attitude softened somewhat. On July 27, 1940, the All-India Congress Committee repudiated the Gandhian policy of non-violence and with it the policy of boycotting the war effort. This was a victory for the moderate and realistic elements in the Congress, which was now prepared to support the war at a price. Britain was asked to make a declaration of India's independence, and, as an initial step, to create a provisional national government. In the face of this Congress gesture Jinnah, backed up by the Muslim League, declared that no new constitution during the war period or after should be set up without the approval of Muslim India.

In the midst of the war crisis and the imminent prospect of German invasion of the British Isles, Gandhi persisted in his pacifism and praised Pétain's armistice and France's surrender to Germany. He declared that India could only be defended "non-violently," and called upon every Briton "to accept the method of non-violence." Specifically, Gandhi wrote in his newspaper:

I do not want Britain to be defeated, nor do I want her to be victorious in a trial of brute strength, whether expressed through the muscle or the brain. I venture to present you with a nobler and a braver way, worthy of the bravest soldier. I want you to fight Nazism without arms. . . . You will invite Herr Hitler and Signor Mussolini to take what they want of the countries you call your possessions. Let them take possession of your beautiful island. . . . If these gentlemen choose to occupy your homes, you will vacate them. If they do not give you free passage out, you will allow yourself, man, woman and child, to be slaughtered, but you will refuse to owe allegiance to them.[13]

Just before the Battle of Britain began, with the German *Luftwaffe* striving mightily to gain control of the air over England and pave the way for a cross Channel invasion, the British government, seeking to end the political deadlock in India, made its significant August 1940 offer. In a statement issued from New Delhi the Viceroy recalled that the previous October the British government had made it quite clear that Dominion status was its objective in India and this goal meant "free and equal partnership in the British Commonwealth." In order to allay and mollify the fears of the Muslim League, the announcement declared that "full weight should be given to the views of the minorities." And, while ruling out the possibility of fundamental constitutional changes during the war, the Viceroy announced: "His Majesty's Government authorize me to declare that they will most readily assent to the setting up after the conclusion of the war . . . of a body representative of the principal elements in India's national life in order to devise the framework of the new constitution."[14] The Viceroy also stated that the expansion of his Executive Council by the addition of representatives of various Indian political parties should not be postponed and that the War Advisory Council suggested by the government in November 1939 should also be constituted without delay.

This "August Offer" utterly failed to eliminate the political deadlock, and President Rajendra Prasad of Congress announced it was "totally at variance" with his party's policy. Other Congress officials declared that the minority problem referred to in the declaration was being made into an insuperable obstacle to Indian progress. Feeling rebuffed, and unable to secure an independent Indian provisional government as a condition to

10- Quoted in Sir Frederick Puckle, "The Pakistan Doctrine: Its Origins and Power," Foreign Affairs, *XXIV* (April 1946), p. 535.

11- A. C. Banerjee, ed., Indian Constitutional Documents (*Calcutta: A. Mukherjee and Co., 1946*), II, p. 408.

12- Ibid., p. 409.

13- T. A. Raman, What Does Gandhi Want? (*New York: Oxford University Press, 1945*), pp. 24-25.

14- Indian Annual Register, 1940, II, pp. 372-373.

its full support of the British war effort, the National Congress turned back again to Gandhi and gave him its backing in a campaign of non-violent civil disobedience, to be waged as a protest against the war. The movement got under way in October 1940, and members of Congress were selected to give anti-war speeches, including the slogan: "It is wrong to help the British war effort with men or money: the only worthy effort is to resist all war with non-violent resistance."[15] In all parts of India the police arrested Congressmen as they delivered anti-war speeches, and at one time more than fourteen thousand were in prison.

The reaction to this Gandhian civil disobedience campaign among the Indians themselves served to demonstrate how confused and divided were the various groups on basic issues such as the war. Jinnah and his League denounced the Congress anti-war campaign, not so much because it might hinder the war effort as because in their view it was a kind of political blackmail for putting pressure on the British government to insure the realization of Congress objectives. The small but brilliantly led Liberal party deplored any action that might weaken the resistance of the British Empire against Germany. The famous Muslim Prime Minister of Punjab Province, Sir Sikander Hyat Khan, said that Gandhi's campaign meant "that while Britain is engaged in a life-and-death struggle, he should be given the freedom to stab her in the back. That the stabbing is to be non-violent makes no difference."[16]

During the summer of 1941, the Viceroy proceeded to carry through the expansion of his Executive Council and the creation of a special War Advisory Council. Five distinguished Indians were added to the Executive Council, making a total of eight Indian and five British members. A new National War Council of thirty-one members was set up, twenty-two from the provinces of British India and nine from the Native States; and in this membership only one was a European. In addition to these gestures, the British Secretary of State for India in London, Mr. L. S. Amery, made a number of important speeches endeavoring to convince Indians of Britain's good faith as far as their country's right to self-government was concerned. Mr. Amery specifically promised India after the war "full and equal partnership in the British Commonwealth." The Secretary also argued that the main obstacle to a free India was com-

munal rivalry, which could only be solved by the Indians themselves. While endeavoring to point out to Indians the seriousness of the Hindu-Muslim problem, Amery at the same time indicated that partition as advocated by Jinnah's League was no solution. Referring to the doctrine of Pakistan, he declared, "It is a counsel of despair and, I believe, of wholly unnecessary despair."[17] The Secretary's emphasis upon the communal problem touched off angry retorts in Congress ranks. Gandhi replied, "It is the British statesmen who are responsible for the divisions in India's ranks."[18]

In addition to the expansion of the Viceroy's Executive Council and the creation of a War Advisory body, another political development of 1941 should be noted. In August of this year the British Prime Minister, Winston Churchill, and the American President, Franklin Roosevelt, met at sea on board the British battleship *Prince of Wales* and affixed their signatures to the Atlantic Charter, a document expressing in rather general terms the international objectives of Great Britain and the United States. Article Three declared: "They respect the right of all peoples to choose the form of government under which they will live; and they wish to see sovereign rights and self-government restored to those who have been forcibly deprived of them."[19]

On September 9, 1941, Winston Churchill proceeded to comment on the Atlantic Charter during the course of a review of the war made in the House of Commons. In his remarks the Prime Minister explained: "The Joint Declaration does not qualify in any way the various statements of policy which have been made from time to time about development of constitutional government in India, Burma or other parts of the British Empire. We have pledged by the Declaration of August, 1940, to help India obtain free and equal partnership in the British Commonwealth. . . ." The Prime Minister continued, "At the Atlantic Meeting, we had in mind primarily the extension of the sovereignty, self-government and national life of the States and nations of Europe now under Nazi yoke . . . That is quite a separate problem from the progressive evolution of self-governing institutions in regions whose peoples owe allegiance to the British Crown."[20]

A furor broke out in India as soon as the Prime Minister's speech was reported in the press, and in the United States, where for many years there had

15- *Sir Reginald Coupland,* India: A Restatement *(London: Oxford University Press, 1942),* p. 205.

16- Quoted in ibid., p. 206.

17- *L. S. Amery,* India and Freedom *(London: Oxford University Press, 1942), p. 87.*

18- Indian Annual Register, 1941, *I, p. 327.*

19- *Louise W. Holborn and Hajo Holborn, eds.,* War and Peace Aims of the United Nations *(Boston: World Peace Foundation, 1943), p. 2.*

20- Indian Annual Register, 1941, *II, pp. 84-85.*

been influential circles highly critical of British policy in India, there were loud outcries against Churchill's "taking India out of the Atlantic Charter."

Regardless of whether it can be argued that Churchill's statement on the Atlantic Charter constituted a limitation on past promises of self-government already made to India, or whether it denied to Indians rights of immediate freedom that they could logically imply from a reading of Article 3 of the Charter, or whether the whole controversy was an unfair and misleading interpretation springing from political opportunism—regardless of these and any other point of view that may be taken, the fact remains that there was wide currency to the view in India that Britain had broken her word. As one British historian sadly admits, "At the end of 1941 there was more disbelief in British honesty than there had ever been before."[21]

Despite the general atmosphere of political frustration and suspicion that was widespread in India in 1941 and which, of course, was strongest in Congress ranks, the country since the war crisis of Dunkirk in the spring of 1940 had continued to make tremendous strides in the war effort. Following the defeat of France and the entrance of Italy into the war, the Mediterranean was closed to British shipping for all practical purposes. As British industries were working night and day for home defense needs, industrial production had to be stimulated east of Suez, so that the part of the Near East and North Africa held by Britain, together with other parts of the Empire ringed around the Indian Ocean, could be made as self-sufficient as possible. In the fall of 1940 a mission under Sir Alexander Roger came to India and remained there for six months to mobilize the country's economic resources for the war. While this mission was in India, the Eastern Group Conference met at Delhi in October 1940. Delegations arrived from New Zealand, South Africa, Burma, Ceylon, Southern Rhodesia, East Africa, Hongkong, Malaya, and Palestine. As a result, the Eastern Group Supply Council was established in February 1941, to coordinate supply and plan production in the vast area represented by these countries with a total population of more than five hundred million.

By the end of 1941 war production in India had made considerable progress. Pig-iron production increased from 1,600,000 to 2,000,000 tons and

finished-steel production grew from 867,000 to 1,250,000 tons, while armor plate began to be produced for the first time in India. Government ordnance factories were expanded to produce field guns, machine guns, bombs, depth charges, and other weapons; and 600,000 shells and 150,000,000 rounds of small-arms ammunition were sent overseas. In trying to put its war effort in high gear India was badly handicapped by the lack of trained men, the scarcity of machine tools, and the lack of electric power. A plan was put into effect to meet the manpower shortage by training 10,000 specialists in technical schools and factories.

In the actual field of combat and military effort a new program of recruitment was initiated in June 1940; one hundred thousand men were called to volunteer for the fighting forces, with an ultimate aim of an army of 500,000 men. Up to this time the process of "Indianization" of the officer ranks had been slow and halting; but now measures for training thousands of Indian officers were formulated.

While the British Isles fought off the efforts of the *Luftwaffe* to force surrender, the main peril to the British Empire in the fall of 1940 was in North and East Africa, where well-equipped Italian Fascist armies threatened to overwhelm Egypt, the Sudan, Uganda, and Kenya. In brilliant campaigns directed by General Sir Archibald Wavell, outnumbered British divisions scored a complete victory over the Italian army in North Africa. Taking the offensive in East Africa against Mussolini's empire, British troops in the spring of 1941 freed British Somaliland and captured Eritrea, Abyssinia, and Italian Somaliland. In all these actions Indian troops, especially the famous Fourth and Fifth Divisions, played a prominent part.

Cripps and Crisis

During the summer and early fall of 1941 the British Empire's prospect appeared much brighter than the year before. The Axis threat to the homeland had been thwarted; the imperial communications in North Africa had been successfully defended against Fascist attack; and, most important, Britain was no longer fighting alone with her Empire. Russia, erstwhile ally of Nazi Germany, was now feeling the full might of Hitler's Panzer Divisions. And from across the Atlantic there was

21- Coupland, India: A Restatement, p. 209.

now coming—both to Britain and to Russia—a vast cargo of American lend-lease material. The auguries seemed favorable.

During the last month of 1941, however, the entire prospect changed. The rapid conquests of Japan reversed for a time the balance of power in the Pacific; threatened to take over the vast British, French, Dutch and American possessions in Southeast Asia; and even extended their menace toward Australia and New Zealand. On December 7 the Japanese attacked Pearl Harbor, Manila, Hongkong, and Malaya. The following day the United States and Great Britain declared war on Japan, and British troops, together with Indian forces, had their first engagement against Japanese forces landing on the coast of north Malaya. A catastrophic blow was dealt to the successful defense of Malaya and its great naval base, Singapore, when the British battleships *Prince of Wales* and *Repulse* were sunk by hostile aircraft while endeavoring to intercept Japanese troop transports. Outnumbered and outmaneuvered by troops who had been specially trained for jungle warfare, the British forces were pushed down the Malayan peninsula and then cooped up on the island of Singapore. The end came in the middle of February 1942, with the surrender of the hapless British army defending this great and supposedly impregnable naval base. The tide of the Japanese conquest now lapped over into Burma.

The Japanese crossed the southeastern frontier of Burma from Siam with an excellent army of sixty thousand men; against it could be pitted only some twenty thousand Indian and seven thousand British troops and in North Burma several divisions of Chinese troops under General Joseph Stilwell. The Allied forces lacked air power, transport, radios, and anti-aircraft guns. On December 23, 1941, Rangoon had been bombed and upwards of 100,000 people fled from the city. Burma is surrounded by a horseshoe of mountains with her roads and railways following the narrow valleys which run north and south. By March 10 the Japanese controlled Rangoon, through which they could funnel reinforcements to the north, where they soon pinned the allied forces against the mountains. Only twelve thousand Indo-British troops were able to escape by crossing the mountains and getting back to India. General Stilwell led the remnants of his Chinese forces through 140 miles of jungle into India.

By May 1942 all of Burma was in Japanese hands. Valuable oil fields had had to be destroyed and the Burma Road to China had been cut. The significance of the victory of Japan was that Burma now could be used as a shield along the west to protect the vast new Nipponese empire in Southeast Asia. Burma was also a wedge, for its conquest had isolated China and made it less defensible against Japanese aggression. Most important, Burma could be a springboard for the Japanese conquest of India and resulting Japanese union with German forces in Iran, for General Rommel with his *Afrika Korps* in the spring of 1942 was poised in the Libyan desert ready to strike for the Nile and the Near East.

In a few weeks the war status of India had been changed from that of a rather complacent and somewhat unwilling ally of Britain, remote from the enemy, to one that was on the front line directly in the path of the rapidly approaching enemy, Japan. There was great astonishment in India over the Japanese victories in the Philippines, the East Indies, and Malaya; there was also growing fear and some people began to flee from Calcutta as they realized that the Japanese were now in control of the waters of the Bay of Bengal. All the while Japan carried on a barrage of radio propaganda, stressing its cultural ties with India, and stating that it was coming as a deliverer to oust the British imperialists.

Within Congress there was some jockeying and maneuvering between various factions as a realization of India's danger became evident. As in the spring of 1940, after Dunkirk, there was another repudiation of Gandhi's pacifism. By this time the civil disobedience campaign had worn itself out. In fact the government had released all imprisoned members of Congress, including such leaders as Nehru and Azad, just before Pearl Harbor. Having decided to support the war against Japan, however, Congress divided into those who were willing to do so on the basis of reasonable British concessions and those, led by Nehru, who would accept only complete independence. Among the former was the Prime Minister of Madras, Chakravarti Rajagopalacharia (usually and understandably referred to in India simply as "C.R."), who was an outstanding member of Congress and a statesman of exceptional talents. "C.R." toured his province rousing his people to be ready to fight invasion. While urg-

ing the British to make some constitutional concessions, such as the grant of some kind of national government, he also called for Hindu-Muslim reconciliation and recognized that the League was one of the two dominant political bodies in India. "C.R." was aided by another Congressman, K. M. Munshi, who, in January 1942, appealed for political unity, declaring, "The dangers of the hour must awaken the wisdom of all communities and interests and ought to make us realize that we should not allow future ambitions to frustrate a program of present safety."[22]

As we will see, the appeals of men like "C.R." had little influence upon Congress policy and the League seemed oblivious to the menace just beyond the borders of India. On the day Singapore fell the most important organ of the League, *The Dawn,* published the following statement:

> Pakistan is our deliverance, defense, destiny. . . . No amount of threats or intimidation will ever deter us from the chosen path. Hints about a "long period of civil war" we will brush aside with contempt . . . Pakistan is our only demand . . . and, by God, we will have it.[23]

Tension mounted rapidly in India. Early in January 1942 the leaders of the moderate Liberal party, always ready to lead the way to reconciliation, cabled Winston Churchill urging him to recognize India's national status and to form a new national government that would hold itself morally responsible to the country. In effect the latter proposal would mean an all-Indian Executive Council at New Delhi.

The month of February was a time of rumor and anxiety in India. In the British Parliament it was evident there was strong feeling that something should be done, and at once, to rally India to the cause of the Empire and the United Nations. On March 10 the leader of the House of Commons, Sir Stafford Cripps, announced that the Prime Minister would make a declaration on India at the next sitting of Commons. At the same time the Viceroy at Delhi issued a message to all the Indian people, regardless of their politics or religion, saying: "You will be invited during the next few weeks to enroll yourselves in the national war front. The land we live in is threatened with danger. . . I confide in your courage."[24]

On March 11, 1942, Churchill made his statement on India, announcing that Sir Stafford Cripps, Lord Privy Seal and leader of the House of Commons, was to go to India immediately. The Prime Minister explained that the crisis in India demanded that all must be done to guard this land from invasion.

The appointment of Cripps for this difficult mission was a happy and a logical choice. Reputed to have one of the most brilliant minds in Parliament, Sir Stafford was a prominent English Socialist who had long championed the cause of India's freedom. In December 1939 he had visited India and discussed its problems with many of its leaders; in the spring of 1940 he went to Moscow as British ambassador, and in February 1942 he was made a member of the British War Cabinet. There could be no doubt that the British government was sending to New Delhi a man who was an ardent sympathizer with Indian aspirations.

Sir Stafford Cripps arrived by air at Delhi on March 22 and immediately called a press conference, where in an informal and friendly fashion he explained the purpose of his mission. During the next three days Sir Stafford met various British officials and showed them the Draft Declaration he had brought to India, containing the proposals which had been approved by the British War Cabinet. Then he began a series of discussions with the leaders of the various Indian parties. Mr. Jinnah represented the League, Nehru and Azad the Congress, while the Indian rulers also sent their representatives. During these interviews Sir Stafford showed the Indian leaders the Draft Declaration, but for the time being they were pledged to secrecy.

Finally, on March 29 Cripps held a large press conference attended by some two hundred journalists. At this historic meeting copies of the Draft Declaration were distributed for publication. This Declaration admitted there were anxieties in India as to the fulfillment of past British promises. It had been decided, therefore, that in the most precise and clear terms the steps by which self-government was to be realized should now be laid down. The aim was the creation of a new Indian Union, "which shall constitute a Dominion, associated with the United Kingdom and the other Dominions by a common allegiance to the Crown, but equal to them in every respect, in no way subordinate in any aspect of its domestic or external affairs."[25]

The new constitution would be drafted by an

22- Indian Annual Register, 1942, *I, p. 40.*

23- *Coupland,* The Indian Problem, *II, p. 267.*

24- Indian Annual Register, 1942, *I, p. 55.*

25- Statement and Draft Declaration by H. M. Government, *Cmd. 6350 (London: His Majesty's Stationery Office, 1942), p. 4.*

Indian body in which the Native States were to be represented, following the conclusion of hostilities. A basic feature of the Draft Declaration was provision for any province of British India to remain out of the proposed Indian Union with the right of formulating its own independent government. This right of "non-accession" was specifically aimed at mollifying Muslim League separatism. The Declaration also stated there should be a treaty negotiated between Britain and the Indian constitution-making body respecting the protection of religious and racial minorities. This Treaty, however, would in no way restrict the power of the Indian Union "to decide in the future its relationship to the other Member States of the British Commonwealth."[26]

The British proposal ruled out any major alteration in India's constitutional position during the war, specifically stating that during the critical period of the conflict the British government must "inevitably bear the responsibility for and retain control and direction of the defence of India."[27] While Britain must be the ultimate authority in India, every effort would be made to associate its people in the counsels of their country and in the war effort. The journalists at Cripps' press conference were given the opportunity to quiz Sir Stafford on every phase of the War Cabinet's proposals. In his answers it was made unequivocally plain that, following the establishment of the new Indian Union, India could secede from the Commonwealth; that no British troops would be left in the country except upon request; that all British authority would be removed immediately upon the framing of the constitution; and that there would be no insistence upon special safeguards for British investments or trade in India.

Outside of India, particularly in Great Britain and the United States, the Draft Declaration was welcomed as a "fair and practicable compromise."[28] Inside India, however, Sir Stafford found the waters of Indian politics more stormy than he had anticipated. From March 29 to April 9 numerous conversations were held by Cripps with representatives of the Muslim League, Congress, the Sikhs, the Depressed Classes, Anglo-Indians, and the Indian States. By the latter date it seemed as if agreement could be reached, but on the following day, April 10, the Congress leaders rejected the Draft Declaration and demanded that a free national government should be set up with full

power immediately. This would have amounted to a fundamental alteration of the Indian constitution before the end of the war, an event that had been specifically denied by the Draft Declaration. In order to meet the demand of Congress at least halfway, however, Sir Stafford Cripps did offer to establish a new executive council in which all members should be Indians, except the Viceroy and the commander-in-chief. Further, this council should proceed to appoint a member to the British War Cabinet and to the Pacific War Council. Under this new arrangement practically all the day-to-day details and administration of government would have been in Indian hands. Only in the actual military phases of the war would the British commander-in-chief have had complete authority, and in theory the Viceroy, if an emergency should arise, could have overridden the decisions of the council.

On April 11 the Congress by formal resolution turned down the Cripps proposals because they failed to give India full independence immediately, because they contained "the novel principle of . . . non-accession for a Province [which] is a severe blow to the conception of Indian unity,"[29] and because defense was not sufficiently turned over to Indian control.

Once Congress had turned down the proposals, other political groups followed suit. The League argued that the terms of non-accession were too indefinite and went on to say:

So far as the Muslim League is concerned, it has finally decided that the only solution of India's constitutional problem is the partition of India into independent zones: and it will therefore be unfair to the Muslims to compel them to enter such a constitution-making body whose main object is the creation of a new Indian Union.[30]

On the other hand, the Mahasabha party, representing Hindu fundamentalism, argued that its basic principle was that India was one and indivisible. Dr. Ambedkhar in a letter to Cripps expressed the reaction of the Untouchables: "We are all of us absolutely convinced that the proposals are calculated to do the greatest harm to the Depressed Classes and are sure to place them under an unmitigated system of Hindu rule."[31] As to the Sikhs of the Punjab, these redoubtable warriors saw the possibility of their homeland, in which the Muslims were in a majority, being cut

26- Ibid., *p. 5.*

27- Ibid.

28- Margaret LaFoy, *"India's Role in the World Conflict,"* Foreign Policy Reports, *XVIII (May 1, 1942), p. 42.*

29- *"The Cripps Mission to India,"* International Conciliation, *Vol. 381 (New York: Carnegie Endowment for International Peace, June 1942), p. 340.*

30- *Quoted in ibid., p. 342.*

31- Ibid., *p. 347.*

154

off from the Indian Union. In their memorandum to Sir Stafford Cripps, therefore, the Sikhs declared: "We shall resist by all possible means separation of the Punjab from the All-India Union. We shall never permit our Motherland to be at the mercy of those who disown it [i.e. the Muslim majority]."[32] The sole exception to this wholesale repudiation of the Draft Declaration was the Liberal party, which gave it a qualified approval.

On April 11 Sir Stafford Cripps made a farewell broadcast to the people of India and expressed, without any rancor, his extreme disappointment that no agreement had been reached between the British government on the one hand and the various Indian parties on the other. He explained that the real and decisive cause of the breakdown had been the Congress demand for a new national government untrammeled by any control by the Viceroy or the British government. Sir Stafford pointed out that "it is easy to understand that great minorities in India would never accept such a suggestion."[33]

Having turned down the proposals brought to India by Cripps, Congress gave up all thought of actively engaging in the war effort and again turned to Gandhi and his policy of non-violence and civil disobedience. Following the departure of Sir Stafford, Gandhi gradually came to the view that Japan was going to win and would invade India; that British and American troops were an ineffectual shield; that as such they were only a bait inviting Japanese aggression; and that the Allied forces should get out of India. Then, reasoned Gandhi, an independent India, unimpaired by any connection with the Allies, could come to terms with Japan. If Japan should invade India after the departure of the Allied forces, then Gandhi proposed that non-violence be used as a defense. All would be well after the exit of the alien imperialists, the British. Gandhi said, "Leave India in God's hands, or in modern parlance, to anarchy. Then all parties will fight one another like dogs or will, when real responsibility faces them, come to a reasonable agreement."[34]

Gandhi was now in complete control of Congress, which on July 14, 1942, passed a resolution demanding that British rule in India cease immediately. If this were not done, a campaign of mass non-violent civil disobedience under the leadership of Gandhi would be initiated. There was widespread opposition to this resolution.

On August 8 the All-India Congress Committee endorsed the "Quit India Resolution" that had been passed by the Working Committee on July 14. This latest statement was carefully worded and indicated some retreat from Gandhi's pacifism, because it came out strongly for armed resistance, in co-operation with Allied powers, against Japanese invasion. This aid, however, was made contingent on the immediate grant of independence.

Sir Stafford Cripps in London declared that a complete change in government at this time was impossible. Other British critics pointed out that there was no guarantee that the Congress would be able to secure the co-operation of other Indian parties in establishing a stable government. Indeed, all the evidence seemed to point to the fact that the most serious differences would develop between the Congress and the League.

Before the Congress could carry out its campaign of mass civil disobedience, the government of India acted and all Congress leaders—including Nehru, Gandhi, and Azad—were arrested on August 9. Immediately serious and widespread disorders broke out, first in Bombay, then in the United Provinces, Bihar, and Madras. Telegraph wires were cut, installations on flying fields destroyed, railway lines torn up, and post offices and railway stations burned. By September the "Congress Rebellion," as it was dubbed by British writers, was practically over, its strength spent; but not before 750 persons had been killed and 1200 injured.

The breakdown of the Cripps proposals and the consequent Quit India movement of the Congress with the imprisonment of its leaders seriously threatened the war effort in India. The British were gravely concerned, as was the United States, which regarded India as one of the important links in the chain of victory for the United Nations. It was natural, therefore, that the United States should fashion new ties with India in 1942 and interest itself in trying, as a friendly third party, to help the British and Indians resolve their differences.

Martial India

Notwithstanding the serious disagreements between the various parties, India did make a noteworthy contribution to the United Nations. In particular, the part it played in the defeat of the Japanese armies in Burma was certainly a significant one.

32- Ibid., p. 352.

33- Ibid., p. 334.

34- Coupland, India: A Restatement, p. 220.

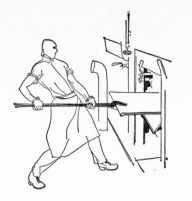

As we have already seen, mobilization for all-out war proceeded slowly in India. For the first eight months the pace was leisurely, but after the fall of France and the Italian Fascist threat in North Africa there was an acceleration of military activity in India. The Indian army was rapidly expanded without the use of the draft. The average number of men recruited was 50,000 monthly, and the peak was reached in July 1942, when 75,000 volunteered. Altogether more than two million men were taken into the Indian army.

All branches of the Indian army were expanded. Before 1939 there were less than two hundred commissioned Indian officers; by the end of the war there were more than ten thousand, including one hundred with the rank of colonel, two brigadiers, and one major general. The Air Force was expanded and a training scheme was instituted at five universities. The personnel of the Royal Indian Navy increased from twelve hundred officers and men to a figure of more than thirty thousand. The Indian navy specialized in escort vessels, minesweepers, and submarine chasers. Ten thousand young women were recruited for a Women's Auxiliary Corps.

Of outstanding importance was the tremendous mass of raw materials and industrial supplies that came from Indian mines, factories, and plantations for the war uses of the United Nations. During the North Africa campaign India was the main supplier of bulk stores. In the year 1944 alone she supplied the armed forces of the United States with seventy-eight million yards of cotton cloth, and she was the third largest consigner of war supplies to Australia.

The Indian government built new ordnance factories, which employed 100,000 men in contrast to the prewar figure of 15,000. These and other factories that were converted to war use increased from ten to fifty times the production of such items as rifles, bayonets, guns and gun carriages, grenades, mines, and bombs. Of the forty thousand articles that are needed for the equipment of a modern army, India managed to produce three-fourths. Auto-assembly plants were set up to manufacture chassis, which then were sent to factories to be armor-plated. The manufacture of such chemicals as soda ash, chlorine, and caustic soda was increased; steel production was stepped up in 1943 by 50 per cent; and the shipbuilding and ship repair industries were so expanded that three hundred vessels were launched in a single year. In addition to munitions, India exported a large and immensely important volume of such raw materials as oil-seeds, timber, mica, manganese, tea and coffee, and jute.

One of the most decisive long-range results of this vast war effort was the transformation of India from a debtor to a creditor nation, with Britain's extensive investments in this country practically canceled out. Early in the war an agreement was worked out between the British and the Indian governments whereby the former accepted responsibility for financing a large measure of the Indian war effort. The agreement stipulated:

That India would pay for the raising, training and equipping from Indian resources of all land forces raised in India, and for their maintenance as long as they stayed in the country and were available for the local defence of India. When they left for overseas, the cost to India of raising and training them, and also of equipping them, would be recovered from H.M.'s Government who would assume all further liability for them. All imported equipment and stores for such expansion measures of the land forces . . . would be provided free by H.M.'s Government.[35]

In 1938 the sterling debt of the government of India was equivalent to about $1,500,000,000. During the war, from 1942 to 1945, the Indian defense expenditure was $6756 million, and of this sum Britain accepted responsibility for $3624 million. Thus it was that India was able to pay off the government's debt to Britain. In speaking of this accomplishment the Indian finance minister declared: "India has completed the transition from a debtor to a creditor country, and extinguished within the space of about three years accumulations over decades of its public indebtedness to the United Kingdom."[36] By the end of the war the Indian government not only had managed to pay off its public indebtedness to Britain but had built up in London an enormous amount of sterling credits, to the extent of five billion dollars. These were "blocked" by the British treasury, to be gradually released at the conclusion of the war in stipulated annual amounts to the credit of the Indian government.

On the battle fronts, the spring of 1942 immediately after the failure of the Cripps Mission was the time of greatest peril to India. The ineffectual armies of Italy in North Africa had been re-

35- *Geoffrey Tyson*, India Arms for Victory *(Allahabad, India: Kitabistan Company, 1943), p. 265.*

36- Ibid., *p. 267.*

placed by those of the German General Rommel, the "Desert Fox." In June the *Afrika Korps* won a decisive battle against British forces defending Egypt and the German forces plunged ahead, only to be halted by a desperate stand of the British at El Alamein. Here the British army stood firm and in October 1942 launched an attack that drove the German army out of North Africa. In this campaign Indian troops figured prominently and later they participated in the bitter fighting in Italy.

A new menace against the British Empire, and India in particular, materialized when Japanese armies, after overrunning Burma, blocked land communications via the Burma Road to China and menaced the borders of India. The battle for Burma was one of the hardest fought of the entire war. In November 1942 Indian forces carried out their first offensive against the Japanese in Burma but were repulsed with heavy losses.

At the Quebec Conference, in August 1943, a new phase of the Burma campaign was planned when Prime Minister Churchill and President Roosevelt appointed Admiral Lord Louis Mountbatten as supreme commander of the Southeast Asia theater. Air power, supplies, and troops were built up in India, and, after the repulse of a last desperate Japanese attack in the direction of Bengal and Assam, the British Fourteenth Army began its victory drive in the fall of 1944. This force was made up of one million men, more than 60 per cent of whom came from India. In March 1945 Mandalay, the capital, was lost by the Japanese, and the Burmese campaign was practically over except for mopping-up operations.

In retrospect, Burma had been reconquered by an international army in which the great preponderance of manpower came from India. In a sense, this war theater was always a sideshow, having to give precedence to other Allied requirements in western Europe and the Pacific. Yet Burma was vitally important, for it controlled in large part the fate of both China and India.

In their invasion of India the Japanese had been joined by a small force known as the Indian National Army. Its story largely concerns the activities of Subhas Chandra Bose, a left-wing leader of the National Congress who has already been mentioned in the previous chapter. On the eve of the Second World War Bose had been arrested and imprisoned by the Indian government, but in December 1940 he had been released for reasons

37. *Hemendranath Das Gupta,* Subhas Chandra *(Calcutta: Jyoti Prokasalaya Co., 1946), p. 222.*

of health. The following January he secretly fled from India and in March was in Moscow. The end of March saw Bose in Berlin, where he had conferences with both von Ribbentrop and Hitler.

Bose followed carefully the capture of Malaya by the Japanese and was aware that in March 1942 an Indian good-will mission, made up of representatives from various parts of Southeast Asia, had been received in Tokyo to start an Indian independence movement with the assistance of the Japanese. The following June a conference was held at Bangkok, where one hundred Indian delegates gathered from Japan, Manchukuo, Hongkong, Java, Malaya, and the Indian army which had been captured at Singapore. As a result of this conclave an Independence League was established with headquarters at Singapore. Relations with the Japanese authorities, however, did not run smoothly, and in July 1943 Bose arrived in Singapore as the new leader.

Training camps for an Indian National Army were immediately opened up and a Provisional Government of Free India was established. In Subhas Bose's first proclamation of the Provisional Government of Azad Hind it was declared:

It will be the task of the Provisional Government to launch and to conduct the struggle that will bring about the expulsion of the British and their allies from the soil of India. . . . We hereby pledge our lives and the lives of our comrades-in-arms to the cause of her freedom, of her welfare and her exaltation among the nations of the world.[37]

This statement was issued on October 21, 1943, and two days later the Provisional Government declared war on the United States and Britain.

When the Japanese attack on Imphal and Kohima was opened, the Indian National Army took part in the offensive. Following the collapse of this attack the "I.N.A." practically disappeared, and many of its officers deserted to the British-Indian Fourteenth Army. In April Bose fled from Rangoon to Singapore and in August moved to Saigon, where he took a plane for Japan. Before the aircraft reached its destination, it crashed, and Bose was killed.

While undoubtedly a sincere patriot, Bose must have caused men such as Nehru acute embarrassment by his pro-Axis sympathies. There were in Bose elements of instability and incipient fascism which had disturbed leaders in Congress even before the outbreak of war. Nehru wrote of Bose in his autobiography:

He did not approve of any step being taken by the Congress which was anti-Japanese or anti-German or anti-Italian. . . . There was a big difference in outlook between him and others in the Congress executive, both in regard to foreign and internal matters, and this led to a break early in 1939. He then attacked Congress policy publicly, and early in August 1939 the Congress Executive took the very unusual step of taking disciplinary action against him, who was an ex-president.[38]

The death of Bose did not conclude his striking story, which was renewed with dramatic consequences after the end of the war when certain of his officers in the I.N.A. were placed on trial for treason in Delhi's Red Fort.

38- Jawaharlal Nehru, The Discovery of India *(New York: John Day Co., 1946), p. 428.*

The Home Front: 1942-1945

While Indian armies had been helping to reclaim both Italy and Burma from the invader, India itself from the latter part of 1942 to the end of the war in 1945 was being internally buffeted and changed by the impact of total war. Thousands of foreign soldiers, many of them American, were quartered in the land, and they brought strange and exciting ways from the outside world. War brought a tremendous upsurge of business activity, as new factories for the war effort were built and others were set up to supply the goods for domestic consumption originally imported from Britain and other countries. The Indian manufacturing and trading classes made enormous profits from war contracts. On the other hand, the life of the masses was seriously disturbed by the economic dislocations of war. There was a serious shortage of goods, prices in some cases increased 300 per cent, and food supplies especially were insufficient. As a result the middle class and white-collar groups suffered a lowering in standards of living and the real wages of the factory laborers decreased.

39- Great Britain, Parliamentary Debates, *5th Series, House of Commons, Vol. 302, p. 1106.*

A tragic reflection of this economic disequilibrium occurred in Bengal, a province with a population of sixty million. Before 1942 great supplies of rice had come to this area from Burma, but the Japanese invasion cut off this source of supply. There was also a poor rice crop in Bengal in 1942-1943, and a food shortage was general in most of the cities of India in 1942. In spite of growing signs of danger, there had been vigorous opposition to government controls and rationing. The central government at Delhi showed little leadership and initiative, and the provincial governments were equally inert and unwilling to co-operate. When the government aroused itself from its lethargy and began to try to move grains and rice, transport problems arose, and the food did not arrive at the stricken areas in time.

The sequel was famine, stark and horrible. In April 1943 an army of refugees poured into Calcutta, the capital of Bengal. Thousands died from starvation in the streets of the great city, and the total number of victims in the province was one and a half million. The Woodhead Famine Inquiry Commission was appointed to investigate the disaster and its report castigated both the government of India and that of Bengal for negligence. It also criticized the selfishness and greed of the merchants who made enormous profits, which according to the Report worked out at one thousand rupees for every death caused by famine. Indian nationalists tended to heap the blame for the disaster upon the British government in India. The basic cause for the famine, however, was not governmental inefficiency, the rapacity of the merchants, or even the loss of the Burma rice crop, but rather the lack of a margin of economic safety in India. In the two decades between 1920 and 1940 the population had grown 27 per cent, but the increase in the acreage of food crops was only 1 per cent, and there had been little improvement in the efficiency of agricultural production. This problem of the bare subsistence of the masses was to be a heritage of independent India, perhaps its greatest challenge.

British policy from 1942 to the war's end was to reiterate that the Cripps Proposals still stood, but it was made clear that the Congress leaders responsible for the Quit India Resolution of 1942 would not be released from prison until they changed their demands. Amery, the British Secretary of State for India, in 1944 stated in the House of Commons that the Cripps offerings remained open "in all their generous amplitude," and "we shall stand by them in the hour of victory as we did in days of adversity."[39]

At the same time Indian leaders of moderate propensities worked to find a way out of the political impasse. They asked the British government to release its Congress prisoners. Rajago-palacharia, himself a Congressman, made many speeches urging a reorientation in his party's policy. In his pamphlet *The Way Out,* he urged that the Cripps Proposals be revived, declaring they were "a bonafide gesture by the British Government to the people of India and not a measure of mere expediency or appeasement."[40] Nothing, however, came of these well-intended efforts and the Congress leaders remained adamant, and also out of circulation, in prison.

The sterilization of Congress gave Jinnah and his Muslim League a heaven-sent opportunity to make up for lost time and to rectify the balance between his organization and Congress. Jinnah would have nothing to do with the Quit India campaign, regarding it as a kind of blackmail directed against the hard-pressed British to force them to agree to a Hindu raj. During the period from 1943 to the conclusion of hostilities, Jinnah worked like a man possessed, motivated by one objective: the achievement of Pakistan. His statements to the press and his speeches were many, and they continued to win converts among the Muslims and to make the League the unquestioned spokesman for the Muslim community in India. Speaking before a group of students in 1941, Jinnah declared:

It is as clear as daylight that we are not a minority. We are a nation. And a nation must have territory. What is the use of merely saying that we are a nation? A nation does not live in the air. It lives on the land, it must govern land, and it must have a territorial state and that is what you want to get.[41]

The Muslim League, under Jinnah's direction, now imitated the tactics of the National Congress. It refused to recognize the right of any other organization to represent Muslims. Jinnah and the League high command formulated basic policies and then demanded that they be implicitly obeyed by all the provincial governments controlled by the League. The League assumed a position of domination in the governments of Bengal, Sind, Assam, and the North-West Frontier Province; and the government of the Punjab, while a coalition, had a majority of members who belonged to the Muslim League.

The able statesman Rajagopalacharia apparently was one of the few members of the Congress who fully appreciated the strength and dynamism of

Muslim nationalism and the growing appeal of the Pakistan idea. Following the release from prison of Mahatma Gandhi in May 1944, Rajagopalacharia was instrumental in paving the way for a meeting between Jinnah and Gandhi in September 1944 at the home of the former in Bombay. After discussions lasting three weeks these leaders announced the failure of their conversations. A clue to the basic obstacles to agreement was given in the twenty-one letters which passed between the negotiators and were later published. Perusal of this correspondence shows that Gandhi would not admit the validity of Jinnah's "two-nation theory." Gandhi wrote: "I can find no parallel in history for a body of converts and their descendants claiming to be a nation apart from the parent stock. If India was one nation before the advent of Islam, it must remain one in spite of a change of faith of a very large body of her children."[42]

Notwithstanding Gandhi's denial of the two-nation theory, he did, nevertheless, admit that India was "one family consisting of many members," and that plebiscites should be carried out to determine what separate states should be formed. Gandhi maintained, however, that the unity of India should be preserved by some form of central government which would take care of defense and other matters of common interest. Gandhi insisted that before anything was done the British must leave India. "I do hold that unless we oust the third party we shall not be able to live at peace with one another."[43] Further, the Congress leader maintained that the separate states would be formed *after India is free of foreign domination.*

For his part, Jinnah made it crystal clear that there could be no matters of joint concern, such as defense, between two sovereign states. The most fundamental difference between the two men, however, was Gandhi's argument that independence must come before partition or separation. Jinnah referred to the famous Quit India Resolution of Congress of 1942, which demanded that Britain turn over its power immediately, declaring that apparently Gandhi still followed this same policy. The Muslim leader also charged that Congress planned a constituent assembly, after independence had been secured, in which its majority would be able to establish any form of government it wished. Notwithstanding the failure of the Jinnah-Gandhi conversations, they served the useful pur-

40- Coupland, India: A Restatement, p. 231.

41- Jamil-ud-Din Ahmad, ed., Some Recent Speeches . . . of Mr. Jinnah (Lahore: Sh. Muhammad Ashraf, 1943), I, p. 213.

42- Sir Frederick H. Puckle, "The Gandhi-Jinnah Conversations," Foreign Affairs, XXIII (January 1945), p. 320.

43- Ibid., p. 323.

Jinnah

pose of indicating the wide gulf of suspicion existing between the League and Congress and in particular indicated what specific issues would have to be resolved before these bodies would be willing to march side by side in a united and independent India. For the first time Jinnah defined the exact geographical boundaries of his proposed Pakistan, for, in the name of the League, he laid claim to five provinces—Bengal, Assam, Punjab, Sind, and the North-West Frontier Province—and also to the administrative district of Baluchistan.

Back in Great Britain, the final months of the Second World War found the Labour party extremely critical of the Coalition Government's India policy and its inability to end the political stalemate in this great dependency. In December 1944, the Labour party conference had passed a resolution urging the resumption of negotiations with the Congress leaders, with the object of securing as quickly as possible a place for India as a self-governing member of the British Commonwealth. Lord Wavell, the Viceroy, spent March of 1945 in London discussing with Churchill and his cabinet how best the deadlock could be ended in India.

After his return to India, on June 14, 1945, Lord Wavell broadcast a new British offer to the Indian people. In this message it was affirmed that, whatever new constitution should be drawn up, it was to be the work of the Indian people themselves. Furthermore, the offer made in 1942 by Sir Stafford Cripps still remained open. As an immediate step, the Viceroy announced that he was prepared at once to make important changes in his Executive Council, whereby all the members except the commander-in-chief were to be Indian. These new members would be selected from among the Indian leaders "in proportions which would give a balanced representation of the main communities, including equal proportions of Moslems and Caste Hindus."[44]

This British offer of June 1945 was designed to demonstrate the good will of the government in London in conceding a generous measure of representative government within the framework of the existing Indian constitution. However, the Viceroy in the legal sense still retained ultimate control if he chose to wield it. In return for this gesture, the British government appealed to Indians to extend their full support in the war against Japan, while in the House of Commons the Indian

Secretary, Amery, announced that imprisoned Congress leaders were to be released.

In order to create the new Executive Council, Lord Wavell invited twenty-two representatives of the various Indian groups to a conference at Simla. At this meeting Wavell appealed for confidence in his good offices, telling the assembled representatives: "You must accept my leadership for the present. Until there is some agreed change in the constitution, I am responsible to His Majesty's Government for the good government and welfare of India. I ask you to believe in me as a sincere friend of India."[45] The Viceroy asked the main Indian parties each to present its list of nominees from which he could select members for the reconstituted Executive Council. All parties except the Muslim League complied. Jinnah, however, rejected this procedure because he demanded that all Muslims appointed to the Council should be members of his League, while Congress insisted on nominating two of its Muslim members and placing them on its list. Jinnah maintained further that Muslim-Hindu parity was not enough, his view being that other minority nominees on occasion would vote with the caste Hindus and thus place the League nominees in the minority. Finally, Jinnah contended that the principle of Pakistan should be recognized, for if the League accepted the Wavell Plan "the Pakistan issue will be shelved and put in cold storage indefinitely."[46] The Simla Conference dragged on until the middle of July, when Wavell reluctantly announced its breakdown. It was now manifest that the basic issue holding up constitutional advances in India was not the question of how much power was to be transferred to Indian hands but, rather, what Indian hands were to get this power.

In the meantime, a national election had been held in Great Britain in July 1945, and Winston Churchill, the Conservative leader, had been displaced as Prime Minister by Clement Attlee. The coming to power of the Labour party with a decisive majority was a good augury for the cause of Indian independence. The party of Harold Laski, Stafford Cripps, and Ramsay MacDonald had long been the traditional champion of Indian freedom. In 1929, for example, the election pledge of the Labourites had stood for "the recognition of the right of the Indian people to self-government and self-determination, and the admission of India to the British Commonwealth of Nations

44- Statement of the Policy of His Majesty's Government, *Cmd. 6652, June 14, 1945* (London: His Majesty's Stationery Office, 1945), p. 3.

45- *The Times (London), June 26, 1945.*

46- *Quoted in Parkin, op. cit., p. 310.*

on an equal footing with the self-governing Dominions."[47] During the election campaign of July 1945 the Labour party came out specifically for the grant of self-government to India in friendly association with Great Britain. When the new parliament opened in August, the King's speech outlining the program of the Labour government specifically promised the "early realization of full self-government in India."

Prime Minister Attlee's government announced on August 21 that the Viceroy was coming to London for fresh discussions. Following Lord Wavell's return to India, after his conversations in London, the Viceroy announced that the British government was now resolved to push forward with plans for the attainment of Indian self-government; that, as soon as possible, a constitution-making body would be convened; and that, as a preliminary step, elections would shortly be held for the central and provincial legislatures. The Viceroy also stated his intention of conferring after the elections with the newly elected representatives, to determine whether the proposals brought by Cripps in 1942 to India were still acceptable or whether some other procedure was desired and could be agreed upon. Wavell further stated his intention of making another attempt to reconstitute his Executive Council. Underlining the British government's desire to know the true situation in India was the announcement made in London on December 4, 1945, that a parliamentary delegation —made up of representatives of the three British parties—was to leave for India at once in order to study the situation at first hand and report back to Parliament.

The Labour government had now made it quite clear that Indian independence was no longer an issue between Britain and the Indian people. For too long, however, Indian nationalism had felt itself frustrated and the advance toward self-government in the past too slow and halting. Consequently, Congress and its leaders found it difficult to realize that victory had been won against Britain on one battlefield and that it was now imperative to transfer attention to problems in another field of controversy that had to be resolved before India could expect to enjoy the full fruits of independence. This problem was the conflict between the Muslim League and the National Congress, and more specifically the demand of the former for partition and Pakistan.

Instead of devoting complete attention to the Pakistan issue, the National Congress proceeded to expend its energy in waging a battle that had already been won and continued to ignore, or at least to underestimate, serious divisive rivalries among the Indian people themselves that threatened the peace and the unity of their native land. In the elections for the Central Legislative Assembly, carried out in December, and in those for the provincial legislatures held early in the spring of 1946, Great Britain was singled out as the enemy. In the Congress election manifestoes reference was made to the Gandhian Quit India Resolution of 1942 and it was declared: "By its demand and challenge the Congress stands today. It is on the basis of this resolution and with its battle-cry that the Congress faces the election."[48]

Such a rallying cry found a response. The end of the Second World War saw nationalism rampant and impatient in India. The conflict had brought in its wake inflated prices, shortages of goods, and even famine. The masses at war's end were restless and disillusioned. To this ferment were added the new ways and attitudes that had been picked up by thousands of men as a result of their service in the Indian army. For the first time many Indians traveled to distant lands. Masses of men were trained to handle mechanized machinery, and officers were educated to be alert and self-reliant. The result of all this was that men in the Indian army "recognized and felt the new trends sweeping across India."[49] Nationalistic susceptibilities were also shocked by the trial of the officers of Bose's Indian National Army in the closing weeks of 1945 in the Red Fort at Delhi. Feeling in India rose to a danger pitch, and Subhas Chandra Bose became canonized as a great national hero. The important thing in the minds of Indian nationalists was not that Bose had co-operated with the Japanese in trying to invade India but that his main purpose had been to drive British authority from India. For this his followers should not be punished. As 1945 ended, the country became more and more tense. Irate mobs periodically paraded in the streets of the large cities insulting all westerners and Britishers in particular. In Calcutta there were serious and widespread student demonstrations against the Indian National Army trials.

Early in 1946 strikes, outbreaks of violence, and demonstrations became more frequent and

47- Quoted in W. Y. Elliott, The New British Empire (New York: McGraw-Hill Book Co., 1932), p. 400.

48- Indian Annual Register, 1945, II, p. 110.

49- Phillips Talbot, "The Independence of India," Foreign Policy Reports, XXIII (June 15, 1947), p. 77.

menacing. In February serious disorders broke out in Calcutta over the Indian National Army trials. Many fires were started and rioting continued for five days. More serious was the mutiny of the sailors of the Indian navy at Bombay. Sailors clashed with the police and several hundred invaded the European business district, where they smashed windows and beat Europeans. A mob also milled around the United States Information Service office, where they tore down the American flag and burned it in the street. This last incident would seem to show there was a general anti-western sentiment prevailing, as well as a specific grudge against Great Britain. The naval strike spread to other port cities, such as Karachi, and in addition the police of several cities went on strike. India seemed on the verge of rebellion.

The League-Congress controversy was also building up to a dangerous pitch. The elections to the Central Legislative Assembly and those for the Provincial Legislatures had shown that there were now only two major parties in India. In the provinces, for example, the League had gained 425 of the available 441 Muslim seats, and in the Central Assembly the League had won all the Muslim seats. There could be no doubt that Jinnah's organization was the mouthpiece for India's Muslim population. It was at the new session of the Legislative Assembly that Jinnah delivered an intransigent fighting speech threatening civil war, declaring that partition was the only issue and that both Britain and Congress must concede Pakistan before anything else. Jinnah warned, "Only over the dead bodies of Muslims will the Congress party flag fly in the Northern Provinces."[50]

Up to the end of 1945, during the first half year of its power, the British Labour government had taken the view that the transfer of power in India could be an orderly and deliberate operation. In its long history of criticizing imperialism, the Labour party had taken the position that the Indian problem was a fairly simple one. All that was needed was the straightforward offer of independence. The events of January and February, 1946, however, shocked the Labour government into the realization that the march of events in India was getting out of hand. There was need of a dramatic and resolute move and one was made when Clement Attlee announced in the House of Commons on February 19 that a Cabinet Mission would shortly leave for India to assist the Indian leaders in drawing up a method of framing a new constitution. At the same time, as an interim measure Indians would be given *de facto* responsibility for their own rule by the creation of a new Executive Council representing the main Indian parties. Three weeks later Attlee, on the eve of the departure of the Cabinet Mission, made it clear in the House of Commons that his government wanted India to be completely free and that it fully appreciated the strength of nationalistic aspirations among its people. Attlee declared: "India herself must choose what will be her future constitution; what will be her position in the world. I hope that the Indian people may elect to remain within the British Commonwealth. . . . But if [they] so elect, it must be by [their] own free will."[51]

This unequivocal statement and the arrival of the Cabinet Mission in India on March 24 halted the trend toward rebellion and induced the main political parties to use constitutional methods as they worked with Lord Pethick-Lawrence, the Secretary of State for India; Sir Stafford Cripps, then President of the Board of Trade; and A. V. Alexander, the First Lord of the Admiralty, the British cabinet members who composed the personnel of the Cabinet Mission.

It was appropriate and logical that a Labour government had taken the decision to give India unfettered freedom. It is doubtful, however, whether any other British government would have made a different decision. The determination of Mr. Attlee's government to give India her freedom is to be explained not only by the traditional belief of his party that this great dependency should be freed but also by the inexorable realities of 1946. The plain truth was that Britain could no longer rule India against the wishes of its people, that Britons indeed had little desire to do so, and that there was hardly any economic justification for their doing so. From an administrative point of view, the government of India had already passed into the hands of the Indian people. Recruitment of British personnel for the all-important Indian Civil Service had been stopped during the war, and by 1946 there were only 520 British officers in the I.C.S. out of a total strength of 1060. At the same time there were some 150 British members of the I.C.S. who were eligible for retirement. Practically the entire personnel of

50- *Quoted in Robert A. Smith,* Divided India *(New York: McGraw-Hill Book Co., 1947), p. 169.*

51- *Quoted in* The Cabinet Mission in India, *compiled by A. C. Banerjee and D. R. Bose (Calcutta: A. Mukherjee and Co., 1946), pp. 17-18.*

the much larger subordinate services, which during the war had assumed more and more administrative responsibilities, was Indian. These Indian civil servants, together with the host of petty local officials and the police, had become very sensitive to the aspirations of the nationalistic movement.

In the 1930's, and even in 1942, the Viceroy and the British Governors of the provinces could enforce a policy which the major political parties opposed. That such a course would be practically impossible now was admitted in January (1946) by the British governor of one Congress-controlled province, and it is reported that the Viceroy advised London to the same effect.[52]

An important factor in Britain's decision to quit India was her weariness of the burdens of an imperialist power, especially in India, where nationalism was so intransigent and at the same time so confused and divided. The average man in Britain was getting "fed up" with the Empire, and during the war British soldiers frequently showed little enthusiasm for fighting for the sake of India. The sacrifices of the Second World War had left Great Britain tired and impoverished and there was in England "an incredible weariness widely exhibited over the Indian problem."[53]

And from the view of pounds, shillings, and pence, Britain no longer had any reason to stay in India. During the course of the war, as we have already noted in this chapter, India was able to pay off her huge public debt owed to Great Britain. She was able not only to do this but to accumulate sterling credits in London to the sum of five billion dollars. All that was left in India of the once imposing British financial stake was the equivalent of a few hundred million dollars of private investment, which as early in the war as 1943 was estimated to be no more than what British capital had invested in Argentine railways.

Independence with Partition

The Cabinet Mission was engaged for three months, from the last week of March to the end of June 1946, in continuous conversations with various Indian leaders. An important press conference was held on March 25 in which Lord Pethick-Lawrence again made it clear that the object was to give India complete, unfettered freedom—inside or outside the British Commonwealth—and

that the aim of the Mission was to help Indians to establish a constitutional structure including the provinces of British India and the Native States. During April the Cabinet Mission conferred with the Viceroy and leading British officials and then with the Indian leaders. On May 5 the so-called Tripartite Conference was opened at Simla where representatives of the Congress and the League conferred with the three British ministers on how best British authority could be wound up in India. The two main Indian parties were violently opposed. Congress, as can be seen from its published correspondence with the Cabinet Mission, insisted upon a strong central government. It also asked for the immediate relinquishment of all authority by Great Britain and its transference to a sovereign interim Indian government. Congress further maintained that the constituent assembly, when it met to frame India's new government, must have perfect freedom to draft the constitution and should not be bound by any previous arrangements.[54]

Jinnah and the League insisted upon a federal system in which the central government would have minimum powers as compared with those exercised by the federated units. There would have to be prior agreement as to the basic features of the new constitution and presumably Britain would stay in India as the ultimate authority until an acceptable constitution was drafted. Jinnah had tersely expressed the League's position to Britain in the slogan "You divide and then quit," whereas the Congress said in effect to Britain, "You quit and then we will divide." There could be no reconciliation, no accommodation, between these two views, and on May 12 the announcement was made of the failure of the Tripartite Conference.

Confronted with the inability of the two main Indian political parties to agree on any plan, the Cabinet Mission drafted a scheme of its own which was announced on May 16. The Cabinet statement, while agreeing there was a genuine anxiety among the Muslims "lest they should find themselves subjected to a perpetual Hindu-majority rule," came out strongly against Jinnah's claim for partition based upon a Pakistan of six provinces. Statistics were cited to show that the non-Muslim population would be 48.31 per cent of the total population in the north-east area and 37.93 per cent in the north-west area of the proposed Pakistan. In the remainder of British India left

52- *Talbot,* op. cit., p. 76.

53- Ibid., *p. 75.*

54- *See the letters of Maulana Azad in* The Cabinet Mission in India.

outside Pakistan there would be a Muslim minority of 20 million amid a total population of 188 million. So important are these statistics that the break-down on Pakistan given by the Cabinet Mission statement should be kept in mind:

North-Western Area	Muslim	Non-Muslim
Punjab	16,217,242	12,201,577
North-West Frontier Province	2,788,797	249,270
Sind	3,208,325	1,326,683
British Baluchistan	438,930	62,701
	22,653,294	13,840,231
North-Eastern Area		
Bengal	33,005,434	27,301,091
Assam	3,442,479	6,762,254
	36,447,913	34,063,345

Obviously the six-province area of Pakistan as envisaged by the League would not solve the religious minority problem, and this fact was strongly underlined by the Commission statement. In addition it was pointed out that the transportation, postal, and telegraph system had been planned and constructed by the British on the basis of a united India. Furthermore, the Indian armed forces had been built up and trained for the defense of the sub-continent as a whole. A final point made was that the two halves of Pakistan, one in the north-west and the other in the north-east, would be separated from each other by seven hundred miles. For these reasons the Cabinet Mission strongly recommended that India should not be divided into two sovereign states.

Having ruled out the practicability of Pakistan, the Cabinet Mission presented an ingenious scheme which retained the unity of India and at the same time made some substantial concessions in the direction of recognizing the League's desire for autonomy for the Muslim-majority provinces. The plan envisaged a "Union of India" made up of the provinces of British India together with the Native States. There was to be a central government endowed with authority in the fields of foreign affairs, defense, and communications. All other powers were to rest with the component parts of the Union—the provinces and the states. In the Union Legislature, as a safeguard for minorities, no communal matters were to be acted upon save by a majority vote of each major community, i.e., the Muslim and the Hindu.

Thus far the Cabinet plan called for a Union at the top tier, so to speak, of the governmental structure and a group of provinces and states at the bottom tier. Midway between the Union and the bottom tier were to be three groups of provinces: one predominantly Hindu India and the other two the Muslim majority provinces in the north-west and north-east of India. The latter Muslim groups would consist of the Punjab, North-West Frontier Province, and Sind on the one hand, and Bengal and Assam on the other. Each of these three groups was to draw up its own regional constitution.

It can be seen that the Cabinet Mission's plan for grouping was an attempt to satisfy in some degree the Muslim demand for Pakistan. Given the limited powers of the proposed Union government, the Muslims could feel reasonably secure in the enjoyment of a wide degree of autonomy in each of their group areas. While the Congress might protest that Assam with its non-Muslim majority should not be joined to Bengal, the Cabinet Mission could point out that there would be some twenty million Muslims in predominantly Hindu India. This figure was in contrast to 47,000,000 non-Muslims in the two "Pakistan areas." In short the scheme, while not achieving a clear cut grouping on the basis of religion, did constitute a nicely balanced plan aimed at securing Muslim-Hindu amity in India. The reasonable treatment of non-Muslims in the two Pakistan areas would call for a similar respect for the rights of the Muslim minority elsewhere in India.

A few additional details of the Cabinet Mission's proposals should be noted. A Constituent Assembly was proposed, to be made up of 292 members from the provinces of British India and 93 from the States. The Legislative Assembly of each province was to elect its representatives on the basis of one for each million of population. Following the convening of the Constituent Assembly at New Delhi the representatives of each of the three groups envisaged by the Cabinet Mission were to meet separately and then decide the nature of their group constitutions. After this action the group representatives were to reassemble in a single body for the drafting of the Union Constitution. The Cabinet Mission further recommended that any province after a period of ten years could call for a reconsideration of the terms of the constitution

Nehru

and that after the new constitutional arrangements had come into operation it should be possible for any province to elect to move out of any group in which it had been placed. Finally, the Constituent Assembly was asked to negotiate a treaty with Great Britain "to provide for certain matters arising out of the transfer of power." In closing its proposals the Cabinet Mission appealed to the Indian people for good will and mutual accommodation in this supreme moment in Indian history.

On May 25, the Cabinet Mission issued a clarifying statement on its proposals. It was intended that there should be immediately set up an interim government, and in this new Viceroy's Executive Council all members were to be Indian. Until the new Indian constitution was adopted the present constitution was to remain in force, and during this time British troops would remain in India, as Great Britain was responsible for the ultimate security of the country until the actual transference of authority had taken place.

The reception of the Cabinet Mission plan was none too encouraging. While it cleared the air by demonstrating that Great Britain was completely serious in her intention of quitting India, it seemed only to exacerbate the existing rivalry between League and Congress. For the next nine months there was a continuous jockeying for position, party maneuvering, and acrimonious debate, with the Congress-League deadlock getting more and more ominous. The Congress after some delay accepted the long-range plan of the Cabinet Mission with some reservations, but refused to accept the conditions laid down for the entrance of its representatives into an All-Indian Executive Council. The Muslim League, on the other hand, had finally accepted the conditions for participating in an interim government and in the Constituent Assembly. At the same time the election had taken place for this latter constitution-making body, and the contest had given the Congress 97 per cent of all the general seats, i.e., all but 7 out of 210 seats, and the League all but 5 of the 78 set aside for the Muslims. There could be no shadow of doubt as to the right of the League to speak for the Muslim community of India, and, equally, no doubt that the Congress represented the remainder of public opinion.

In spite of the confusing barrage of criticisms, proposals, and counter-proposals that had ema-

nated from the League and Congress headquarters following the announcement of the Cabinet Mission plan, the last week of June 1946 was a brief period of high hope for the success of the Cabinet plan and for the preservation of the unity of India. With both the League and Congress accepting the long range plan, i.e., the three-tier system of government and the Constituent Assembly that was to blueprint its form, the British Cabinet Mission felt its work was done, and accordingly left for England.

The rising confidence of the closing days of June, however, was soon succeeded by the grim despair and deadlock of mid-July, 1946. Jinnah and his League during this time made a clear turnabout and repudiated the Mission proposals, lock, stock, and barrel. It is difficult to assess blame for this grievous disappointment, but it would seem that a strong case can be made out for blaming the intemperate remarks of Congress leaders, especially Pandit Nehru. As the spokesmen for the overwhelming majority party in India these leaders, one would think, would have been particularly careful not to excite the already strong fears of the minority party of the League.

On July 6, 1946, Pandit Nehru was inducted as president of the National Congress, and as its spokesman he proceeded to make a number of statements defining the position of Congress in the plans for the taking over of authority in India. On July 7, before the All-India Congress Committee, Nehru stated:

There is a good deal of talk of the Cabinet Mission's long-term and short-term plan. So far as I can see, it is not a question of our accepting any plan long or short. It is only a question of our agreeing to go into the Constituent Assembly. We will remain in the Assembly so long as we think it is good to India. We are not bound by a single thing except that we have decided for the moment to go into the Constituent Assembly.[55]

Three days later Nehru had declared at a press conference that, as far as the constitution-making body was concerned, *"What we do there, we are entirely and absolutely free to determine. We have committed ourselves to no single matter to anybody."*[56] Another Congress leader, Maulana Azad, had also declared in a speech that when the Constituent Assembly met it would have the "unfettered right to make a constitution; it would be

55- The Cabinet Mission in India, *pp. 312-313.*

56- Ibid., *p. 315. The italics are mine.*

sovereign; and would legislate for a united, not a divided India."[57]

Such utterances completely doomed the Cabinet Mission proposals. The worst fears of Jinnah were realized. To his mind, once the League went into the Constituent Assembly the overwhelming majority of Congress would scrap the scheme formulated by the Cabinet Mission and then proceed to set up just the kind of government they desired, one in which there would be little guarantee of Muslim rights. The best expression of the Muslim League's position in regard to the Constituent Assembly and its "brute majority" of Congress was given in these words of Jinnah:

It is a majority of one nation that can overrule the unanimous decision of any other nation because they are 79 and the Congress are 292. In the perilous position that the Muslims will be, we don't want any outside interference in this sense that somebody should tinker with us, but there must be some provision within the scheme itself which will prevent a brute majority taking the bit in its mouth and running away. But to treat it as a sovereign Constituent Assembly taking decision after decision and then presenting the poor Muslim minority, the British Government, and the world with a *fait accompli*—there is the real danger.[58]

A few days after Nehru's statements, Jinnah reacted strongly, declaring that the Congress leader's interpretation of the Constituent Assembly was a complete repudiation of the long-term scheme of the Cabinet Mission. On July 27 the League Council met in Bombay. Amid tumultuous scenes it reversed its acceptance of the Cabinet Mission Plan and announced that the time had come to resort to direct action to achieve Pakistan. August 16 was announced as Direct Action Day, when a Muslim hartal, or general strike, was to be observed against both Congress and Britain, who were accused of trying to trick the League. Jinnah, amid cheers, defiantly declared "Today we bid good-bye to constitutional methods. Today we have also forged a pistol and are in a position to use it."[59]

The inflammatory result of such exhortations soon became tragically evident. On August 16 the Muslims observed their Direct Action Day. In Calcutta riots broke out and for four days frenzied mobs milled in the streets. This was the most bloody communal outbreak in modern Indian history. In what was called "the Great Calcutta Killing," there were 4700 deaths, 15,000 injured,

and 150,000 refugees fleeing the city. This Muslim-Hindu affray was just the beginning. Rioting spread to various other areas—to east Bengal, to Bihar, and early in 1947 to Punjab—with a total loss of life from August to February of 12,000.

Meanwhile, in September Lord Wavell had succeeded in getting Nehru to form an interim government. The Viceroy's Executive Council at last was all Indian, but Jinnah and the League refused to come in. Finally, at the end of October Wavell succeeded in getting Jinnah and four colleagues to enter the government. The members of the interim government, however, were just as much divided among themselves as before. The crux of the matter was that Jinnah refused to have anything to do with the Constituent Assembly scheduled to convene in December. In desperation Prime Minister Attlee called for Congress and the League each to send two representatives to London, and the Sikhs one, for a conference. The meeting was fruitless, however, and when the Constituent Assembly opened on December 9, no League representatives attended. As the troubled new year opened, the breach between the two main parties remained as wide as ever. It was not now a question of rebellion against the British raj; the country teetered on the brink of civil war.

It was at this critical point that Mr. Attlee grasped the nettle. On February 20, 1947, speaking in the House of Commons, the Prime Minister stated that "His Majesty's Government wish to make it clear that it is their definite intention to take necessary steps to effect the transference of power to responsible Indian hands not later than June 1948." Attlee urged Indians to sink their differences, for "administration had broken down to the point where Britain was no longer effective." Another item of considerable importance was contained in the dramatic announcement that Lord Wavell was recalled as Viceroy and Lord Louis Mountbatten was to take his place.

Lord Mountbatten was sworn in as the new Viceroy on March 24 and immediately plunged into the task of arriving at some agreed plan that would push aside the mounting danger of civil war. Conferences were held with the various leaders and at the end of May the Viceroy was back in London explaining why the Cabinet Mission plan would not meet the emergency and what an alternative might be. On June 2, back in India, Mountbatten met with various leaders and outlined

57- The Constituent Assembly of India, *compiled by A. C. Banerjee (Calcutta: A. Mukherjee and Co., 1947), p. 105.*

58- *Ibid., p. 264.*

59- The Cabinet Mission in India, *p. 363.*

Britain's final plan for the liquidation of her rule. The following day he made a broadcast to the country in which he expressed his great regret that no plan for preserving the political unity of India was acceptable and said there would be no coercion. The solution to the dilemma was the transfer of British power to two governments, each having Dominion status, the change-over to be made "within the next few months."

In the plan as outlined by Mountbatten the Muslim majority provinces not represented in the Constituent Assembly should have their Legislative Assemblies vote to determine whether their Constitution would be framed by the Constituent Assembly already in session or by another body. Jinnah, it will be recalled, had demanded all of the Punjab, Bengal, and Assam as part of Pakistan. The population statistics cited on page 163 show that such a claim would mean that a huge non-Muslim minority would have been created in Pakistan. In the case of Bengal and the Punjab, therefore, the Legislative Assemblies met in two sections—one Muslim and the other non-Muslim—to give the latter an opportunity, if they wished, to join the Constituent Assembly that had been in session since December 1946. As for Assam, provision was made in this Hindu-majority province for one district, predominantly Mohammedan, to join the Muslim area of eastern Bengal.

By this time the Congress leaders had come to realize that partition was inevitable, and they accepted the plan. The Muslim League by the proposals got much less than it had demanded. India was to be divided, but self-determination was also to be invoked in Bengal and the Punjab, which would now have to be dissected. There was, however, no choice, and reluctantly the League also tendered its acceptance.

It was no easy matter to unscramble the old governmental system that had presided over a united India and to set up two distinct and independent governmental structures in its place. A Boundary Commission under Sir Cyril John Radcliffe was created to define the frontiers of the provinces that were to be divided. There was also the matter of the division of the Indian army and the small navy. There had to be a division of the old regime's assets and liabilities, agreement on the public debt, and arrangements made in the realm of currency, exchange, and coinage. International agreements had to be duplicated, office equipment and records divided, and arrangements made for the division of office and administrative personnel. All of these details were turned over to ten expert committees made up of senior Indian officials, plus some British in the case of the army, and these bodies in turn presented their recommendations to a supreme Partition Council that was responsible for fundamental policy and decisions.

In all the matters pertaining to the complex arrangements necessary for partition, Lord Mountbatten took the lead as a disinterested and friendly third party. During July 1947 the Viceroy announced that his interim government would divide into two groups. These would meet separately, to work on their own particular problems, and from time to time jointly under the chairmanship of Mountbatten as they were forced to consider matters of joint concern. The process of partition had now begun.

The Mountbatten plan reiterated the policy on the Indian States expressed in the proposals of the Cabinet Mission of May 1946. The British government took the view at that time that the former overlordship, or paramountcy as it was called, exercised by the British Crown over the Native States would lapse once Britain ceded her authority and would not be transferred to any new government. In theory, at least, each native state had three choices: it could join with Pakistan, enter the Indian Union, or remain unattached from either and endeavor to go it alone. Once British power had been removed from India, however, it was inevitable that the states would have to join one or the other governments of Pakistan or the Indian Union. Practically, there was no other choice. They were not strong enough to stand on their own. The only question to be solved was on what conditions they would be united and how much autonomy they would be permitted to enjoy. The final outcome of this matter of the states will be discussed in the next chapter.

On July 4, 1947, the Indian Independence Bill was introduced into Parliament and quickly passed. Speakers all deplored the sundering of Indian unity but agreed that this was a matter for the people themselves to decide. Final discussion on the Bill took place in the Commons on July 15, at which time a number of eloquent valedictory speeches were made as members bade farewell to India and the responsibility Great Britain had exercised since Lord North's Regulating Act of 1773. On July 18 the Bill for the transfer of power to two Dominions on August 15 became law.

Independence became a reality at midnight, August 14, for both Pakistan and the Union of India. In New Delhi the Constituent Assembly, meeting in an exultant yet solemn mood, paid tribute to Gandhi, sent friendly greetings to the new sister state of Pakistan, and observed two minutes of silence for patriots who had died for freedom in India. Equally impressive ceremonies were being carried out in Karachi, capital of Pakistan. The following day, the 15th, Lord Mountbatten became Governor-General of the new dominion of the Union of India and swore in his cabinet with Pandit Nehru as Prime Minister. In Karachi, Mr. Jinnah assumed office as Governor-General and Liaquat Ali Khan then took the oath as Prime Minister. Independence for the two new domin-

ions was celebrated in many parts of the world. Impressive ceremonies were observed at the headquarters of the United Nations at Lake Success, New York, as the flag of the Indian Union was raised to join those of fifty-four other member nations. In the West Indies and in South Africa Independence Day was celebrated by Indian communities with parades and displays of the flags of the two new dominions. In Great Britain, the London *Daily Mail* signalized the new dispensation by changing its traditional masthead from "For King and Empire" to "For King and Commonwealth." And at the ceremony held in London for the hoisting of the flag of the new Dominion of India, A. V. Alexander, who had been a member of the Cabinet Mission, declared: "The Indian Empire dissolves—the British Commonwealth of free nations welcomes two free peoples into their association."

*Throughout India and Pakistan
patriots rejoiced in their
new-found independence, which had
seemingly been achieved so peacefully. A feeling of spiritual
exaltation suffused the people
as they listened to the hopes
and programs for national
greatness propounded by their
leaders. Unfortunately,
this mood of nationalistic
exuberance was soon shattered
by the impact of violence
and wholesale slaughter in
the Punjab and the dark prospect
of war between Pakistan and
India. Never in modern times
have two nations in the first
hours of freedom been confronted
by such serious problems. As
we will see, this initial
emergency was surmounted, and
India and Pakistan happily
were able, toward the end of
1947, to turn to the tasks of
constitution making, social
reform, and economic advancement.
By 1950, both Pakistan and
India were sobered and chastened
by the responsibilities of
statehood. The world was not
quite so simple, kindly, or
secure as it had appeared in
August 1947, and there was
the realization that Gandhian
Soul Force of itself would
not bring national security, nor
the mere exit of alien rule
guarantee the solution of
fundamental domestic problems.*

India and Pakistan

since independence

chapter 10

ENGLISH NEWSPAPERS in the summer and fall of 1947 were filled with reports describing the end of British rule in India and the details of "packing up." The world in general and India in particular had been amazed at the rapidity with which Britain had pushed the arrangements for complete independence. Lord Mountbatten was largely responsible for insisting that the British departure be carried out as soon as possible. Mountbatten, the last of the British Viceroys, has described how the Law Officers of the Crown in London, together with the Lord Chancellor, worked all night on the draft of the Indian Independence Bill to insure its passage in Parliament during the summer of 1947.[1]

This rapidity of abdication of British power may be criticized by later historians. It should be kept in mind that Attlee's original plan called for a transfer of power to Indian hands by June 1948. This date had been moved up to August 15, 1947, and, as the decision was announced on June 3, only seventy-two days were available for the division of the country. While intransigent and frustrated Indian nationalism may have been responsible to a large extent for the speed with which the independence plan was carried out, there are observers who believe Britain could have slowed down the process and thus have helped to avoid the confusion and later the bloodshed that was visited upon India in the fall of 1947. One Indian judge is said to have declared, "The British are a just people. They have left India in exactly the same state of chaos as they found it."[2]

Whether or not the British withdrawal was at the end too precipitous, all observers agreed that no imperial rule had ever before ended like this. Jinnah declared, "Such voluntary and absolute transfer of power and rule by one nation over others is unknown in the history of the world."[3] British officials stayed on to assist the new Dominions either as administrators or as officers in the armed forces. The first British troops to leave India after the transfer of power were sent a message by Prime Minister Nehru in which he said, "I know the good qualities of the British soldier and I should like our own army to develop those qualities. . . . It is rare in history that such a parting takes place not only peacefully but also with goodwill. We are fortunate that this should have happened in India. That is a good augury for the future."[4]

The British left behind them the two nascent states of Pakistan and India. During the previous decade numerous warnings and arguments had been advanced to prove that the former would be an economic impossibility and a political anachronism, with its two main areas separated from each other by a thousand miles. In spite of all these arguments, however, Pakistan had become a reality because in essence "the Indian Muslims felt themselves to be Muslims before they were Indians."[5] The new state had a population of seventy million, it was estimated by the census taken in 1941, but this figure had probably reached eighty million in 1948, thus making Pakistan the fifth nation in the world on the basis of population. Official Pakistan statistics give 360,000 square miles as the area, a figure apparently including the western part of Kashmir, then under Pakistan control. As will be seen shortly, the status of Kashmir became a bitter issue between Pakistan and India.

The New Pakistan

A political map of the Indian sub-continent after 1947 (see the last page of the first picture section) shows the Union of India occupying its great central bulk with Pakistan separated into two peripheral areas, one in the north-west and the other in the east. The larger, Western Pakistan, has an area of over 300,000 square miles with 34,000,000 inhabitants. It embraces the valley of the Indus River and its tributaries, stretching from the coastal plain fronting on the Indian Ocean and running back to the slopes of the great mountain wall of north India. This area is mainly dry country and, in the Sind province for example, the rainfall averages only eight inches a year. Western Pakistan, however, has extensive irrigation systems which have turned arid and desert land into some of the most productive agricultural areas in the world.

East Pakistan, created mainly from the eastern areas of Bengal, is completely different in topography and climate from the region just described. A flat alluvial plain of 53,000 square miles traversed by many streams and rivers, notably the Ganges and the Brahmaputra, it is a wet country with dense tropical jungles. The rainfall averages from 75 to as much as 160 inches a year. East Pakistan is a fertile area producing great quantities of rice and the world's largest supply of jute. It is

1- *Earl Louis Mountbatten of Burma,* Time Only to Look Forward *(London: Nicholas Kaye, 1949), p. 266.*

2- *Richard Symonds,* The Making of Pakistan *(London: Faber and Faber, 1950), p. 74.*

3- *Ibid., p. 169.*

4- *Mountbatten, op. cit., p. 74.*

5- *Symonds, op. cit., p. 191.*

Liaquat Ali Khan

heavily populated, having 46,000,000 inhabitants and a population density which in some areas equals 1200 people to the square mile.

In August 1947 the Pakistanis secured an extensive land area for their new nation, but they did not obtain the necessary governmental structure for their state. This had to be built up almost overnight. The old capital of British India at New Delhi, with its great public buildings and many offices, as well as the bulk of its staff, went to the Union of India. Karachi, the main city and seaport of the province of Sind, was chosen as the capital of Pakistan. Here offices and bureaus were improvised in tents and barracks. Meanwhile, an exodus was taking place from New Delhi, from which 25,000 government employees with their families and more than 50,000 tons of personal belongings had to be moved to Karachi. This was just at the time when massacres and train derailments had broken out in north-west India. With great difficulty the Pakistan government succeeded, partly with the help of forty English airplanes, in transporting the bulk of its civil servants to their new capital. Arriving in Karachi, these transplanted officials established themselves in either tents or temporary buildings. Crude tables purchased in the bazaars were their desks, boxes their chairs, and packing cases their files. Somehow the necessary files of records were set up, government departments established, and administrative machinery set in motion.

As hundreds of Pakistani civil servants streamed into Karachi, they brought with them a share of the assets and liabilities of the old undivided India. Pakistan was to receive stipulated amounts of war materials, and 150,000 troops out of a total of 420,000 were transferred to her command. Final arrangements for the division of Indian assets were not reached until December, when Pakistan secured 17.5 per cent of the sterling balances owed India by the United Kingdom, a like percentage of the cash balances of undivided India, and the same ratio of its uncovered debt.

Independence Day for Pakistan found this new state with a serious shortage of trained administrators and army specialists. British experts, therefore, were urged to remain. In three out of four provinces British officials were retained as governors, and in Karachi British civil servants were placed at the head of four of the governmental departments as permanent secretaries. Many Brit-

ish officers remained in the Pakistan army, and as late as the spring of 1949 the commanders of the army, navy, and air force were from the British Isles. In addition, there were about 750 British officers and technical specialists in the Pakistan armed forces.

By provision of the Indian Independence Act, passed by the British Parliament in July 1947, Pakistan was to be governed by the provisions of the Government of India Act of 1935 until such time as a new constitution could be prepared and without, of course, any authority being possessed by the British government. The legislature at Karachi was a Constituent Assembly of seventy members chosen by the provincial assemblies, and a cabinet following the traditions of ministerial responsibility was subject to the will of the federal legislature. Since Pakistan was a Dominion in the British Commonwealth of Nations, the Pakistan Governor-General represented the Crown; he was nominated by the Pakistan cabinet and formally appointed by the King. Pakistan as a federal state consisted of four Governor's Provinces (West Punjab, Sind, North-West Frontier Province, and East Bengal), the area of Baluchistan, the Tribal Territories on the North-West Frontier, and the six Native States which elected to join the new government.

As it began its independent existence, Pakistan was confronted with serious handicaps and problems, the most important being the division of its territory into two disconnected parts. The people in East and West Pakistan were followers of Mohammed, but they spoke different languages and belonged to entirely different culture patterns. In West Pakistan there were three main types: the Sindhis, the Punjabis, and the Pathans, with little love lost between the last two. The Pushtu-speaking Pathans, comprising a group of a little more than three million, posed a serious problem in the Tribal Districts of the North-West Frontier. These restless, belligerent, and fiercely individualistic tribes had never been pacified by the British; in 1947 their status became uncertain, for across the Pakistan border were another five million Pushtoons in Afghanistan, and there were Afghan patriots who envisaged the opportunity of creating a greater Afghanistan by the union of all the Pushtu people under its rule. This irredentist movement was checked, however, when a plebiscite among the tribes of the Frontier District registered the overwhelming desire of the people to remain with Pakistan. When Jinnah, the first Governor-General of Pakistan, visited the area in the spring of 1948, the various tribes—the Wazirs, Afridis, and Mahsuds—greeted him with friendship. The Pushtu issue, however, was to emerge later on and was to cause deep antagonism between Kabul and Karachi.

The North-West Frontier, apparently, was safely under the administration of Pakistan, but other problems remained, of which the status of the minorities and the necessity of rapid industrialization were most important. Muslim self-determination had been achieved, but it had not been a clean break. In western Pakistan 76 per cent of the inhabitants were Muslim and in eastern Pakistan the figure was 71 per cent. Translating these percentages into figures, there were twenty million non-Muslims in Pakistan, mainly Hindus; at the same time in the Indian Union there existed a huge minority of forty million Muslims. These large minority groups in 1947 were like hostages challenging each nation to protect minority rights, thus insuring like treatment for all. In the event, however, that fanaticism were to override reason and communal rioting should break out, the minority groups would be completely helpless, an easy prey to violence.

In the realm of economics, Pakistan fortunately enjoyed a food surplus, together with large yields of jute, cotton, hides, and wool. But it had practically no industries, no factories to process its jute, no mills for its cotton, and no tanneries for its hides. If Pakistan were to become a modern nation, industrialization would have to be one of the first aims.

The Muslim League controlled the new state, and its leaders were not as numerous or as well known as those of its counterpart, the Congress, in India. During the first year of independence the main burden was carried by Mohammed Ali Jinnah, who had assumed the post of Governor-General. A weary old man of seventy-one, Jinnah yet proved to be a tower of strength for the new nation; but his heavy responsibilities became too great a burden, and he succumbed to a heart attack in September 1948. He was buried with impressive ceremonies and honored as the Quaid-i-Azam (The Great Leader) because the Pakistanis realized that their new state stood as his monument. Yet he was only the skillful leader rather

than the creator of the forces that ultimately brought about Pakistan, and it has been said, "If there had been no Jinnah, it still seems probable that there would have been a Pakistan."[6]

Associated with Jinnah and well prepared to carry on his work was a group of capable administrators. Liaquat Ali Khan, the Prime Minister, had been Jinnah's chief associate. Born in the Punjab in 1895, he had been educated at Aligarh and Oxford and had a long record of political experience in India, both in the legislature and as Secretary of the Muslim League from 1936 to 1947. Pakistan's Foreign Minister was Sir Mohammad Zafrullah Khan, who had received a legal education in Britain, had been a judge in the Indian Federal Court, had held various posts in the Viceroy's Executive Council, and had represented India at several international conferences. He was to uphold Pakistani national interests with eloquence and skill before the United Nations.

Following Jinnah's death, the post of Governor-General went to Khwaja Nazimuddin, formerly the Prime Minister of East Bengal. A statesman whose long experience went back to the post of provincial minister under the Government of India Act of 1919, the Governor-General performed his official tasks with dignity and high-minded patriotism.

The Union of India

Beginning the new state of the Indian Union did not pose as many difficulties as did the establishment of Pakistan. There was no need to search for a new capital, and the bulk of the civil servants, the army, and the navy remained. India also possessed the largest cities, government buildings, most of the museums, colleges, laboratories, banks, and practically all the industries of the subcontinent. With an area of 1,246,000 square miles and a population estimated at 337,000,000, the Indian Union was one of the greatest states in the world. The main territories comprising India when Britain transferred power were nine Governor's Provinces, including Bombay, Madras, Central Provinces, the United Provinces, Orissa, Assam, Bihar, East Punjab, and West Bengal. In addition there were some relatively small areas known as Chief Commissioner's Provinces.

The Native States posed a serious problem to India. The great majority of them were mixed up in and around Indian provincial territory. What was to be their status? Unless they could be in some manner effectively assimilated, India would be Balkanized and fragmented. Some of the Native States desired complete independence, a course which, the government of the Indian Union declared,

threatened to bespatter the country with a vast number of independent enclaves, large and small, an eventuality which if not prevented . . . could have wrecked the economy of the country, broken its unity as a nation, menaced its security every moment of its existence, vitiated its resurgent democratic spirit and brought about Balkanisation whose effects would be irreparable.[7]

The British Labour government had consistently refused to encourage any idea of complete independence on the part of the Native States. The Governor-General, Lord Mountbatten, took a leading role in convincing the States that their proper destiny lay in joining one of the two Dominions. In an important meeting of the Chamber of Princes, held in July 1947, Mountbatten explained that two States Departments had been set up, one for each Dominion, to conduct negotiations with the States, and that a Draft Instrument of Accession had been prepared, under which only three basic powers would be surrendered by the Native States when they merged with a Dominion, these powers being defense, foreign affairs, and communications. Mountbatten explained to the Princes that the power of paramountcy had lapsed, that it could not be retained or transferred, and thus technically the Native States had now become independent political units. The Governor-General pointed out, however, "You cannot run away from the Dominion which is your neighbor."[8] He added that "there are certain geographical compulsions that cannot be evaded."[9] Under the capable direction of Sardar Vallabhbhai Patel, who made a conciliatory appeal to the States, all of the States within what might be regarded as the geographical confines of the Indian Union had signified their intention of coming into the Union. There were three states, Junagadh, Kashmir, and Hyderabad, whose status was uncertain, and serious difficulties were to arise in each of them. At the outset of independence, the problem of the majority of the States had been settled in principle, with only the details left to be cleaned

up, and, while India had lost the territory of Pakistan, she had effectively consolidated the great heartland of the sub-continent.

India faced many internal problems. Politically this new nation would have to consolidate its peoples into one nation and its provinces and Native States into a unified governmental structure. India's inhabitants were extremely diverse: Sikhs, Jats, Tamils, Bengalis, Mahrattas, and Punjabis, all with different languages and cultural traditions. In the past, before the advent of the European invader, we have seen that no native ruler had ever succeeded in uniting all of the country; and that, when it had been politically unified in part, the forces of disintegration were not long held in check. Would the new militant Indian nationalism, born in the late nineteenth century, prove an effective deterrent to the age-old political defect of India—political fragmentation?

Economically also the new India had difficulties. It had lost its richest granary to Pakistan, and disturbed conditions in independent Burma cut down the bountiful amounts of rice which Burma had exported to India in the past. India had important industries to be developed, while it had at the same time a huge population, the second largest in the world, which had already in 1947 outstripped its food supply. The rationalization of agriculture and the modernization and expansion of industry were the two prime economic goals in the minds of India's new statesmen.

These leaders were better known throughout the world than their counterparts in Pakistan. It was logical that Jawaharlal Nehru should be Prime Minister, but close at his side, as Deputy Prime Minister, was Sardar Vallabhbhai Patel. If Gandhi was the mystic, Nehru the socialist reformer and national idealist, Patel was the new India's man of action. Born in 1875, he had grown up to become a successful lawyer and then, like Motilal Nehru, gave up a lucrative practice to follow Gandhi. Becoming active in the nationalist crusade in the 1920's, he was imprisoned several times for his part in civil disobedience movements and during the Second World War he spent most of the period from 1940 to 1945 in prison.

While Patel was perhaps not as influential as his two distinguished colleagues, Gandhi and Nehru, he nevertheless deserves to be included with them in the outstanding triumvirate in contemporary Indian leadership. A man of the political right,

7- Indian Information, Independence Number *(New Delhi: Government of India, 1948), p. 5.*

8- *Mountbatten, op. cit., p. 56.*

9- Ibid., *p. 53.*

Alice Schalek from Three Lions

India and Pakistan: The Land and the People

Govt. of India Information Service

THE LANDSCAPE *of the Indian sub-continent offers vast contrasts, from the Himalayas, where farmers must terrace the* hills, *to the Pakistan salt marshes, where primitive implement raise water from which salt will be obtained. The oxen belo*

Three Lions

e being driven in the barren, hilly North-West Frontier area. ear Bombay tropical trees furnish palm leaves from which

the hut above is made. India has flat plains, too, like that in Rajputana, just above, where a Hindu fair is being held.

Govt. of India Information Serv

IN TOWNS *and cities cattle and people mingle, while forms of dress range from traditional to western styles. The town above is in Travancore, and the cities below are Karachi, left, and Bombay.*

Photo Almasy, Three Lions

Henri Cartier-Bresson (Magnu

NDUSTRIAL LIFE *in India offers great contrasts, for while skilled mechanics handle modern machinery, the potter still fashions his copper wares by hand. Despite Gandhi's campaign for hand spinning, factory production of cotton textiles is on a large scale. The two Hindu girls below are bobbin carriers in a Bombay textile mill.*

THESE PAGES *show the peoples of India and some aspects of their religious life and customs today, as well as religious centers held sacred by them from the past. The camel-men shown on this page are Mohammedans from the North-West Frontier near Afghanistan and the Khyber Pass. The camels are used both as pack animals and as means of transportation. The shepherds below are leading their sheep to the grazing grounds outside a village in Palitana, in Bombay province. At the bottom of this page are natives and cattle bathing together in the Janini River at Delhi. The strange light on the river is accounted for by the fact that the picture was taken during the time of the monsoon.*

ONLY A *few features of the varied religious life of India and Pakistan today can be shown here, and the pictures on the next page are merely representative. The first picture section (between pp. 60 and 61) has shown earlier examples of religious architecture and sculpture.*

Three Lions

Three Lions

Three Lio

Evans from Three L

TWO OF *the most beautiful temples in India are the Jain temple in Calcutta, shown on the opening page of this picture section, and the Golden Temple at Amritsar (above), the Holy City of the Sikhs. The Jains are a Hindu sect who carry the respect for all life to an extreme, and the Sikhs are a separate religious group founded in the fifteenth century (see p. 26). At the left are Muslims praying at the Agra mosque; this is the third phase of their ceremonial prayer. Below are Hindus practicing two of their religious customs. At the left the body of an old man is being prepared for cremation at Calcutta and at the right Hindus are bathing in the holy waters of the Ganges River, the banks of which are crowded with believers. Mohammedan prayers are everywhere the same and their mosques contain no representations of God. Hindu observances are many and a multitude of gods adorn their temples.*

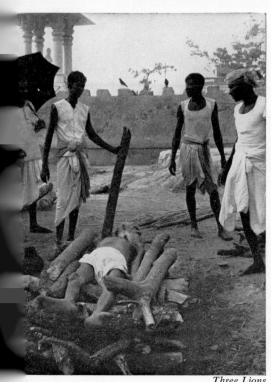

EDUCATION IN *India may mean the training of children in home spinning of raw cotton, a result of Gandhi's campaign for homespun, or it may mean college training of well-to-do women. The girls shown are at a college in Mysore.*
INDIA'S MAHARAJAS *often live in splendid surroundings, such as this reception room, below, of the Maharaja of Kolhapur.*

Patel

Manchester Guardian Week-
December 21, 1950, p. 8.
a recent evaluation of
' see K. Shridharani,
re," New Republic,
IV (February 26, 1951),
10-12.

deeply conservative, realistic and practical, Patel was what John Gunther called the "party-boss" of the Indian National Congress. In the tumultuous days just before independence it was Patel who dominated the arrangements for the transfer of power from Britain. Like Gandhi, Patel did not live to see the Indian state reach an even keel (he died late in 1950), but in the early years of independence this strong and sometimes ruthless man rendered great service to his country. Even the liberal *Manchester Guardian*, which might be expected to shy clear of Patel's authoritarian tactics, remarked on his death, "it can be said that the only disservice which he did his country since it gained its independence was to die at a very critical moment."[10]

Another leader high in the ranks of Indian statesmen was Chakravarti Rajagopalacharia, whom we have already discussed in connection with the Quit India campaign of Gandhi in 1942. With Patel and Nehru he was the leader closest to Gandhi, although on occasion he disagreed completely with the Mahatma's tactics. A good administrator with a keen mind, "C.R." was deeply religious but in no way mystical. During the Second World War he had realistically called for an all-out effort against Japan. He was the foremost political leader in the province of Madras, and was to be India's last Governor-General.

A few other leaders deserve mention. Dr. John Mathai, India's Finance Minister, was an economist and author of note who had been educated at Madras, the London School of Economics, and Oxford University. He was a Christian and had been a professor of economics and a member of the Indian Tariff Board. Maulana (Very Reverend) Abul Kalam Azad was a Muslim theologian and philosopher, the author of one of the most famous commentaries on the Koran. Born in Mecca in 1888, Azad had been educated at the Al Azhar University in Cairo and had founded an Urdu newspaper in India in 1912. Azad sought to bring Indian Muslims into the Congress movement, which he regarded as a non-religious, nationalistic organization. Azad became Minister of Education in the new Union government.

Another scholar high in the circles of Indian leadership was Dr. Rajendra Prasad, who early in his career had made a name for himself at Calcutta University and then proceeded to gain fame as a lawyer. In 1920 he became a disciple of Gandhi and was imprisoned several times. Prasad was named president of the Congress on four occasions and in 1947 became president of the Indian Constituent Assembly. In 1946 his book *India Divided* was published; it contained a strong indictment of Britain for helping to create what was charged to be artificial Muslim nationalism and of Muslim leaders, including Jinnah, for their Pakistan program.

The only important Indian leader educated in the United States was Jayaprakash Narayan, the founder of the Indian Socialist party. Early in the 1920's Narayan came to America, where he earned his living at a variety of jobs, being in turn a waiter, a farm laborer, and a salesman. He attended five universities in the United States and became an ardent Marxist. In 1929 he returned to India, and with the help of Jawaharlal Nehru he organized the Labor Research Department for the Indian Congress. Gradually the young socialist became the leader of the left wing in Congress and in 1934 he helped to found the Congress Socialist party. For a few years the small socialist group continued to work within the framework of the more conservative Congress. The rift between the right and left wings widened, however, and in 1948 the Socialists led by Narayan cut all ties with the larger organization and set about trying to bring "democratic socialism" to India.

Leadership in both India and Pakistan in 1947 seemed quite adequate, in some cases brilliantly so, for the tasks at hand. In both states, however, there was too much reliance upon three or four leaders and, further, the leaders in the main were old men. Young men were not being encouraged and trained to take over from the aging team of patriots who had fought the long campaign against British imperialism.

The Period of Great Expectations

During the latter part of the war, as India paid off its debts to Britain and even ran up a huge credit account of blocked sterling in London, and as Great Britain began to evince unmistakable signs of her impending departure, Indian nationalists viewed the future with expectancy and complete confidence. In many of the countries allied together as the United Nations there was considerable discussion about postwar planning and the necessity of raising the standard of living. In the

11- *Quoted in Jawaharlal Nehru,* The Unity of India, Collected Writings of Jawaharlal Nehru, 1937-1940 *(London: Lindsay Drummond, 1948), p. 406.*

12- *P. S. Lokanathan,* India's Post-War Reconstruction and Its International Aspects, *published for the Indian Council of World Affairs (Bombay: Oxford University Press, 1946), p. 57.*

13- *Bimal C. Ghose,* Planning for India *(Calcutta: Oxford University Press, 1945), p. 11.*

United Kingdom in particular there was considerable activity in preparing schemes for full employment, educational reform, and social security. India was no exception to this general interest in postwar planning, for the National Congress since 1931 had been seriously advocating comprehensive schemes of socio-economic reform. It had resolved that the state should own or control the key industries and services and that "political freedom must include real economic freedom for the starving millions."[11] At the end of 1938 Congress created a National Planning Committee of fifteen members under the chairmanship of Nehru. This body, after setting up twenty-nine subcommittees to investigate special problems, prepared a ten-year plan which called for the improvement of nutrition, the provision of more clothing for the masses, the improvement of housing facilities, the increase of agricultural and industrial production, and the elimination of illiteracy. Before the details of the plan could be worked out, the Second World War had broken out and most of the members of the Planning Committee had been sent to prison.

Up to 1939 the government of India had little interest in planning. The orthodox view was held that the function of government was to enforce law, protect property, collect taxes, and defend the country, and that all other functions of society were better handled by private hands. In June 1941, however, the government of India created a Postwar Reconstruction Committee, which was enlarged in 1943; and when Lord Wavell became Governor-General in 1944 he proceeded to establish a new department responsible for planning and development.

This step was taken in May 1944. Only a few months before—in January—the Indian people had been startled by the publication of the so-called Bombay Plan (*A Plan of Economic Development for India*). The work of eight of India's most prominent industrialists, the scheme provided for three successive Five Year Plans involving the expenditure of thirty billion dollars, the doubling of agricultural production, and the quintupling of industrial output in fifteen years. The Plan aroused widespread interest, and one Indian economist rightly observed, "It has made the entire nation planning-conscious."[12] So enthusiastic was Indian public opinion over the Bombay Plan and national programs for reform that an-

other economist wrote, "The whole world including ourselves is today mad about planning."[13]

The authors of the Bombay proposals laid down minimum standards to be secured in food, clothing, housing space, education, and health. Every village was to have its school, dispensary, and doctor. It is important to keep in mind that the Plan assumed the economic unity of India, as its makers expected that the partition proposals of the Muslim League would not be successful. Priority was given to the expansion of basic industries, such as electrical power, mining, chemicals, and transport. While agriculture was to be improved, the main emphasis was upon industry, nearly half of the entire thirty billion dollars being earmarked for this purpose. The Bombay Plan necessitated the expenditure of huge sums of money, and it was this aspect of it that many economists criticized as unrealistic. In short, the money was to be obtained by tapping the huge supply of hoarded wealth in the country and from sterling securities, foreign loans, the savings of the people, a favorable balance of trade, and by the creation of new money. The last source, in particular, was strongly rejected by many leading Indian economists.

Another ambitious postwar reform project was the People's Plan, issued in April 1944 by the Indian Federation of Labour. In this document there was much greater emphasis upon the intervention of the state, for the government was to control industrialization and nationalize all the farm lands. The Bombay Plan, while accepting the principle of a planned economy, would maintain a large measure of private enterprise. The People's Plan would have instituted a socialist state.

Meanwhile, the Department of Planning and Development of the Indian government under Sir Ardeshir Dalal, who had been one of the authors of the Bombay Plan, encouraged government officials to scan the possibilities of postwar planning in each of their respective fields. As a result numerous schemes were devised, one of the most discussed being the Sargent Plan for a system of universal and compulsory education for boys and girls between six and fourteen. This was to cost thirty million dollars in the first five years and by the fortieth year the cost was to rise to the huge sum of $832,000,000. In the field of public health, the Bhore Committee in its report laid down a blueprint for a healthier India, rightly concentrating upon the village. The plan was commendably ambitious, calling for a great increase in the number of doctors, the expansion of hospitals, and the building up of a network of public health agencies all over the country.

In April 1945 the Department of Planning and Development issued a statement that left no doubt that after the war independent India would follow the policy of a planned economy in which the government would direct and control industry; it might nationalize basic industries, while all others "will be left to private enterprise under varying degrees of control."[14]

As Indian leaders feverishly set about initiating the measures that would bring about a planned, and at least a semi-socialist, economy, it became quite apparent that there was little use, with independence just around the corner, in continuing to harp on the evil economic consequences of British imperial rule. Realistic thinkers, especially economists and sociologists, now began to warn that while a political revolution would soon be achieved, and with it national freedom, there was a comparably important revolution that would have to take place in the social and religious customs and habits of the Indian people. One of these economists wrote: "Rural poverty is not a social disease which large-scale public expenditure can cure nor . . . is it a problem which can be met through the indirect influence of industrial expansion. It is rooted deeply in the present structure and economic basis of our rural society."[15]

Obstacles to Reform in India

The general framework of caste, outworn custom, and traditionalism in India has already been discussed. At this point in our narrative, where we find India and Pakistan eager to initiate economic reforms and to raise the standard of living of their people, it is important to understand just what are some of the specific evils and uneconomic customs that required abolition.

One of the most serious obstacles to raising living standards in India is the sanctity enjoyed by practically all animals, especially the cow. Cow protection is one of the main tenets of Hinduism, and Gandhi has said, "Man through the cow is enjoined to realize his identity with all that lives. She is the mother to millions of Indian mankind. The cow is a poem of pity."[16] This belief in the sanctity of all life springs from the belief in rein-

carnation and means that the animal world rather than man rules India. Monkeys, rats, crows, peacocks, and pigeons, and all kinds of rodents multiply unchecked, consuming tremendous quantities of food. The depredations of rats alone have been calculated at 200,000,000 dollars a year.

India supports 215,000,000 out of the world's total of 690,000,000 cattle. This means 60 cows for nearly every 100 people. Yet these cattle have little economic value. Hindus will not consent to the control of their cow population or to the practice of selective breeding. Millions of aged and maimed cows continue to exist miserably and in general all the cattle are small and under weight by western standards. In Bengal, for example, the live weight runs from 425 to 750 pounds while in the United States a herd often has an average weight of 1400 pounds. Most Hindus will not eat beef, and, because of the poor quality of the cattle, milk production is limited. An American missionary who attracted much attention by his attempts to teach efficient stock management in India has declared, "Over 90 per cent of the cows of India do not pay for their keep. They are an economic drain on the country."[17] This statement is born out by the testimony of the Indian Board of Agriculture, which has put the annual loss incurred by the maintenance of useless cattle at $585,000,000.

Closely related to this cow problem and the sanctity-of-life complex is the difficulty of providing the average peasant with secondary occupations. In many areas it has been estimated that the work done by the farmers consumes only 150 days a year. The small farmer in Europe, on the other hand, can always be busy. He has his dairying, poultry, calf raising, and his pig pen. In Japan there has also been the cultivation of silkworms. All of these rural projects, however, are ruled out for the great majority of farmers in India because of their poverty.

One of the most serious evils in the structure of Indian life is the expenditure of relatively large sums of money by the Hindu peasants for uneconomic festivals and ceremonies, such as weddings and funerals. Men will spend the equivalent of twenty years of their land rent for a marriage feast for their daughter. On occasion the peasant must feast his caste-fellows, pay the priest for some service, or spend a large sum on a pilgrimage. So strong is the tyrannical force of custom that no one dares to reduce the customary expenditures.

14- Press Release, *Government of India Information Services, Washington, D. C.*, April 30, 1945, p. 8.

15- Tarlok Singh, Poverty and Social Change *(Calcutta: Longmans, Green and Co., 1945), p. 16.*

16- John Gunther, Inside Asia *(New York: Harper and Brothers, 1939), p. 393.*

17- Sam Higginbottom, "The Cattle Drain in India," Asia, XXVIII (1938), pp. 473-482.

This unproductive borrowing gives the money-lender, the bania, his opportunity and it has been estimated that the total rural debt runs to the incredible figure of four billion dollars. Excessive rates of interest are charged and, once in debt, the ryot usually stays there the rest of his life. No wonder the peasants have a saying, "The bania goes in like a needle and comes out like a sword."[18]

Two other conditions which spring from belief and custom are the maintenance of a large number of unproductive mendicants and beggars and the practice of hoarding wealth. One Indian writer estimates that in undivided India the Muslim and Hindu communities supported about three million holy men and beggars, a heavy burden for a poor country. This writer states that these people must be turned to useful vocations, observing that "when young men are able to earn a living the elders are ashamed to beg."[19] From time immemorial large amounts of gold and silver have been placed in temples, or buried, or fashioned into women's jewelry. The value of this immobilized wealth is tremendous, and it could be used to finance extensive schemes of economic development.

The great central problem of India is the pressure of its people upon the land. In the sixteenth century its population was perhaps 100,000,000; by 1881 it had reached 250,000,000; by 1911 it was 302,000,000; and by 1941 it totaled 388,000,000. As modern sanitation began to make some impression in India, the mortality rate fell while the birth rate remained the same. Thus it was that between 1931 and 1941 the population increase was nearly 51,000,000. The Indian sub-continent now supports 20 per cent of the world's people and has a population one and one-half that of all North and South America. This population increase in India has not been something unique in comparison with other countries. In India between 1872 and 1941 the rate of increase was 54 per cent, but in the United Kingdom it was 56 per cent and in Japan during the same period it was more than 130 per cent. The distinctive element in the Indian situation has been that this country experienced a large population increase without at the same time developing its economic productivity to keep pace with the people's needs. It is not too much to say that independent India's most fundamental problem is one of population. A well-known English authority on Indian economic history has observed;

It is difficult to avoid the conclusion that no matter how productivity is increased, economic organization is improved, public health is promoted, or industrialization progresses, the standard of the masses will not and cannot be raised to a satisfactory level until changes have been introduced which will enable the size of the population to be better adjusted to economic resources.[20]

In India, however, the marriage customs and associated religious beliefs make it almost impossible to exert control over population. Marriage is a social and religious necessity. Hindu belief has it that girls should be married before puberty, and the necessity of having a son to perform the *sraddha* ceremony at the funeral of the father, thereby insuring his salvation, helps explain the universality of parenthood among Hindus. The unmarried state is practically unknown, divorce is rare, and there is the lowest proportion of unmarried women in the world. Too many girls are married at an early age; in the 1920's it was estimated that 40 per cent were married before fifteen, that two million were married before the age of ten, and that 100,000 were already widowed at this age. Of course, child couples do not live together immediately after marriage, the usual age being fourteen or fifteen. This means the first child is born when the mother is sixteen or seventeen, and thousands are mothers of six children before thirty. Early marriage and the burden of too many children explain the high maternal mortality in India and, contrary to the situation in western countries, the lower life expectancy of women than men. "It is clear," writes one Indian student of this problem, "that such a universality of marriage, especially early marriage, must tend to shorten the Indian woman's period of education, affect her health and restrict both her professional and public activities."[21]

Actually in India there is a serious disparity in the ratio between the sexes, for there are about 930 women to every 1000 men. This problem is made worse by Hindu law, which prohibits the remarriage of widows. It is this shortage of marriageable women that further encourages child marriage.

Springing from this population problem in India is the pressure of the people upon the land and its subdivision into uneconomic holdings. Roughly throughout the country one half of the holdings are under five acres and three fourths of them are

18- Sir Edward Blunt, ed., Social Service in India (London: His Majesty's Stationery Office, 1939), p. 109.

19- Singh, op. cit., p. 35.

20- Vera Anstey, The Economic Development of India (London: Longmans, Green and Co., 1936), pp. 474-475.

21- L. N. Menon, "The Position of Women," Oxford Pamphlets on Indian Affairs, No. 2 (Bombay: Oxford University Press, 1944), p. 18.

under fifteen. Many surveys have been made, and all tell the same story of farmers making a bare subsistence on three or four acres, indifferently tilled, and usually not fertilized. Among Hindus land is generally equally divided among the heirs, and the laws of inheritance among the Muslims lead to the same result. A greater evil than land subdivision is that of fragmentation. The fields are broken up so that various heirs may secure a small portion of the several types of crop or wood land. In the Punjab there are fields only a few yards wide but over a mile long. The prevalence of small farm holdings in India makes it almost impossible to carry on modern, mechanized farming without the equivalent of an agrarian revolution. It is not surprising that there is a great gap between agricultural productiveness in India and in the United States.

Two final factors influencing the Indian economic picture demand comment. The Indian peasant has insufficient land to support him in a reasonably comfortable living, while out of the pitiably small yield that is his, he must often hand over a large sum to the landlord, the zamindar. In Bengal, for example, there are many parasitic landlords who take £3,750,000 annually from the tillers of the soil. This zamindar class has been described as "an incubus on the working agricultural population, which finds no justification in the performance of material services, so far as agricultural improvements are concerned and fails to provide any effective means for the development of the resources of the land which is the greatest asset of the province."[22]

As already indicated, the lot of the urban worker is no better than that of the rural villager. The second serious economic problem is the overall maldistribution of wealth in India, the tragic gulf which exists between opulence and dire want. In the entire country it has been calculated that 33 per cent of the wealth is owned by 5 per cent of the people, another like amount by 30 per cent, and the last third by more than 60 per cent. Or the picture can be described another way, by stating that in India 20,000,000 people are very wealthy or enjoy substantial middle-class status, some 130,000,000 live in respectable poverty, and 240,000,000 endure a bare subsistence.

It was these economic problems of Indian life that demanded study and rectification if the governments of India and Pakistan were to secure for their people the better life that had been an essential objective of the nationalist movement before independence.

The Shadow of Conflict

Unfortunately, in the first few months of their national existence both Pakistan and India were confronted by a state of crisis that left little opportunity for study and work on social reform and economic development. In the fall of 1947 there was real danger that the entire sub-continent would be convulsed by massacres and suffer the collapse of law and order.

Sporadic communal rioting had been going on ever since the major outbreak in Calcutta in August 1946. Just before the partition, August 15, 1947, numerous reports of riots and killings were received from Delhi and Calcutta, and from Amritsar and Lahore in the Punjab. This last-named province was a tinderbox of suspicion and even hatred, with the Muslims pitted against the Sikh and Hindu communities. In western Punjab the Muslim majority could vent their antagonism against the Sikh and Hindu minority, but the reverse was true in eastern Punjab, where the Muslims were outnumbered. No clear picture can as yet be drawn of how the rioting began, and each side accuses the other of premeditated massacre.

Religious fanaticism and mob violence were unchecked in the last two weeks of August and throughout September. On both sides of the Pakistan-Indian border in the Punjab, village after village went up in flames, their inhabitants, regardless of sex and age, butchered without mercy or compunction. A gigantic movement of people now began as hundreds of thousands of terrified villagers and townspeople tried to flee to safety— Muslims rushing out of East Punjab and Hindus and Sikhs fleeing to the sanctuary of Indian territory. As this migration got under way, trains were derailed, their passengers were dragged off and killed, and refugee columns were ambushed along the road. The Punjab Boundary Force had to be disbanded as its soldiers took sides and refused to fire on rioters of their own communal group.

Faced by one of the most terrible disasters in modern times, India and Pakistan momentarily forgot their differences and pooled their resources to set in motion a joint military evacuation organization. Relief camps were established, refu-

22- Quoted in Gyan Chand, *"The Problem of Population,"* Oxford Pamphlets on Indian Affairs, *No. 19 (Bombay: Oxford University Press, 1944),* p. 16.

gees were evacuated by an air shuttle service, and in little more than two months special trains carried nearly 2.5 million refugees. Huge foot convoys were organized, some numbering as many as 60,000. Moving slowly across the countryside, these convoys were guarded front and rear by men on horseback armed with spears and swords, with regular troops not far away, and with a system of bugle calls that warned of attack. There was much marauding, however, and many stragglers were picked off. Food had to be dropped from planes from time to time when a column was beleaguered. The outbreaks subsided in October, and by November 21 more than eight million refugees had crossed the India-Pakistan borders. All in all it has been estimated that by the end of the year 6,500,000 refugees crossed into Pakistan territory and that 500,000 Muslims were killed or, in the case of many women, abducted. More than five million Hindus and Sikhs fled from the Punjab, and large numbers of them were massacred en route.

Outside the Punjab there was a serious outbreak in Delhi, and for a brief period it seemed that partitioned Bengal would follow the terrible example of north-west India. It was Gandhi who almost single-handed prevented this holocaust by an appeal and fast; never had non-violence won a more important victory. Nehru also displayed personal courage and magnificent leadership in appealing to the people of India to control their communal antipathies.

These massacres aroused resentment and anger in both dominions, but the very enormity of the tragedy forced both governments to co-operate in the saving of thousands of lives. But other events were taking place which brought Pakistan and India to the verge of conflict by the end of the year and in the spring of 1948 into a state of limited but undeclared war. This added acrimony sprang from rivalry and disagreement over the status of certain Native States, namely Junagadh, Kashmir, and Hyderabad. The first of these was a small State on the Kathiawar coast where 800,000 inhabitants were ruled by a Muslim Nawab although they were more than 80 per cent Hindu. Although Junagadh was entirely surrounded by the territory of the Indian Union, the ruler acceded to Pakistan in September 1947. This action brought a strongly worded protest from the government of India, which declared that it violated the facts of

geography stressed by Lord Mountbatten in his speech to the Chamber of Princes on the eve of partition and, furthermore, that Junagadh's ruler was bound to follow the wishes of his subjects, 82 per cent of whom were non-Muslim. Dismissing the argument of sheer legality, the Indian government stated: "Every Ruler claiming sovereignty over his people can have the sanction of law even now for oppressing his people as much as he pleases. Legal sanction is not everything."[23]

Following the Nawab's accession to Pakistan, disturbances broke out in Junagadh, and the ruler fled to Karachi. On November 11, 1947, Indian troops entered the State and took over the administration, promising an early plebiscite to determine the real wishes of the people. Pakistan immediately protested, declaring the ruler's action legal and stating that Junagadh had acceded to Pakistan voluntarily and freely. The plebiscite was duly held, however, and the great majority of Junagadh's people voted for union with India. This incident aroused widespread feeling in Pakistan against India, but its real importance, as will be seen shortly, is its connection with the Kashmir controversy.

Located well within the center of the territory of the Indian Union was the important Native State of Hyderabad, the largest area in the sub-continent where medieval Muslim rule and government institutions had been perpetuated with little change down to modern times. Most of the people were Hindu peasants and over them was a small Muslim elite of landowners and civil servants. As the date of the British exodus drew near, the Congress party in Hyderabad was determined that this State should accede to the Union of India. On the other hand, the Nizam and the Muslim aristocracy were equally resolved that Hyderabad would not come under the control of India. Most determined to block this eventuality was an organization called Ittehad-ul-Muselmin, which sought to protect Islamic culture in the Deccan. This group had come under the leadership of a militant Muslim, Qasim Razavi, who created a private army called the Razakar Volunteers.

In the spring of 1947 the Nizam toyed with the idea of Hyderabad securing recognition from Great Britain as an independent Dominion in the British Commonwealth of Nations. This possibility was firmly ruled out by the Labour government. At any rate, in June 1947 the Nizam stated

23- Press Release, New Delhi, October 10, 1947 (Washington, D. C.: Government of India Information Services).

that for the time being his government would not accede either to Pakistan or to India. He added:

> When the British go I shall become an independent sovereign. But this does not mean that I wish Hyderabad to stand aloof either from old allies or old neighbors . . . I greatly hope that some kind of Standing Conference may soon be established, with regular meetings which may assist the new Dominions and such States as may decide to remain autonomous to co-operate actively in all matters concerning their common welfare.[24]

This announcement touched off a civil resistance campaign on the part of the Congress party in Hyderabad and led to the arrest and imprisonment of several thousand of its members.

Negotiations between the Nizam's government and that of India were carried on just prior to the resignation of British authority and continued on into the fall of 1947. New Delhi demanded nothing short of accession. It was argued that the facts of geography demanded Hyderabad's incorporation into the Indian Union. India could not countenance an independent state located as Hyderabad was in the very center of its territory. As the London *Times* put it, "Hyderabad is regarded as a possible ally of Pakistan deep in the heart of India."[25] Indians also argued that the will of the people had expressed itself in favor of accession. In reply, the Nizam's negotiating committee stood mainly upon the legalistic aspects of the matter, stressing that, once British paramountcy had been withdrawn, Hyderabad was automatically a sovereign state. As in the Junagadh imbroglio, the Indian government discountenanced the strictly legalistic arguments put up by Hyderabad, and maintained:

> The future of political communities and States is not governed by such declarations. An issue like this involving the defence of India, the integrity of her territory, the peace and security of the country . . . could not be allowed to be solved by mere legalistic claims of doubtful validity.[26]

The Nizam's position in the fall of 1947 seemed to be a strong one. India was beset with crises and there was the possibility of its soon being at war with Pakistan. There was the prospect that the sub-continent might break up into a number of political units, and that Hyderabad might eventually emerge as one of the strongest powers.

While agreeing, therefore, to a treaty with India which would give this state adequate control of foreign relations, communications, and defense, the Nizam absolutely refused to accept accession. Finally, in November 1947, a Standstill Agreement was signed for one year, whereby India was given the same rights over foreign affairs and defense as had been formerly exercised by Great Britain, but India was not given the right to send her own troops into Hyderabad. The agreement also provided that any dispute that might arise between the two signatories was to be settled by arbitration.

In this dispute the Pakistanis naturally were sympathetic with their co-religionists and with the Nizam, for his State was the most important center of Islamic traditions and culture in the Indian sub-continent. What particularly aroused the Pakistani statesmen at Karachi, however, was what seemed to them the open hypocrisy of the Indian government at New Delhi. To Pakistanis all the arguments based upon the facts of economics and geography and the will of the people seemed to be completely repudiated by the Indian government in the case of Kashmir. According to Pakistan, legalism was being made the foundation for India's claim to Kashmir, while the will of the people and the compulsions of geography were being completely ignored. It seemed to Karachi that India was resolved to have her Junagadh and get Hyderabad and Kashmir too.

Just as India naturally looked forward to the accession of Hyderabad, so Pakistan believed that Kashmir logically belonged to her. All the rivers and the roads that are open the year round go into West Punjab from Kashmir. The main import and export trade of this State is also with Pakistan and the most important commodity produced for export by Kashmir, timber, was marketed by floating it down the streams into Pakistan. Referring again to the logic of geography, the Pakistanis pointed out that their huge irrigation works, servicing nineteen million acres of land, depended upon rivers rising in or flowing through Kashmir, i.e., the Indus and its tributaries, the Jhellum, Chenab, and the Ravi. The economic life of Pakistan depended upon the control of these rivers.

It was also argued that 80 per cent of the inhabitants of Kashmir were Muslims who had long been oppressed by their Sikh maharajas, who had obtained the throne only by an accident of history,

24- *Quoted in* Chronology of International Events and Documents, *Vol. III, No. 16, August 4 to August 24, 1947 (London: Royal Institute of International Affairs, 1947), pp. 466-467.*

25- The Times *(London), September 27, 1947.*

26- White Paper on Hyderabad *(Government of India, 1948), p. 6.*

when the British in the 1840's turned over the country to a Sikh nobleman. The ruling clique in Kashmir was Hindu. Laws discriminated against the Muslims and there was continual popular unrest punctuated by sporadic revolts. Early in the 1930's politically-minded Muslims in Kashmir organized their Muslim Conference to undermine the absolute power of the ruler, Sir Hari Singh. A few years later the Muslim leader Sheikh Abdullah seceded from this organization and founded the Kashmir National Conference. This body accepted the aims of the Indian National Congress and was in close touch with such leaders as Nehru, Gandhi, and Azad. In 1946 Sheikh Abdullah launched a Quit Kashmir movement against the Kashmir ruler and was imprisoned as a result. On the eve of partition and the departure of the British there were, therefore, two popular and anti-Maharaja movements, the Muslim Conference, tied to the Muslim League, and the Kashmir National Conference, oriented to the Indian Congress.

Following independence day on August 15, 1947, the Kashmir ruler gave no indication of what his choice would be—accession to Pakistan or union with India. As an interim measure, however, he did sign with the former a Standstill Agreement providing for the management of the railway line, the postal services, and the customs by the government of Pakistan. During the third week of October reports were received of revolts and severe fighting in Kashmir, and on October 27 an official statement that Kashmir had acceded to India was issued by New Delhi. This action, it was explained, had been taken in order to secure the assistance of India in re-establishing law and order, and it was planned that just as soon as normal conditions were restored the will of the Kashmiris would be ascertained by plebiscite.

There has been much conflicting testimony as to what actually happened during the latter part of October in Kashmir. Pakistan claims that it was apparent to the Muslim tribesmen in Jammu and Poonch that their unpopular ruler was setting the stage for union with India in order to save his position. A spontaneous revolt thereupon broke out, which was put down with extreme severity by the soldiers of the Maharaja. There was pillaging and terrorism, and large numbers of Muslim Kashmiris, fearing for their lives, fled to Pakistan. The news of this terror reached the fanatical Muslim tribesmen of the North-West Frontier, and they immediately rushed to the aid of their co-religionists in Kashmir. Most of these tribesmen had to cross Pakistan territory, and there is little doubt that their movement was expedited by the Pakistan authorities. Pushing into the Vale of Kashmir, they defeated bodies of the Maharaja's army, rescued columns of Muslim refugees, and regrettably were unable to resist the temptation of looting any property that came their way. These Muslim tribesmen got within eighteen miles of Srinigar, the state capital; in the meantime, in order to give his government the semblance of popular support, the Maharaja had released Sheikh Abdullah from prison and made him the head of a new provisional government. The pro-Pakistan Kashmiris proceeded to establish their own regime, known as the Azad Free Government.

In reply to the Maharaja's plea for assistance, the Indian government immediately dispatched armed forces by air to Kashmir. These troops managed to hold back the tribesmen and save Srinigar. The news of the accession stunned the Pakistan leaders, and Jinnah for a time considered moving his regular troops into Kashmir. Such an action would have meant war with India and, fortunately, his British military advisers dissuaded the Governor-General from taking this course.

During November and December heavy fighting took place between the tribal invaders and Indian battalions. At this time Sheikh Abdullah declared, "If present conditions continue, conflict between India and Pakistan is inevitable."[27] Relations between the two nations rapidly deteriorated as heated recriminations were exchanged. Liaquat Ali Khan declared that India wanted to outflank Pakistan so that she could be in a position to throttle its very existence, and, further, that India had welched on its partition arrangements in not turning over the cash balances and military stores due Pakistan. Nehru on the other hand accused Pakistan of assisting the tribesmen to invade Kashmir and of using force to gain their objectives.

Feeling that it had the better case, the Indian government appealed the issue to the United Nations, invoking Article 35 of the Charter and charging Pakistan with aggression. On January 15 Pakistan filed countercharges, and two days later the Security Council asked both parties to refrain from any action that might worsen the situation. India had expected the United Nations

27- Chronology of International Events and Documents, *Vol. IV, No. 1, December 22, 1947, to January 9, 1948, p. 13.*

to support its action in Kashmir and, consequently, to condemn the action of Pakistan. Instead the Security Council was concerned more with investigating the basic elements in the problem than with trying to assign blame for the civil war. Nehru, deeply disappointed, complained in the Indian Parliament of the "strangely narrow view that people in the Security Council have taken in this matter."[28] Finally, in April 1948, the Council established a Commission to study conditions on the spot in Kashmir with the purpose of bringing about a free and impartial plebiscite to determine the wishes of the inhabitants.

It is interesting to compare the arguments used by both sides in the Kashmir controversy. Indian leaders took the view that the Kashmiris were not justified in revolting against the constituted authority of their Maharaja and that the tribesmen had no right to come to their assistance. Nehru in supporting this view stated: "The issue in Kashmir is whether violence and naked force should decide the future or the will of the people."[29] Again he observed, " . . . there has been aggression, aggression of a shameless kind and this has to be resisted. There should be no surrender to aggression."[30]

Above all, the legal aspects of the case have been used to buttress the Indian position. Speaking before the Security Council the Indian representative, Sir Benegal Rau, declared:

The Maharajah of Kashmir executed an instrument of accession in favor of India on October 26, 1947 and Lord Mountbatten accepted it the next day. This completed all legal and constitutional requirements for accession to the Indian Dominion. Nothing more was required. . . . Therefore, it is elementary that Kashmir now is legally a part of India; that Indian troops are legally in Kashmir, going there to restore law and order.[31]

Pakistani spokesmen stressed the economic, geographical, religious, and cultural ties of Kashmir and Pakistan and argued that India played the game with two different sets of rules, one for Junagadh and Hyderabad, the other for Kashmir. Sir Zafrullah Khan pointed out that while India dismissed all arguments based on legality in the first two states mentioned and took her stand on the wishes of the people and the facts of geography, she made legalism sacrosanct in the case of Kashmir, ignored the traditions and wishes of the people, and denied the plain implications of geography.[32]

The intervention of the United Nations in the Kashmir dispute early in the spring of 1948 may be thought of as marking the conclusion of this period of great tension and danger of war. Tempers cooled somewhat, and both Pakistan and India, reprieved from the possibility of destructive conflict, now began to inaugurate another phase in their recent history which might be called the Period of Recovery and Promise.

In January 1947, the very same month in which the U.N. became concerned with Kashmir, an event of a tragic nature took place which in a sense also served to mark an end to an unhappy period of confusion and strife and the beginning of a new era of confidence and progress. During the holocaust of blood in the Punjab, Gandhi almost singlehanded had prevented a similar outbreak in Calcutta and from there all over Bengal. The Mahatma's appeal for forbearance, for mutual respect and tolerance between the Muslim and Hindu communities, enraged extremists in the latter group.

Amid the passions of the massacres in the Punjab and the acrimony of the Kashmir dispute the Hindu Mahasabha was violently anti-Muslim, espousing a Hindu empire covering the entire Indian sub-continent and passionately defending caste and cow protection. Closely associated with the Mahasabha was the R.S.S.S. (the Rashtriya Swayam Sewak Sangh), a highly disciplined group whose numbers wore uniforms and drilled in military formation. Both these organizations were regarded with deep suspicion by Indian liberals who regarded them as fascists willing, if the opportunity arose, to use force for the establishment of a Hindu theocracy. Some of these ultra-Hindu nationalists made the following demands:

Remove the present government, which is composed of men of straw and replace it by men who would be strong Hindus . . . declare the Indian Union a Hindu State; prepare the country on a basis of war with Pakistan; impose conscription on all Hindus; treat all Muslims as fifth columnists; and declare the professing of Islam as unlawful.[33]

On January 13, 1948, Gandhi started his last fast to induce Indian leaders to pledge their opposition to any anti-Muslim program. Five days later a solemn promise was made by outstanding leaders including Nehru and Azad that the life and property of Muslims in India were not to

28- Lawrence K. Rosinger, *India and the United States* *(New York: The Macmillan Co., 1950), p. 107.*

29- *Jawaharlal Nehru,* Independence and After, A Collection of Speeches, 1946-1949 *(New York: John Day Co., 1950), p. 65.*

30- India Record *(October 11, 1950), II, p. 7.*

31- *Quoted in* Pakistan Affairs *(Washington, D. C.), March 3, 1950.*

32- Kashmir Question, *pamphlet of the Pakistan Government, published in New York, 1950.*

33- The Times *(London), September 19, 1950.*

be molested. Meanwhile, a plot had been hatched, and a Brahman editor of a Mahasabha weekly was picked to assassinate Gandhi. The deed was done on January 30, when the Mahatma was shot to death by four pistol bullets fired at close range as he walked to a prayer meeting in the grounds of Birla House in New Delhi. The assassination was linked to extremist elements in both the Mahasabha and the R.S.S.S. For the time being the former suspended its political activities, while the latter was outlawed by the government.

All the world paid tribute to the frail, diminutive man whose biography had been so much the history of India during the preceding thirty years. In death he made one of his great contributions, for the murder brought many people in both Pakistan and India to their senses and made them realize that this evil act was the symptom of chaos waiting to be unleashed upon the sub-continent of India. Gandhi occupied an important place in Indian and world history, and many books and hundreds of articles have attempted to evaluate his contributions and appraise his worth. It may be said that in too many of them Gandhi ceases to be a man and becomes a myth. He was too great a leader and patriot not to have all the truth told about him.

The Great Awakener of Indian nationalism, Gandhi transformed the Congress movement from a limited crusade of intellectuals and bourgeois professional and business classes to a great mass movement in which the common man played an important part. His championship of *Ahimsa,* or non-violence, while at times utterly devoid of solid reason and practicality, was at least a salutary corrective in a world increasingly convinced of the rightness of sheer force. Gandhi correctly saw the snares and evils inherent in the gadget civilization and materialism of the West. He called upon his people to be aware of the western Mammon. Finally, Gandhi always stood by the side of mercy and love. Compassionate above all, he was the spokesman of the lowly and downtrodden all over the world, and more particularly of the Untouchables in his own land.

But Gandhi suffered from the defects of all these virtues. Only a holy man, a mystic, could so strongly influence the Indian people. It would be a mistake, however, to identify this situation as part of a democratic process. An American historian sagely observes: "Hindus looked upon Gandhi as the mouthpiece of their gods. When your gods told you to vote the Congress ticket, you did not disobey. It was an effective argument, but it cannot be called democratic."[34] The trouble with a mystic and saint as a leader is that his followers must accept with his religiosity a confused ideology made up of worship of the past, medieval economics, attacks on modern science and medicine, and hazy goals. As Nehru has sadly commented, "What, after all, was he aiming at? In spite of the closest association with him for many years, I am not clear in my own mind about his objective. I doubt if he is clear himself."[35]

Gandhi's civil disobedience campaigns and his attacks on constituted authority tended to bring all government into contempt, not only the British but later that of an independent India. And after 1947 on several occasions fanatics seriously embarrassed the government by resorting to civil disobedience and other extrademocratic techniques to force the authorities to their will. For example, a new political party was formed in West Bengal in the fall of 1950, dedicated to the attainment of a "democratic classless society." Its spokesmen declared that this goal would be sought by constitutional means, but if these failed "mass satyagraha might be necessary."[36]

The charge of inconsistency may also be leveled against Gandhi. The Mahatma asked Britain to surrender to Hitler in 1940, thus scoring a victory for non-violence, but in 1947 he found it possible to support the dispatch of Indian soldiers to fight against the Muslim tribesmen in Kashmir. Furthermore, he always sought to assuage communal differences, yet it was his authoritarian attitude at the Second Round Table Conference, his insistence that he alone could speak for the Indian people, that violently aroused the Muslim community and did much to make Pakistan possible. Gandhi fulminated against western materialism and its factories, but had no compunction about making a strong alliance with industrialists in his own country. He violently attacked western medicine, but permitted an English doctor to save his life by surgery early in the 1920's.

Gandhi at his best was the Holy Man subtly combining the wisdom of the ancient Vedas with the doctrines of John Locke and Thomas Jefferson. He awakened his people and set them in motion toward a noble yet distant objective, the real nature of which was never clarified in Gandhi's own

34- Lennox A. Mills, "Problems of Self-Government," The New World of Southeast Asia, ed. Lennox A. Mills (Minneapolis: University of Minnesota Press, 1949), p. 304.

35- Jawaharlal Nehru, Toward Freedom (New York: John Day Co., 1942), p. 313.

36- The Statesman (Calcutta), November 25, 1950, p. 5.

mind. In truth, as India neared independence day, the country no longer needed a seer or mystic as a leader but rather a statesman who could think clearly and precisely. During the negotiations between the Muslim League, the Congress, and Britain in the fateful spring months of 1947, Gandhi seemed ineffectual. As he himself ruminated in September of this year, "There was a time when India listened to me. Today I am a back number. I have no place in the new order where they want an army, a navy, and an air force and what not."[37]

Yet Gandhi, with all these inconsistencies and what to the western mind seem to be serious defects, was a noble and heroic character great enough to be revered as the Father of the New India. And even Englishmen, who might be expected to dismiss the Mahatma with a jeer or a growl, on the whole treat his memory with sincere respect. One of them has written:

And time will enable us to see the triumphs and blunders of Gandhi in a gentler light. He has harboured no enmity against us. Posterity will certainly number him among the friends of England. One day we shall raise a statue to his memory, as we have raised statues to Washington and Lincoln, and to the memory of others whose universal spirit transcended the conditions of their time. Perhaps that statue will be placed within one of our great cathedrals . . . It would not be more incongruous than the statue raised in Winchester Cathedral to the memory of St. Joan.[38]

Recovery and the Return of Confidence

In the spring of 1948 the stream of refugees had practically ended, all-out war had been averted between Pakistan and India, and both nations could now turn their attention more to the urgent problems of economic development and social reform. On the whole, the refugee problem was handled remarkably well. At one time the Indian Union was running 160 camps accommodating as many as 1,250,000 homeless refugees. A tremendous amount of food, tents, clothing, medicine, and other supplies had to be furnished by both nations to their homeless migrants. Housing schemes and programs of vocational and technical training were worked out, and hundreds of thousands were settled on the land. While this refugee problem was handled better than one might expect, considering its dimensions, hundreds of thousands of displaced persons remained stranded

and homeless in the cities. It was natural that they should become restless and disgruntled with the government. Furthermore, tension at times mounted between the newcomers bent on obtaining jobs and the old residents who saw their employment jeopardized.

The United Nations Commission on Kashmir arrived in India in July 1948 and immediately set about its task of bringing an end to hostilities and setting up plebiscite machinery to determine the wishes of the inhabitants. This Commission ran into an intransigent attitude on the part of both disputants and had to report its failure to the Security Council. Negotiations continued, however, and in January 1949 a cease-fire agreement was achieved. On January 15 the commanders of both armies met and agreed to exchange prisoners, and in March Admiral Chester W. Nimitz was named as Plebiscite Administrator by the Secretary-General of the U.N. The outlook for a peaceful settlement of the Kashmir issue seemed promising.

India in 1948 registered considerable achievement in the drafting of a new constitution, the integration of the Native States, the study and formulation of numerous plans for economic development, and the introduction of social reform. In Pakistan, the less than one dozen princely states harbor only 4 per cent of the total population, but in India there are more than five hundred states and they contain 25 per cent of the population. Under the vigorous leadership of Sardar Patel, the Indian government laid down three fundamental principles to guide policy on the status of the Native States: (1) Despotism, however benevolent, must be displaced by democratic government. (2) The States must be effectively subordinated to the central government. (3) The absurd multiplicity of States, large, small, and minuscule, must give way to an integration into larger and more economically viable units.

By the spring of 1950, 216 states had been merged with the former British provinces; 61 states had been taken over by New Delhi to be centrally administered; and 275 states had been joined to make new political units called Unions of States. While the original word of the Indian government in 1947 had been that the States would only yield the powers of defense, foreign affairs, and communications to the central government, by 1950 the old States had been completely subordinated

[37] Chronology of International Events and Documents, *Vol. III, No. 19, September 22 to October 5, 1947, p. 568.*

[38] *Glorney Bolton, The Tragedy of Gandhi (London: George Allen and Unwin, 1934), p. 322.*

to a position no different from that of the old provinces of British India. In this process the Princes naturally have lost their earlier powers and privileges. A few have remained as the constitutional heads of States, but the great majority have been "pensioned off" and bereft of any influence.

In this process of state integration, Hyderabad posed a serious problem to Indian statesmen. The Nizam was determined to maintain his State's independence. However, as India became stronger in the spring of 1948, its government began to apply pressure upon Hyderabad demanding its accession. Tension mounted, border raids took place along the Nizam's frontiers, and Communists took advantage of the uncertainty to harry and raid villages in Hyderabad. As the crisis developed, fanatical Razakars terrorized Hindu villages, looted shops, and took the law into their own hands. Negotiations between the Nizam and Nehru's government broke down in June 1948, and India thereupon initiated a complete economic blockade of the State. The Nizam appealed to the Security Council for its good offices in settling the dispute, but India immediately insisted that Hyderabad was not competent as a sovereign state to bring the matter before the U.N. Finally, on September 13 the Indian army invaded Hyderabad and after five days of fighting took over the Nizam's government. It has been claimed that many Muslim civilians were killed, one authority putting the number as high as fifty thousand.[39]

In the Hyderabad quarrel, legality was undoubtedly on the side of the Nizam, but facts of geopolitics—defense, economics, communications— were on the side of India. The use of force, albeit in the name of restoring law and order, weakened the case of India in Kashmir, especially in the minds of Pakistanis. It must also be said that the press in Europe and America was critical of India's action. Said the London *Times*, "Its present use of force against a weaker neighbour which resists its claims comes badly from a government that owes its existence to the principles embodied in the Charter of the United Nations."[40]

The Draft Constitution for India was published in the spring of 1948. It was presented to the Constituent Assembly early in November, was approved late in the same month, and became the law of the land on January 16, 1950. India, or Bharat as it is called, became a sovereign, demo-cratic republic. The new constitution owes much to the political liberalism of Europe and the United States, and Nehru acknowledged this fact when he spoke before the American Congress on October 13, 1949. It is also apparent that the lessons of federalism in Canada, Australia, Switzerland, and the United States have been studied.

In form a federation with powers divided between a central and state governments, the Indian Union is almost unitary in function, with emphasis placed upon the authority of the central government. Although there is a list of state subjects, the central government can legislate upon any subject it may consider to be in the national interest. Furthermore, the President in Delhi can promulgate ordinances and suspend any state constitution. The central Parliament is bicameral, consisting of the House of the People and the Council of States. Heading the Union's executive is a President who is the constitutional head, together with a Prime Minister and Cabinet responsible to the House of the People.

The Constitution contains an imposing Statement of Fundamental Rights, which abolishes untouchability and guarantees such rights as free speech, free assembly, religion, and due process of law. An interesting feature is the section on Directive Principles of State Policy, which asserts that the government should be guided by certain principles in making its laws. Among them might be mentioned equal pay for the sexes, humane conditions of work, free education, adequate nutrition, and a living wage. It is also stated that the economic system must not result in the concentration of wealth and "that the health and strength of workers, men and women, and the tender age of children are not abused and that citizens are not forced by economic necessity to enter vocations unsuited to their age or strength."[41]

The Constitution makes Hindi the official language of the Union, and the government has zealously propagated it as the national language. There has been strong opposition to this policy, especially in south India, where Hindi is regarded as a foreign tongue.

Constitution making has proceeded slowly in Pakistan, the only important achievement being the publication of "Fundamentals of Freedom," containing the basic aims and objectives guiding the Constituent Assembly. While this statement endorses such principles as representative govern-

39- William Cantrel Smith, "Hyderabad: Muslim Tragedy," Middle East Journal, *IV* (January 1950), p. 47.

40- The Times *(London)*, September 14, 1948.

41- The Constitution of India *(New Delhi: Government of India, 1949)*, pp. 19-20.

ment, social justice, equality, and the protection of the rights of minorities, the implication is that Pakistan is to be a Muslim state. Some fundamentalist circles assert that non-Muslims cannot expect to hold positions of great trust under the new constitution but, on the other hand, the Prime Minister, Liaquat Ali Khan, has stated that a non-Muslim could be the head of the government. While, in theory at least, the Indian Union is based on the principle of a secular state, it remains to be seen whether Pakistan will tend to be theocratic.

In the realm of industry, agriculture, transportation, medical and educational progress, India and Pakistan could each be termed a Planner's Paradise, as economists, reformers, and statesmen enthusiastically set to work to achieve a richer livelihood for their people. In India the economic picture was not gloomy or discouraging. The financial position was sound, with the total public debt less than half the national income and with a huge credit account amounting to several billion dollars held in blocked sterling in London. The great need of the country was to increase its food output. In industry, India was more fortunately situated than Pakistan, for following partition practically all the industry remained with the former, together with those resources necessary to support an ambitious program of industrialization. In particular, India had great deposits of coal and iron and on the whole could be said to possess industrial resources potentially greater than those of any other country except the United States and the Soviet Union.[42]

Numerous industrial projects were either actually initiated or planned in the Indian Union in 1948. These included two large steel mills, a newsprint factory, fertilizer and gasoline plants, and three automobile assembly factories. In textiles, the largest industry, the plan was to import thousands of spindles and looms from Japan. A Seven Year Plan for modernizing the railroads at a cost of one billion dollars was blueprinted. The rapid expansion of air services was planned, together with a five year scheme for highways, and another for creating two million tons of shipping. Most spectacular were the Multi-Purpose Power Schemes based on the American Tennessee Valley Authority model. These projects aimed at flood control, irrigation, better navigation on the rivers, and the generation of electric power. In India at present only 6 per cent of the water resources are

being used, and it is estimated that ultimately more than thirty million kilowatts yearly can be produced. In 1950 the annual production of electric power was equal to only one week's output in the United States.

The most critical economic problem in India is the shortage of food, and after independence a goal was laid down of an increase in agricultural production of ten million tons of food grains yearly. Hundreds of tube wells were planned, better seeds were procured, and various schemes were initiated to reclaim fallow land, the most ambitious being a plan to reclaim some ten million acres in central India. Assisted by a loan of ten million dollars from the World Bank, India obtained special machinery from Britain and the United States to dig up and destroy the insidious kans grass, whose root system penetrates more than three feet below the ground surface.

Public sanitation, education, and labor also received the attention of the planners. There was talk of eradicating illiteracy in five years, training two million teachers, and increasing the amount spent on elementary education from a pre-war figure of ninety million to five hundred million dollars yearly. The recommendations of the Bhore Committee on public health were accepted, and a target was envisaged of 300,000 doctors, 778,000 nurses, and 70,000 health visitors. There was also a Five Year Plan for labor which called for better working conditions, more housing, social security, and other benefits.

A similar pattern of economic planning reform was being worked out in Pakistan. This nation, while very productive in certain raw materials and enjoying an adequate food supply, was seriously deficient in industrial resources. It produced large amounts of wheat, cotton, rice, and jute, but had no coal or iron. The most pressing need was to develop power resources for the new industries it planned. Oil surveys were therefore undertaken and huge water power projects planned to harness the rivers of West Punjab. In December 1947 plans were laid for twenty-seven new industries. During the next two years various projects were initiated: jute mills; cotton factories; a large sugar mill; tanning, silk, and tobacco factories.

During 1948, as India and Pakistan embarked upon an amazingly ambitious project of economic development, the mood of both governments was strongly socialistic, with faith in national planning,

- Kingsley Davis, "India and *kistan: The Demography of rtition*," Pacific Affairs, *XXII eptember 1949), p. 256.*

a distrust of private enterprise, and consequently a strong intention to nationalize as much of their industry as possible. In a statement of the Indian government made in April 1948 the following principles were enunciated:

(1) The generation and distribution of electric power will be regulated, and in certain instances, will be the function of the government. (2) The state will have an exclusive monopoly in the case of munitions, atomic energy, and the railways. (3) All new projects in such fields as coal, iron, steel, aircraft, oil, shipbuilding, radio, telegraph, and telephone apparatus will be the concern of government; and, after ten years, private enterprise in all these fields will be reviewed by the government. (4) The state must have the power to plan and regulate certain basic industries, listed in eighteen categories, in addition to those mentioned above. (5) Foreign capital will be welcomed but the major interest and effective control of all projects financed from abroad must be in Indian hands.[43] Nehru, speaking in June 1948, declared: "We would rather delay our development, industrial or ortherwise, than submit to any kind of economic domination of any country. That is an axiom which is accepted by everyone in India. . . ."[44]

This policy of semi-socialization, together with a fear of foreign economic imperialism, could be found in Pakistan as well as in India. In the former, certain industries were to be run by the state and twenty-seven categories of industry were to be subject to the central planning of the state. And even in private industry the government was to lay down production goals and determine the location of factories. Foreign capital was to be carefully controlled, and there were to be facilities for the remittance of *reasonable* proportions of the profits back to the foreign country.

Considering the terrible riots in the Punjab, the subsequent mass of refugees, the threat of war in Kashmir, and the difficulties of establishing and setting in motion a new machinery of government, it is remarkable not only that Pakistan and India were able to formulate so many social reforms and industrial projects but that in the first two years of independence they were able to plan at all.

Meanwhile, the mood in both nations was one of hope and confidence, as illustrated by the remarks of an Indian professor visiting the United States. This visitor declared in a press interview that India is

witnessing the beginnings of a renaissance in agricultural and rural sanitation, a rising tempo in industry, mining and transportation, an improvement in the general standard of living and expectation of life on a sub-continental scale, a vast educational expansion . . . and a steady introduction of people to constitutional and democratic institutions.[45]

43- Economic and Commercial Conditions in India *(London: His Majesty's Stationery Office, 1949), pp. 220-224.*

44- *Rosinger, op. cit., p. 53.*

45- Press Release, *April 21, 1949 (Washington, D. C.: Government of India Information Services), p. 5.*

Indian prospect

epilogue: INDEPENDENCE FOR Pakistan and India coincided with one of the most troubled and menacing periods in world history. Unlike the United States, Canada, and Australia, nations whose infancy was more or less insulated from the interplay of power politics, these new Asian powers were plummeted at birth in 1947 into the very center of gigantic revolutionary forces and rivalries. They faced not only the difficulty of avoiding entanglements in the world rivalry between Russia, its satellites, and the American-Western bloc, but also the problem of protecting themselves against the dangers and complications stemming from the Asian revolution.

In the light of this Asian revolution and the concomitant expansion of Soviet imperialism, India and Pakistan in the 1950's assumed a new significance in world affairs and a special importance to the United States. Because of their traditions of parliamentary government bequeathed by British rule, their political stability, and the fact that they were relatively untouched by Communism, there was substantial ground for belief that these nations might act as an effective barrier to further Soviet expansion in Southeast Asia. Furthermore, they might stand as a hope to other Asian peoples that good government and economic progress can be secured without tyranny. Finally, Pakistan and India might also serve as a kind of bridge, assisting the East and the West to an understanding of each other's fundamental values and ways of life.

India and Pakistan thus might play a decisive role in the affairs of one billion Asians, half the world's population. It also follows that the growing importance of these two new states should elicit from the United States and its western partners and allies, especially Britain, every effort to understand their problems and to aid in solving them. If India and Pakistan are to meet the challenge of their times, substantial progress must be made in four distinct fields, the first of which is the assurance of livelihood for their people.

As we have already seen in the last chapter, a good start was made by both New Delhi and Karachi in the direction of increasing food output, providing new sources of power, launching industrialization, and improving the health and education of the people. However, it soon became apparent to both governments that it was one thing to plan oneself into prosperity but quite

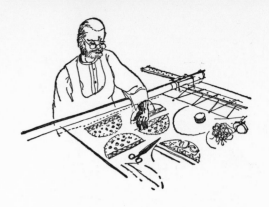

a different matter to bring the plans to fruition. In both India and Pakistan there was a decided decline in confidence as plans failed to reach their goals and as capital was not forthcoming to finance the new schemes. India in particular experienced acute disillusionment, not so much because there was a failure to achieve substantial economic progress as because there were many ominous signs that the economic situation was deteriorating. In the fall of 1949 one observer noted, "Not even the gloomiest of political Jeremiahs had predicted the serious and rapid deterioration of the Indian economy and the almost complete suspension of industrial expansion, which have been so marked in recent months."[1]

This economic setback was attributable to the fact that grandiose plans had not correctly estimated the available natural resources, the existing technical personnel, and the amount of capital that could be procured from domestic sources. In the case of India, the Federation of Chambers of Commerce, in an analysis of government planning released in January 1950, maintained that most of the plans were unrealistic and unrelated to the financial and physical resources of the country, and were in many cases being abandoned or drastically cut down. The total cost of central and provincial government projects, it was estimated, would run to an annual cost of 200 crores of rupees, an expenditure that could not possibly be made except through the use of huge amounts of foreign capital, which thus far had not been obtained. As for the great multi-purpose irrigation projects, many of which called for completion in five years, it was stated that it would be difficult enough to complete them in twenty years. On November 14, 1950, in a broadcast to the nation, the late Sardar Patel, then Deputy Prime Minister, declared: "I can tell you quite frankly that the time for preparing paper schemes has gone; we cannot indulge any longer in the pastime of conjuring before our vision idealistic utopias."[2]

It should also be pointed out that political considerations in both Pakistan and India were allowed to take precedence over economic needs and realities. The tragic quarrel over Kashmir, and with it the constant possibility of full scale war, forced Pakistan to earmark more than 60 per cent of its budget for military purposes, and caused India to devote 50 per cent to military

needs. And, as we will see shortly, a disastrous trade war broke out between Pakistan and India, almost completely disrupting commercial relations. The huge expenditure on arms and the cessation of mutually profitable trade relations made it almost impossible for either India or Pakistan to carry through an economic program of development and reform commensurate with the needs of their people.

It is charged by many critics that industrial development in the Indian Union is being throttled by the government's policies of nationalization of industry, limitation of dividends, and interference in labor relations. In the spring of 1948 Nehru had declared that the conflict between the social state and the profit motive would go on, and that only one would survive. He added, "It is clear that the State will survive and not that group which represents the private motive in industry."[3] Indian businessmen protested that while they were not against economic planning they were resolutely opposed to bureaucratic control. Whether justified or not, investors refused to place their funds in new enterprises, and since 1947 virtually no subscriptions of fresh capital have been forthcoming. Stock markets have remained sluggish, and in September 1948 an Indian financial reporter observed, "A sepulchral silence has settled on the hall of the exchange; and the marking up of a single quotation has become quite an occasion for the handful of brokers who now meet where dozens used to congregate to shout their prices a year or two ago."[4]

It has been estimated that India must save at least 8 per cent of her national income for new investment if she is to maintain even the present low standards of living. Since 1947, however, the country has been living on its reserves, disinvesting nearly two billion rupees in 1947. If this trend continues, the decline of production will become serious because of the lack of replacement of capital equipment.

Foreign capital has proved as shy as domestic capital. The new Indian government manifested a deep suspicion of economic imperialism and with it a determination to lay down rigorous rules governing the investment of foreign capital. Nehru and his colleagues apparently were under the impression that, regardless of any limitations they might lay down, the business interests in the United States, Britain, and other western nations

1- "The Economic Outlook in India," The World Today, V (September 1949), p. 397.

2- The Statesman (Calcutta), November 14, 1950, p. 6.

3- The Statesman (Calcutta), April 16, 1948, p. 9.

4- The Statesman (Calcutta), September 20, 1948, p. 14.

would be eager to invest capital in Indian enterprise. Such investment, however, has not been forthcoming. The amount of foreign capital secured by both Pakistan and India has been relatively small. American capital has been especially difficult to secure, and in commenting on this fact Dr. Henry F. Grady, the American ambassador to India, bluntly explained:

If a country fears "domination of foreign capital," it is perfectly logical for it to pass laws and make administrative provisions keeping foreign capital out. But it is inconsistent for the leaders of a country to complain that capital does not come in when they are taking measures and announcing policies which have no other effect than to keep it out.[5]

In the Indian Union it was quite apparent by the end of 1950 that grandiose plans had been conceived in an atmosphere of undue optimism, that funds which should be spent to build up the economic sinews of the state were being drained away in military expenditures, and that capital for new enterprise was not available in adequate amounts, either from domestic or from foreign sources.

Added to these disturbing features were other alarming conditions in the general economic malaise. Industrial production, which had increased 20 per cent during the war, was steadily dropping back to 1939 levels; and at the same time that industrial output for Indian needs was quite inadequate, only two thirds of the factories were operating at full capacity. Agricultural production also declined from 3 to 7 per cent below the figures for the period 1936 to 1939. There was also little substantial progress in social and economic reform. Imperative economies forced by lack of funds have resulted in drastic reductions in health, education, and labor welfare budgets. For the same reason long overdue agrarian reform, especially the buying out of the landlords, has lagged, and such schemes as have been passed call upon the peasants themselves to bear the chief cost.

More important than any long range reforms are the problems of inflation and the growing deficit in food supplies. Since 1939 the wholesale price index in India has climbed fourfold, from an index of 100 to that of 458 in December 1949. In 1950 prices declined a trifle, back to 413, but then began advancing at the rate of 1.4 per cent

a month. This skyrocketing of prices has placed an intolerable burden upon the industrial workers in the cities and threatens to destroy the white collar and lower middle classes. An American economist and student of Southeast Asia sums up the situation in India in a somber statement: "The general picture in post-war India is that of the rich getting richer, the middle groups shrinking, and the poor getting relatively, and perhaps absolutely, poorer."[6]

This dark economic panorama is not yet complete, however, for in 1950 India suffered severely from a series of natural calamities, drought, floods, and earthquakes, which destroyed more than six million tons of food grains in the field. In 1947 the new Indian government set up the goal of food self-sufficiency by 1951, but each year has witnessed larger and larger importations of foreign food grains—in 1948 nearly three million tons and in 1949 close to four million. In 1949 food imports cost more than £113,000,000, and a large share of them had to be purchased with dollars. Largely because of the necessity of buying these huge food stocks India has had an unfavorable balance of trade, which in 1949 was close to 600,000,000 dollars. This deficit has been met only by using up the sterling balances held for India in London. And so, instead of using the important credits for purchase of the capital equipment so vital in building up the industrial structure, India has been forced to use them for food. By the end of 1950 the country was facing the dread prospect of famine, with food rations reduced 25 per cent, and with the necessity of securing six million tons of food grains from abroad. If such a huge quantity of food had to be secured by outright purchase, it would mean that India would be forced to discontinue all other imports. In 1951 a proposal to ship grain to India was laid before the United States Congress.

In this economic discussion, main emphasis has been placed on the Indian Union, where the situation is much more serious than in Pakistan. In this latter country, as in India, there has been too much faith in economic planning and too much expenditure for the army, but the country still has enough food for its people and produces several excellent cash crops that give it a substantial overall favorable balance of trade. Unlike India, therefore, Pakistan faces no immediate

5- The Statesman *(Calcutta),* *June 12, 1948, p. 11.*

6- *Daniel Thorner, "Prospects* *for Economic Development in* *Southern Asia,"* Foreign Policy Reports, *XXVI (April 15, 1950),* *p. 24.*

economic crisis but, as in the case of her neighbor, the long term problem of economic reform and development remains, calling for a higher standard of living for the masses, land reforms, and more extensive health and educational services. Thus far "the country's resources are going down the military drain and little is being spent on constructive development."[7]

Turning from the problem of livelihood and the field of economics, we find that the second basic challenge before Pakistan and India is that of establishing a reasonably sound, efficient, and responsible system of parliamentary government based upon the traditional two-party system. Self-government in the newly emancipated colonial areas of Asia is a daring experiment, and, as we have earlier indicated, the results in such areas as the Philippines, Burma, and Indonesia have not been too encouraging. Colonial nationalism has been prone to regard democratic constitutions as ends in themselves, capable of providing almost automatically honest and stable popular government. But an American student of Indian history warns:

Until India and Pakistan have had greater political experience and a longer existence independent of each other and Great Britain, no written constitution, however wisely framed, can guarantee against the emergence of a type of oligarchic rule more akin to the past than to the democratic future which the framers have envisioned.[8]

Thus far, both Pakistan and the Indian Union have been one-party states, the Muslim League and the Congress dominating practically all segments of politics without the challenge of an effective opposition. In Pakistan a stable and moderately efficient government has been created, still based upon the 1935 Government of India Act. At the top there are a few outstanding statesmen in the national ministry, but there is a serious shortage of superior leaders in the highest political posts, and among the members of the civil service the percentage of poorly trained men is too high. While the dominance of the Muslim League was perhaps desirable in the critical days following partition, the time is now overdue for the building up of a healthy parliamentary opposition. Unlike the situation in India, there is no immediately serious economic crisis, the people have enough to eat, and the siren call of the Communists has been largely unheeded. If extremism in politics does develop, it will probably be not from the left but from the right. There are Muslim extremists, such as Maulana Maududi, who champion a militant orthodoxy, regarding Hindus in Pakistan as second-class citizens, and demanding that there be no separation between church and state.

The state of politics in India is much more fluid and more critical, largely because Congress promised so much to the masses before independence and because the economic situation is much more serious. Congress "is discovering it is much easier to be a popular revolutionary than a popular national government."[9] While food prices soar, educational reforms lag, and land reforms scarcely get beyond the blueprint stage, resentment and disillusionment are spreading among the peasants and city workers. There is widespread complaint against the corruption and maladministration of the various Congress governments in the provinces and in the central government. Dr. Rajendra Prasad, the President of the Republic, has inveighed in public speeches against the bribery, corruption, and blackmarketing, and against "a general deterioration in our moral life."[10]

There is abundant testimony to prove that the Congress has lost much of its former reformist zeal and that it has moved in the direction of the right since independence. Some observers in interpreting this fact declare Congress has become the tool of big business; and, in support of this contention, they point to the government's reduction of tax rates in the higher income brackets, the slowing down of the nationalization program, and the watering down of many plans for economic reform.[11] There is undoubtedly truth in these assertions, but it is equally true that Congress has faltered and slowed down on its pre-1947 program of social and economic revolution because of the very complexity of its task and because obduracy to change is found in several important quarters outside of big business. Nehru has become more conservative and cautious in his approach to reform, because his government must pick its way cautiously forward amid the conflicting interests of the industrialists, the peasant agrarian reformers, the Hindu religious extremists, moderate Socialists, and militant Communists.

In November 1951 India will hold its first general election, and 170 million voters are qualified to go to the polls. In this first national political

7- Ibid., p. 23.

8- Holden Furber, "Constitution-Making in India," Far Eastern Survey, XVIII (April 20, 1949), p. 89.

9- Christian Science Monitor (Boston), September 8, 1948, p. 2.

10- The Statesman (Calcutta), October 28, 1950, p. 5.

11- See D. R. Gadgil, "The Economic Prospect in India," Pacific Affairs, XXII (June 1949), pp. 115-129, and Phillips Talbot, "India and Pakistan: A Progress Report," Foreign Policy Reports, XXV (June 15, 1949).

contest it is unlikely that Congress will be defeated unless there is a major famine catastrophe. Congress is losing strength both to new groups that are breaking away from its own organization and to parties like the Mahasabha and the Socialists. Just how much strength it will lose and to which rivals is conjectural.

The Socialists, led by Jayaprakash Narayan, are numerically small, perhaps numbering no more than 120,000. Yet they have been scoring some important successes in municipal and by-elections. The Socialist party espouses large scale industrialization, land reform, immediate nationalization of key industries, and the retention of private enterprise in small businesses. Democratic methods are to be used in reaching these goals. Narayan and his colleagues are at present trying to gain the support of the peasants and are working in some 200 villages on a program of rural reconstruction involving the building of roads and the improvement of water supplies and sanitary conditions. There are substantial numbers in India to whom the Socialists would seem "to offer the only hope of India evolving a two-party system of democracy."[12]

On the extreme political fringes there are several groups. In 1948, following the International Youth Conference of Communists held in March at Calcutta, the Indian Communists under instructions from Moscow began a campaign of terrorism against the Indian government. These tactics were duplicated in all other countries in Southeast Asia. There was a mounting toll of bomb outrages, murders of landlords, and sabotage on the railroads. Thousands of Communists were imprisoned, and Prime Minister Nehru left no doubt that he and his government regarded the Indian Communists as enemies of the state. The mass of people reacted against Communist terrorism, and as a result the party's membership (never more than 100,000) and its influence declined throughout 1950.

As we have seen in Chapter X, the Mahasabha and the R.S.S.S. (Rashtriya Swayam Sewak Sangh, the National Voluntary Service Association) are extremist Hindu parties, the latter having a disciplined and uniformed membership somewhat reminiscent of fascist organizations in the 1930's in Europe. These exponents of Hindu domination stand for no appeasement of Muslims, the ultimate incorporation of as much of Pakistan into the Indian Union as possible, the preservation of caste, and the perpetuation of orthodox Hinduism. Immediately after the assassination of Gandhi, a wave of popular denunciation descended upon these extremist organizations. During the next two years, however, the quarrel with Pakistan tended to exacerbate Hindu nationalism, and both the Mahasabha and the R.S.S.S. found increasing popular support. It may be significant that in October 1949 the government ban against the R.S.S.S. was removed, and it was accepted as part of the Congress party. The Indian Socialist party was vehement in its denunciation of this action, declaring it was characteristic of the drift of the country toward fascism.

The Indian political situation on the eve of the first national election was delicately balanced. The government needed the support of the industrialists, the peasants, and the urban workers. But could adequate economic and social reforms be achieved at the behest of the two latter groups without alienating the ranks of the wealthy and the privileged? And, outside these groups, the Mahasabha and the R.S.S.S., strengthened by disgruntled Hindu refugees and the anti-Muslim feeling occasioned by the deadlock in Kashmir, increased their following. There was, therefore, the possibility that the economic right and the religious right might see the mutual advantage of joining forces.

Perhaps the best hope for a stable and democratic government in India is that Congress will be able to develop within itself a strong liberal or left-of-center group ready when necessary to co-operate with the Socialist party in the realization of social gains and in effectively uniting against both the extreme right and the extreme left.

As new nations seeking eagerly to carry out domestic reforms and to consolidate their strength, Pakistan and India are vitally interested in world peace and, more specifically, in the political stabilization of Asia. The defense of India and Southeast Asia had been the responsibility of Great Britain for the 150 years preceding independence. The whole area of the Middle East, Southeast Asia, and the great Indian Ocean basin was guarded by British sea power. Following the liquidation of British rule in a large segment of Southeast Asia, a new defense arrangement became essential for what an Indian publicist has defined as "the Indian Ocean area with Afghani-

12- *"Socialism in India,"* The Times *(London), September 18, 1950, p. 5.*

stan, Sinkiang and Tibet as the outer northern ring constituting the real security region of India."[13] This same scholar, just before the grant of independence to India and Pakistan, pointed to the Soviet power controlling all of the Eurasian heartland and insisted that only by the organization of the maritime rim of Asia in an alliance with Great Britain could Russian power in Southeast Asia be contained. Said Panikkar, now Indian ambassador to Communist China, "A permanent alliance for security between England and India is a primary necessity."[14]

While India and Pakistan have not made military alliances with Great Britain, they have continued to be members of the British Commonwealth. When India proceeded to draft a constitution that would make her a sovereign republic, the question arose as to how this republican status could be squared with allegiance to the Crown, the one common feature that had, heretofore, united the Dominions in the Commonwealth. During the course of the first two years of independence, it became more apparent to Pakistanis and Indians that their association with the other members of the Commonwealth would be on the basis of complete equality, and that there were a number of important reasons for remaining in what one might think of as an informal association of nations. British advisers were playing an important role in both the Pakistan and Indian armed forces; Britain was still the leading nation in India's foreign trade; Britain's war debts tied India to the sterling bloc; and there were also important ties with British shipping, banking, and insurance.

In April 1949 the prime ministers of the various Dominions met in conference in London to see if some formula could be devised that would keep the republic of India within the Commonwealth. Agreement was reached in six days whereby India could remain a full member, giving up her former allegiance to the Crown but now acknowledging the King "as a symbol of the free association of its independent member nations and, as such, the Head of the Commonwealth."[15] This agreement was ratified by the Indian Constituent Assembly with only one dissenting vote. Representatives of the Indian republic on numerous occasions have defended their Commonwealth membership and have referred to its constructive influence in world affairs.

Pakistan was happy to continue as a Dominion, with close ties to Britain as a kind of protection against her much larger neighbor India. As we will now see, however, in connection with the discussion of the Kashmir affair, the failure of Britain and the other Dominions to exert pressure on India in securing a solution severely weakened the Commonwealth connection in Pakistan.

It was encouraging that India and Pakistan continued their co-operative association with Britain and the other Dominions, but it was doubly disappointing that where co-operation was most vital, on the Indian sub-continent, the two new nations continued what can be called the "Little Cold War." A cease-fire agreement had been secured in Kashmir in January 1949, and for two years negotiations continued fruitlessly. It was agreed that a plebiscite should be held, but India maintained that Pakistan had been the aggressor and that there could be no voting until all her troops were withdrawn and the forces of the pro-Pakistan Azad Free Government disbanded.

Admiral Chester W. Nimitz failed to secure agreement as the Plebiscite Administrator, and in the spring of 1950 an Australian jurist, Sir Owen Dixon, was named by the Security Council as mediator. While Dixon in his Report did agree that on the basis of international law Pakistan had committed aggression, he declared on the matter of the plebiscite that India's agreement would never be obtained for an arrangement which would insure a fair and unintimidated expression of opinion in Kashmir. Dixon had to report failure to bring India and Pakistan together.

In January 1951 the Commonwealth Prime Ministers again convened in London, primarily with the view of surveying the threatening war situation in the Far East. At the outset, Liaquat Ali Khan refused to attend the Conference unless the question of Kashmir could be formally placed on the agenda. Finally the Pakistan Prime Minister was induced to come to London, and Mr. Attlee and his colleagues strove mightily to help the disputants arrive at agreement. Various suggestions were made, the most important being that Commonwealth forces from outside the Indian sub-continent should take over the policing of Kashmir while a plebiscite was undertaken. But Nehru was unable to accept this offer on behalf of the Indian government, and the Kashmir problem remained as menacing as ever.

13- K. M. Panikkar, The Basis of an Indo-British Treaty, Pamphlet of Indian Council on World Affairs (Bombay: Oxford University Press, 1946), p. 44.

14- Ibid., p. 37.

15- Quoted in Gwendolen M. Carter, "The British Commonwealth in the Asian Crisis," Foreign Policy Reports, XXVI (October 1, 1950), p. 107.

Not only did this feud continue to poison Indo-Pakistan relations but other irritants were added, such as Pakistan's belief that India supported the Afghans against her. Again, in the fall of 1949 Great Britain devalued her pound. India followed suit with the devaluation of her currency, but Pakistan, fortified by a strong favorable balance of trade, did not think it essential to cheapen her rupee. Instead of parity of currencies with her neighbor, Pakistan could now ask for 140 Indian rupees to match 100 of her own. The result was a trade war, and commerce between the two states virtually halted. Furthermore, in the spring of 1950 there was an outbreak of Hindu-Muslim rioting in both East and West Bengal. Three thousand fell victims to religious fanaticism, and again, as in the fall of 1947, refugees began their march across the borders. It is estimated that 750,000 Muslims and 500,000 Hindus were uprooted. The situation became so critical that Jawaharlal Nehru and Liaquat Ali Khan sought to halt the threat of imminent war between their two states and signed the Delhi Pact on April 8, 1950. This agreement provided for elaborate machinery for the protection of minority groups in both countries.

Both Pakistan and India urgently need peace and stability in Asia to enable them to concentrate upon their domestic problems, but as long as the canker of their rivalry continues, especially in Kashmir, neither country can contribute to the new defense system so vitally important to them both after the departure of much of Britain's power in Southeast Asia. Membership in the Commonwealth is something, but it is not enough; it is no substitute for Indo-Pakistan mutual assistance and co-operation in defense and foreign relations. The Pakistan Prime Minister had this in mind when he said:

Together we could play an important role in stabilizing Asia because we possess the two strong and stable Governments in this continent. But divided by the suspicions which the Kashmir dispute keeps alive, it is unrealistic to talk of either Pakistan or Bharat [India] successfully playing their role in Asia.[16]

In the general field of foreign policy, Pakistan and India have followed certain common objectives. Both states have given firm support to the United Nations and its Charter and have been vigilant in championing the Asian point of view in the councils of the world. They have also been eager to support oppressed peoples and to encourage the liquidation of the remaining vestiges of colonialism in Asia. Any slight directed against Asians in general and Indians in particular is deeply resented. This championing of Asian interests and point of view is illustrated by the calling of the First Asian Relations Conference at New Delhi in April 1947, at which time representatives from all over Asia met to discuss problems and issues of common interest. Again, in January 1949, Nehru issued invitations to the Asian governments to send representatives to a conference in New Delhi to see what could be done to assist the Indonesian Republic's cause against the Netherlands government.

By reason of her size and the world reputation of her main spokesman, Jawaharlal Nehru, India has become a more significant factor than her neighbor, Pakistan, in international affairs. In foreign policy India has attempted to follow a course of non-involvement, steering clear of entangling commitments with either Russia and her satellites on the one hand, or the United States and the western democracies on the other. This policy has been defined as "constructive non-alignment with other power blocs and not as neutrality."[17]

In the case of China and the Korean crisis, Nehru as the spokesman for India not only has followed the independent policy already defined between the so-called Soviet and American power blocs but, much more important, has taken on the position of the interpreter and defender of Asian nationalism. Nehru maintains that revolutionary movements in Asia are basically nationalistic, and that their utilization of Communist techniques and their orientation toward Moscow have occurred because for many Asians there was no other alternative. Once the revolution is successful and consolidated, countries such as China will stand on their own as independent Asian national entities, not subordinate to any other nation. Nehru always stresses the sensitiveness and pride of Asians and the inability of westerners to understand these characteristics of the new Asia. Specifically in the case of China it is maintained that the Chinese People's Republic at Peiping has been motivated by understandable and sincere suspicions and fears, stemming from

- Pakistan Affairs *(Washing-*
1, D. C.), December 22, 1950,
2.

- Press Release, *March 29,*
48 (Washington, D. C.:
overnment of India Informa-
•n Services).

American aid to Chiang Kai-shek at the close of World War II, the refusal to seat Communist China in the United Nations, the protection of Chiang and his army by the American fleet around Formosa, and the crossing of the 38th parallel in Korea by United Nations forces and their approach to the Manchurian border.

Following the invasion of South Korea by its northern neighbor in June 1950, India supported the U.N. action branding the North Koreans as aggressors but neither India nor Pakistan felt prepared to send a contingent to join the U.N. forces in Korea. Nehru constantly championed the course of mediation and cautiousness, and the Indian delegate, Sir Benegal Rau, in the Security Council especially warned of the danger of crossing the 38th parallel.

Following the intervention of Chinese Communist armies in Korea in November 1950, India assumed the leadership of an Asian and Near Eastern group of thirteen countries seeking to achieve a cease-fire in Korea and the solution of all basic issues in the Far East, such as the seating of the Peiping regime in the United Nations, the Formosa problem, and the re-establishment of a popular and united government in Korea. Two cease-fire proposals were adopted but were rejected by Mao Tse-tung's Communist government. On February 1, 1951, despite the arguments put forward by Sir Benegal Rau, the United Nations General Assembly formally found Communist China guilty of aggression in Korea. In the voting, nine Near Eastern nations abstained, as did Pakistan, while Burma and India joined the Soviet bloc of five members in voting against the resolution.

The diplomatic line followed by India in the U.N. irritated and even angered many Americans, who called its policy one of appeasement. There were also important circles of Indian opinion that were growing increasingly dissatisfied with Nehru's "in between" policy. Growing criticism became quite marked after Communist Chinese forces invaded Tibet in October 1950 and after India's note to Peiping protesting against this action was rejected by the Chinese. One Indian critic declared, "We are preaching to the world high sounding principles which are not followed at home and are behaving like innocents abroad. We are nobody's darling. The Communist Powers regard us as a stooge of the Anglo-American bloc, and that bloc regards us as blockheads who want to have the best of both worlds."[18]

In the spring of 1951 no one could easily guess whether Nehru was right in his main contention that China, suffused with its new nationalism, would remain Chinese in the long run and would not be a wheel of the chariot of Soviet imperialism. Back of Nehru's views is the desire not to alienate China, for in the near future, as this potentially great world power gains strength, he believes it will also be able to adopt an independent policy vis-à-vis Russia. India and China might then, as Asian powers speaking for Asia, constitute a third force in world affairs.

In this prospect for the Indian sub-continent the fourth and final challenge is perhaps the most fundamental, for it concerns the inner conflict of India and Pakistan, involving tensions of the spirit and of the mind, as they seek to achieve a satisfactory balance and accommodation between their traditional ways of life and the new forces brought by the impact of western culture. With British rule and India's growing contact with the outside world came the influence of parliamentarianism, nationalism, science, and industrial technology, all calling for some kind of adjustment from traditional beliefs and behavior patterns.

On every hand one observes in India the clash of cultures, of the old and the new. There are Gandhian pacifism and the realities of the world of power politics; the paradox of public servants trying to give their complete allegiance to the state and at the same time carrying out their old traditions of loyalty to the family. There is the antithesis between creating a political democracy with a constitution and leaving practically unchanged the social compartmentalism and inequalities of a caste system. There is the illogicality of trying to raise standards of living while at the same time retaining such expensive beliefs as the sanctity of animal life, especially that of the cow.

Perhaps the best hope lies in following the middle path, which seeks to find the best in both the traditional culture and that of the West and to blend them into a meaningful synthesis. Jawaharlal Nehru may be said to represent this happy balance between the old and the new, and it has been sought by the late Rabindranath Tagore, who believed that there should be "a collaboration of East and West, each giving its best and taking the best the other can offer."[19]

18- The Statesman (Calcutta), October 21, 1950, p. 5.

19- L. S. S. O'Malley, Modern India and the West (London: Oxford University Press, 1941), p. 782.

reading list: IN THE preparation of this volume, most of the significant books on India written in English and published since 1900 have been consulted, together with numerous articles from periodicals and newspapers. To these sources have been added the more important documents published by the British government and, after August 1947, by the governments of India and Pakistan. A representative sampling of the author's bibliography may be secured by scanning the sources cited throughout the book. Many of these references are, unfortunately, either out of print or, when published in India, not easily available for the general reader in the United States. The following titles are especially recommended as a basic library on the history and culture of the Indian sub-continent, with emphasis upon the modern period.

Indian history during the past two centuries, that is, the period of British rule, has been full of controversial issues. In the reading list a variety of views and attitudes are represented, such as the ultra-nationalist or the very pro-British or, in very recent times, the Pakistani as opposed to the Indian point of view. There are in addition volumes written by those authors who endeavor to transcend faction and to follow only the truth.

Anstey, Vera. *Economic Development of India.* London: Longmans, Green and Co., 1937.

The Cambridge History of India. 6 vols. Cambridge: Cambridge University Press, 1922-1932.

Coupland, Sir Reginald. *India: A Restatement.* London: Oxford University Press, 1945.

Darling, Malcolm L. *At Freedom's Door.* London: Oxford University Press, 1949.

Desai, A. R. *Social Background of Indian Nationalism.* Bombay: Oxford University Press, 1949.

Dodwell, H. H. *A Sketch of the History of India from 1858 to 1918.* London: Longmans, Green and Co., 1925.

Dodwell, H. (ed.). *Cambridge Shorter History of India.* New York: The Macmillan Co., 1934.

Dunbar, Sir George. *A History of India.* 2 vols. London: Nicholson and Watson, 1943.

Gandhi, Mohandas K. *The Story of My Experiments with Truth.* Ahmadabad: Navajivan Publishing House, 1940.

Garratt, G. T. (ed.). *The Legacy of India.* London: Oxford University Press, 1937.

Goshal, Kumar. *The People of India.* New York: Sheridan House, 1944.

Keith, A. B., *A Constitutional History of India, 1600-1935.* London: Methuen and Co., 1936.

Khan, Liaquat Ali. *Pakistan the Heart of Asia.* Cambridge: Harvard University Press, 1950.

Majumdar, R. C., Raychaudhuri, H. C., and Datta, K. *An Advanced History of India.* 2nd ed. London: Macmillan and Co., 1950.

McKelvie, Roy. *The War in Burma.* London: Methuen and Co., 1948.

Mills, Lennox A., et al. *The New World of Southeast Asia.* Minneapolis: University of Minnesota Press, 1949.

Mitchell, Kate. *India Without Fable.* New York: Alfred A. Knopf, 1942.

Muehl, John Frederick. *Interview with India.* New York: The John Day Co., 1950.

Nehru, Jawaharlal. *The Discovery of India.* New York: The John Day Co., 1946.

Nehru, Jawaharlal. *Toward Freedom.* New York: The John Day Co., 1942.

O'Malley, L.S.S. (ed.). *Modern India and the West.* London: Oxford University Press, 1941.

Panikkar, K. M. *A Survey of Indian History.* London: Meridian Books, 1948.

Parkin, Raleigh. *India Today.* Rev. ed. New York: The John Day Co., 1946.

Prasad, Rajendra. *India Divided.* Bombay: Hind Kitabs Ltd., 1947.

Rawlinson, H. G. *India: A Short Cultural History.* New York: D. Appleton-Century, 1938.

Rosinger, Lawrence K. *India and the United States, Political and Economic Relations.* New York: The Macmillan Co., 1950.

Sen, Gertrude Emerson. *The Pageant of India's History.* Vol. I. New York: Longmans, Green and Co., 1948.

Sheean, Vincent. *Lead, Kindly Light.* New York: Random House, 1949.

Smith, Wilfred C. *Modern Islam in India.* London: Victor Gollancz, 1947.

Smith, W. R. *Nationalism and Reform in India.* New Haven: Yale University Press, 1938.

Spear, Percival. *India, Pakistan, and the West.* London: Oxford University Press, 1949.

Symonds, Richard. *The Making of Pakistan.* London: Faber and Faber, 1950.

Talbot, Phillips (ed.). *South Asia in the World Today.* Chicago: University of Chicago Press, 1950.

Thompson, Edward, and Garratt, G. T. *The Rise and Fulfilment of British Rule in India.* New York: The Macmillan Co., 1934.

2 3 4 5 6 7 8 9 10 11 12 13 14 15 16 17 18 19 20 21 22 23 24 25   60 59 58 57 56 55 54 53 52